Written for Our Instruction:
Essays in Honor of William Varner

WRITTEN FOR OUR INSTRUCTION: ESSAYS IN HONOR OF WILLIAM VARNER

ABNER CHOU AND CHRISTIAN LOCATELL
EDITORS

Fontes

CONTENTS

Contributors

ABNER CHOU (Th.D., The Master's Seminary) is the John F. MacArthur Endowed Fellow and professor of biblical studies at The Master's University. He is head translator of the Legacy Standard Bible, the author of *The Hermeneutics of the Biblical Writers* (2018), *Lamentations* (Evangelical Exegetical Commentary, 2014), and *I Saw the Lord* (2013) and has authored articles on biblical theology, hermeneutics, and Christian thought.

DANIEL FORBES earned his BA and MA in Biblical Studies from The Master's University and his ThM from Southeastern Baptist Theological Seminary.

HERALD GANDI earned a BA in biblical languages from The Master's University and MDiv from The Master's Seminary. He is currently working on a doctorate in Old Testament at the University of Oxford.

WYATT GRAHAM (Ph.D., Southern Baptist Theological Seminary) is the executive director of The Gospel Coalition Canada.

MICHAEL A. GRISANTI (Ph.D., Dallas Theological Seminary) is the Distinguished Research Professor of Old Testament and Chair of Old Testament Department at The Master's Seminary. He is the co-editor of *Giving the Sense* (Kregel, 2004); *Deuteronomy* commentary in the revised Expositor's Bible Commentary (2012); and co-author of *World and the Word: An Introduction to the Old Testament* (Broadman & Holman, 2011), and has authored articles and essays on Deuteronomy, Isaiah, the history of Israel, ethical issues, and biblical theology.

CLIFF KVIDAHL earned a BA in biblical languages from The Master's University and a MTh from the South African Theological Seminary.

DREW LONGACRE (Ph.D., University of Birmingham) is postdoctoral researcher on the ERC project "The Hands that Wrote the Bible: Digital Palaeography and Scribal Culture of the Dead Sea Scrolls" at the Qumran Institute of the University of Groningen. He specializes on the texts and manuscripts of the Greek and Hebrew Bibles.

GEOFF KIRKLAND (Ph.D., Baptist Bible Seminary) serves as pastor of Christ Fellowship Bible Church in St. Louis, Missouri. He has served in pastoral ministry for over fifteen years. He also teaches New Testament at Brookes Bible College (St Louis) and travels to teach and train indigenous pastors in east Asia. Geoff is a graduate of The Master's University (BA) and The Master's Seminary (MDiv and ThM).

CHRISTIAN LOCATELL (Ph.D., Stellenbosch University) is Golda Meir post-doctoral fellow in the Linguistics Department at The Hebrew University of Jerusalem. He is co-editor of *Ancient Texts and Modern Readers* (Studia Semitica Neerlandica, 2019), author of *Grammatical Polysemy in the Hebrew Bible* (Studia Semitica Neerlandica, forthcoming), and has published articles in the fields of biblical languages, linguistics, biblical interpretation, and archaeology.

CHRIS MCKINNY (Ph.D., Bar-Ilan University) is a Research Fellow at Gesher Media. Passionate about the archaeology, history, and geography of the Biblical world, he has written extensively on these subjects in both academic and popular publications. Chris is a senior staff member at the Tel Burna Archaeological project and regularly leads study tours to the lands of the Bible.

STANLEY E. PORTER (Ph.D., University of Sheffield) is President and Dean, Professor of New Testament, and Roy A. Hope Chair in Christian Worldview at McMaster Divinity College, Hamilton, Ontario, Canada. Porter has authored thirty volumes and edited over ninety others. He has published on most areas of New Testament studies and related subjects, including Greek language and linguistics, hermeneutics, Paul, historical Jesus, and papyrology and textual criticism, among others.

TODD A. SCACEWATER (Ph.D., Westminster Theological Seminary) is Assistant Professor of International Studies at Dallas International University and a member of Wycliffe Bible Translators.

Abbreviations

2 Clem	2 Clement
AB	Anchor Bible Commentary
ABD	*Anchor Bible Dictionary.* Edited by David Noel Freedman. 6 vols. New York: Doubleday, 1992.
ANE	Ancient Near East
ANT	Anteriority
Ant.	*Jewish Antiquities*
AThANT	Abhandlungen zur Theologie des Alten und Neuen Testaments
BAGL	*Biblical and Ancient Greek Linguistics*
BBR	*Bulletin for Biblical Research*
BCOTWP	Baker Commentary on the Old Testament Wisdom and Psalms
BDAG	*Bauer, W. A Greek-English Lexicon of the New Testament and Other Early Christian Literature.* Revised and edited by F. W. Danker. 3rd ed. Chicago: University of Chicago Press, 2000.
BDB	*A Hebrew and English Lexicon of the Old Testament.* Edited by Francis Brown, S. R. Driver, and Charles A. Briggs.
BDF	*A Greek Grammar of the New Testament and Other Early Christian Literature.* Edited by F. Blass, A. Debrunner, and R. W. Funk. Chicago: University of Chicago Press, 1961.
BECNT	Baker Exegetical Commentary on the New Testament
BGBE	Beitrage Zur Geschichte der Biblischen Exegese
Bib	*Biblica*
BKKWS	Bible Knowledge Key Word Study
BNTC	Black's New Testament Commentary
BSGRT	Bibliotheca scriptorum Graecorum et Romanorum Teubneriana
BST	Bible Speaks Today
BTB	*Biblical Theology Bulletin*
BTCP	Biblical Theology for Christian Proclamation
BZNW	Beihefte zur Zeitschrift für die neutestamentliche Wissenschaft
CBNT	Coniectanea Biblica, New Testament Series
CBQ	*Catholic Biblical Quarterly*
CCC	cause, condition, concession, etc.
CDA	Critical Discourse Analysis
CJT	*Canadian Journal of Theology*
COMACC	comment-accord
COMPAR	comparison
ConBNT	*Coniectanea Neotestamentica or Coniectanea Biblica: New Testament Series*

ConC	Concordia Commentary
CurBR	*Currents in Biblical Research*
CurBS	*Currents in Research: Biblical Studies*
DA	Discourse Analysis
Det.	*Quod deterius potiori insidari soleat*
DSD	Dead Sea Discoveries
DSS	Dead Sea Scrolls
EBC	The Expositor's Bible Commentary
EKKNT	Evangelisch-katholischer Kommentar zum Neuen Testament
ESV	English Standard Version
ETL	Ephemerides Theologicae Lovanienses
EvQ	*Evangelical Quarterly*
FAT	Forschungen zum Alten Testament
FIOLT	Formation and Interpretation of Old Testament Literature
FOTL	The Forms of the Old Testament Literature
GE	*The Brill Dictionary of Ancient Greek.* Franco Montanari. Leiden: Brill, 2015.
HALOT	*The Hebrew and Aramaic Lexicon of the Old Testament.* Edited by L. Koehler, W. Baumgartner, and J. J. Stamm. Translated and edited under the supervision of Mervyn E. J. Richardson. 4 vols. Leiden: Brill, 1994–2000.
HBAI	*Hebrew Bible and Ancient Israel*
HBT	*Horizons in Biblical Theology*
HCOT	Historical Commentary on the Old Testament
Herm	Hermeneia
HNT	Handbuch zum Neuen Testament
HTR	*Harvard Theological Review*
HUCA	*Hebrew Union College Annual*
ICC	International Critical Commentary
Ign. Rom.	Ignatius, To the Romans
Il.	*The Illiad*
IMANTE	immediate anteriority
In Joh.	*Interpretation or Comment on the Gospel According to John,* Cyril of Alexandria
INSTRU	instrumental
Int	*Interpretation*
INTF	Institut für Neutestamentliche Textforschung
ISBE	*International Standard Bible Encyclopedia.* Edited by Geoffrey W. Bromiley. 4 vols. Grand Rapids: Eerdmans, 1979–1988.
ISI/RR	*Information Sciences Institute Research Report*
ITC	International Theological Commentary

JBL	*Journal of Biblical Literature*
JETS	*Journal of the Evangelical Theological Society*
Jos. Asen.	Joseph and Aseneth
JPS	The Jewish Publication Society Torah Commentary
JSHJ	*Journal for the Study of the Historical Jesus*
JSJSup	*Journal for the Study of Judaism in the Persian, Hellenistic, and Roman Periods Supplement Series*
JSNTSup	*Journal for the Study of the New Testament Supplement Series*
JSOT	*Journal for the Study of the Old Testament*
JSOTSup	Journal for the Study of the Old Testament Supplement Series
JTS	*Journal of Theological Studies*
K&D	*Biblical Commentary on the Old Testament.* Carl Friedrich Keil and Franz Delitzsch. Translated by James Martin et al. 25 vols. Edinburgh, 1857–1878. Repr., 10 vols., Peabody, MA: Hendrickson, 1996.
LBS	Linguistic Biblical Studies
Leg.	*Legum allegoriae*
LHBOTS	The Library of Hebrew Bible/Old Testament Studies
LNTS	The Library of New Testament Studies
LSJ	Liddell, H. G., R. Scott, and H. S. Jones. *A Greek-English Lexicon. 9th edition with revised supplement.* Oxford: Clarendon, 1996.
LXX	*Septuaginta: SESB Edition.* Edited by A. Rahlfs and R. Hanhart. Stuttgart: Deutsche Bibelgesellschaft, 2006.
Migr.	*De migratione Abrahami*
MT	Masoretic Text
NA[28]	*Novum Testamentum Graece.* 28th ed. Edited by K. Aland, B. Aland, J. Karavidopoulos, C. M. Martini, and B. M. Metzger. Stuttgart: Deutsche Bibelgesellschaft, 2012.
NAC	New American Commentary
NASB	New American Standard Bible
NCV	New Century Version
NET	New English Translation
NIBC	New International Biblical Commentary
NICNT	New International Commentary on the New Testament
NICOT	New International Commentary on the Old Testament
NIDOTTE	*New International Dictionary of Old Testament Theology and Exegesis.* Edited by Willem A. VanGemeren. 5 vols. Grand Rapids: Zondervan, 1997.
NIGTC	New International Greek Testament Commentary

NIV	New International Version
NJPS	New Jewish Publication Society Tanakh
NKJV	New King James Version
NLI	National Library of Israel
NLT	New Living Translation
NovT	*Novum Testamentum*
NovTSup	Novum Testamentum Supplement Series
NRSV	New Revised Standard Version
NSBT	New Studies in Biblical Theology
NT	New Testament
NTC	New Testament Commentary
NTL	New Testament Library
NTM	New Testament Monographs
NTS	*New Testament Studies*
NTTC	New Testament Textual Criticism
NTTSD	New Testament Tools and Studies
Od.	*The Odyssey*
Onom.	*Onomasticon*
OT	Old Testament
OTL	Old Testament Library
OTTC	Old Testament Textual Criticism
P&BNS	Pragmatics & Beyond New Series
PG	*Patrologia Graeca* [= *Patrologiae Cursus Completus: Series Graeca*]. Edited by Jacques-Paul Migne. 162 vols. Paris, 1857–1886.
PNTC	Pillar New Testament Commentary
RB	*Revue biblique*
RBS	Resources for Biblical Study
REL	relative pronoun
Rep.	*The Republic*
RevExp	*Review and Expositor*
RST	Rhetorical Structure Theory
SAA	Semantic Structural Analysis
SBJT	*Southern Baptist Journal of Theology*
SBLAcBib	Society of Biblical Literature Academia Biblical
SBLDS	Society of Biblical Literature Dissertation Series
SFL	Systemic Functional Linguistics
SIMIL	similarity
SIOVER	simultaneous overlap
SJOT	*Scandinavian Journal of the Old Testament*
SNTSMS	Society of New Testament Studies Monograph Series

SOTBT	Studies in Old Testament Biblical Theology
SPCK	Society for Promoting Christian Knowledge
Spec.	*De specialibus legibus*
STDJ	Studies on the Texts of the Desert of Judah
T-S NS	Taylor-Schechter New Series Genizah Collection
T. Dan	Testament of Dan
TC	Textual criticism
TCSt	Text-Critical Studies
TDNT	*Theological Dictionary of the New Testament.* Edited by Gerhard Kittel and Gerhard Friedrich. Translated by Geoffrey W. Bromiley. 10 vols. Grand Rapids: Eerdmans, 1964–1976
TDOT	*Theological Dictionary of the Old Testament.* Edited by G. Johannes Botterweck and Helmer Ringgren. Translated by John T. Willis et al. 8 vols. Grand Rapids: Eerdmans, 1974–2006
Tg. Ps.	Targum Psalms
The Message	*The Message: The Bible in Contemporary Language*
Them	Themelios
TOTC	Tyndale Old Testament Commentaries
TSAJ	Texts and Studies in Ancient Judaism
TWOT	*Theological Wordbook of the Old Testament.* Edited by R. Laird Harris, Gleason L. Archer Jr., and Bruce K. Waltke. 2 vols. Chicago: Moody Press, 1980
TynBul	*Tyndale Bulletin*
VT	*Vetus Testamentum*
VTSup	Supplements to Vetus Testamentum
WBC	Word Biblical Commentary
WMANT	Wissenschaftliche Monographien zum Alten und Neuen Testament
WTJ	Westminster Theological Journal
WUNT	Wissenschaftliche Untersuchungen zum Neuen Testament
ZNW	*Zeitschrift für die neutestamentliche Wissenschaft und die Kunde der älteren Kirche*
תנ״ך	Tanakh: Torah, Nevi'im, Ketuvim

"If Any of You Lacks Wisdom":
An Introduction to the Volume

T HE ADMONITION GIVEN IN JAMES 1:5 to all who lack wisdom is
to "ask." Dr. William Varner embodies this disposition. What
has impressed colleague and student alike is his never ceasing
drive to grow and learn. As a scholar-pastor, he has been characterized
by the desire to pursue wisdom and the humility to ask and search
for it. Indeed, the work and interests of Dr. Varner span multiple disciplines and subdisciplines from discourse analysis to the Messiah in
the Old Testament, from the history of ancient Israel to early Christian
literature, from hermeneutical theory to the modern Messianic movement and many other topics. This present volume recognizes the contribution Dr. Varner has made to these subjects both in his writing and
teaching in which he has inspired subsequent generations to engage
in these various disciplines.

The contributions of this volume come from Dr. Varner's colleagues with whom he has interacted and engaged on various subjects, and former students on whom he has had a marked impact
and have gone on to do graduate work in several of these areas. As a
background to his productive career, Herald Gandi presents a short
biographical sketch, summarizing just a few of the highlights in the
life of Dr. Varner by tracing some of the defining trajectories of his life
which served to shape his scholarship and church service. Because of
the breadth of Dr. Varner's academic engagement, the subjects covered in this volume are wide-ranging. These essays deal with topics
within linguistics, the exegesis, theology, intertextuality, and textual

criticism of Old and New Testament texts, early Christian literature, and the land of the Bible. In line with the interdisciplinarity of Dr. Varner's work, many of these essays explore and develop the relationship between several of these topics at once. The diverse topics addressed in the following pages make any categorization difficult. Nevertheless, an attempt has been made to arrange the contributions beginning with essays focused on theoretical and methodological foundations in studying the texts of Scripture and then proceeding to more concrete essays which deal with particular texts and topics.

The essay by Stanley Porter surveys two theoretical approaches to textual interpretation which have been applied to the New Testament over the past several decades: discourse analysis and literary criticism. He defines each and synthesizes their main commitments, goals, and difficulties, boiling each down to a list of defining characteristics. Porter also traces the development of these approaches by summarizing many of the works from a plethora of fields which had their part in the formation of each discipline. These approaches are then compared in terms of their respective strengths for approaching the text of the New Testament. While discourse analysis (for better or for worse) can be perceived as more objective and literary criticism more indeterminate, Porter notes several shared philosophical and hermeneutical underpinnings of both approaches to reading a text. However, there are also significant differences, such as the definition of a "text" and where its meaning resides. In the end, each approach comes to the text of the New Testament in similar, yet distinct ways, each affording a different perspective of analysis.

The essay by Christian Locatell explores the often-debated topic of polysemy—the idea that words have multiple (sometimes seemingly unrelated) meanings and functions which haunt the first-year Greek student. Locatell presents the theory of grammaticalization (the universal process by which lexical words develop grammatical functions and by which grammatical words develop additional grammatical functions) as a way of making sense of the various meanings and uses of polysemous and multifunctional words. The notoriously multifunctional word ὡς is taken as a test case. Locatell proposes a reconstruction of the development of some of the main functions of ὡς as well as the inferential processes in communication responsible for its extended uses which are known to facilitate such developments crosslinguistically. It is suggested that such a perspective on how words develop and how such a development shapes their meanings provides a better understanding of how meaning works and a surer footing when approaching the interpretation of the New Testament (and beyond).

The next contribution by Drew Longacre takes up the topic of Old and New Testament textual criticism. Longacre observes that these two disciplines are often seen as so different as to be methodologically incompatible and exclude the possibility for collaboration and cross-pollination between students and scholars of each. On the contrary, Longacre maintains that the great chasms often thought to separate the two on closer examination turn out to not really be there. It is argued that neither the sources (e.g. types, content, date, and number of manuscripts) nor methods of Old and New Testaments criticism are fundamentally different enough to exclude fruitful collaboration.

In the following contributions, the volume turns from a focus on theory to application in discussions of particular texts and topics. Michael Grisanti's chapter discusses the nature of heart circumcision spoken of in many biblical texts, but specifically in Deuteronomy 10:16 and 30:6. In 10:16 God commands Israel to circumcise their hearts and in 30:6, God says he will do it for them. After covering the conceptual background of circumcision and considering the meaning of "heart" circumcision, Grisanti considers different approaches to this problem. Rejecting as inadequate interpretations such as thinking that Israel's relationship with God was merely external until a later time of heart circumcision, or that God was asking of Israel an impossible task, Grisanti argues the way to understand these two texts is in light of the concepts of the remnant and the New Covenant restoration of Israel. While the remnant was circumcised in heart (and regenerate) in ancient Israel, a national heart circumcision awaits a future time.

Abner Chou's essay presents a biblical theological study of Jesus' wilderness wanderings. Looking above the level of the sentence (a defining feature of discourse analysis) and sensitive to intertextual clues, Chou concurs that Matthew's account of Jesus' wilderness does indeed present him as the fulfillment of Israel, Moses, and Elijah, but that this is not the whole picture. Chou shows that the account of Jesus in the wilderness in Matthew 4 shares intentional parallels with king David's wilderness wanderings in 1 Sam 21–26. As such, king David recapitulated the wilderness wandering of Israel and Moses, this time as the national representative and pattern after which the messianic king would follow. In this way, Matthew presents Jesus as the true heir to the Davidic dynasty and the fulfillment of redemptive history.

Taking up again the topics of intertextuality and the New Testament use of the Old Testament, Geoffrey R. Kirkland looks at the use of Psalm 69:9 in Romans 15:3. Kirkland explores the way in which Paul takes the Davidic words of Ps 69:9 and interprets them in relation to Christ's earthly ministry and the experience of the Christian community in Rome and in light of this offers several practical applications for a modern audience.

The chapter by Daniel Forbes also looks at the intertextuality of Scripture by examining the use of Psalm 118 and its "gate" motif in the Gospel accounts of the triumphal entry and elsewhere in Passion Week. In addition to Psalm 118, Forbes examines several "gate-entry" texts in Scripture and detects in each the theme of encountering and overcoming opposition. Forbes argues that this background illuminates the strategic use of Psalm 118 by the Gospel writers and Jesus himself who emerged victorious despite the rejection he experienced.

Next, Wyatt Graham presents a philosophical and theological exploration of the Synoptic Gospels by considering possible traces of their conception of metaphysics in relation to the deity of Christ. Graham notes the debate among New Testament scholars concerning whether an affirmation of Jesus' divinity can be detected in the synoptics. Graham argues that an appreciation for the "metaphysical awareness" of the Synoptics inherited from an Old Testament worldview can be seen in their treatment of topics such as angels and the heavenly versus earthly sanctuary and that this supports the case for an early high Christology. Graham detects the same metaphysical orientation in the more explicit high Christology of John which also employs sanctuary imagery in relation to Christ's hypostatic nature. Therefore, he maintains, this shared metaphysics also suggests a shared Christology, even if less explicit in the Synoptics.

Clifford Kvidahl's essay explores the Christology of the Letter to the Hebrews. The presentation in Hebrews of Christ as high priest is examined and compared to the descriptions of Christ in the Gospels. Kvidahl argues that the author of the Letter to the Hebrews uniquely focuses on the heavenly locale of Christ's high priestly office and ministry according to the order of Melchizedek vis-à-vis the Levitical priesthood and its function in the earthly sanctuary.

The chapter by Chris McKinny brings to bear the tools of archaeology and historical geography in the interpretation of biblical texts in an examination of the account of Gideon's pursuit of the Midianites in Judges 7–8. This essay offers new proposals and refinements of old proposals concerning the identification of the sites and routs referred to in this account. McKinny then uses this background to illuminate the meaning of Gideon's interaction with the Ephraimites in the passage, especially in Judges 8:3 when Gideon quells their anger against him with the rhetorical question, "What have I done in comparison with you?"

Finally, moving beyond the texts of Scripture, but adjacent to biblical studies and very much within the interests of Dr. Varner's own work, Todd Scacewater presents a study of the Didache which applies discourse analysis to the text in order to discern its major topics. After a brief overview of discourse analysis and a summary of the structure of the Didache as a whole, Scacewater argues that economic ethics is a central part of the message which also permeates other major concerns expressed in this ancient Christian manual, such as its well-known dichotomy of the way of life and the way of death, proper worship, community relations, and false teachers who would threaten to lead new converts astray from the way of life.

The breadth of topics in these chapters reflects Dr. Varner's lifelong endeavor to seek wisdom. He is a model scholar who never stops learning and expanding his field of understanding. He is a model teacher who sparks curiosity in his students to delve into the areas he has taught. He is a model churchman who does not remain in the ivory tower but serves amongst God's people. He is a model pastor who brings academic depth and devotional insight to his people. This collection of essays is a tribute to Dr, Varner's labors in the classroom as a teacher-mentor, his contributions to the academy as a scholar, and his shepherding in the church as a minister.

We are delighted to present this volume to Dr. Varner in appreciation for his labors and would like to thank all of the contributors to the volume. It has been a pleasure crafting this tribute together. Many more of Dr. Varner's former students and colleagues could have been added to this volume who, for one reason or another, were unable. Among them we would like to especially mention Kai Akagi, Rodney Decker, Ben Gladd, Rob Plummer, Will Ross, and Laney Stroup who share the deep appreciation of Dr. Varner's work that lies at the heart of this project. We would also like to make mention of several others who have helped in the production of this volume. Helen Varner's assistance in providing biographical information on Dr. Varner (while keeping the project a surprise) was extremely helpful. Todd Bolen and especially Eric Dean provided expert help in developing the cover art for which we are very grateful. We extend our deep appreciation to Jenny Greiner and the Chester Beatty Library digital services team for granting us use of the fragment of Romans 15:4 from P[46] on the cover of the volume. We are very thankful to Kris Udd who generously allowed us to use his Greek papyri font from BiblePlaces.com for the cover. We would also like to make special acknowledgment of Deborah Gandi who graciously compiled the index and provided excellent proofing assistance. A very big thanks goes to Clifford Kvidahl and Todd Scacewater of Fontes Press, who have acted as both contributors and publishers, for their labor in copy editing, typesetting, and otherwise giving this volume physical form. Their enthusiasm for the project and efforts in bringing it to press have been indispensable.

Yom Hakkippurim 2020
Santa Clarita and Jerusalem

Abner Chou
Christian Locatell

2

"Who Is Wise and Understanding among You?"

A Biographical Sketch of Dr. William Varner

Herald Gandi

"IT'S NOT IF YOU GO TO IBEX, IT'S WHEN YOU GO TO IBEX." These come from none other than Dr. William Varner as he encourages all his student at The Master's University to experience the Bible in the land of the Bible, Israel, and often also other Bible lands such as Egypt, Jordan, Greece, and Italy during travel study break. He would know the value of this experience after all of his study of Scripture, Jewish culture, the books he's written, and the many trips he has led to the Holy Land (a total of 52 times!). But this motto is a world away from the one William Varner grew up in.

Born in 1947 in Spartanburg, South Carolina, Dr. Varner grew up in a secular home. His dad was an alcoholic who also umpired at minor league baseball games. As a result, Dr. Varner played on the baseball team whenever possible. When his father passed away, he and his mother went to live with his godly grandparents. It was while he lived with his grandparents that Dr. Varner committed his life to the Lord's service. But baseball was still his main focus.

He continued playing throughout high school as a pitcher. During his senior year in 1964, his team went on to win the South Carolina state championship. Dr. Varner then earned a full-ride scholarship, based on his merit, to Wofford college. There he would continue his successful baseball career and study chemistry.

The summer before he was to set off for college, his missionary uncle visited him while on furlough from Japan. Dr. Varner would spend many evenings with his uncle during that summer, discussing

Scripture and ministry. As the summer came to a close, Dr. Varner felt that the Lord was working in his heart to lead him away from baseball and into ministry. Just three days before he would start his freshman year at Wofford college, his uncle drove him to see Bob Jones University. It must have been a good visit, because before they left Dr. Varner had enrolled to major in Bible with a minor in Greek. There were no collegiate sports teams at the time, and that meant he left his baseball career behind to study God's Word. His mother was astounded at this decision. When she heard the news, she had two questions, "Who will listen to you?" and "How will you pay for it?!"

One would not know it now, but Dr. Varner had stuttered from a very early age. This was the reason for his mother's first question. Due to this stutter, she could not see him preaching and teaching to crowds of people. But, by God's grace, this has not been a problem in his preaching and teaching ministry to this day. Consequently, his mother's reservations were resolved after witnessing her son's teaching and preaching.

As to his mother's second question, God's grace came through again. Dr. Varner worked assiduously at three different jobs during the school year and others during the summer. Any other needs were met by the unexpected checks he received in his mailbox which made ends meet.

Dr. Varner earned his BA in Bible from Bob Jones University in 1969. He met a beautiful girl from Pennsylvania, Helen, and married her in 1971. He then began his first pastorate at Independent Bible Church, where he taught for 7 years. During this time, he completed both his Master of Divinity and Master of Sacred Theology at Biblical Theological Seminary in Hatfield, Pennsylvania.

It was at this seminary that Dr. Varner met Gary Cohen, a professor and a Jewish believer. This friendship inspired a deep interest in Israel and Jewish studies, so much so that Dr. Varner went on to earn a third Master's degree in Jewish Studies at Dropsie College for Hebrew and Cognate learning (now the Center for Judaic Studies at the University of Pennsylvania). Dropsie, the first accredited academic institution in the world to confer PhD degrees in Judaic studies, attracted world-renowned faculty and produced some of the best scholars in the field, including notable evangelical scholars like E. J. Young, R. L. Harris,

Meredith Kline, Ronald F. Youngblood, Raymond Bryan Dillard, and of course, William Varner who distinguished himself as valedictorian of his class.

Dr. Varner's interest in Judaic studies would continue to grow into a life-defining pursuit. After he finished his master's program, he went to minister as a Field Evangelist with the Friends of Israel Gospel Ministry in 1979. He became a prominent figure at the ministry and served as Dean of the Institute of Biblical Studies from its founding in 1987 until 1996. He also designed and wrote the curriculum, taught many courses, and formed the library for the institute. Because of his position as dean, he felt the need to complete a doctoral degree in higher education which he completed at Temple University in Philadelphia.

One day as Dr. Varner was working as dean, he got the call of a lifetime. "Would you like to move to California, teach at The Master's College (now University), and start the Israel Bible Extension Program?" said Doug Bookman on the other end of the line. Of course, this was a dream for Dr. Varner! The chance to travel to the land of the Bible and direct a college program there was an epic opportunity. His answer was a resounding, "Yes!"

He moved with his family, three children in tow at this point, out to sunny Santa Clarita, California. Dr. Varner began teaching at the university in 1996 and just three years later was awarded the Teacher of the Year Award. It is no surprise as there are many reports of Dr. Varner climbing up on desks, bringing outrageous props, asking unexpected questions, putting students on the spot, all to help his pupils learn and love the Bible. He went on to win the award two more times. Until recently, Dr. Varner served as the director of IBEX (Israel Bible Extension program) at The Master's University during which time he provided leadership to countless study trips to Israel. His popularity among IBEX students earned him the affectionate nickname "Dr. IBEX," which you can find on his Mini Cooper's licence plate. His vast experience in the Holy Land was evident when even the local tour guides began to listen and follow him around on his tours.

When Dr. Varner moved with his family, he also began teaching at the Sojourners' Fellowship at Grace Community Church in Sun Valley, California. This group of saints (around 400 people total) meet regularly on Sundays and study the Old Testament book-by-book under

Dr. Varner's leadership. Over the years, Dr. Varner preached through the Old Testament numerous times in Sojourners, earning him the affectionate title, "Rabbi" (no doubt encouraged by the fact that he even presents a Passover Seder in Sojourners annually).

In 2005, Dr. Varner's youngest daughter, Lynda Joy, was in a fatal car accident. While Lynda's untimely death was a difficult test of faith, Dr. Varner showed exemplary faith throughout the ordeal. He stood at Lynda's funeral and said, "The LORD gave, and the LORD has taken away; blessed be the name of the LORD" (Job 1:21). This display of faith continued into his pastorate at Sojourners and his classroom at The Master's University.

As it may be evident from his educational and professional background, Dr. Varner is a renaissance man. He is just as adept at teaching advanced Koine Greek and elaborating on Jewish mysticism in the middle ages as he is at pastoral counseling and preaching Old Testament prose. He is also consistently *au courant* with the latest developments in biblical studies. His varied research interests and capabilities led him to author many popular and academic books along with numerous journal articles. These range from books on Old Testament characters[1] to New Testament exegetical works.[2] During the recent global pandemic, he finished writing a major exegetical commentary on 2 Clement[3], which is now in press, as well as a book on Advent.[4] Concurrently, he also translated the New Testament for the upcoming *Legacy Standard Bible*. Of note is another recent publication on the Passion Week,[5] which he wrote as a result of being left behind from his fifty first trip to Israel. He had lost his passport at the airport! But he turned that loss into gain by producing a fresh work

---

1 *The Chariot of Israel: Exploits of the Prophet Elijah* (Friends of Israel Gospel Ministry, 1984); *Jacob's Dozen: A Prophetic Look at the Tribes of Israel* (Friends of Israel Gospel Ministry, 1987).

2 *The Book of James-A New Perspective: A Linguistic Commentary Applying Discourse Analysis* (Kress Biblical Resources, 2010).

3 *Second Clement: A Commentary* (Cascade Books, Forthcoming).

4 *Anticipating the Advent: Looking for Messiah in All the Right Places* (Fontes, 2020).

5 *Passionate About the Passion Week: A Fresh Look at Jesus' Last Days* (Fontes, 2020)

that reexamines the last days of Jesus on earth. One can only hope for more missed flights in his future.

Many more details beyond this brief sketch can be given of the events which God used to shape Dr. Varner's life into the exemplary scholar-pastor he has become, and the myriad of ways in which he has contributed to the life of the church and the academy. Dr. Varner's multi-faceted interests and specialties in biblical studies coupled with his unparalleled pedagogical capabilities have inspired many of his students to pursue academic careers. This volume is only a small representation of the many successful scholars who owe their first spark of interest in academia to Dr. Varner.

"It's not if you go to IBEX, it's when you go to IBEX"—these famous words sum up Dr. Varner's passion for quality education and scholarship. Perhaps this brief sketch of his life explains why Dr. Varner has devoted his life to bringing the scriptures alive through his teaching, preaching, and writing and encourages every student, colleague, and friend to visit Israel. He knows that there is nothing quite like learning about the God of the Bible, whom he knows and loves, in the land of the Bible.

3

Discourse Analysis and Literary Criticism: A Comparison of Two Interpretive Models

Stanley E. Porter

INTRODUCTION

I HAVE KNOWN WILL VARNER FOR A NUMBER OF YEARS, and have always appreciated his enthusiasm for the study of New Testament Greek and his making available various opportunities for others to share in his excitement and study it along with him. Will is unusual in the sphere of New Testament scholars, because he is always wanting to learn new things, whether these are simply new individual facts or individual items or, and much more importantly, entirely new methods and approaches to studying the Greek text of the New Testament. I had the opportunity of finally meeting Will for the first time in 2005, when McMaster Divinity College hosted the Linguistic Institute for Ancient and Biblical Greek. Will made the trip all the way from California to be with us at the Institute for its inaugural meeting during that summer. Although the Institute only lasted two years—but has in many ways been replaced by the linguistic focus of the Bingham Colloquium every second year on matters of linguistics and the inauguration and regular publication of *Biblical and Ancient Greek Linguistics* (*BAGL*) an online and print journal—it had a significant impact on a number of scholars, and apparently not least of these was Will. Even though Will is a senior scholar, he enthusiastically entered into the atmosphere of the conference. He readily asked questions when he didn't know, and queried assertions or suggestions made by others when he found himself unconvinced by the claims or arguments being made. In other words, Will got maximal benefit from his attendance at the Institute. In fact, and probably unbeknownst to most of us at the time, Will was drinking deeply from the heady mixture of papers that were offered and discussions that were held. These events included a culminating formal dinner, at which the entire complement of the Institute gathered in my home and we enjoyed both good food and further conversation over the broad topic of linguistics. On the basis of the questions Will asked during his time in Hamilton, Ontario, and in subsequent conversation, I realized that he was not just curious about discourse analysis but interested in pursuing it further, much further than I think anyone at the time realized he was prepared to go. It was not that much later that Will was following up with further questions related to research and writing that he was doing on the letter of James. This work culminated in his commentary published in 2010, a mere five years after the Institute.[1] Will had not just been following along with the various strands of discussion during the Institute but he had been convinced that some of the linguistic ideas that were being thrown around regarding texts, discourse, and various approaches to them could be of benefit in his own long-standing work on James, a letter in which he has been interested for some time. I was very happy to receive an inscribed copy of the commentary soon after it was published. I am only sorry that we have not been able to lure Will back to MDC since that initial visit, so that we could continue the conversation that we began during that late summer of 2005.

It is in recognition of his faithful life of Christian scholarship that I offer this paper to my friend Will Varner. In commemoration of his work, I am going to try to push the agenda that he advocated in his commentary on James further than his initial steps in publishing it. In this paper, I am going to examine the premises of discourse analysis and of literary criticism, two models of textual interpretation that have been utilized in New Testament studies over the last thirty or so years. I will lay out their basic approaches and contributions, and then use these to compare how they might approach a text within the New Testament as a means of assessing their relative strengths and values for New Testament interpretation. I realize that my approach

---

1 William Varner, *The Book of James: A New Perspective* (Kress, 2010).

is much more theoretical than practical, especially compared to the research and writings of my friend, Will. Whereas he has done excellent work in applying the results of DA in his writings, I wish to step back and explore some of the fundamental questions that underlie his undertakings.

DISCOURSE ANALYSIS

Discourse analysis (DA) has been a concept in linguistic circles since at least the middle or so of last century, although some would argue that it has been known, even if under different terms, since before that. Within biblical studies, in particular in New Testament studies, its emergence was relatively a bit later, with its gradual yet increased implementation occurring in different forms in the last third or so of the last century. Although no one would pretend that DA has replaced historical criticism, it certainly has established itself as one of the accepted, even if still relatively little implemented, alternative methods being regularly employed by some New Testament scholars.

One of the major problems in discourse analysis, whether biblical or otherwise, is defining the discipline. An examination of several recent handbooks and companion volumes on the topic illustrates the difficulty. The renowned Blackwell handbook takes a concentric approach by way of four sections expanding in scope.[2] The first part defines DA in relation to linguistics, the second connects theory with practice, the third addresses broader socio-political topics, and the fourth explores cross-disciplinary work. Apart from the first part, in which DA is seen in relationship to more traditional linguistic categories (e.g. discourse markers and semantics, among others), the other categories represent DA as, if not inclusive, at least touching on most everything else. In that regard, DA is seen to be a linguistically based but expansive model of textual examination. Linguistics forms the basis of DA, but DA has a legitimate function in appreciating the role of context and how it might relate to and inform and be informed by other disciples (a suggestive stance for an essay concerned with the relationship between DA and literary criticism).

---

2 Deborah Schiffrin, Deborah Tannen, and Heidi E. Hamilton, eds., *The Handbook of Discourse Analysis* (Blackwell, 2003).

By contrast, the Bloomsbury companion to DA comprises only two parts, methods and areas upon which DA inevitably touches, a simple division between DA proper and DA in extension.[3] Although part one of the Bloomsbury volume is not as attentive to the nitty gritty of linguistics as is part one of the Blackwell volume, part one in the Bloomsbury volume treats DA in relation to big questions, such as conversation, genre, narrative, and the like. Many of these topics clearly resonate with topics within the field of literary criticism. The second part of the Bloomsbury volume has a number of the same topics as in the third part of the Blackwell volume, such as DA and race and gender. The Bloomsbury volume on DA is less overtly linguistic and much more literarily interpretive. It establishes DA in relation to many of the well-established topics of critical analysis, and uses this common interpretive platform to move into the expanded interests that DA seems to readily connect with. The third example, the Routledge handbook, is divided into six parts that segment the field into sections of various lengths and significances, or, if one is to ignore the contents and reconceptualize the various essays, one might divide the contents into theory and application.[4] Part one covers various approaches to DA, part two the areas of register and genre, part three issues for spoken discourse, part four educational applications, part five institutional applications, and part six various culturally important topics. There are several recognizable differences between the Routledge handbook and the other two volumes outlined above, in both scope and application. The areas covered in the Routledge volume touch on topics central to Systemic Functional Linguistics (SFL), such as register and genre, education, institutional applications, and culture and context. In fact, SFL is offered, along with Critical Discourse Analysis (CDA) and several other models of DA, as a specific approach to DA. In that sense, the Routledge handbook sees DA as less a generalizing rubric for other forms of linguistics and more a means of appreciating and even identifying the discourse implications of already developed methods in linguistics. And there are a number of methods

---

3 Ken Hyland and Brian Paltridge, eds., *The Bloomsbury Companion to Discourse Analysis* (Bloomsbury, 2011).

4 James Paul Gee and Michael Handford, eds., *The Routledge Handbook of Discourse Analysis* (Routledge, 2012).

in linguistics that have in various ways influenced and been taken up in various ways in models of DA.

In these definitions, based upon three recent reference volumes, we may observe several broader generalizations that help us to understand DA. The first is that DA is seen as either assumptively linguistic or abstractly linguistic, by which I mean that, apart from the first parts of several of the volumes, there is not much discussion of the traditional areas of linguistics, if by these we mean the usual categories of phonology, morphology, syntax, semantics, and even pragmatics. This indicates that DA is not typically or usually conceptualized simply as analysis that is extended beyond the sentence or clause, but as if DA were simply a heightened or expanded form of language study that must accept the presuppositions of others. This is the way that DA was once conceived, especially in an earlier stage when it was more readily equated with text-linguistics (although that term remains ambiguous and is still widely used). The second observation is that there is a sense in which DA is not a definable *thing*, but it is "things," things requiring special attention or apparently requiring that the resources of DA be applied to them. The handbooks contain numerous essays in which DA engages with other areas or disciplines that illustrate its malleability. A third observation is that what might well be called method in other disciplines is not so narrowly defined in these handbooks. These handbooks have moved away from DA as focusing upon lower levels of language and are much more interested in the surrounding issues that intersect with DA, such as culture, ideology, and context defined in various ways. There is little in any of the books that remotely resembles instruction in or exemplification of any specific method of linguistics. The fourth observation is that, even after surveying these various handbooks, one might still wish to ask the question regarding what DA is, because it appears to be encompassing of many other things but also something much more narrowly circumscribed as a result of its associations and relations, a narrower entity that is difficult to grasp and adequately define.

A way through this potential tangle of expansive thoughts regarding DA may be found in attempting to narrow down some of the major ideas that recur in discussions of it by briefly presenting some of the major models of DA used outside of New Testament studies.[5] DA is often said to have begun with the work of Zellig Harris, who presented a systematic means of examining what he called "connected speech" or writing,[6] a highly computational approach without a place for the meaning of language. Some of the earliest approaches to DA developed from the traditional area of linguistics called pragmatics. Most linguistic models were concerned with the sentence as the highest level of analysis, but even with this unit, one observed a difference between sentence meaning (or semantics) and utterance meaning (or pragmatics). The philosopher H. Paul Grice addressed this disparity through what he called conversational implicature, that is, the implications when humans converse.[7] The implicatures involved various maxims, include maxims of cooperation, relevance, and other forms of sufficiency.[8] Grice's principles were akin to those developed in natural language philosophy that came to be known as speech-act theory, identified with J. L. Austin and John R. Searle.[9] Speech-act theory

---

5 I have provided an earlier summary in Stanley E. Porter, "Discourse Analysis," in *The Dictionary of the Bible and Ancient Media*, ed. Tom Thatcher et al. (Bloomsbury, 2017), 83–87, esp. 83–84; cf. also Porter, "Defining Discourse Analysis as an Important New Testament Interpretive Framework," in *New Testament Philology: Essays in Honor of David Alan Black*, ed. Melton Bennett Winstead (Pickwick, 2018), 194–211. See Deborah Schiffrin, *Approaches to Discourse* (Blackwell, 1994). Cf. the similar, though in some ways limited, approach (but treating the Old Testament) in Terrance R. Wardlaw, Jr., "Discourse Analysis," in *Words and the Word: Explorations in Biblical Interpretation and Literary Theory*, ed. David G. Firth and Jamie A. Grant (InterVarsity, 2008), 266–317.

6 Zellig Harris, "Discourse Analysis," *Language* 28.1 (1952): 1–30; followed by "Discourse Analysis: A Sample Text," *Language* 28.4 (1952): 474–94; both reprinted in Harris, *Papers in Structural and Transformational Linguistics* (Reidel, 1970), 313–48, 349–72; and Harris, *Discourse Analysis Reprints* (Mouton, 1963). His form of DA was dependent upon constituent analysis and introduced such notions as kernels and transformations. Cf. the related Harris, *String Analysis of Sentence Structure* (Mouton, 1962).

7 H. Paul Grice, "Logic and Conversation" (1967), repr. in *Studies in the Way of Words* (Harvard University Press, 1989), 22–40, along with other essays.

8 Relevance Theory, although it is not so much a language theory as an orientation, is a direct development from Grice's ideas. See Dan Sperber and Dierdre Wilson, *Relevance: Communication and Cognition*, 2nd ed. (Blackwell, 1995 [1986]). See Margaret G. Sim, *A Relevant Way to Read: A New Approach to Exegesis and Communication* (Pickwick, 2016).

9 J. L. Austin, *How to Do Things with Words*, 2nd ed., ed. J. O. Urmson and Marina Sbisà (Oxford University Press, 1975) and John R. Searle, *Speech Acts: An Essay in*

recognizes that language is performative rather than simply informative. A locution may have various illocutionary forces, such as naming, promising, or introducing, and various perlocutionary effects. The field of sociolinguistics has been an even more productive area for development of DA. The Interactional Sociolinguistics of John Gumperz examines the interaction between participants in communication, and recognizes that dialogue is situated in a social context and that the social situation is responsible for the construction of the verbal interaction.[10] Conversation Analysis is another sociolinguistic DA model. Growing out of ethnomethodology, which examines how people know and do things, conversation as a creator and reflector of the person was developed by Irving Goffman.[11] He examines how conversation is adjusted in anticipation of a response to the conversational environment. The Ethnology of Communication of Dell Hymes grows out of linguistic anthropology and focuses upon communication as an important part of culture. Influenced by Prague School linguistics (see below), Hymes analyzes communication with reference to various factors: setting/scene, participants, ends, act sequence, key, instrumentalities, norms, and genre (Speaking).[12] Some recent work in multilingualism, diglossia, and code-switching has made use of these various sociolinguistic/anthropological theories. Variation analysis of William Labov understands how speakers vary their language for different purposes, and hence language is both social and functional.[13] Major areas for examination relate to ethnicity, where Labov questions the notion of language deficiency as caused by any factor other than social situation.

The final group of methods of DA is Systemic Functional Linguistics (SFL), and its related Critical Discourse Analysis (CDA). Michael Halliday, building on the linguistics of John Firth and anthropology of Bronislaw Malinowski, examines language according to its function

---

the Philosophy of Language (Cambridge University Press, 1969). Anthony Thiselton, among a few others, has frequently attempted to utilize speech-act theory to inform his exegesis.

10   John J. Gumperz, *Discourse Strategies* (Cambridge University Press, 1982).

11   Irving Goffman, *Forms of Talk* (University of Pennsylvania Press, 1981).

12   Dell Hymes, *Foundations in Sociolinguistics: An Ethnographic Approach* (University of Pennsylvania Press, 1974).

13   William Labov, *Sociolinguistic Patterns* (University of Pennsylvania Press, 1972).

in context. Halliday differentiates three (or four) (meta-)functions of language, related to its thought (ideational), participants (interpersonal), and conveyance (textual).[14] Critical Discourse Analysis draws heavily upon SFL, as well as the critical theory of Jürgen Habermas and the Frankfurt School, politics, and economics.[15] CDA examines language and its relationships to power, identity formation, and social construction. Multimodal Discourse Analysis, as propounded by Gunther Kress and developed by many others, examines the communicative potential of various social semiotic systems in their various modes such as music, art, and electronic media.[16] Biblical studies has been highly influenced by SFL, as will be noted below, but not so much by the other related forms of DA.

There are also a group of introductions to DA that are not as easily categorized according to the above schema. These introductions—of which there are many and they continue to grow in number—may best be described as eclectic, or at least integrative and inclusive in approach. They often emphasize pragmatics, making use of speech-act theory, but they also may draw upon any number of other elements of DA or textlinguistics, including various cognitive theories. Here is not the place to treat them individually, except to note that they often provide the author's own approach to text or discourse, drawing upon various strands of the above theories, as well as other approaches, to create what is represented as a model of DA. Their titles often indicate their areas of interest within DA.[17]

---

14 M. A. K. Halliday and John J. Webster, *Text Linguistics: The How and Why of Meaning* (Equinox, 2014). Halliday wrote many things much earlier, but this is a clear identification of his linguistic approach to DA.

15 Norman Fairclough, *Discourse and Social Change* (Polity, 1994). CDA has had a huge influence upon sociolinguistics as a form of DA.

16 Anthony Baldry and Paul J. Thibault, *Multimodal Transcription and Text Analysis* (Equinox, 2006).

17 A few of these volumes, in rough alphabetical order, are Malcolm Coulthard, *An Introduction to Discourse Analysis*, 2nd ed. (Longman, 1985 [1977]); Teun A. van Dijk, *Text and Context: Explorations in the Semantics and Pragmatics of Discourse* (Longman, 1977); Robert de Beaugrande and Wolfgang Dressler, *Introduction to Text Linguistics* (Longman, 1981); Gillian Brown and George Yule, *Discourse Analysis*, Cambridge Textbooks in Linguistics (Cambridge University Press, 1983); Michael Stubbs, *Discourse Analysis: The Sociolinguistic Analysis of Natural Language* (Blackwell, 1983); Alexandra Georgakopoulou and Dionysis Goutsos, *Discourse Analysis: An*

I have spent some time on these non-biblical forms of DA to illustrate the difference between them and DA in New Testament studies. There is some overlap, especially in more recent research, but New Testament studies has also appropriated and developed some of its own forms of DA. DA in New Testament studies was probably first developed within the ambit of the Summer Institute of Linguistics (SIL) on the basis of the Tagmemics of Kenneth Pike, and then developed further by his student and fellow linguist, Robert Longacre.[18] SIL has developed in different directions since then into a more cognitive-functional approach as seen in the work of Stephen Levinsohn.[19] Nevertheless, both Tagmemics and at least some parts of the cognitive-functional approach are functional in focus, emphasizing the functions of language over its formal characteristics. The functional side of this equation has been influenced by the Continental Functionalism of Simon Dik and the cognitive dimension by a variety of scholars reacting to Chomskyanism in varying ways.[20] Continental DA, including the Scandinavian and continental forms, was probably the next major form of DA to emerge in New Testament studies. This form of DA emphasized the relationship of syntax, semantics, and pragmatics, while also incorporating communications theory and rhetorical theory, and is found in the work of scholars such as Birger Olsson and Cilliers Breytenbach.[21] Around the same time, but in relative isolation in South Africa, J. P. Louw was responsible

---

Introduction, 2nd ed. (Edinburgh University Press, 2004 [1997]); John Paul Gee, *An Introduction to Discourse Analysis: Theory and Method* (London: Routledge, 1999); Barbara Johnstone, *Discourse Analysis*, 2nd ed. (Blackwell, 2008 [2002]); and Brian Paltridge, *Discourse Analysis* (Continuum, 2006).

18 Kenneth L. Pike, *Language in Relation to a Unified Theory of the Structure of Human Behavior*, 2nd ed. (Mouton, 1967); Robert E. Longacre, *The Grammar of Discourse*, 2nd ed. (Plenum, 1996).

19 Stephen H. Levinson, *Discourse Features of New Testament Greek: A Coursebook on the Information Structure of New Testament Greek*, 2nd ed. (SIL, 2000).

20 Simon Dik, *The Theory of Functional Grammar*, 2 vols., ed. Kees Hengeveld (de Gruyter, 1997); Vyvyan Evans and Melanie Green, *Cognitive Linguistics: An Introduction* (Edinburgh University Press, 2006).

21 Birger Olsson, *Structure and Meaning in the Fourth Gospel: A Text-Linguistic Analysis of John 2:1–11 and 4:1–42*, CBNT 6 (Gleerup, 1974); Cilliers Breytenbach, *Nachfolge und Zukunftserwartung nach Markus: Eine methodenkritische Studie*, AThANT 71 (Theologischer Verlag, 1984).

for developing South African colon analysis, as a means of identifying Subject-Predicate structures (cola) and describing their semantic relations in ever-expanding configurations.[22] He has been followed mostly by other South Africans, although enthusiasm seems to have waned in recent years. It was only in the 1990s that Systemic Functional Linguistics emerged as an important framework in New Testament DA, with its emphasis upon a stratified view of language and the relationship of lexicogrammar and semantics within a robust view of context. Around this same time, evidently because of the diversity within New Testament DA, along with other critical theories, an eclectic form of DA also emerged, reflected in the DA of George Guthrie.[23] This eclectic model drew upon various forms of DA, other linguistic theories, and other interpretive approaches such as literary criticism. There have been a number who have continued to develop their own eclectic models.

Within such a panoply of critical practice, it would appear difficult to identify the major factors within DA. Some time ago, I tried to identify some of the major concepts within DA. Some of the important terms that define DA are (1) bottom-up versus top-down analysis, (2) movement beyond the clause or sentence, (3) examination of whole texts, (4) the role of semantics, (5) levels of linguistic description, (6) markedness and prominence, (7) the sociolinguistic dimension or the importance of language in use, and (8) the meaning of a text.[24] Let me say a little about each one, and illustrate it from some recent work in DA in New Testament studies.

1. *Bottom-Up and Top-Down Analysis.* This distinction captures the importance of moving from the smallest analyzable units of structure to the largest structures, and from the broadest generalizations to the most particular. SFL captures this well in its stratification of language from context to semantics to lexicogrammar to expression, in which there is an interplay among the strata (SFL has a similar movement in the lexicogrammar called the rank scale). Jeffrey Reed displays how

---

22 J. P. Louw, *A Semantic Discourse Analysis of Romans* (University of Pretoria, Department of Greek, 1987).

23 George H. Guthrie, *The Structure of Hebrews: A Text-Linguistic Analysis* (Brill, 1994; repr., Baker, 1998).

24 Stanley E. Porter, *Linguistic Analysis of the Greek New Testament: Studies in Tools, Methods, and Practice* (Baker Academic, 2016), 133–44.

one must, especially in dealing with an epigraphic language, move from the lexicogrammar to the semantics and from semantics to lexicogrammar.[25] He does this so as to study the question of the integrity of Philippians, a question that requires attention to individual verbal configurations (e.g. Phil 3:1–2) and the entire letter and its context. Most forms of DA appreciate the necessary interplay between the levels of language, and there is often a movement from individual components, such as the noun group or clause, to larger levels of meaning, such as larger structural units and especially conceptual units such as the text or a discourse type. Some other types of discourse analysis are often bottom-up oriented, such as Stephen Levinsohn's when he is examining various phenomena such as conjunctions in a particular book.[26] We often see such movement from bottom to top and in reverse within Will's DA of James.

2. *Movement beyond the Clause or Sentence.* In his *Grammar of Discourse*, Robert Longacre develops a model that reflects elements of Tagmemics, in which he develops categories beyond the clause that he then transfers to his study of the Bible. In an essay on the Gospel of Mark, entitled "A Top-down, Template-Driven Narrative Analysis, Illustrated by Application to Mark's Gospel," Longacre identifies elements of plot—stage, inciting incident, mounting tension, climax, denouement, and closure—and then within the individual units identifies the various episodes into which the Gospel is divided.[27] Along the way he is able to identify what he calls the discourse peak (Mark 11:1–16:8), the didactic peak (Mark 11:12–13:37), and the action peak (Mark 14:1–16:8), as well as other analytical categories that give shape to his examination of the Gospel. In some people's minds, DA is defined by this principle of movement beyond the clause, and in many respects it is a sound principle. However, this is not to say that DA cannot take place below the clause, only that often such analysis must also appeal to levels above.

---

25 Jeffrey T. Reed, *A Discourse Analysis of Philippians: Method and Rhetoric in the Debate over Literary Integrity* (Sheffield Academic, 1997).

26 E.g. Levinsohn, *Discourse Features*, 71–93.

27 Robert E. Longacre, "A Top-Down, Template-Driven Narrative Analysis, Illustrated by Application to Mark's Gospel," in *Discourse Analysis and the New Testament: Approaches and Results*, ed. Stanley E. Porter and Jeffrey T. Reed (Sheffield Academic, 1999), 140–68.

3. *Examination of Whole Texts.* DA is not necessarily concerned with whole texts, as it can often involve studies of corpora larger than a single text or even several texts (as well as portions of texts), as Matthew Brook O'Donnell so effectively has shown.[28] However, when we think of the most insightful DA we think of description or analysis not of incidental clauses but of entire texts, even if these texts, as they often are in linguistics, are relatively short. As James Martin has said, the vast majority of texts discussed in linguistics fit on a single sheet of paper each.[29] This means that there are increased challenges with examining entire texts, when these texts are even as large as a New Testament book. Jae-Hyun Lee shows the profitability in a rigorous analysis of even eight chapters in Romans.[30] However, a number of recent works of DA have tackled entire books, such as Mark's Gospel by Cilliers Breytenbach and by John Cook, John by Steve Booth, Philippians by Jeffrey Reed, Hebrews by Cynthia Westfall and by George Guthrie, 2 Corinthians by Christopher Land, and Romans by Johannes Louw and by Stanley Porter,[31] as well as Will's DA of James.

4. *The Role of Semantics.* Early DA, as noticed above, was very formal in orientation, concerned with sentence strings and the like. One of the major developments of DA is attention to semantics. For some this means making a useful distinction between semantics and pragmatics, with DA concerned more with pragmatics as the utterance meaning or meaning in use. However, some other DA models conflate levels of meaning into a single semantics stratum, sometimes simply referred to as semantics and sometimes as discourse semantics.

---

28 Matthew Brook O'Donnell, *Corpus Linguistics and the Greek of the New Testament* (Sheffield Phoenix, 2005).

29 J. R. Martin, "Macro-Genres: The Ecology of the Page" (1994), repr. in *Systemic Functional Linguistics*, ed. J. R. Martin and Y. J. Doran, 5 vols. (Routledge, 2015), 4:206–55, here 206.

30 Jae-Hyun Lee, *Paul's Gospel in Romans: A Discourse Analysis of Rom 1:16–8:39*, LBS 3 (Brill, 2010).

31 Breytenbach, *Nachfolge*; John G. Cook, *The Structure and Persuasive Power of Mark: A Linguistic Approach* (Scholars Press, 1995); Steve Booth, *Selected Peak Marking Features in the Gospel of John* (Peter Lang, 1996); Reed, *Discourse Analysis*; Cynthia Long Westfall, *A Discourse Analysis of the Letter to the Hebrews: The Relationship between Form and Meaning* (T&T Clark, 2005); Christopher D. Land, *The Integrity of 2 Corinthians and Paul's Aggravating Absence*, NTM 36 (Sheffield Phoenix, 2015); Louw, *Romans*; Stanley E. Porter, *The Letter to the Romans: A Linguistic and Literary Commentary*, NTM 37 (Sheffield Phoenix, 2016).

In his examination of 2 Corinthians, Christopher Land examines the semantics of 2 Corinthians in light of arguments that the letter's diverse elements indicate that it is a composite letter.[32] He instead examines the various "meanings" within 2 Corinthians in an attempt to find a coherent text that can indicate a context in which such meanings could form a single text.

5. *Levels of Linguistic Description.* An examination of a number of different attempts at DA shows that various levels of linguistic description are to be found. There are, for example, those who examine the structure of the text, such as George Guthrie in his treatment of Hebrews or Mark Edward Taylor in his investigation of James.[33] Some scholars differentiate a number of levels of description, so that Ray Van Neste discusses cohesion, which exists beyond the clause level in SFL, and structure in the Pastoral Epistles, examining both lower and higher levels of analysis; and John Cook studies the structure and the persuasive power in Mark's Gospel, thereby treating both structural and semantic categories; and the same is claimed by Birger Olsson in his examination of the structure and meaning in John's Gospel—although I note that all of these DA volumes speak in relationship to structure, obviously a major interest in DA.[34] In other words, DA is diverse in the data that it gathers and attempts to find various levels of appropriate linguistic description whereby it can comment upon the text.

6. *Markedness and Prominence.* Markedness and prominence are, together, one of the most widely discussed topics in New Testament studies. Markedness and prominence originated in the Prague School of Linguistics (see below), but have come to be used in a variety of ways within linguistics, including within DA. As a result, the terms are defined differently and there is discussion of whether categories developed for phonetics can be applied to other ranks or strata. Despite the technical difficulties, most discourse analysts believe that markedness and prominence are useful categories because they identify and provide a mechanism for describing the fact that not all features of

---

32 Land, *Integrity.*

33 Guthrie, *Structure*; Mark Edward Taylor, *A Text-Linguistic Investigation into the Discourse Structure of James* (T&T Clark, 2006).

34 Ray Van Neste, *Cohesion and Structure in the Pastoral Epistles* (T&T Clark, 2004); Cook, *Structure*; Olsson, *Structure.*

text are expressed on the same level, and that differentiation is made between linguistic elements—and some of these are marked and thus in some sense have prominence, whether that prominence derives from statistical or morphological or other means or is simply a function of context and accumulation of marked features. Two essays on the notions of markedness and prominence are found in a collection of essays on language, by Stanley Porter and Cynthia Westfall, where they examine the means of linguistic marking.[35] Even though they arrive at varying conclusions, they illustrate that the concepts are important and worth defining.

7. *Sociolinguistic Dimension/Language in Use.* As the survey above illustrates, much DA originates in sociological/anthropological environments, that is, out of concern for how people or people groups use language. Hughson Ong has published a major treatment of multiligualism and the languages of Jesus, in which he draws upon the ethnography of communication model of Hymes, as well as other theories of multilingualism, to explain the linguistic situation of first-century Palestine.[36] One of the features of Ong's treatment is his identification of various social domains within the first-century sociolinguistic landscape, and then his evaluation of the language of use within each domain. Ong's study addresses how one uses sociolinguistic data to inform language usage, and thereby how one connects the wider sociolinguistic context with language use, in his instance the languages of Jesus and his contemporaries.

8. *Meaning of a Text.* The concept of meaning is complex, and no less complex in DA. The kinds of analysis that one may perform in DA may result in various estimations of what constitutes meaning. In other words, there is no single sense of "meaning" in DA. For example, the meaning of a text may be expressed as the result of examination

---

35 Stanley E. Porter, "Prominence: A Theoretical Overview," and Cynthia Long Westfall, "A Method for the Analysis of Prominence in Hellenistic Greek," both in *The Linguist as Pedagogue: Trends in the Teaching and Linguistic Analysis of the Greek New Testament*, ed. Stanley E. Porter and Matthew Brook O'Donnell, NTM 11 (Sheffield Phoenix, 2009), 45–74 and 75–94. Cf. Paul L. Garvin, ed. and trans., *A Prague School Reader on Esthetics, Literary Structure, and Style* (Georgetown University Press, 1964), esp. the section on theory and standard language and departure from it.

36 Hughson T. Ong, *The Multilingual Jesus and the Sociolinguistic World of the New Testament*, LBS 12 (Brill, 2016).

of cohesion and cohesive harmony of a text within a SFL framework, the analysis and consequent hierarchical arrangement of colon relationships within South African colon analysis, descriptions of various syntactic, semantic, and pragmatic patterns, and perhaps even statements regarding rhetorical impact, within continental DA, and the like. I note how several of the volumes of DA speak of meaning in their titles, but each means a different thing by it.[37] Each of these analyses has the potential for fulfilling the criteria for establishing meaning within a text, according to the standards of a particular model of DA, but the question of what that meaning is in relation to wider theories of meaning remains unanswered.

More could and definitely should be said about what DA is and how it is used in New Testament studies, but the above survey should help to define how DA is already being used by some of its current practitioners.

LITERARY CRITICISM

I turn now to literary criticism, or, as some prefer to call it, literary approaches to reading the New Testament. Literary criticism of the New Testament, a field that trailed behind Old Testament studies, emerged in New Testament studies in the early 1980s and continued to flourish for some time, to the point of promulgating several derived forms of criticism, such as reader-response criticism and deconstruction, among some others, such as some canonical approaches and narrative criticism. However, over the last ten to fifteen years, literary criticism of the New Testament has apparently severely receded in importance, apart from character studies, which seem to be thriving in many quarters, and a recent resurgence of interest in some of the mechanics of literary study. Character studies are an important part of traditional literary criticism, so it is perhaps not out of place to see such studies, although the number of them does raise questions about the factors that have prompted their emergence. The field of literary

---

37 E.g. Olsson, *Structure*, from a Continental DA perspective; and Westfall, *Discourse Analysis*, from a SFL framework, with very different conceptions of syntax, semantics, and pragmatics, in which the three of Olsson are rolled into the one of Westfall.

studies is, and always has been, a very large, complex, and expansive field of intellectual endeavor. Thus, one should be suspicious when one hears the term "the literary approach" to the Bible. Instead, it is better to see literary criticism as a complex of various approaches.[38]

The history of literary criticism is a long and complex one. Statements about the nature of literature and its purpose or function go back to the ancients. One finds comments about literature in Plato, Aristotle, Horace, Quintilian, and Longinus, to name the best known who are always referred to. The history of literary criticism from ancient to modern times can be summarized as a debate over the purpose of literature—whether it was to instruct or delight—and the recognition that literature was mimetic in nature, that is, literature was in one form or another an attempt to imitate life.

Major advances in literary criticism emerged with the rise of Romanticism.[39] Romanticism is one of the great intellectual movements

---

38 There are many summaries of the field of literary criticism, including introductions to the field and anthologies of representative statements by various literary theorists. I have found especially helpful in my summary below Anne H. Stevens, *Literary Theory and Criticism: An Introduction* (Broadview, 2015); Irena R. Makaryk, ed., *Encyclopedia of Contemporary Literary Theory: Approaches, Scholars, Terms* (University of Toronto Press, 1993); Raman Selden, Peter Widddowson, and Peter Brooker, *A Reader's Guide to Contemporary Literary Theory*, 4th ed. (Harvester Wheatsheaf, 1997); and Mads Rosendahl Thomsen et al., eds., *Literature: An Introduction to Theory and Analysis* (Bloomsbury, 2017), who also provide a very useful "An Overview of Schools of Criticism" (pp. 409–23); and whose approach is somewhat mirrored in Douglas Estes and Ruth Sheridan, eds., *How John Works: Storytelling in the Fourth Gospel* (SBL Press, 2016). A previous effort in this regard on my part is Stanley E. Porter, "Literary Approaches to the New Testament: From Formalism to Deconstruction and Back," in *Approaches to New Testament Study*, ed. Stanley E. Porter and David Tombs (Sheffield Academic, 1995), 77–128. See also Stanley E. Porter and Jason C. Robinson, *Hermeneutics: An Introduction to Interpretive Theory* (Eerdmans, 2011). I draw on all of these in what follows. I do not write as if there is as much connection between linguistics and literary theory as does David Birch in *Language, Literature and Critical Practice: Ways of Analysing Text* (Routledge, 1989); an approach taken in a more limited way by Douglas Mangum and Douglas Estes, eds., *Literary Approaches to the Bible* (Lexham Press, 2016). However, having said that, I believe that Birch does an excellent job of bringing many different linguistic, literary, and philosophical approaches together in a coherent account worth further examination. For a somewhat similar, though more limited, attempt, see Grant R. Osborne, "Literary Theory and Biblical Interpretation," in *Words and the Word*, 17–50.

39 See Roy Porter and Mikuláš Teich, eds., *Romanticism in National Context* (Cambridge University Press, 1988), which surveys the movement by major countries.

that swept much of western thinking along with it, and as a result is very difficult to define even though it exerted a great influence upon contemporary thought. Romanticism emerged in the eighteenth century as a reaction to many of the developments during the Enlightenment, with the rise of rationalism and empiricism. The emphasis upon rationalism and empiricism, while helpful and necessary to establish the basis for modern scientific thought, was viewed by some as inhibiting the nature of the human being by subjecting all of human experience to the strictures of empirical evidence and only those things that can be rationally explained. The result was an intellectual reaction but also extension of Enlightenment thought that corresponded with the rise of democratic movements, appreciation of the common and ordinary, recognition of and even a return to an uninhibited nature, and the role of experience, including the role of the sublime. Romanticism took various forms, but was influenced in Germany by the idealistic thought of Immanuel Kant and Georg Hegel, and seen in the writings of Friedrich Schiller and Johann Goethe. The Germans had an effect upon English Romanticism, especially by means of Samuel Taylor Coleridge, and resulted in the work of William Wordsworth and Percy Bysshe Shelley, among others. In his writings upon the Bible, which became the basis of modern hermeneutics, Friedrich Schleiermacher was one of the most important thinkers of Romanticism, and his views of involvement of the subject in understanding resulted in focus upon the role of the author and intentionality as a means of interpreting literature, and with it an emphasis upon biographical and historical criticism.[40] Schleiermacher contended that one must understand the author better than the author understood him- or herself. That is, one must know the inner thoughts and intentions of the author. This emphasis carried over into the rise of realism, which was an extension of romantic notions of the common person and encouraged by the enduring legacy of the mimetic view of art as imitation from classical times.

The focus upon the author as the center of meaning began a progressive movement of literary critical re-evaluation of the center of authority within literary interpretation, one that ended up involving

---

40 Friedrich Schleiermacher, *Hermeneutics and Criticism and Other Writings*, ed. Andrew Bowie (Cambridge University Press, 1998).

the triad of author, text, and reader. The debate over the center of authority in interpretation has continued to have relevance to the present. Schleiermacher argued for the author as the center of authority, a position that continued to be emphasized in various successive movements, up until the turn of the nineteenth to twentieth centuries. There were two major intertwined movements that led to the de-centering of the author and the emergence of the text as the center of authority. These two movements were one literary and the other linguistic. The linguistic movement I will summarize first as the supporting background framework for discussing the literary movement.

The comparative philology movement, which had developed along with the rise of Romanticism in the early nineteenth century, was concerned with applying theories of progress and development to an optimistic view of human development, including language.[41] As a consequence, there was increased attention to the interrelatedness of human languages, especially those of the West. The result was the description of major language families, such as the Indo-European language family that extended from the far east to the west, and encompassed the vast majority of the known languages, at least of Europe. Language study at the time was concerned with diachronic relationships and deducing fixed rules of language change. A major shift began with some earlier thought of scholars such as Wilhelm von Humboldt and his concern for historicism,[42] his recognition of the historical embeddedness of language and culture, but emerged most fully in the work of Ferdinand de Saussure, who lectured in the first decade of the twentieth century, and the writings of the Prague Linguistics Circle (1926–1948).[43] Saussure, who himself was a comparative philologist, recognized several important features about language that caused a major shift in orientation. These included the arbitrary relationship of the sign and its signification, the difference between one's language system and one's individual use of language,

---

41 R. H. Robins, *A Short History of Linguistics*, 3rd ed. (Longman, 1990) 180–217.

42 Wilhelm von Humboldt, *On Language*, ed. Michael Losonsky, trans. Peter Heath (Cambridge University Press, 1999 [1840]).

43 Ferdinand de Saussure, *Course in General Linguistics*, ed. Charles Bally and Albert Sechehaye with Albert Riedlinger, trans. Wade Baskin (McGraw-Hill, 1959 [1916]); and on the Prague School, F. W. Galen, *Historic Structures: The Prague School Project, 1928–1946* (University of Texas Press, 1985).

the difference between synchrony and diachrony, the recognition of language as difference, the importance of language as system, and language as social system. Similar ideas were being developed by members of the Prague Linguistics Circle, under the influence of Russian Formalism (see the next paragraph). The Prague school not only accepted synchrony over diachrony (without rejecting diachrony), they also emphasized the systematic nature of language and its functional potential. Out of these two major movements emerged structuralism, which, like Romanticism, came to be an equivalent dominant intellectual movement within the twentieth century.[44] One of the founders of the Prague Circle, Jakobson, apparently first used the term "structuralism" in reference to literature in 1929, and then Jan Mukarovsky, another of the major figures, regularly used it in a literary/linguistic sense from 1934 on.[45]

The Russian Formalists (1915–1923) consisted of two major literary groups, one in Moscow and the other in St. Petersburg, both of which formed just before the Russian Revolution, around 1915–1916.[46] The Russian formalists were called "formalists" by others as a derogatory term because of their emphasis upon the formal features of literary texts, indicating a clear shift to the text as the center of authority. Two of the fundamental distinctions of the Russian formalists are differentiation between the story of actual events and the discourse that conveys them (various terms are used to describe this), and the notion of "defamiliarization," in which that which is familiar or usual is de-familiarized and made strange and thereby noteworthy so as to be experienced anew. Both ideas had a major influence upon subsequent text-centered thought. The former influenced views of narrative and became a staple of narratology, the French influenced form

---

44 For a brief introduction that shows some of the extent of its reach, see David Robey, ed., *Structuralism: An Introduction* (Clarendon, 1973), with essays on structuralism and linguistics, social anthropology, semiology, literature, science, philosophy, and mathematics.

45 For representative essays, see Jan Mukarovsky, *The Word and Verbal Art: Selected Essays*, trans. and ed. John Burbank and Peter Steiner (Yale University Press, 1977).

46 See Lee T. Lemon and Marion J. Reis, eds. and trans., *Russian Formalist Criticism: Four Essays* (University of Nebraska Press, 1965); and S. Bann and J. E. Bowlt, eds., *Russian Formalism* (Edinburgh: Scottish Academic Press, 1973), with an insightful opening essay by Tzvetan Todorov, "Some Approaches to Russian Formalism," 6–19.

of structuralist literary criticism that has continued to thrive in various ways in the work of A. J. Greimas and Seymour Chatman,[47] among others, including entering a post-structuralist phrase (see below),[48] and the latter influenced the Prague linguists and the development of theories of markedness and foregrounding. Vladimir Propp's *Morphology of the Folk Tale* (1928),[49] in which he identifies 31 types, is probably the most well-known of the works of the formalists, with Mikhail Bakhtin, with his emphasis upon intertextuality, heteroglossia, dialogism, etc., being a descendant of the movement once it had been suppressed by the rise of Communism within the Soviet Union.[50] Two of the most important members of the Russian formalist school were Roman Jakobson and René Wellek. Jakobson left Moscow in 1920 for Prague and then fled to the US in 1939 because of Hitler (he was Jewish), and had an influence upon both literary criticism and structuralism in North America (he greatly influenced Claude Lévi-Strauss).[51] Wellek, a member of the Prague school but who was a literary scholar, emigrated to the US in 1939 and held important positions in literary studies at the University of Iowa and Yale University, and brought the influence of Russian formalism by way of Prague to North American literary criticism.[52]

The rise of the New Criticism in the US and practical criticism in the UK is the result of the influence of especially Russian formalism

---

47 A. J. Greimas, *Structural Semantics: An Attempt at a Method*, trans. Daniele McDowell, Ronald Schleifer, and Alan Velie (University of Nebraska Press, 1983 [1966]); and Seymour Chatman, *Story and Discourse: Narrative Structure in Fiction and Film* (Cornell University Press, 1978).

48 See Patrick O'Neill, *Fictions of Discourse: Reading Narrative* Theory (University of Toronto Press, 1994).

49 Vladimir Propp, *Morphology of the Folktale*, trans. Laurence Scott, rev. Louis A. Wagner (University of Texas Press, 1968).

50 Among many works, M. M. Bakhtin, *The Dialogic Imagination: Four Essays*, ed. Michael Holquist, trans. Caryl Emerson and Michael Holquist (University of Texas Press, 1981).

51 There are many works of linguistics to cite by Jakobson. Some of those on literature appear in Roman Jakobson, *Language in Literature*, ed. Krystyna Pomorska and Stephen Rudy (Harvard University Press, 1987).

52 René Wellek, *Discriminations: Further Concepts of Criticism* (Yale University Press, 1970), who provides many insightful chapters, including one on "The Literary Theory and Aesthetics of the Prague School," 275–303, that has influenced my thinking.

but also of structuralism and found philosophical support in both phenomenology and logical positivism. Phenomenology, founded by Edmund Husserl and manifested in Roman Ingarden,[53] emphasized the nature of perception of the thing itself, and logical positivism, which emerged from the Vienna Circle and spread to the English-speaking world, argued that the basis of verifiable knowledge was empiricism and axiomatic truths (such as of mathematics).[54] The literary movement came to be identified with the text as the center of authority, the text as a self-contained artifact, and the necessity of close readings of the text. I. A. Richards, a Cambridge scholar who later taught at Harvard, in the 1920s wrote several important works, one on the *Principles of Literary Criticism* (1924) and the other on *Practical Criticism* (1929).[55] *Practical Criticism* was the result of his experience of having students respond to unattributed poems, as experiments in dealing directly and only with the text. Richards's student, William Empson, continued this tradition in his *Seven Types of Ambiguity* and other works that emphasized the types of meaning within texts.[56] T. S. Eliot and F. R. Leavis in their emphasis upon the great tradition of literature are also often associated with this text-centered movement.[57] In the US, there were several streams that came together in the New Criticism, all of them emphasizing in varying ways the text as the center of interpretive authority. A number of American scholars came under the influence of the European movements noted above, including such a highly educated northern scholar as Austin

---

53 Edmund Husserl, *Ideas: General Introduction to Pure Phenomenology*, trans. W. R. Boyce Gibson (Collier, 1962 [1913]) and Roman Ingarden, *The Literary Work of Art: An Investigation on the Borderlines of Ontology, Logic, and Theory of Literature, with an Appendix on the Functions of Language in the Theater*, trans. George G. Grabowicz (Northwestern University Press, 1973).

54 A. J. Ayer, ed., *Logical Positivism* (Free Press, 1959), a collection of important essays by some of its leading thinkers.

55 I. A. Richards, *Principles of Literary Criticism* (Routledge and Kegan Paul, 1924) and *Practical Criticism: A Study of Literary Judgment* (Kegan Paul, Trench, Trubner, 1929).

56 William Empson, *Seven Types of Ambiguity* (Hogarth, 1984 [1930]).

57 T. S. Eliot, *The Sacred Wood: Essays on Poetry and Criticism* (Methuen, 1920), with his classic essay "Tradition and the Individual Talent," 47–59; and F. R. Leavis, *The Great Tradition* (New York University Press, 1960). However, Eliot and Leavis did not agree on many things.

Warren. Warren and Wellek wrote one of the most important books to arise out of the New Criticism, their *Theory of Literature* (1942).[58] Another major impetus for the New Criticism was the southern agrarian movement, a group of scholars who were focused around a number of southern universities, especially Vanderbilt.[59] These scholars, such as John Crowe Ransom, who published *The New Criticism* in 1941 and gave the movement its name,[60] Robert Penn Warren, and Allen Tate, were part of a retroversion movement to southern simplicity, including focusing upon close reading of the unencumbered text. A third strand of this movement was the Chicago School of criticism, originated in the 1930s by R. S. Crane and best known in the work of Wayne Booth.[61] This school is recognized for its Neo-Aristotelian approach to literary criticism, in which emphasis is placed upon the elements that Aristotle examined, such as plot, action, and character. Even though the Chicago School was in some respects a response (and even opposition) to the New Criticism, in its attempt at greater precision and rigor it took the New Criticism further.

The influence of close readings of the text remains in literary criticism, even if another shift occurred from text to reader. There were several reasons for this shift, one literary and the other philosophical. The philosophical shift came about as the revolt against the ontological implications of structuralism. At a conference on structuralism at Johns Hopkins University in 1966, Jacques Derrida delivered a stinging critique of Lévi-Strauss that undermined the structuralist underpinnings of his thought.[62] Derrida in this and later works effectively

---

58 René Wellek and Austin Warren, *Theory of Literature*, 3rd ed. (Harcourt, Brace and World, 1956 [1942]).

59 See William L. Andrews et al., "The Southern Agrarians," in *The Literature of the American South: A Norton Anthology* (Norton, 1998), 389–91.

60 John Crowe Ransom, *The New Criticism* (New Directions, 1941).

61 R. S. Crane, *The Languages of Criticism and the Structure of Poetry* (University of Toronto Press, 1953); and Wayne C. Booth, *The Rhetoric of Fiction*, 2nd ed. (University of Chicago Press, 1983 [1961]).

62 Jacques Derrida, "Structure, Sign, and Play in the Discourse of the Human Sciences," in *The Structuralist Controversy: The Languages of Criticism and the Sciences of Man*, ed. Richard Macksey and Eugenio Donato (Johns Hopkins University Press, 1972 [1970]), 247–65, along with other essays. The primary journal of the rise of post-structuralism was *Tel Quel*. See Patrick French and Roland-François Lack, eds., *The Tel Quel Reader* (Routledge, 1998).

argued for a severing of the sign/signified relationship and this led to the rise of what is called post-structuralism and with it deconstruction. The dissolution of the sign/signified relationship inevitably leads to destabilization of not just meaning but of texts themselves, and the result is emphasis upon difference and play and deconstruction, with texts always open, never closed, and full of aporias that are never settled. The results of deconstruction were more immediately accepted in North America, with the rise of major deconstructive interpreters, such as Harold Bloom, Geoffrey Hartman, the displaced (and later discredited) European Paul de Man, and J. Hillis Miller.[63] In Europe, authors such as Roland Barthes—one time a strong structuralist—who came to be known for promoting the death of the author, and Michel Foucault, who also left authors behind and emphasizes the way language was used as a form of power (Foucault became a major influence upon CDA), became proponents of various forms of post-structuralism.[64] The literary rebellion against the text took the form of the rise of reader-response criticism. Reader-response criticism, although it also was influenced by the structuralist/post-structuralist environment, took more of its impetus from the phenomenology of Hans-Georg Gadamer and the reception criticism of the Konstanz school, including Hans Robert Jauss and Wolfgang Iser, all of whom came to be identified with the history of influence and how interpretation is the product of the response of readers to the text.[65] The reader-response movement took both textual and psychological forms, with one of the most influential being Stanley Fish.[66] On the

---

63 Harold Bloom, Paul de Man, Jacques Derrida, Geoffrey Hartman, and J. Hillis Miller, *Deconstruction and Criticism* (Continuum, 1979).

64 Roland Barthes, *Image–Music–Text*, trans. Stephen Heath (Hill & Wang, 1977); and Michel Foucault, *The Archaeology of Knowledge and the Discourse on Language*, trans. A. M. Sheridan Smith (Pantheon, 1972).

65 Hans Georg Gadamer, *Truth and Method*, trans. Joel Weinnsheimer and Donald G. Marshall, 2nd rev. ed (Continuum, 2002 [1960]); Hans Robert Jauss, *Toward an Aesthetic of Reception*, trans. Timothy Bahti (Harvester, 1982); Wolfgang Iser, *The Implied Reader: Patterns of Communication in Prose Fiction from Bunyan to Beckett* (Johns Hopkins University Press, 1974); Iser, *The Act of Reading: A Theory of Aesthetic Response* (Johns Hopkins University Press, 1978).

66 Stanley Fish, *Is There a Text in This Class? The Authority of Interpretive Communities* (Harvard University Press, 1980).

continent, Umberto Eco acknowledged the place of both open and closed texts.[67]

The result of such movement was a major shift in literary criticism. On the one hand, many departments of English and literature came to become departments of cultural studies. Cultural studies of various sorts thrived in the highly ideological environment of post-structuralism, in which the authority of the text had been replaced by the authority of the reader and the reader's situatedness.[68] As a result, a variety of movements came into varying grades of recognition, not necessarily prominence, as a reflection of the loss of the grand narrative associated with modernism.[69] These movements include the re-emergence of historicism, a nineteenth-century movement that emphasized that each historical or cultural epoch has its own character, in the New Historicism, a historicism influenced by Marxism.[70] Political criticism was heavily influenced by Karl Marx, and seen especially in the Frankfurt School of Jürgen Habermas.[71] Other types of political criticism involved postcolonial studies and ethnic studies. These studies stemmed from similar political concerns that some people were privileged and others were marginalized by the political, social, and economic system. Edward Said, and later Homi Bhabha, were responsible for drawing attention to the way in which colonialism had influenced views of others, even in the use of language such as "oriental" to characterize those from the east, and Henry Louis

---

67 Umberto Eco, *The Open Work*, trans. Anna Cacogni (Harvard University Press, 1989).

68 Cultural studies originated in the English department of the University of Birmingham in 1964 and came to be an encompassing term for a variety of ideological criticisms.

69 See Jean-François Lyotard, *The Postmodern Condition: A Report on Knowledge*, trans. Geoff Bennington and Brian Massumi (University of Minnesota Press, 1984 [1979]).

70 Wesley Morris, *Toward a New Historicism* (Princeton University Press, 1972); H. Aram Veeser, ed., *The New Historicism* (Routledge, 1989); and Brook Thomas, *The New Historicism and Other Old-Fashioned Topics* (Princeton University Press, 1991), three distinct books tying in to another major intellectual movement.

71 John Frow, *Marxism and Literary History* (Harvard University Press, 1986); and Jürgen Habermas, *The Theory of Communicative Action*, 2 vols., trans. Thomas McCarthy (Beacon, 1984–1987).

Gates raised issues regarding race and ethnicity.[72] In North America especially, but also elsewhere, ethnic studies brought to the fore the same kinds of problems but often discovered closer to home, where various groups were marginalized and disenfranchised simply on the basis of ethnicity. Feminist and gender studies, and in their trail queer studies and the like, were concerned with defining matters of gender and sexuality, their respective roles, and how these were defined within the languages and literatures in which they were or were not treated. Some such studies examined the texts themselves and others were concerned with the interpreters of those texts and their perspectives. Elaine Showalter examined feminism with the same critical lens as had been focused upon colonial and ethnic studies, and Eve Sedgwick pioneered queer theory and its examination of sex and gender and their distinctions (or not).[73] Finally, various types of psychoanalytic criticism, influenced by the writings of Sigmund Freud, made major inroads in literary criticism, especially in the psychoanalytic writings of Jacques Lacan and his student Julia Kristeva.[74]

With so much literary theory on offer during such a short amount of time (all of this had happened within the span of a single century), it was perhaps inevitable that there would be a rebellion against theory. A number of literary scholars, including some major theorists, raised questions about what formalist, and even some might say positivist, literary scholars were doing when they were reading and they re-introduced concern for traditional notions such as theme, even if they were introduced in conjunction with various ideologies that promoted them,[75] and some even went so far as to rebel against

---

72 Edward W. Said, *Orientalism* (Vintage, 1978); Homi K. Bhabha, *The Location of Culture* (Routledge, 1994); Henry Louis Gates, Jr., ed., *"Race," Writing, and Difference* (University of Chicago Press, 1986), in a volume of essays by many of those who regularly write on ideological issues.

73 Elaine Showalter, *A Literature of Their Own: British Women Novelists from Brontë to Lessing* (Princeton University Press, 1977); and Eve Kosofsky Sedwick, *Between Men: English Literature and Male Homosocial Desire* (Columbia University Press, 1985).

74 Jacques Lacan, *Écrits: The First Complete Edition in English*, trans. Bruce Fink, with Héloïse Fink and Russell Grig (Norton, 2006); and Julia Kristeva, *The Kristeva Reader*, ed. Toril Moi (Columbia University Press, 1986).

75 Werner Sollors, ed., *The Return of Thematic Criticism* (Harvard University Press, 1993); Claude Bremond, Joshua Landy, and Thomas Pavel, eds., *Thematics: New Approaches* (SUNY Press, 1995).

the dominance of theory.[76] Their objections were focused upon how theory had distracted from reading and the appreciation of literature, including such basic elements as simply understanding what literature was about. The reactions to this have been several. These include a recognition that, like Pandora's box, once theory is with us, it is hard to think of literature without theorizing, and that even a post-theory age is dependent upon previous theory.[77] There have also been movements such as the rise of interdisciplinarity as a recognized theoretical stance, in which the boundaries of theories are dissolved and theory becomes much more eclectic and reconfigured in various ways.[78] In conjunction with the rise of cognitive science, a form of cognitive criticism has emerged, with a particular emphasis upon theories of metaphor. The work of the linguist George Lakoff and the philosopher Mark Johnson has been influential in this area.[79] Despite such calls and cautions and new trends, however, theory has persisted, even if it is theory in a period after theory.

In the field of New Testament literary criticism, the first inroads were probably made by structuralism, before various formalist criticisms emerged and have continued to be the most lasting and enduring criticisms. This was followed by a few quick flirtations with reader-response criticism and deconstruction. Few of such flirtations have continued apart from a few individual scholars, although the notion of cultural studies has remained in effect.

Throughout much of the twentieth century the Bible as literature movement has maintained literary approaches to reading the Bible. Beginning with such scholars as Richard Moulton and continuing

---

76   E.g. Thomas Docherty, *After Theory* (Edinburgh University Press, 1996); Valentine Cunningham, *Reading after Theory* (Blackwell, 2002); Terry Eagleton, *After Theory* (Penguin, 2003). See for further discussion Daphne Patai and Will H. Corral, eds., *Theory's Empire: An Anthology of Dissent* (Columbia University Press, 2005), with a surprising and surprisingly large group of contributors. The discussion was anticipated in W. J. T. Mitchell, ed., *Against Theory: Literary Studies and the New Pragmatism* (University of Chicago Press, 1985).

77   Jean-Michel Rabaté, *The Future of Theory* (Blackwell, 2002).

78   E.g., Nancy Easterlin and Barbara Riebling, eds., *After Poststructuralism: Interdisciplinarity and Literary Theory* (Northwestern University Press, 1993).

79   George Lakoff and Mark Johnson, *Metaphors We Live By* (University of Chicago Press, 1980); Lakoff and Johnson, *More than Cool Reason: A Field Guide to Poetic Metaphor* (University of Chicago Press, 1989).

with Mary Ellen Chase through to Kenneth R. R. Gros Louis and Leland Ryken, there have been a number of advocates of reading the Bible as literature.[80] This has usually meant English and literature departments hosting courses in the Bible, often organized by the study of genres. The usual result is the application of the current literary critical paradigm in an accessible form for those studying the wider fields of literature. Serious study of the Bible from a literary standpoint, especially by those within the literary and theological guild, seems to have begun under the influence of structuralism, especially in studying the parables. A variety of structuralists as well as biblical scholars, and most especially Daniel Patte, read the Bible with attention to structure, organization, actantial oppositions, narrative and story, and other structuralist conventions.[81] The philosopher Paul Ricoeur, with his phenomenological and narratival views, also read a number of biblical texts in productive ways, ways in many regards reflecting the concerns of phenomenology, the structuralists, the New Critics, and some other influences.[82] Such readings were not persistent, and with the poststructuralist rebellion tapered off significantly.

Formalism in its various realizations, such as the New Criticism and practical criticism, had a more enduring legacy within New Testament literary studies. There are two major types of formalist criticism to note. There are first the methodologically relatively naïve common sense readers of the Bible. They often dissociated their readings

---

80 Richard G. Moulton, *The Modern Reader's Bible for Schools: The New Testament* (Macmillan, 1931); Mary Ellen Chase, *The Bible and the Common Reader* (Collins, 1946); Eric Auerbach, *Mimesis: The Representation of Reality in Western Literature*, trans. Willard R. Trask (Princeton University Press, 1953); Kenneth R. R. Gros Louis et al., eds., *Literary Interpretations of Biblical Narratives*, 2 vols. (Abingdon, 1974–1982); Leland Ryken, *The Bible as Literature* (Zondervan, 1974).

81 As representative, see R. Barthes, F. Bovon, F.-J. Leenhardt, R. Marti-Achard, and J. Starobinski, *Structural Analysis and Biblical Exegesis: Interpretational Essays*, trans. Alfred M. Johnson, Jr. (Pickwick, 1974); Daniel Patte, *What is Structural Exegesis?* (Fortress, 1976); Patte, *Structural Exegesis for New Testament Critics* (Fortress, 1990); Patte, *The Religious Dimensions of Biblical Texts* (Scholars Press, 1990); Patte, *Paul's Faith and the Power of the Gospel: A Structural Introduction to the Pauline Letters* (repr., Wipf & Stock, 2006 [1983]).

82 Paul Ricoeur, *Interpretation Theory: Discourse and the Surplus of Meaning* (Texas Christian University Press, 1976); and *Essays on Biblical Interpretation*, ed. Lewis S. Mudge (Fortress, 1980).

from historical and authorial background and focused upon the text. Their readings consequently were concerned with such examples as the Gospels as stories, including the development of plot, character, and setting. Scholars such as Charles Talbert and Robert Tannehill offered numerous readings of biblical books from this perspective, to the point of writing entire commentaries that attempted to take such formalist approaches.[83] The second type of formalist scholarship was much more methodologically aware and made attempts to read in the light of developments within literary criticism, especially as found in various text-oriented methods even as they developed toward readerly interests. One of the early works in this light was not by a New Testament scholar, but by a Renaissance literature scholar, Frank Kermode, whose *The Genesis of Secrecy* was a study of Mark and the revelation of his message, patterned in some ways on Kermode's previous work regarding the endings of texts with eschatological implications.[84] The two major works by New Testament scholars were the work on Mark by David Rhoads and Donald Michie (Michie being a literary scholar) and by Alan Culpepper on John.[85] Rhoads and Michie directly drew upon the structuralist-influenced narratology of Seymour Chatman, who had captured and exemplified narratology for a North American audience. The second and subsequent editions of their volume, however, switched from Chatman's model to one that was less narratological and more literary-theological. Culpepper's work on John is an eclectic model influenced by numerous literary-critical scholars, such as the New Critic Murray Krieger, Seymour Chatman, Wayne Booth, and the formalist Boris Uspensky, among others.[86] In other words, Culpepper's approach is in the formalist narratological framework.

---

83 C. H. Talbert, *Reading Luke: A Literary and Theological Commentary on the Third Gospel* (Crossroad, 1982); Robert Tannehill, *The Narrative Unity of Luke–Acts: A Literary Interpretation*, 2 vols. (Fortress, 1986–1990)

84 Frank Kermode, *The Genesis of Secrecy: On the Interpretation of Narrative* (Harvard University Press, 1979); cf. Kermode, *The Sense of an Ending: Studies in the Theory of Fiction* (Oxford University Press, 1967).

85 David Rhoads and Donald Michie, *Mark as Story: An Introduction to the Narrative of a Gospel* (Fortress, 1982; 2nd ed., 1999 with the additional author Joanna Dewey; 3rd ed., 2012); and R. Alan Culpepper, *Anatomy of the Fourth Gospel: A Study in Literary Design* (Fortress, 1983).

86 Murray Kreiger, *The New Apologists for Poetry* (Indiana University Pres, 1963); and Boris Uspensky, *A Poetics of Composition: The Structure of the Artistic Text and*

There were numerous subsequent scholars who followed in the path of these biblical innovators, with the 1980s and 1990s being very productive times in literary New Testament scholarship. Some of the most important work during this time was written by scholars such as Mark Stibbe on various approaches to John's Gospel and John Darr on character in the Gospels.[87] Although formalism is no longer as overtly practiced as it was, close readings of texts continue to be produced, as is seen in the work on sequential reading by Peter Phillips.[88] Numerous character studies have also come to the fore as a means of performing literary readings of elements of texts, thereby focusing upon one of the elements of formalist criticism, as opposed to plot or setting, even if these are acknowledged and involved.[89]

By this time, even if it was not at first obvious, in New Testament studies formalism had been replaced, at least in name, by what is now called narrative criticism, to the point that narrative criticism has come to be identified as a form of criticism unique to New Testament studies and its literary studies in particular.[90] The major elements of

---

Typology of a Compositional Form, trans. Valentina Zavarin and Susan Wittig (University of California Press, 1973).

87 Mark W. Stibbe, *John as Storyteller: Narrative Criticism and the Fourth Gospel*, SNTSMS 73 (Cambridge University Press, 1992); John A. Darr, *On Character Building: The Reader and the Rhetoric of Characterization in Luke–Acts* (Westminster John Knox, 1992); cf. Darr, *Herod the Fox: Audience Criticism and Lukan Characterization* (Sheffield Academic, 1998).

88 Peter M. Phillips, *The Prologue of the Fourth Gospel: A Sequential Reading* (T&T Clark, 2006).

89 The works in this area are becoming numerous especially of late (and I only mention a few). See Joel Williams, *Other Followers of Jesus: Minor Characters as Major Figures in Mark's Gospel* (JSOT Press, 1994); David Rhoads and Kari Syreeni, eds., *Characterization in the Gospels: Reconceiving Narrative Criticism* (Sheffield Academic, 1999); Christopher W. Skinner, ed., *Characters and Characterization in the Gospel of John* (Bloomsbury, 2013); Steven A. Hunt, D. Francois Tolmie, and Ruben Zimmermann, eds., *Character Studies in the Fourth Gospel: Narrative Approaches to Seventy Figures in John* (Eerdmans, 2013); Cornelis Bennema, *A Theory of Character in New Testament Narrative* (Fortress, 2014); Christopher W. Skinner and Matthew Ryan Hauge, eds., *Character Studies and the Gospel of Mark* (Bloomsbury, 2014); and Frank Dicken and Julia Snyder, eds., *Characters and Characterization in Luke–Acts* (Bloomsbury, 2016).

90 See Mark Allen Powell, *What Is Narrative Criticism? A New Approach to the Bible* (SPCK, 1993); James L. Resseguie, *Narrative Criticism of the New Testament: An Introduction* (Baker Academic, 2005). The term "narrative criticism" was formulated by

narrative criticism consist of such things as the study of plot, character, setting, and point of view. These sound much like the elements of concern in previous formalist criticism—and they are. The major difference is that, whereas in previous work scholars were engaged in defining their method as they developed their literary readings, in narrative criticism the set of expectations for reading is already established by the method. I suspect that narrative criticism has come about for two major reasons. The first is in response to the text-centeredness of New Testament literary criticism in light of the adoption of the authorial intentionality of E. D. Hirsch.[91] In literary criticism, Hirsch had in some ways resisted the move from author to text to reader, and his views had been widely adopted in some New Testament circles. I am not convinced that all who adopted Hirsch's views fully understood the nature of his argument. His argument recognized that a text could be construed to mean a number of different things, but that the control on these meanings was the author, but especially as understood through the notion of genre.[92] In other words, this made genre determinative for meaning, and hence in some ways begged the question of meaning by simply displacing it with the genre question. Many scholars in biblical studies have adopted genre-oriented approaches to reading the Bible, but such genre criticism tends to be based on fixed forms of texts in order to arrive at definitive meanings, rather than recognizing that genres exist with fuzzy boundaries as various socially conditioned ways in which a culture organizes its literature, and cannot be seen to be the determiner of meaning. The second reason for the adoption of narrative criticism was in reaction to a number of New Testament literary scholars who made a shift from text to reader. A relatively fixed method of interpretation, such as narrative criticism, could be seen to preserve textual certainty against reader-based uncertainty.

David Rhoads in "Narrative Criticism and the Gospel of Mark" (1982), repr. in Rhoads, *Reading Mark: Engaging the Gospel* (Fortress, 2004), 1–22.

91 E. D. Hirsch, Jr., *Validity in Interpretation* (Yale University Press, 1967).

92 Some examples are Richard A. Burridge, *What Are the Gospels? A Comparison with Graeco-Roman Biography*, 2nd ed. (Eerdmans, 2004); Sean A. Adams, *The Genre of Acts and Collected Biography*, SNTSMS 156 (Cambridge University Press, 2013); and Justin Marc Smith, *Why Βίος? On the Relationship between Gospel Genre and Implied Audience* (Bloomsbury, 2015).

Reader-response criticism in New Testament studies became very popular for a relatively short time. There was always ambivalence about the adoption of it. For some, reader-response criticism was interpreted to mean how the first-century audience would have responded to the text.[93] In some ways, this is simply a relabeling of traditional historical-critical interpretation, but without the textual dissections that often went with source and form criticism. Such reader-response criticism would generally have been unrecognizable outside of New Testament studies by literary scholars. For others, there was a genuine engagement with reader-response theories, although these usually involved relatively narrow and constrained forms of it, such as that practiced by Iser and others in the reception history movement.[94] The more extreme forms of reader-response, such as by Fish, were generally not utilized. Akin to reader-response was deconstruction. There were a few New Testament scholars who fully embraced the post-structural agenda and engaged in deconstructive criticism, but those have been relatively few. Stephen Moore is probably the best known of these, although not the only one.[95] He began as a post-structuralist and has continued to migrate to cultural studies and a variety of ideological perspectives, along the way producing some of the most stimulating and also infuriating essays fully attuned to developments in literary critical studies.[96] He has also been one of the leading advocates of cultural studies within New Testament studies, including writing on many of the topics mentioned above, including

---

93 Mary Ann Beavis, *Mark's Audience: The Literary and Social Setting of Mark 4:11–12* (Sheffield Academic, 1989).

94 E.g. Jeffrey Lloyd Staley, *The Print's First Kiss: A Rhetorical Investigation of the Implied Reader in the Fourth Gospel*, SBLDS 82 (Scholars Press, 1988); Mary Ann Tolbert, *Sowing the Gospel: Mark's World in Literary-Historical Perspective* (Fortress, 1989); and Robert M. Fowler, *Let the Reader Understand: Reader-Response Criticism and the Gospel of Mark* (Fortress, 1991).

95 E.g. David Seeley, *Deconstructing the New Testament* (Brill, 1994).

96 Stephen D. Moore, *Literary Criticism and the Gospels: The Theoretical Challenge* (Yale University Press, 1989); Moore, *Mark and Luke in Poststructuralist Perspectives: Jesus Begins to Write* (Yale University Press, 1992); Moore, *Poststructuralism and the New Testament: Derrida and Foucault at the Foot of the Cross* (Fortress, 1994); Moore, *The Bible in Theory: Critical and Postcritical Essays* (SBL Press, 2010); Moore, *Gospel Jesuses and Other Nonhumans: Biblical Criticism Post-poststructuralism* (SBL Press, 2017).

not just post-structuralism but feminism, gender theory, queer theory, and others. There have been others within New Testament studies who have adopted various ideologically influenced critical stances, such as feminism and other gender studies, but these have remained a relatively small portion of New Testament scholars.[97]

The defining characteristics of literary criticism are: (1) the value of close reading; (2) the integrity of the text; (3) the relationship of story and discourse; (4) the writing, reading, and reception process; (5) text, canon, and reading; (6) the importance of context; and (7) the uncertainty of meaning.

1. *Close Reading*. The close reading of texts is one of the great legacies of formalism, especially the New Criticism and practical criticism. Close reading requires a text-oriented focus, even if other factors are brought into play, such as the response of the reader or even the internal tensions within the text determined on the basis of such a close reading. Most character studies are close readings of the characters involved. John Darr's readings of Herod are fleshed out discussions of not the historical information about Herod, which is surprisingly small and insignificant, but the role that Herod plays within the narrative itself. The same kinds of close readings are found in a variety of the volumes of character studies in Mark, Luke, and John's Gospels.

2. *Integrity of the Text*. Cleanth Brooks's most well-known work was entitled *The Well Wrought Urn*, and this image captures one of the most important dimensions of the New Criticism.[98] Just as John Keats in his poem "Ode on a Grecian Urn" speaks of the shape and lines and features of the urn, reading of the text ever since the formalists has in varying ways attempted to capture the shapes and contours of the text as itself a well-formed artifact, even if one then goes on to dispute these fine features, their meaning, and their implications for both the text and the readers. Culpepper's *Anatomy of the Fourth Gospel* reveals such a perspective. He uses the analogy of anatomy as a way of speaking of the dissection of John's Gospel, not with the idea of harming

---

97 E.g. F. Scott Spencer, *Salty Wives, Spirited Mothers, and Savvy Widows: Capable Women of Purpose and Persistence in Luke's Gospel* (Eerdmans, 2012).

98 Cleanth Brooks, *The Well Wrought Urn: Studies in the Structure of Poetry* (Harvest/HBJ, 1974 [1947]).

the text but discovering how it constitutes a text, that is, how it forms a text of integrity and unity. This notion has recently been criticized for the biblical texts,[99] but the principle of textual integrity seems to be present in much literary reading.

3. *Story and Discourse*. This distinction is a legacy of the Russian formalists. An important reading of Philemon was made by Norman Petersen in his *Rediscovering Paul: Philemon and the Sociology of Paul's Narrative World*.[100] In his reading of this short letter, Petersen goes to great pains to distinguish between the story and the discourse. In other words, he maps out the events that occur within the historical account of Paul and his relationship with Onesimus, Philemon, the church in his home in Colossae, and others, and then he examines how Paul conveys his discourse, so that Paul takes the events and reshapes the story into the discourse of power that he creates to effect the results he seeks of having Philemon released back to him, the now-manumitted slave.

4. *Writing, Reading, and Reception Process*. Informed readers from the Romantic period to the present have often combined attention to the writing, reading, and reception process, even if they have not always been aware of this process, and the center of authority has shifted, as noted above, from the author to the text to the reader, and now to what is hard to say. Even some of the most well-known historical and biographical critics, such as C. S. Lewis, were attentive to the integrity of the text and the role of the reader. The well-known essay by the New Critic W. K. Wimsatt and the philosopher Monroe Beardsley on the intentional fallacy is aware of the fact that writers produce texts that require reading within a context—their strictures on the notion of intentionality are limited to particular kinds of poetry, but they recognize the need to understand the language of the author when the author used it, even if intentionality is not decisive or determinative.[101]

---

99 See Petri Merenlahti, *Poetics for the Gospels? Rethinking Narrative Criticism* (T&T Clark, 2002).

100 Norman R. Petersen, *Rediscovering Paul: Philemon and the Sociology of Paul's Narrative World* (Fortress, 1985).

101 W. K. Wimsatt, Jr., and Monroe C. Beardsley, "The Intentional Fallacy" (1946), in Wimsatt, *The Verbal Icon: Studies in the Meaning of Poetry* (Noonday, 1954), 3–18, along with other emblematic essays.

5. *Text, Canon, and Reading.* Fish argues that reading occurs within a community and that readings are community products. Interpretive communities play an important role in establishing how texts are read and the kinds of readings that are acceptable to that community. Stibbe in his book on John's Gospel offers four different readings: what he calls practical criticism (the New Criticism of North America), genre criticism, social function (a type of narratology), and narrative-historical (where he attempts to ground his readings in history, a constant concern of biblical scholars).[102] He shows that the various approaches to a single text yield different results. He does not necessarily privilege one reading over the other, but illustrates that the various readings offer different insights into the text. A major issue in literary studies concerns the canon of literary works, as it is typically criticized as not being representative of all writers by ethnicity, gender, etc. Although similar issues have not to my knowledge arisen in a major way in New Testament studies, some ideological criticisms might well have views on the more or less acceptability of some texts or portions of texts over others.

6. *Context.* Despite the stance of the New Critics and the practical critics—especially evidenced in I. A. Richards's own comments regarding the readers of his poems—context is important for any reading.[103] For many literary readers context constitutes the immediate textual context, one that requires and demands close reading. For others, context extends beyond the text into a variety of layers of cultural, political, and ideological context. For all readers, there is a recognition that context matters. Even for the New Critics there was a recognition that understanding of the language of a text implied understanding the language at the time of composition, that is, within its context.

7. *Uncertainty of Meaning.* One of the major criticisms of literary readings by New Testament scholars is that such meanings are, if not unhistorical at least ahistorical, and that such readings are not appropriate to historical texts. This is one of the issues that Stibbe and Merenlahti attempt to address from the position of those sympathetic

---

102 Stibbe, *John as Storyteller,* divided into two parts with four chapters within each on these topics.

103 Richards, *Practical Criticism,* esp. 13–17.

to literary methods.[104] Such critics fail to realize that the meanings of texts are based upon much more than simply historical referentiality and involve a variety of factors that must be taken into account, many of which have been noted above. The result is that textual interpretation is difficult, and is often influenced by a variety of factors, such as context, ideology, belief systems, and even one's view of how to understand a text. If one learns anything from studying the developments in literary theory, one sees that it is difficult to escape the complexity of reading because all readings are contextually situated and language, rather than reflecting reality, is a mediator of it.

Some Random Final Thoughts Comparing Discourse Analysis and Literary Criticism

These two relatively brief summaries of DA and literary criticism are designed to illustrate some of the significant similarities and differences between the two. Let me offer a few more or less random thoughts in response to what this exploration has found. I will begin with some similarities between them. They are similar in that they are both concerned with understanding how language is used by various writers, for the most part literary writers for New Testament studies, even if not such writers for DA and sometimes even for literary critics. In that regard, both have been influenced by a variety of common cultural and philosophical factors, including such broad and important movements as Romanticism, structuralism, and even post-structuralism. To the extent that they co-exist in New Testament criticism today, they are often seen to be incompatible or even at odds with each other. In some circles, DA may be viewed as an objective means of deciding meaning, whereas literary criticism is indeterminate in its meanings; while in others, literary criticism may be seen to be more closely attuned to reading the text, rather than simply providing lists of data (such as key words in context).

There are numerous places where DA and literary criticism intersect. Some of the eighteenth- and nineteenth-century philosophers and hermeneuts had influence over both language study and literary study of their times, such as Kant, Hegel, and Schleiermacher, among

---

104 Stibbe, *John as Storyteller*, 67–92; and Merenlahti, *Poets for the Gospels?*

others. Some later philosophers also have had influence upon these areas, such as Gadamer, Derrida, and Ricoeur. Structuralism, in its close relationship with Russian formalism, and its later developments through the Prague School of linguistics into such things as French literary structuralism, narratology, and even the New Criticism through the work of Jakobson, Wellek, and others, had a major influence upon literary theory and criticism.

Despite these similarities, literary criticism and DA usually evidence striking differences in their approaches to the text. One is not the other. There are many possible reasons for this. One possible reason is the nature of their definitions of text. For DA, a text is an occasional configuration of meanings put into wordings and has no necessary literary pretension, while for literary criticism—although this notion, as is the literary canon, is subject to radical debate—the text is usually seen to be a literary artifact. This does not mean that DA cannot be applied to written and especially literary texts—it can—but it does not assume an aesthetic dimension to the text in the same way that literary criticism often, if not usually, does. A second reason for differentiation is the difference of opinion over where meaning resides in texts. DA, like most linguistics, functions from an assumption of some kind of recoverable intention, not necessarily an authorial but at least some type of textual intention, implied in the language of the text, whereas literary criticism has moved from the author to the text to the reader to the death of the author, until the nature of authors is uncertain and their intentions are suspect and difficult to know, if they are even something to speak about. A third reason is that the procedure for analysis is radically different. DA attempts to identify structures—structures of meaning or structures of form—and see their configurations and, on the basis of these configurations, arrive at notions of meaning. These meaningful components may be seen as functions or forms, but they are seen to be in some way describable, and even meaningful within the parameters of that term for each respective model. There is a presumption of intelligibility as is illustrated in positive discussions of cohesion and coherence, features assumed to be found in texts. Literary criticism offers readings of texts, within the constraints of reading communities, on the basis of a variety of less well-defined and estimable features, such as character, plot, setting, point of view, audience, the traditional textual features, but also more recent ones such as implied and (un)trustworthy narrators and readers, ideologies of various types, and the presumption of uncertainty, even skepticism, regarding authors and their readers.

The fourth and final reason to note here is that one of the major problems for both DA and literary criticism, and one that is often not touched upon, is the ability of the model to deliver what might be described as a definitive-transferable meaning. One of the major advances of philosophical hermeneutics, especially of Gadamer, is the recognition that the horizon of the text and the horizon of the reader are not easily or ever fused. The act of horizonal identification is complex and fraught with interpretive difficulty. This difficulty functions at two levels. The first concerns definitive meaning. By this term I do not mean a definite meaning, but one that is definable and specific to a text. This is commonly seen when someone asks, "what is this poem about?" or "what did Paul mean when he wrote to the Corinthians?" Both DA and literary criticism engage in a variety of exercises in describing texts, but these descriptions are often confused with definitive meanings. The two are not the same. Describing all of the features of a text, or describing the various components of plot, etc., is not the same as creating a definitive meaning of the text. Both do not have obvious mechanisms for doing this. This does not stop discourse analysts or literary critics from offering such meanings, however, and they must to the best of their abilities on the basis of the understandings that they have. They do so, even if the foundations upon which they are laid are suspect, and they must pretend to have a more substantial foundation for such belief than they do. One merely needs to observe the variety of DA frameworks and the wide range of literary critical models to see that one has not arrived at a univocal sense of definitive textual meaning. Meanings are constantly being negotiated within the various models, and across disciplines. However, even if it may be possible to arrive at a satisfactory estimation of a definitive meaning—by that indicating that one may agree as to how someone may in the past have read a text—the act of interpretation is not complete without a transferable meaning, that is, a meaning that understands the text in the contemporary context of the interpreter. On this account, both DA and literary criticism do not have clear mechanisms or answers.

This situation is not necessarily regrettable, but instead offers an opportunity for the community of interpreters as they engage in constructive debate over both the models that they use and the results that these models drive them to. I think that there are some potential ways forward in such discussion, as there is a recognition that meaning operates on several different levels. The levels that have mostly been explored have been attentive to, in fact mostly focused upon, the text and its immediate environment, rather than extending the scope of meaning beyond such limitations. However, the result of extending such spheres of estimation leads to proportional decrease in certainty as connections between variables become less tightly defined as immediacy recedes.

Conclusion

I wish to congratulate my friend Will Varner for the work that he has done in New Testament studies. His work in DA has been an act of adventure and exploration that has taken him beyond the confines of traditional exegesis and offered a new perspective on the Bible, in particular the letter of James. For this he is to be commended, as traditional exegesis is itself a model of interpretation. I have not described it here, although one can probably see how it does or does not fit within the definitions and descriptions that I have offered. Will has instead taken the less well-trodden path into using DA as a means of explicating the book of James. I am sure that he would not claim that he has arrived at definitive and transferable meanings in all of the various avenues that he has explored. However, I commend him for the work that he has done, and I am confident that his work—and the example that he has set—will help to stimulate others to similar explorations.

4

Puzzling Out Polysemy:
The Relationship between Seemingly
Unrelated Meanings and Functions of ὡς

Christian Locatell[1]

1. INTRODUCTION[2]

STUDENTS OF GREEK OFTEN FEEL OVERWHELMED by the dizzying
complexity of the language. This is hardly alleviated in the
experience of scholars. In fact, the more one learns, the more
complexity is revealed. This feeling is highlighted in the tongue-in-
cheek use of the category "aporetic genitive" from the word ἀπορέω
which expresses the experience of being "in a confused state of mind"
because you simply cannot figure out what the genitive is doing.[3]
This is especially the case with smaller words like the Greek particles,
prepositions, and conjunctions. For example, the word ὡς has a wide
range of semantic meanings and syntactic functions, such as its use
as a comparative preposition "as," a complementizer "that," a comparative adverbial conjunction "as," a temporal adverbial conjunction
"after, while, as soon as," a final adverbial conjunction "so that," a causal adverbial conjunction "since, because," an exclamative "how," and

1 I would like to thank the Golda Meir Fellowship fund for awarding me a post-
doctoral fellowship at The Hebrew University of Jerusalem during which I was able
to carry out this research.

2 It was during my several years in Dr. Varner's Greek classes that I developed a
love for the language and was first introduced to the application of linguistics to the
Greek NT. His contagious enthusiasm in the classroom (even climbing on his desk on
more than one occasion and taking a knee whenever he mentioned the name of J. B.
Lightfoot), his labor in the academy, and his care as a minister have been an inspiration to me. It is my great pleasure to dedicate this chapter to him.

3 D. B. Wallace, *Greek Grammar Beyond the Basics* (Zondervan, 1996), 79.

actually began as a an ablative relative pronoun "by means of which, the way in which." Thus, not only does it have a variety of meanings within a particular word class (e.g. adverbial conjunction with comparative, temporal, final, and causal meanings) it also functions across word classes (e.g. relativizer, conjunction, preposition, complementizer, exclamative).[4]

Treatments of such words, especially in grammars and lexica, have tended to use what may be called the "taxonomy" method. That is, they simply list out each of the uses. While helpful in their descriptiveness, it is difficult to perceive any coherence between uses and can leave the impression of arbitrariness. More recently, calls have been made for what may be called methodological monosemy.[5] That is, when approaching the language of the NT, it is argued that one must adopt a monosemic bias and make every effort to define the meaning of a word as "the common denominator that can be identified in all of its contexts."[6]

However, rather than simply listing out all the uses of a word or trying to strip them down to a "lowest common denominator," when viewed through crosslinguistically consistent patterns of language change in the process of grammaticalization, what initially seems to be an arbitrary list of disconnected meanings and syntactic functions is revealed to be an organic whole with complex but interconnected branches of form and function. To borrow the analogy of the elephant and the blind men, if the taxonomy method seeks to define

---

4 The former has been termed "polysemy" and the latter "heterosemy." For the sake of simplicity, I will use the term "polysemy" more broadly to refer to both.

5 Monosemy meaning "one meaning". See Ryder A. Wishart, "Monosemy in Biblical Studies: A Critical Analysis of Recent Work," *BAGL* 6 (2017): 99–126; Ryder A. Wishart, "Monosemy: A Theoretical Sketch for Biblical Studies," *BAGL* 7 (2018): 107–39. Also see Stanley Porter, "θαυμάζω in Mark 6:6 and Luke 11:38: A Note on Monosemy," *BAGL* 2 (2013): 75–9 and Gregory P. Fewster, *Creation Language in Romans 8: A Study in Monosemy*, LBS 8 (Brill, 2013). Note that Fewster oddly identifies monosemy as coming from cognitive linguistics (e.g., p. 17), even though approaching semantic analysis with a "bias" toward monosemy (to use Fewster's characterization) is clearly opposed to a cognitive linguistic perspective, as will be seen throughout this paper (also see the definition of "monosemy" given in Vyvyan Evans, *A Glossary of Cognitive Linguistics* [Edinburgh University Press, 2007], 147). From a general linguistic perspective, see Charles Ruhl, *On Monosemy: A Study in Linguistic Semantics* (SUNY Press, 1989), on whom these applications to biblical (especially NT) studies rely.

6 Wishart, "Monosemy: A Theoretical Sketch," 122–23.

the elephant by simply listing out its parts without showing how each relates to the others (ears, tail, trunk, etc.) giving the impression of an assortment of dismembered appendages, and the monosemy method seeks to define the elephant as some common denominator found in every part (dry skin?, in which case an elephant and a rhino are really the same thing), a grammaticalization approach seeks to define the elephant as a whole, to understand how its parts are related, and to uncover the processes that guided their development. As Bybee explains with a different analogy:

> Comparing grammatical categories across languages from only a synchronic perspective is something like comparing an acorn to an oak tree: They appear to have distinct and unrelated properties. Only when we observe these entities across the temporal dimension do we see the relationship between them. Similarly with grammatical categories and constructions: New relationships are observable when we take into account where particular grammatical constructions and categories come from and where they are going.[7]

Grammaticalization theory is based on extremely robust observations of a huge and constantly growing number of languages.[8] Such a diachronic perspective on synchronic polysemy has already been proposed as a way past the entrenched positions surrounding the well-known debate over the meaning of the verbal forms in Greek.[9] While the application of cognitive linguistics and grammaticalization research has begun to make its way into the study of Greek more

---

7 J.Bybee, "Cognitive Processes in Grammaticalization," in *The New Psychology of Language: Cognitive and Functional Approaches to Language Structure*, vol. 2, ed. M. Tomasello (Lawrence Erlbaum Associates, 2003), 151.

8 Landmark examples of this include the study of the development of tense, aspect, and modality by J. Bybee, R. Perkins, and W. Pagliuca, *The Evolution of Grammar* (University of Chicago Press, 1994), 29–32; 302–315, which is based on 76 languages representing the world's major linguistic phyla. Another is B. Kortmann, *Adverbial Subordination: A Typology and History of Adverbial Subordinators Based on European languages* (de Gruyter, 1997), based on 53 languages from the Indo-European, Uralic, Altaic, Caucasian, and Semitic language phyla, as well as one language isolate.

9 A. Andrason and C. Locatell, "The Perfect Wave: A Cognitive Approach to the Greek Verbal System," *BAGL* 5 (2016): 7–121.

broadly, it has been surprisingly underutilized in NT scholarship.[10] Commenting on the need for such application to the study of Greek, Bentein maintains that, "adopting such a cross-linguistic perspective may shed new light on questions which have concerned classical philologists since Wackernagel and Chantraine, and beyond."[11]

In this essay, I would like to demonstrate the use of grammaticalization theory to help clarify and explain synchronic polysemy, using ὡς as an illustration. As noted by Jannaris, "If any particular section of Greek grammar were taken as a specimen to illustrate the historical evolution of the Greek language, no better representative could be selected than the section of the particles."[12] I will begin by providing an overview of grammaticalization theory in section 2. I will then discuss how this can be applied to a word like ὡς in section 3. There I will propose a path of development that explains its synchronic polysemy along with examples which may shed light on the cognitive processes that facilitated its semantic extensions. In section 4 I will summarize the uses of ὡς discussed and visualize their relationship to one-another in a semantic map. Finally, I will offer some concluding remarks on implications this perspective has for how we approach the study of Greek in the NT and beyond.

To express up-front the main idea I wish to advance, which I hope will be of use to students of the language of the NT, it is this. Language is too dynamic and complex to allow us to force semantic meaning into tidy abstract cores which fit every use of a word or form. We also need not assume that the various uses of a word or form are simply

---

10 See A. Sansò, "Cognitive Linguistics and Greek," in *Encyclopedia of Ancient Greek Language and Linguistics*. Vol. 1: A–F, ed. G. K. Giannakis (Brill, 2014), Online Edition, https://referenceworks.brillonline.com/entries/encyclopedia-of-ancient-greek-language-and-linguistics/cognitive-linguistics-and-greek-COM_00000062. In linguistics in general, P. Hopper and E. C. Traugott, *Grammaticalization*, 2nd ed. (Cambridge University Press, 2003), 25, have noted an "amnesia" about grammaticalization.

11 K. Bentein, "The Periphrastic Perfect in Ancient Greek: A Diachronic Mental Space Analysis," *Transactions of the Philological Society* 110, no. 2 (April 2012): 176.

12 A. N. Jannaris, *An Historical Greek Grammar: Chiefly of the Attic Dialect as Written and Spoken from Classical Antiquity down to the Present Time, Founded upon the Ancient Texts, Inscriptions, Papyri, and Present Popular Greek* (MacMillan and Co., 1897), 365. He primarily has in mind here the general process by which older forms are replaced by novel ones. However, his comments apply equally well to the phenomenon of polysemy so often seen in small grammatical words.

arbitrary with no conceptual relation, and which we must simply memorize off the pages of grammars and lexicons. Rather, the semantics of even a highly multifunctional word or form is made up of conceptually related meanings which develop in cognitively motivated and constrained ways. Much like the way that the topography of the land directs the flow of a river, following the path of least resistance, so too our cognitive topography directs the flow of semantics with its various tributaries and outlets. While the relationship between the temporal meaning of "since" and the causal meaning of "since" may not be immediately obvious to us, as will be discussed below, one is the source and the other the goal in the flow of meaning. Rather than being a static thing, these branches of meaning ebb and flow. One branch of a word's meaning may dry up, while others form. It is this sort of flow of meaning that characterizes all of language. Grammaticalization studies helps us to see the connections between these branches and the direction of flow.

2. An Overview of Grammaticalization

Grammaticalization refers to the universally observed process by which lexical words develop grammatical function, and the process by which already grammatical words develop new grammatical functions.[13] A well-known example of a lexical word developing a grammatical function is the word *while*.[14] This began in Old English as a

---

13 Cf. Hopper and Traugott, *Grammaticalization*, 1. The recognition of and research on the phenomenon of grammaticalization has a long history that can be traced back several centuries. See H. Narrog and B. Heine, "Introduction," in *The Oxford Handbook of Grammaticalization*, ed. H. Narrog and B. Heine (Oxford University Press, 2011), 1–18. Cf. C. S. Locatell, "Grammatical Polysemy in the Hebrew Bible: A Cognitive Linguistic Approach to כִּי" (PhD diss., Stellenbosch University, 2017), 107. The term itself was coined by A. Meillel, "L' Évolution des Formes Grammaticales," 1912, reprinted in *Linguistique Historique et Linguistique Générale*, by A. Meillet, Collection Linguistique Publiée par la Société de Linguistic de Paris, vol. 8. (Champion, 1982), 130–48. However, its emergence as a distinct program of linguistic research can be identified with the publication of the textbooks on grammaticalization by B. Heine, U. Claudi, and F. Hünnemeyer, *Grammaticalization: A Conceptual Framework* (University of Chicago Press, 1991) and Hopper and Traugott, *Grammaticalization*, now in its second edition.

14 See E. C. Traugott and E. König, "The Semantics-Pragmatics of Grammaticalization Revisited," in *Approaches to Grammaticalization. Vol. I: Focus on Theoretical*

noun *hwile* meaning "time" in the construction *Þa hwile Þe* "at the time that," as in example 1a) below. This construction consisted of "the dative distal demonstrative, the dative noun *hwile* 'time', and the subordinator *Þe*, a highly explicit coding of simultaneity."[15] Through use in this construction, the noun *hwile* "time" became so strongly associated with the head of a temporal clause that by late Old English it could be used as a temporal conjunction all by itself, as in sentences like 1b), or like sentences as 1c) which we hear and use today.

1. a. ChronA (Plummer) 913.3[16]

& *wicode Þær Þa hwile Þe man Þa burg   worhte*
and camped there that time that one that fortress worked-on

& *getimbrede*
and built

"and camped there while the fortress was worked on and built"

 b. ChronE (Plummer) 1137.36

ðæt lastede Þa [xix] wintre wile   Stephne was king
That lasted those 19   winters while Stephen was king

 c. While I was walking home, I found a million dollars.

However, remnants of its original nominal origin can still be seen in fossilized expressions like "once in a while" and "all the while" where it is still a noun meaning "time," even being able to take a definite and indefinite article as a noun. After the emergence of the temporal conjunction *while*, it continued itself to serve as the input for further developments. The German cognate *weil*, shares the same origin as English *while*. However, the temporal meaning of German *weil* has given way to a causal meaning. In English, *while* has developed a subsequent concessive (i.e. "although") meaning.[17]

---

and Methodological Issues, ed. E. C. Traugott and B. Heine (John Benjamins, 1991), 200–201, and Hopper and Traugott, *Grammaticalization*, 90–92. Compare the development of the French noun *pas* "step" (as in *Il ne vas pas* "He does not go a step") into a negator "no" as in (*Il sait pas* "He does not know"). See Meillet, "L' Évolution," 139–41, and Hopper and Traugott, *Grammaticalization*, 65–66.

15 Traugott and König, "The Semantics-Pragmatics of Grammaticalization," 200.

16 This and the next Old English examples taken from ibid.

17 This divergence between English *while* and German *weil* illustrates the that the potential for grammaticalization does not mean words will necessarily undergo

Another often-cited example of grammaticalization is *going to* > *gonna* (space > time). The construction *going to* was originally a spatial expression as in example 2a) but came to be used as a future auxiliary as in example 2b). Due to phonological reduction (a hallmark of grammaticalization), it became *gonna*.[18] Since *gonna* is more advanced on the cline of grammaticalization, it can only be used as a future auxiliary and is no longer compatible with its original spatial meaning, as seen in example 2c).

2. a. I am going to the store.

   b. I am going to/gonna go to the store.

   c. # I'm gonna the store.

The processes by which these developments happened illustrate two major cognitive processes in communication which drive grammaticalization: metonymic (part for whole) and metaphorical extension. In the change from noun to adverbial conjunction, *hwile* as part of the construction meaning "at the time that" came to stand for the whole construction. This sort of metonymic extension is also referred to as "context induced reinterpretation."[19] The development of *going to* into a future auxiliary illustrates the mechanism of metaphorical extension. In this case, a spatial trajectory is metaphorically construed as a temporal trajectory.[20]

These extensions begin as pragmatic inferences which are

---

the process and that there are usually multiple developmental paths a word may take. It may develop along one or another, multiple paths simultaneously, or none at all. But when natural change does occur, it is characterized by a constrained set of cognitively motivated paths. More on this below.

18 Compare the process by which θέλω ἵνα "I want that" became the future tense morpheme θα in Modern Greek. This occurred in the following stages: θελω ινα > θελω να > θενα > θα. Hopper and Traugott, *Grammaticalization*, 24–25, 99–100.

19 Heine, Claudi, and Hünnemeyer. *Grammaticalization*, 65–97.

20 The space = time metaphor is pervasive across languages. This can be seen in such English expressions as "Christmas is just ahead of us" and "I'm glad the exam is behind me." The word *before* in contemporary English is primarily temporal (e.g. "You cannot go to the movies before you clean your room."), even though its older spatial use continues to be used in higher registers as a preposition (e.g. "Before the throne of God above"). See further S. Svorou, *The Grammar of Space* (John Benjamins, 1994), 158–61; Hopper and Traugott, *Grammaticalization*, 85.

gradually strengthened until they become part of a form's semantic make-up. From a neurological perspective, initially pragmatic meaning extensions which arise "on the fly" in communication gradually become semanticized through Hebbian learning, summarized as, "neurons that fire together wire together."[21] In other words, in the process of semanticization, the more a word or construction becomes associated with an extended interpretation through synaptic co-activation in language use, the more they become neurologically connected in the brain and condition future uses of and encounters with the form. Through this process, called entrenchment, the extended use becomes less inferential and more automated (i.e. less pragmatic and more semantico-syntactic).[22] For example, in the sentence "While I was walking home I found a million dollars," English speakers no longer process *while* as a noun meaning "time" which simply combines with certain contexts to produce a merely pragmatic use as a temporal conjunction. Rather, it is now this use as a temporal conjunction that is most strongly and automatically associated with *while*. Since frequency of use is constantly driving entrenchment, we may say that today's semantics is yesterday's pragmatics.[23]

A test for the "semanticization" of an initially pragmatic inference is "semantic uniqueness."[24] Since a pragmatic implicature co-exists as an interpretively enriched reading along with the more concrete meaning from which it can be inferred, cases in which the inferentially enriched meaning is the only one possible do not fit that profile.

---

21 D. Divjak, and C. L. Caldwell-Harris, "Frequency and Entrenchment," in *Handbook of Cognitive Linguistics*, ed. E. Dąbrowska and D. Divjak (de Gruyter, 2015), 62. Cf. E. Ahlsén, *Introduction to Neurolinguistics* (John Benjamins, 2006), 172; J. A. Feldman, *From Molecule to Metaphor: A Neural Theory of Language* (MIT Press, 2008), 78–82.

22 R. W. Langacker, *Cognitive Grammar: A Basic Introduction* (Oxford University Press, 2008), 38; Divjak and Caldwell-Harris, "Frequency and Entrenchment"; J. R. Taylor, "Prototype Effects in Grammar," in *Handbook of Cognitive Linguistics*, ed. Dąbrowska and Divjak, 567.

23 This trades on the insight of Givón who observed a similar phenomenon on the spectrum of morphology and syntax when he said, "Today's morphology is yesterday's syntax." T. Givón, "Historical Syntax and Synchronic Morphology: An Archaeologist's Field Trip," *Chicago Linguistic Society* 7 (1971): 394–415, cited in Hopper and Traugott, *Grammaticalization*, 26. The case of the construction θέλω ἵνα developing into a future auxiliary θα is a case in point (see footnote 18 above).

24 Kortmann, *Adverbial Subordination*, 91–92.

This would reveal that such an enriched meaning is not merely pragmatic, but rather has become semanticized. For example, the Old English ancestor of *since* could only express anteriority "after" and possibly an accompanying causal implicature. This was therefore merely a pragmatic polysemy at that stage. However, in contemporary English, *since* can express a causal meaning independently of any temporal meaning, illustrating the change temporal > causal.[25] Consider the following examples.

3. a. He has been working here since he was 18 years old.
   b. Since [i.e. from the time that > because] Mary left John, he has been depressed.
   c. Since [i.e. from the time that > because] she is drinking wine, she must not be pregnant.

In 3a), since has a purely temporal *terminus a quo* meaning without any causal implicature. In 3b) a causal meaning can be inferred from the temporal meaning of *since* via the inferential process *post hoc ergo propter hoc* "after this therefore because of this" common to human reasoning based on our universal experience that causes precede (or temporally overlap with) their effects. However, in 3c) *since* is only compatible with a causal meaning and not a temporal one. This shows that the causal pragmatic implicature of utterances like 3b) has become semanticized in *since* so that it can now be used in utterances like 3c) independently of any temporal meaning as an inferential spring-board.

Crucially, such diachronic processes result in two related phenomena. One is that the source meanings and functions which give rise to polysemous extensions in the process of grammaticalization continue to persist alongside those extensions (and even extensions of extensions). This is called layering, in which multiple uses exist side-by-side at different levels of semanticization and entrenchment.[26] Geeraerts explains: "As a consequence of the semantic changes it undergoes, a

---

25 See Kortmann, *Adverbial Subordination*, 320–21; E. C. Traugott and E. König, "The Semantics-Pragmatics of Grammaticalization," 194–99.

26 See further Divjak & Caldwell-Harris, "Frequency and Entrenchment," 60. It is not unusual for older uses in a polysemous set to die out at some point, but they

word acquires multiple meanings, and polysemy, as the situation resulting from such semantic shifts, is so to speak the natural condition
of words."[27] This is especially the case for smaller grammatical words,
since "there exists an inverse relation between morphological complexity and semantic as well as functional versatility."[28]

Another result is that we cannot expect to find a single meaning
from which all uses are directly derived. To return to the example of
while, what abstract core could we come up with as the "real" meaning
that would be common to its uses as a noun and a temporal and concessive adverbial conjunction (not to mention the causal meaning of
German *weil*)? Any such abstract definition would be so vague as to
be unrecognizable by speakers and so broad as to inevitably include
a whole host of other words as synonyms with equally abstract core
meanings. Rather, the extension of *while* in English as a concessive
conjunction (meaning "although") and a causal conjunction (meaning "because") in German has no direct connection to its original
nominal origin. It is only after its development into a temporal conjunction (itself a complex process) that it was able to develop these
later meanings. This is because extensions in grammaticalization proceed in a unidirectional fashion (more on this below) and only develop between conceptually adjacent functions and meanings. Meaning extensions proceed from less to more grammatical function (e.g.
noun > preposition > conjunction) and from more concrete to more
abstract meaning (e.g. space > time > causation). In other words, a
word or construction cannot "jump" stages in the process of development.[29] This means that the conceptual unity of polysemous forms
cannot be found in a common core to which all uses are directly connected. In the words of Haspelmath, "it is not a good strategy to look
for one single central sense in all cases."[30]

---

also commonly persist for long periods alongside newer uses (cf. J. D. Denniston, *The
Greek Particles*, 2nd ed. [Clarendon, 1954], lvi).

  27   D. Geeraerts, *Theories of Lexical Semantics* (Oxford University Press, 2010), 42.

  28   Kortmann, *Adverbial Subordination*, 113.

  29   Kortmann, *Adverbial Subordination*, 187; M. Haspelmath, "The Geometry of
Grammatical Meaning: Semantic Maps and Cross-Linguistic Comparison," in *The
New Psychology of Language*, ed. Tomasello, 233; Andrason and Locatell, "The Perfect
Wave," 29.

  30   Haspelmath, "Grammatical Meaning," 232.

Along with the characteristics discussed above, the process of grammaticalization has several further properties that we can utilize in the study of Greek. Firstly, grammaticalization paths which have been found to be crosslinguistically pervasive show that they are driven by cognitive processes common to human cognition rather than language-specific idiosyncrasies.[31] Therefore, known grammaticalization paths involving the same uses of a given word or construction in the Greek NT can be heuristically employed to locate the conceptual relationship between seemingly unrelated uses. This is especially useful with words like ὡς which had already developed a wide range of usage in the early layers of its textual history, making it impossible to directly observe when each use emerged (see section 3 below).[32] Secondly, as mentioned above, grammaticalization has been repeatedly confirmed to be a robustly unidirectional process.[33] That is, with very few exceptions, the source > goal development never occurs in the opposite direction (see further section 3 below). This allows us to order uses according to their time of emergence relative to one another. This can also provide clues as to which uses are still emerging and gaining ground semantically and which may be waning in a form's synchronic profile. So, mapping a word's functional profile onto known grammaticalization paths generates plausible hypotheses about how each use is related to the others and how they developed.

Finally, these hypotheses generated by the heuristic application of grammaticalization paths can be corroborated by testing them against a form's synchronic usage. Consider Figure 4.1 below. This represents the fashion in which extended uses emerge gradually in certain contexts that are compatible with both a source meaning "A"

---

31 Some grammaticalization paths are only attested in a few languages while others can be observable across dozens of areally and genetically distinct languages with no contact and constitute an essentially universal process of change. See, for example, the locative > temporal development in B. Heine and T. Kuteva, *World Lexicon of Grammaticalization* (Cambridge University Press, 2002), 205–06.

32 Robertson makes a similar observation when he comments, "Some conjunctions are so early as to elude analysis, like δέ, τέ, etc." A. T. Robertson, *A Grammar of the Greek New Testament in the Light of Historical Research*. 3rd ed. rev. and enlarged (Hodder & Stoughton, George H. Doran Company, 1919), 301.

33 See Hopper and Traugott, *Grammaticalization*, 130–38 for a discussion of this issue and proposed counter examples.

as well as an extended meaning "B." However, even after this development takes place, such "A/B" bridging contexts continue to persist alongside earlier use "A" and extended use "B." Such lingering "seams" of development can help illuminate the conceptual processes responsible for these extensions. Thus, the examples of ὡς discussed below are not presented as the very moments in which its various extensions emerged, but rather the persisting "A/B" bridging contexts that may have initially served as the locus of those extensions.

Diachronic development

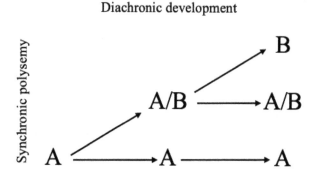

Figure 4.1: Grammaticalization schema

Recall example 3 above in light of the crosslinguistically robust observation that temporal words often develop causal meanings but never the other way around. Even if we only had synchronic uses of *since*, we could see certain uses that were only temporal ("A"), others that were only causal ("B"), and bridging contexts that were temporal with a causal implicature ("A/B"), and we could reconstruct the development time > cause and the inferential process that drove that development. Taken together, the various elements of this approach allow us to reconstruct a word's diachronic history and uncover the conceptual relationships of its synchronic polysemy. In the next section, I will employ specific grammaticalization paths that overlap with the polysemy pattern of ὡς in order to propose a reconstruction of its diachronic development. I will also discuss various examples of ὡς which lie at the conceptual seams of its uses and can be used to illuminate the cognitive processes at work in its syntactico-semantic development. Such bridging contexts in the processes of change can then clarify the relationship between its synchronic uses in the NT.

3. The Diachronic Development and Synchronic Polysemy of ΩΣ

Classical philologists consistently trace ὡς back to the old Indo-European instrumental/ablative case form of the relative pronominal y/jo-,[34] used to communicate manner, i.e. "by means of which, the way in which."[35] Ventris and Chadwick have identified possible examples

---

34 The original y/j became the rough breathing in Greek. J. Wright, *Comparative Grammar of the Greek Language* (Oxford University Press, 1912), 78.

35 Janaris, *Historical Greek Grammar*, 352; Robertson, *Grammar*, 953; E. Schwyzer, *Griechische Grammatik, auf der grundlage von Karl Brugmanns Griechische Grammatik. 2. Bd. Syntax und syntakitische Stilistik*, vervollständigt und herausgegeben von A. Debrunner (C.H. Beck, 1950), 662; P. Monteil, *La Phrase Relative en Grec Ancien*, Thèse, Études et Commentaires, vol. 47 (Librairie C. Klincksieck, 1963); LSJ, 239–40; BDAG 1103; M. Haspelmath and O. Buchholz, "Equative and Similative Constructions in the Languages of Europe," in *Adverbial Constructions in the Languages of Europe*, ed. J. V. D. Auwera and D. Ó. Baoill (de Gruyter, 1998), 293; S. Cristofaro, "Grammaticalization and Clause Linkage Strategies: A Typological Approach with Particular Reference to Ancient Greek," in *The Limits of Grammaticalization*, ed. A. G. Ramat and P. J. Hopper (John Benjamins, 1998), 80; R. Beekes, *Etymological Dictionary of Greek*. 2 vols, with the assistance of L. van Beek. Leiden Indo-European Etymological Dictionaries 10/1–2 (Brill, 2010), 1683. This is also the source of the Greek relative pronoun ὅς. Compare P. Chantraine, *Morphologie Historique du Grec*. Dieuxième Édition, revue et augmenteé, nouveau tirage (Klincksieck, 1984), 121 on the adverbial ending -ως attached to many adverbs. Before this, "The relative ὅς, as is well known, was first an anaphoric substantive pronoun." Robertson, *Grammar*, 953; cf. A. Sihler, *New Comparative Grammar of Greek and Latin* (Oxford University Press, 1995), 187. Note that the ὡς being discussed here should be distinguished from three other similar looking but likely etymologically distinct words. The word being considered here is labeled ὡς 1 in Beekes, *Etymological*, 1683, having the glosses "as, so far as," "when," "because," and final "therewith." LSJ groups them together under a single entry, though it does note at the end that these are not all the same word. Compare P. Chantraine, *Dictionnaire Étymologique de la Langue Grecque: Histoire des Mots. Avec un Supplément* (Klincksieck, 1999), 1305, who gives each a separate entry. However, it is not implausible that these etymologically distinct words began to merge over time. Compare Jannaris, *Historical Greek Grammar*, 365.

as early as Linear B.[36] Robertson notes its use in Homeric Greek.[37] An example of this use is found in Plato's *Rep.* 365d, as cited in LSJ:[38]

4. ἀλλ' ὅμως, εἰ' μέλλομεν εὐδαιμονήσειν, ταύτῃ ἰτέον, ὡς τὰ ἴχνη τῶν λόγων φέρει.

    But all the same if we expect to be happy, we must pursue the path to which the footprints of our arguments point.[39]

Even though the original use, the relative function is quite rare in the NT, if clearly present at all. For a possible lingering example, consider Luke 22:61:[40]

5. καὶ ὑπεμνήσθη ὁ Πέτρος τοῦ ῥήματος τοῦ κυρίου ὡς εἶπεν αὐτῷ[41]

    And Peter remembered the saying of the Lord which he spoke to him ...[42]

Translations almost always render this as "how," which is to say, "the way in which" corresponding to the original ablative relative use discussed above.[43]

---

36 M. Ventris and J. Chadwick, *Documents in Mycenaean Greek: Three Hundred Selected Tablets from Knossos, Pylos and Mycenae with Commentary and Vocabulary* (Cambridge University Press, 1959), 206–07, 307. But see J. T. Hooker, *Linear B: An Introduction* (Bristol Classic Press, 1980), 63.

37 Robertson, *Grammar*, 954. For examples see LSJ, 2038b.

38 LSJ, 2038a.

39 Plato, *Plato in Twelve Volumes*, Vol. 5, trans. Paul Shorey (Harvard University Press, 1969), Perseus Digital Library, http://www.perseus.tufts.edu/hopper/text?doc=Perseus:text:1999.01.0168. Emphasis mine.

40 Cf. Mark 14:72 with a variant reading in which ὅ stands in the place of ὡς. While such variant readings are by definition marginal, they are especially illustrative of conceptual seams between uses since they reveal the (conscious or unconscious) grouping of conceptually similar forms. Also see Acts 11:16; Rom 11:2. Also see LXX Ex 8:8 (8:12 Eng) and the alternative text of Judg 9:38, which render relative אשׁר with ὡς. Cf. T. Muraoka, "The Use of ὡς in the Greek Bible," *Novum Testamentum* 7, no. 1 (1964): 62.

41 NT texts are taken from the NA[28].

42 Translations mine unless otherwise indicated.

43 For similar uses, cf. LXX 3 Kgdms 20:29 (1 Kgs 21:29 Eng); Mark 4:27; Rom 1:9; 1 Cor 12:2; Phil 1:8; Col 3:18; 4:4; 1 Thess 2:10–11. However, these uses do not have an antecedent as in Luke 22:61. Cf. H. G. Liddell, *An Intermediate Greek-English Lexicon*,

In addition to its original relative use, ὡς had developed a wide variety of meanings already in the early layers of Greek. For example, Jannaris identifies uses in Classical Attic as a causal adverbial conjunction, complementizer, final adverbial conjunction, and temporal adverbial conjunction.[44] Compare Cristofaro who gives examples from Homeric Greek of its use as the head of purpose, result, temporal, causal, and manner clauses, as a comparative preposition, and as a complementizer.[45]

In the NT, ὡς also spans a set of semantically distinct meanings within its use as an adverbial conjunction (e.g. comparative "as," temporal "after, as soon as, when, while," and causal "since, because"). It also functions across different words classes (e.g. relative, preposition, adverbial conjunction, complementizer).[46] As summarized by Robertson: "Often the same conjunction is used indifferently in a number of different kinds of clauses. So ὡς in comparative, declarative, causal, temporal, final, consecutive, indirect interrogative, exclamatory."[47] How is it that an originally relative pronoun developed such a wide usage profile?

Founded upon the Seventh Edition of Liddell and Scott's Greek-English Lexicon (Clarendon Press, 1889), 907.

44 See Jannaris, *Historical Greek Grammar*, on uses as a causal adverbial conjunction (408), complementizer (412–13), final adverbial conjunction (416–17), and temporal adverbial conjunction (422). Cf. F. C. Babbitt, *A Grammar of Attic and Ionic Greek* (American Book Company, 1902) which notes uses as an exclamative preceding wishes (292), final conjunction (294–95), causal conjunction (299–300), and complementizer (338). Also see H. W. Smyth, *A Greek Grammar for Colleges* (American Book Company, 1920), 670–71.

45 Cristofaro, "Clause Linkage Strategies," 69–72.

46 See uses listed in BDAG, 1103–1106. See J. H. Moulton and N. Turner, *A Grammar of New Testament Greek. Vol. 3: Syntax* (T&T Clark, 1963) for its use as a final (105, 135–36), comparative (320), causal (with ptc. 320), and temporal (321) conjunction. See BDF for its use as a comparative (236–37) and temporal (237–38) conjunction. Uses identified by Robertson, *Grammar*, include exclamative (302), causal (963–64), comparative (967–68), temporal (974), final (987), and consecutive (1000–1001) conjunction, and indirect question marker (1021). Uses identified by Wallace, *Greek Grammar*, 674–78 include causal, comparative, result, and temporal conjunction, and complementizer. S. E. Porter, *Idioms of the Greek New Testament*, 2nd ed. (JSOT, 1999), 217 lists comparative, temporal, and purpose/result uses, among others. Compare Muraoka's extensive study on the use of ὡς in biblical Greek and several other Koine corpora. Muraoka, "The Use of ὡς."

47 Robertson, *Grammar*, 980.

Due to space limitations, I will only discuss some of the main developments of ὡς in order to illustrate the potential application of grammaticalization paths to the Greek of the NT and its implications for an understanding of how meaning works. Specifically, in the following I will propose grammaticalization paths and their driving cognitive processes which trace a development from an original relativizer use into comparative conjunction and complementizer uses. This will illustrate how a word's development often spans multiple word classes. I will then propose a path from its use as a comparative conjunction into temporal and then causal meanings. This will illustrate the complex developments that words often undergo within a given word class (e.g. adverbial conjunction). Other uses and developments will need to be left for further study.[48] However, it is hoped that these examples will be sufficient to illustrate how cognitively driven grammaticalization paths can help illuminate how meaning develops and how such an approach may be applied to the study of the Greek NT.

Initial Extensions as a Comparative Conjunction and Complementizer

In this section I will describe the ways in which an originally relative ὡς could have been reanalyzed in certain contexts as a comparative conjunction and a complementizer. Thus, the original relativizer ὡς would have had at least two direct extensions which themselves then served as the locus for further extensions of their own (discussed under the following heading).

Kortmann has shown that the most common sources for adverbial conjunctions in Greek are interrogatives and relativizers, followed by adverbs.[49] In fact, Kortmann has shown that such uses fall on various points along several major category continua, many of which are

---

48 Note that I will also be discussing the use of ὡς by itself rather than the numerous collocations and more complex constructions in which it can occur.

49 Kortmann, *Adverbial Subordinators*, 108–12; 346. Cf. B. Kortmann, "Adverbial Subordinators in the Languages of Europe," in *Adverbial Constructions in the Languages of Europe*, ed. J. V. D. Auwera and D. Ó. Baoill (de Gruyter, 1998), 482; B. Kortmann, "Adverbial Conjunctions," in *Language Typology and Language Universals*, ed. M. Haspelmath, E. König, W. Oesterreicher, and W. Raible (de Gruyter, 2001), 845;

realized by a single word. See Figure 4.2 below.

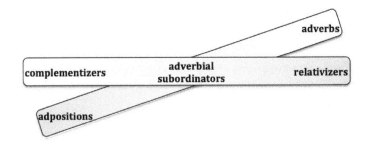

Figure 4.2: Intersecting Category Continua[50]

This visualizes the robust crosslinguistic observation that words which function as adverbial subordinators are regularly polysemous with other functions along these intersecting continua, both in their diachronic history and synchronic usage. It is precisely these functions that grammarians have consistently observed in ὡς in the various stages of its history.

For example, Haspelmath and Buchholz show specifically that comparatives (words like English *as*)[51] across languages often develop from words that were originally relativizers.[52] This same diachronic

---

Cristofaro, "Clause Linkage Strategies," 70–72; Haspelmath and Buchholz, "Equative and Similative Constructions."

50 Adapted from Kortmann, *Adverbial Subordinators*, 59.

51 Haspelmath and Buchholz use more specific designations such as similative, equative, accord, and role constructions to distinguish the various types of related "comparative" constructions (which ὡς is also capable of expressing). For a discussion of these terms with examples, see Haspelmath and Buchholz, "Equative and Similative Constructions," 277–81. I will generally use the terms "comparison" and "comparative" as a blanket term for these subcategories.

52 For example, it has been widely observed that English *as* originally came from the relative pronoun *swá*. This was later reinforced with *all* as *all swá*. Through unitization and phonological reduction (hallmarks of grammaticalization), this gradually progressed as follows: *all swá* > *also* > *alse* > *als* > *as*. See Kortmann, *Adverbial Subordinators*, 315–19; Haspelmath and Buchholz, "Equative and Similative Constructions," 292–93. In fact, the polysemy pattern of English *as* and ὡς have considerable overlap (e.g. as comparative, temporal, and causal conjunctions). Examples from many other languages can be multiplied. For example, German *wie*, Swedish *som*, Russian *kak*, Lithuanian *kaip*, Slovene *kot*, French *que*, Portuguese *como*, Georgian *rogorc*, Albanian *si/siç*, Friulian *come/come che*, Serbian/Croatian *kao/kao što*. Haspelmath and

relationship holds within the development of Greek ὡς.[53] Haspelmath and Buchholz illustrate the derivation of comparative (specifically equative) constructions from relative clauses with the following Latin example:[54]

6. Claudia *tam* docta   est *quam*[REL] Julius.
    Claudia so   learned is how[REL]   Julius
    'Claudia is as learned as Julius.'

The second part of this comparative construction was originally a relative clause as in, "Claudia is as learned *to the extent to which* Julius (is learned)." When combined with a parameter clause (marked here by *tam* "so"), the relative clause becomes functionally equivalent to and can be reanalyzed as a comparative clause communicating the standard which is compared to the parameter. Compare the example above to the following from the NT:

7. οὕτως γάρ ποτε καὶ αἱ ἅγιαι γυναῖκες αἱ ἐλπίζουσαι εἰς θεὸν ἐκόσμουν
    ἑαυτὰς ὑποτασσόμεναι τοῖς ἰδίοις ἀνδράσιν, 6 ὡς Σάρρα ὑπήκουσεν τῷ
    Ἀβραὰμ κύριον αὐτὸν καλοῦσα ...
    For thus formerly also the holy women who hoped in God would
    adorn themselves by submitting to their own husbands, 6 **as [i.e. the
    way in which]** Sarah submitted to Abraham by calling him lord ...
    1 Pet 3:5–6[55]

Here, οὕτως marks the parameter (the quality being compared) and ὡς marks the standard of the comparison. As one can see, the way in

---

Buchholz, "Equative and Similative Constructions," 304–5. In all, the study of Haspelmath and Buchholz is based on 47 different languages. They conclude that this phenomenon characterizes most languages in the Standard Average European group (e.g. Romance, Germanic, Balto-Slavic, and Balkan languages). Haspelmath and Buchholz, "Equative and Similative Constructions," 315. But see R. Hendry, *Relative Clauses in Time and Space: A Case Study in the Methods of Diachronic Typology* (John Benjamins, 2012), 89–96.

53 Haspelmath and Buchholz, "Equative and Similative Constructions," 293. Cf. Schwyzer, *Griechische Grammatik*, 662.

54 Haspelmath and Buchholz, "Equative and Similative Constructions," 287–88.

55 Cf. Matt 1:24; Acts 23:11; Rom 5:18; 2 Cor 11:3; 1 Thess 2:11. For a string of these, see 1 Clem 13:2.

which an originally relative pronoun can be reanalyzed as a comparative adverbial conjunction in such contexts is somewhat transparent.[56] Due to the pressure of economy in communication, comparative constructions such as those in example 7 can also appear with only the standard marker ὡς with an elided predicate.[57]

Relativizers are also a common source of complementizers.[58] Cristofaro has shown how relativizer ὡς could have been reinterpreted as a complementizer.[59] In cases where a manner relative pronoun is used with a verb (or substantive with a verbal idea) of speech or perception, it can be reanalyzed as a complementizer. Consider the following example from Homer:[60]

8. ἤειδεν δ' ὡς ἄστυ διέπραθον υἷες Ἀχαιῶν
   He sang **how/that** the sons of the Acheans destroyed the city *Od.* 8.514

---

56 Cf. Haspelmath and Buchholz, "Equative and Similative Constructions," 304.

57 These sorts of constructions are categorized as elliptical, where the finite clause headed by ὡς may be fully understood and supplied. BDAG, 1103–04; cf. Robertson, *Grammar*, 968. See, for example, Matt 7:29; 10:16; 17:2; Mark 1:22; Rom 5:18; 1 Cor 13:11. For a discussion of a similar examples from Homeric Greek, see Cristofaro, "Clause Linkage Strategies," 70.

58 B. Heine and T. Kuteva, *World Lexicon of Grammaticalization* (Cambridge University Press, 2002), 254. Hendry, *Relative Clauses*, 108–15; B. Fagard, P. Pietrandrea, and J. Glikman, "Syntactic and Semantic Aspects of Romance Complementizers," in *Complementizer Semantics in European Languages*, ed. K. Boye and P. Kehayov (de Gruyter, 2016), 122; P. Kehayov and K. Boye, "Complementizer Semantics in European languages: Overview and Generalizations," in *Complementizer Semantics in European Languages*, ed. K. Boye and P. Kehayov (de Gruyter, 2016), 876; C. Lehmann, "Relativesätze," in *Syntax: Ein Internationales Handbuch zeitgenössischer Forschung / An International Handbook of Contemporary Research*. 2 Halbband / Vol. 2, ed. J. Jacobs, A. Stechow, W. Sternefeld, and T. Vennemann (de Gruyter, 1995), 1213–14. A parade example is the Hebrew relative pronoun אֲשֶׁר which began as a noun meaning "place." This original nominal function can be seen in cognates such as Akkadian *ašrum*, Ugaritic *atr*, and Aramaic אֲתַר (borrowed in Modern Hebrew to mean "site"). This then developed into a relative pronoun and later into a complementizer and adverbial conjunction. For a detailed discussion of various analyses, see R. Holmstedt, "The Etymologies of Hebrew *'ăšer* and *šeC-*." *Journal of Near Eastern Studies* 66, no. 3 (2007): 177–91. Cf. HALOT, 98 and references there.

59 Cristofaro, "Clause Linkage Strategies," 72. Cristofaro, "Clause Linkage Strategies," 71 also suggests that relativizer ὡς was the source for the later development of its use to mark a result clause.

60 Cf. Cristofaro, "Clause Linkage Strategies," 72.

Here, the interpretation of ὡς as a manner relative can still be recovered. The manner in which the sons of the Acheans destroyed the city coincides with the content of what was sang. Thus, the collocation with the verb of speech (ἤειδεν "he sang") contextually induces the reanalysis of ὡς as a complementizer introducing the content of what was sung.

Such contexts are ripe grounds for the semanticization of an extended function. Indeed, Blass reports that this extension becomes strengthened in later Greek.[61] However, this use does not appear to have become fully entrenched in the NT corpus, since there are little to no unambiguous cases where it can only be interpreted as a complementizer.[62] There are several cases in the NT where the seam between the conceptual categories of relativizer and complementizer can be seen. That is, in these cases a complementizer use can be inferred while still leaving the relativizer function as a recoverable reading.[63] One of the clearer examples of complementizer ὡς in the NT is perhaps Acts 10:28:[64]

9. ἔφη τε πρὸς αὐτούς· ὑμεῖς ἐπίστασθε ὡς ἀθέμιτόν ἐστιν ἀνδρὶ Ἰουδαίῳ
    κολλᾶσθαι ἢ προσέρχεσθαι ἀλλοφύλῳ ... [65]

---

61 F. Blass, *Grammar of New Testament Greek.* 2nd ed., rev. and enlarged. Trans. H. St. John Thackeray (Macmillan and Co., 1911), 230–31. Cf. Cristofaro "Clause Linkage Strategies," 79–84. However, Jannaris, *Historical Greek Grammar,* 412–13 says that this use was actually in a phase of retreat since the classical period. It could be that this use did clearly emerge earlier, then dropped in use as seen in the Koine period, before picking up again in later Greek. Cf. Muraoka, "The Use of ὡς," 63–64.

62 Cf. Robertson, *Grammar,* 1032. Schwyzer, *Griechische Grammatik,* 645 however, identifies ὡς as a complementizer in the NT. Other examples of this use may be found outside the NT corpus. See W. W. Goodwin, *Syntax of the Moods and Tenses of the Greek Verb* (Macmillan and Co, 1889), 258. For example, see Tob 11:15 in the LXX alternate text for a case where ὡς is used in parallel within a string of complementizer ὅτι clauses. Compare 2 Macc 2:1–2; 4 Macc 4:22.

63 The reason for the complementizer use of ὡς not gaining more ground can be attributed (at least in part) to the strength of complementizer ὅτι which, already filling that function, mitigated the encroachment of ὡς.

64 Cf. Robertson, *Grammar,* 1032. Contrast this with the very similarly worded use in Acts 20:18 where the complementizer meaning seems to overlap much more with that of a manner relative.

65 Cf. Luke 6:4; 8:47; 16:1 22:61; 24:6; Acts 10:28; 17:22; 20:18; Rom 1:9; Phil 1:8. Also see LXX Dan 1:8. Robertson, *Grammar,* 1032 also notes variant readings where ὡς is

And he said to them; "You yourselves know **that/how** it is unlawful for a Jewish man to associate with or to visit a foreigner …

The manner of "how" the thing is unlawful does not appear to be as prominent here. The use of ὡς seems to come closer rather to complementizer ὅτι. Yet, even in these cases, a relative of manner can still be possibly recoverable as a reading.[66] Thus, at least based on the NT data, complementizer ὡς does not clearly pass the test of "semantic uniqueness." Therefore, as an extension it may only qualify as part of the word's pragmatic polysemy, rather than its semantic polysemy. I will now turn to some secondary extensions which arose from the earlier extension of ὡς as an adverbial conjunction of comparison.

Additional Extensions as a Temporal and Causal Adverbial Conjunction

As described in section 2 above, once an extension becomes entrenched, it can itself serve as the locus for further extensions. In this section, I will present examples showing how the extension of ὡς from relativizer into a comparative conjunction itself became the locus of further extensions of temporal and causal meanings.

From a crosslinguistic perspective, there is an extremely strong cognitively motivated (and therefore language-independent) tendency for comparative conjunctions to develop subsequent temporal and causal uses. This is drawn from Kortmann's study of adverbial conjunctions covering 50 living languages and three extinct languages (including Greek) from 6 different language families.[67] The strongest developmental paths observed from this data are presented in Figure 4.3 below.[68]

---

put in place of complementizer ὅτι. Compare this to Luke 14:22, where there is a variant reading with ὡς instead of the complementizer use of the relative pronoun ὅ. Compare Mark 14:72 where ὅ is a variant reading for ὡς. Additionally, see LSJ, 2039a for cases where an interrupted ὡς clause is resumed by a ὅτι complement clause.

66 Robertson, *Grammar*, 1032.

67 Kortmann, *Adverbial Subordination*. This study included 2,043 different conjunctions from the 53 languages representing Indo-European, Uralic, Altaic, Caucasian, Semitic, and one Isolate, and covering a maximum time-depth of 2,500 years.

68 Note that these broad semantic domains (i.e. locative, temporal, modal, and CCC) are themselves internally complex and contain various subcategories. See

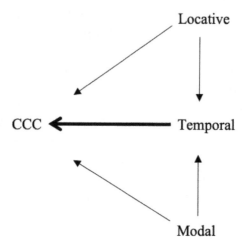

Figure 4.3: Strongest Paths Between Adverbial Subordinators[69]

This figure can be read as follows. Locative and modal (e.g. comparison) adverbial conjunctions are the typical source domain for temporal conjunctions as well as causal, conditional, concession, and related logical relations (labeled CCC).[70] The strongest source of CCC conjunctions is temporal conjunctions. Furthermore, the arrows indicate unidirectionality. As Kortmann explains: "It is crucial to stress that for none of these links does the reverse hold, i.e. neither are CCC subordinators found to develop temporal, locative or modal readings, nor do temporal subordinators come to serve as locative or modal markers."[71]

This unidirectionality is a result of the direction of informativeness. Speakers invite and hearers infer the most informative interpretation of an utterance, based on the communicative maxim to be as informative as possible.[72] Relating this to Figure 4.3 above, speakers

---

further Kortmann, *Adverbial Subordination*, 210. For a detailed look at the temporal subsenses of כ in Biblical Hebrew and their developmental trajectory into causal and concessive adverbial conjunctions, see C. S. Locatell, "Temporal כ and Its Semantic Extensions," *Journal of Semitic Studies* (2020).

69   Adapted from Kortmann, *Adverbial Subordination*, 178.

70   Schwyzer, *Griechische Grammatik*, 661 anticipated this in noting several of these developmental paths among Greek conjunctions.

71   Kortmann, *Adverbial Subordination*, 178.

72   Traugott and König, "Semantics-Pragmatics of Grammaticalization," 190.

invite and hearers infer richer logical interpretations of temporal relations as more informative causal relations. This is an example of the universal tendency in language change to move from the more concrete to the more abstract (e.g. *q* happened when/after *p* happened > *q* happened because *p* happened).[73] This unidirectionality allows us to order such uses in terms of developmental history, even from a synchronic usage profile. These unidirectional paths support the reconstruction that after extending from a relative pronoun into the class of adverbial conjunction heading comparative (i.e. modal) clauses, there would be a strong tendency for it to develop subsequent temporal and CCC senses, such as causation.

The functions of ὡς can be mapped onto these grammaticalization paths to reconstruct the most likely trajectory of development that produced its synchronic usage profile. This points to its function as an adverbial conjunction of comparison as the source for its temporal and causal uses.[74] Beginning with the development from comparative into temporal, it is specifically the modal senses of manner, similarity, comment accord, and comparison that have the strongest tendency to develop temporal senses of immediate anteriority and simultaneous overlap. Consider the following Figure 4.4:

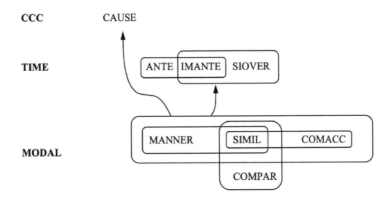

Figure 4.4: Developmental paths of Modal Subordinators[75]

---

73 In these schematized definitions, "*q*" represents the main clause and "*p*" the adverbial clause.

74 Cf. Schwyzer, *Griechische Grammatik*, 662.

75 Adapted from Kortmann, *Adverbial Subordination*, 196, 210. ANTE = anteriority; COMACC = comment-accord; COMPAR = comparison; IMANTE = Immediate

This figure can be understood as a more detailed look at the modal semantic space of Figure 4.3 and its relationship to the temporal and CCC spaces. The boxes enclosing certain subsenses indicate stronger semantic affinity. As it turns out, the usage profile of ὡς in the NT corresponds with this at several points. Consider the following examples along with parallel uses of ὡς from the NT:

10. Similarity[76]
    a. It was (just) as I imagined.
    b. Matt 15:28[77]
       γενηθήτω σοι ὡς θέλεις
       Let it be to you as you desire.
11. Comparison[78]
    a. She treats me as if I am a stranger.
    b. 1 Cor 4:7[79]
       τίς γάρ σε διακρίνει; τί δὲ ἔχεις ὃ οὐκ ἔλαβες; εἰ δὲ καὶ ἔλαβες, τί καυχᾶσαι ὡς μὴ λαβών;
       For who sees you as any different? What do you have that you did not receive? And if indeed you received it, why do you boast as if not receiving?
12. Comment/Accord[80]
    a. As you said, George has no children.

---

anteriority; INSTRU = instrumental; SIMIL = similarity; SIOVER = simultaneous overlap.

76 This can be represented as "*q*, (just) as *p*" where "the character of a situation *q* is described by comparing it to a (typically) real past or present situation *p*." This and other definitions below can be found in Kortmann, *Adverbial Subordination*, 84–87.

77 Compare example 7 above, Matt 1:24; 6:12; 8:13; 26:19; Mark 4:36; Acts 2:15; 23:11; Eph 6:20; Col 2:6; 1 Tim 3:9; 2 Pet 2:1.

78 Note that this is a more specific use of the term "comparison" than the way it has been generally used so far. See fn. 51 above. This relationship can be represented as "*q*, as if/as though *p*" where *p* is typically, but not necessarily, hypothetical. Kortmann, *Adverbial Subordination*, 88.

79 In this use, ὡς consistently governs a participle or infinitive, rather than a finite verb. Cf. Acts 3:12; Col 2:20; 1 Pet 4:12; Rev 5:6.

80 This relationship can be schematically represented as "as *p*, *q*" where "*p* expresses the speaker's comment on the content of the matrix clause, typically with the aim of affirming the truth (and thus reliability) of *q*; e.g. *p* may identify the source of the speaker's information, or express agreement with somebody else's opinion." Kortmann, *Adverbial Subordination*, 87–88.

b. Acts 17:28[81]

ἐν αὐτῷ γὰρ ζῶμεν καὶ κινούμεθα καὶ ἐσμέν, ὡς καί τινες τῶν καθ᾽ ὑμᾶς ποιητῶν‧ εἰρήκασιν· τοῦ γὰρ καὶ γένος ἐσμέν.

For in him we live and move and exist, as also some of your poets have said; "For we are his offspring."

13. Anteriority[82]

a. **After** I went for a jog, I ate breakfast.

b. Luke 5:4[83]

ὡς δὲ ἐπαύσατο λαλῶν, εἶπεν πρὸς τὸν Σίμωνα· Ἐπανάγαγε εἰς τὸ βάθος καὶ χαλάσατε τὰ δίκτυα ὑμῶν εἰς ἄγραν.

Now, **when** [**i.e. after**] he finished speaking, he said to Simon, "Put out into the deep and let down your nets for a catch."

14. Immediate anteriority[84]

a. **When** you're ready, give me a call.

b. Luke 1:44[85]

ἰδοὺ γὰρ ὡς ἐγένετο ἡ φωνὴ τοῦ ἀσπασμοῦ σου εἰς τὰ ὦτά μου, ἐσκίρτησεν ἐν ἀγαλλιάσει τὸ βρέφος ἐν τῇ κοιλίᾳ μου.

For behold, **when** [**i.e. as soon as**] the sound of your greeting came to my ear, the baby in my womb leaped in joy.

15. Simultaneous overlap[86]

a. **When** she fell, he caught her.

b. Luke 19:29 (cf. ὅτε in Matt 21:1; Mark 11:1)[87]

Καὶ ἐγένετο ὡς ἤγγισεν εἰς Βηθφαγὴ καὶ Βηθανία[ν] πρὸς τὸ ὄρος τὸ καλούμενον Ἐλαιῶν, ἀπέστειλεν δύο τῶν μαθητῶν

And it happened that **when** he approached Bethphage and Bethany to the Mount of Olives, he sent two of the disciples ...

---

81 Cf. Acts 13:33; 22:25; Rom 9:25. Also see 1 Clem 32:2.

82 This relationship can be schematically represented as "after *p*, *q*" where the conjunction signals that clause *p* simply precedes clause *q* in time.

83 Cf. Luke 11:1; John 2:9; 4:44; 6:12; 7:10; Acts 10:7; 14:5; 16:15; 19:21; 1 Cor 11:34.

84 This relationship can be schematically represented as "as soon as *p*, *q*" where *p* immediately precedes *q*. Kortmann, *Adverbial Subordination*, 84.

85 Cf. Luke 1:23; 22:66; John 11:20, 29; 21:9; Phil 2:23. This can be strengthened with τάχιστα (e.g. Acts 17:15).

86 This relationship can be schematically represented as "when *p*, *q*" where *p* overlaps temporally with *q* without necessarily being temporally co-extensive.

87 Cf. Luke 22:66; John 2:23; Acts 22:25.

Modal uses such as those given in examples 10 through 12 above have the strongest, crosslinguistically pervasive tendency to develop into the temporal uses given in examples 14 and 15.[88] This has been observed by Robertson who noted that "The temporal use is closely allied to the comparative."[89] Heuristically employing crosslinguistically pervasive grammaticalization paths provides strong evidence for the directionality of this relationship (i.e. from modal/comparative to temporal). Also note that ὡς has temporal uses which do not admit a modal reading, especially examples like 13. This passes the test of semantic uniqueness indicative of semanticized uses rather than pragmatic meanings inferred from an underlying semantic meaning simultaneously present in the text.[90]

In terms of possible paths connecting these senses, a comparative conjunction can be reinterpreted as a temporal conjunction when it is comparing the timeframe, point in time, or temporal duration of the verb in the adverbial clause with the verb in the main clause (recall Figure 4.3). Depending on the temporal idea being compared, this can be reinterpreted as a number of different temporal subsenses. Deutscher notes the following example:

16. 'Thus pleyneth John as he gooth by the way' (Canterbury Tales I. 4114)[91]

Here, the temporal duration of John "complaining" is compared with the temporal duration of him "going by the way." This comparative

----

88 The temporal semantic space also has a complex internal structure of several different subtypes. See Kortmann, *Adverbial Subordination*, 185–86, 191.

89 Robertson cites Mark 9:21; Luke 24:32, John 12:36. Robertson, *Grammar*, 974. Another common source of temporal meaning is the locative semantic space. S. Luraghi, *On the Meaning of Prepositions and Cases: The Expression of Semantic Roles in Ancient Greek*, Studies in Language Companion Series, vol. 67 (Benjamins, 2003), 320; P. Bortone, *Greek Prepositions from Antiquity to the Present* (Oxford University Press, 2010), 57–62, 303.

90 The collocation with ἐγένετο is also common, especially in Lukan writings, e.g. Luke 1:23, 41, 44; 2:15; Acts 21:1. Also note that ὡς can be used in parallel with ὅτε, confirming its temporal sense. For example, see LXX Deut 32:8 (cf. 2 Clem 29:2).

91 Cited in Guy Deutscher, *Syntactic Change in Akkadian: The Evolution of Sentential Complementation* (Oxford University Press, 2001) 39. For other cases of this pathway of development, see F. Heberlein, "Temporal Clauses," in *New Perspectives on Historical Latin Syntax, Volume 4: Complex Sentences, Grammaticalization, Typology*,

meaning invites a temporal inference that John played "while" he went by the way. Indeed, this is one of the stages in the history of the development of English "as," which in Present Day English has comparative, temporal, and also causal meanings.[92] Such a bridging context appears to be seen in Luke 24:32 below:[93]

17. Οὐχὶ ἡ καρδία ἡμῶν καιομένη ἦν [ἐν ἡμῖν] ὡς ἐλάλει ἡμῖν ἐν τῇ ὁδῷ, ὡς διήνοιγεν ἡμῖν τὰς γραφάς;
Wasn't our heart burning within us **as/while** he was speaking with us in the way, **as/while** he was opening up to us the scriptures?

Here, both a comparative and temporal reading are recoverable, with the temporal reading being inferable from the comparative. That is, just as in the example of "as" in 16 above, the timeframe in which the disciples' hearts were burning is compared as corresponding to the time-frame in which Jesus was speaking and opening the scriptures to them. This yields an inference in which the comparative relation communicated by ὡς can be reinterpreted as a temporal relation. Again, through increased frequency of use and entrenchment, this extended meaning would become semanticized via Hebbian learning so that ὡς can also communicate a temporal relationship with no clearly recoverable comparative meaning, such as in 13 above.[94]

Once semanticized, the clear temporal uses of ὡς themselves could then serve as the locus for further semantic extension. Recalling Figure 4.3 above, temporal interclausal relations have the strongest affinity for development into CCC relations, such as causal. As Kortmann observes, "the temporal relations exhibit more and stronger semantic

---

ed. Philip Baldi and Pierluigi Cuzzolin, 235–371 (de Gruyter, 2011), and Y. Treis, "Similative Morphemes as Purpose Clause Markers in Ethiopia and Beyond." In *Similative and Equative Constructions: A Cross-linguistic Perspective*, ed. Y. Treis and M. Vanhove, 133 (Benjamins, 2017).

92 See references in footnote 52 above.

93 Cf. Luke 12:58; 15:25; 19:41; John 8:7; 12:35, 36; Acts 7:23; 13:25; 16:4; 19:9; Gal 6:1; LXX Josh 8:5.

94 Note that the use of ὡς as a comparative preposition has developed a temporal use in Modern Greek, further attesting to the development of temporal uses from prior modal ones. D. Holton, P. Mackridge, and I. Philippaki-Warburton, *Greek: A Comprehensive Grammar*, 2nd ed., revised by V. Spyropoulos (Routledge, 2012), 495.

affinities to CCC relations than to any other type of nontemporal interclausal relations."[95] Rijksbaron has observed that causal ὡς was already present in Herodotus, but not commonly so (governing a participle, though uses with an indicative are found elsewhere).[96] Bridging contexts for this extension can be seen, for example, in the following passage from the Iliad:

18. Ἕκτωρ δ' ὡς οὐκ ἔνδον ἀμύμονα τέτμεν ἄκοιτιν ἔστη ἐπ᾽ οὐδὸν ἰών, μετὰ
     δὲ δμῳῆσιν ἔειπεν· 'εἰ δ᾽ ἄγε μοι δμῳαὶ νημερτέα μυθήσασθε: πῇ ἔβη Ἀνδ
     ρομάχη λευκώλενος ἐκ μεγάροιο;
     So Hector when [i.e. because] he found not his peerless wife within, went and stood upon the threshold, and spake amid the serving-women: "Come now, ye serving-women, tell me true; whither went white-armed Andromache from the hall? *Il.* 6.374–77[97]

Here, the temporal succession of events (i.e. when Hector did not find his wife inside, he then asked where she was) can be understood as the cause-and-effect structure of events (i.e. Because Hector did not find his wife inside, he asked where she was). This conceptual similarity is so relevant to the human mind because the temporal succession of events corresponds to the cause-and-effect structure of events in our experience. Therefore, due to the *post hoc ergo propter hoc* ("after this, therefore because of this") fallacy in reasoning, speakers universally invite and hearers infer causal relationships from temporal expressions.[98] Cristofaro likewise identifies this as the route in the

---

95 Kortmann, *Adverbial Subordination*, 188. Cf. Heine and Kuteva, *World Lexicon*, 291–93.

96 A. Rijksbaron, *Temporal and Causal Conjunctions in Ancient Greek: With Special Reference to the Use of ἐπεί and ὡς in Herodotus* (Adolf M. Hakkert, 1976), 160. For examples in Classical texts with the indicative, see LSJ, 2039a and F. Montanari, *Brill Dictionary of Ancient Greek* (Brill, 2015), 2426c. Babbitt, *Attic and Ionic Greek*, 299–300 lists the causal use of ὡς, though he does not cite examples.

97 Homer, *The Iliad with an English Translation by A.T. Murray, Ph.D. in Two Volumes* (Harvard University Press, 1924), Perseus Digital Library, http://www.perseus.tufts.edu/hopper/text?doc=Perseus:text:1999.01.0134. Emphasis mine.

98 E. C. Traugott, "Conditional Markers," in *Iconicity in Syntax*, ed. J. Haiman (John Benjamins, 1985), 297; Traugott and König, "Semantics-Pragmatics of Grammaticalization," 194; Kortmann, *Adverbial Subordination*, 190; D. Haug, "From Resultatives to Anteriors in Ancient Greek: On the Role of Paradigmaticity in Semantic

development of causal ὡς.[99]

This can also be seen in the NT corpus. Consider, for example, John 19:33 below:[100]

19. ἐπὶ δὲ τὸν Ἰησοῦν ἐλθόντες, ὡς εἶδον ἤδη αὐτὸν τεθνηκότα, οὐ κατέαξαν αὐτοῦ τὰ σκέλη
And coming to Jesus, **when/because** they saw that he was already dead, they did not break his legs.

Here, the temporal order of events coincides with the cause-effect structure of those events.[101] This invites the audience to infer the informatively richer causal reading.[102] In addition to cases in which the temporal order of events corresponds to a cause-effect relationship inferable from the context, another factor that facilitates this extension is the placement of the ὡς clause after the main clause to which it stands related. Temporal clauses typically prefer position before the main clause, while causal clauses prefer position after the main clause.[103] When a temporal ὡς clause appears in a context inviting a

Change," in *Grammatical Change and Linguistic Theory: The Rosendal Papers*, ed. T. Eythórsson (John Benjamins, 2008), 289–90; L. Degand, "Describing Polysemous Discourse Markers: What Does Translation Add to the Picture?" in *From Will to Well. Studies in Linguistics Offered to Anne-Marie Simon-Vandenbergen*, ed. S. Slembrouck, M. Taverniers, and M. Van Herreweghe (Academia Press, 2009), 173–83.

99 Cristofaro, "Clause Linkage Strategies," 72–73. Cf. S. Cristofaro, *Subordination* (Oxford University Press, 2003), 161–62.

100 Cf. Acts 22:11. BDF, 238 notes "points of contact" between temporal and causal uses of ὡς at 2 Clem 8:1; 9:7; and Ign. Rom. 2:2.

101 Cf. Robertson, *Grammar*, 963.

102 Another temporal subsense that has an especially strong affinity for developing into causal meanings is anteriority (Kortmann 1997:210). This can be schematically represented as "after *p*, *q*" where *p* simply precedes *q* in time (Kortmann 1997:84). This temporal subsense of ὡς can be seen in examples such as Luke 1:23; 2:39; 5:4; John 7:10; Acts 16:15. Cf. LXX Ex 13:11; Lev 14:34; Deut 30:1. An example with a relatively strong causal implicature may be Acts 19:21. Cf. the causal use of καθὼς which also likely emerged from its earlier temporal use (cf. BDAG 494).

103 H. Diessel, "The Ordering Distribution of Main and Adverbial Clauses: A Typological Study," *Language* 77, no. 3 (September 2001): 446. For an explanation of the cognitive processes responsible for these preferences, see B. Dancygier, and E. Sweetser, *Mental Spaces in Grammar: Conditional Constructions* (Cambridge University Press, 2005), 180. Of course, temporal ὡς can also appear after the main clause, e.g. Luke 24:32; John 12:35 (vis-à-vis verse 36).

causal interpretation as described above, such a causal interpretation will be further facilitated if the ὡς clause appears after the main clause as preferred by causal clauses.

As shown in Figure 4.4, another likely path for the development of causal ὡς is directly from its use as a modal adverbial conjunction. A context for this extension can be seen when comparing the synoptic accounts of the Lord's Prayer. Consider the following texts.[104]

20. a. Matt 6:12

καὶ ἄφες ἡμῖν τὰ ὀφειλήματα ἡμῶν, ὡς καὶ ἡμεῖς ἀφήκαμεν τοῖς ὀφειλέταις ἡμῶν

And forgive us our trespasses, **(in as much) as/because** we have also forgiven our debtors.

b. Luke 11:4

καὶ ἄφες ἡμῖν τὰς ἁμαρτίας ἡμῶν, καὶ γὰρ αὐτοὶ ἀφίομεν παντὶ ὀφείλοντι ἡμῖν

And forgive us our sins, **for** we ourselves also forgive everyone indebted to us.

In the context of Matt 6:12, a modal reading of ὡς would understand ἄφες to be requesting forgiveness that corresponds to the likeness of the supplicant's forgiveness toward others. It is not difficult to see how this comparative clause "as we have also forgiven our debtors" can be interpreted as the basis for the request "because we have also forgiven our debtors." Here, a comparative relationship can be reanalyzed as a causal relationship when the degree or extent of the verbal idea in the adverbial clause is compared to that in the main clause.[105] In other words, "*q*, (in as much) as / to the extent that *p*" in these contexts

---

104 While Muraoka does not find Matt 6:12 a convincing case of causal ὡς, he cites several other cases he considers unambiguously causal. Muraoka, "The Use of ὡς," 66–67. Cf. LXX 1 Ch 19:2; 2 Macc 7:23; Matt 5:48. Compare this to LXX Lev 11:44 which uses casual ὅτι in the place of ὡς. Also note that 1 Pet 1:15–16 paraphrases the causal relationship of LXX Lev 11:44 with a modal relationship expressed by κατά. For cases of causal ὡς with a non-finite verb, see the second occurrence in Heb 13:3 (with a participle); 1 Pet 3:7 (with verbless clause); 2 Pet 1:3 (with a participle).

105 Cf. Kortmann, *Adverbial Subordination*, 317–18; José Miguel Baños, "Causal Clauses," in *New Perspectives on Historical Latin Syntax, Volume 4*, ed. Baldi and Cuzzolin, 212–14.

yields the inference "*q*, because *p*". Indeed, this is how it is unambiguously expressed in the Luke 11:4 parallel employing γὰρ.[106] The causal reading of ὡς in Matt 6:12 is further supported in the context itself when in verses 14–15 it is restated as a conditional relationship, conditionality itself being hypothetical causation (cf. Matt 7:1).[107]

Of course, one need not always be forced to take one reading or the other. That is the point. Here we see a context in which the conceptual categories of comparison and causation overlap. It is precisely in such contexts that comparative conjunctions like ὡς have the potential to develop causal meanings. Since a causal reading is more informative than mere succession or modal correspondence of events without an explicit logical relationship, it is the causal interpretation that tends to be invited by the speaker and inferred by the audience as the most relevant reading. Through the process of entrenchment via Hebbian learning as described in section 2 above, this can gradually become part of the semantic potential of ὡς. However, like the complementizer use discussed above, it is difficult to find a causal use in the NT that fulfills the criteria of semantic uniqueness. Contributing to this is the fact that this meaning does not seem to have been employed with a sufficient frequency to become thoroughly entrenched within the profile of ὡς as a clearly semanticized use.[108] This can even be observed in its distribution. That is, it is mainly when governing a

---

106 Compare T. Dan 3:1 which has a variant reading replacing γὰρ with causal ὡς. M. De Jong, *The Testaments of the Twelve Patriarchs: A Critical Edition of the Greek Text* (Brill, 1978), 104.

107 Of course, the comparative and/or causal relationship communicated here need not be read as if forgiveness from God is somehow meritoriously based on our forgiveness of others. Rather, forgiveness toward others is evidence of the spiritual humility that characterizes the faith of one who has received forgiveness (cf. Col 3:13). It is this evidence of faith that forms the basis of the request. Cf. J. R. W. Stott, *The Message of the Sermon on the Mount (Matthew 5–7): Christian Counter-Culture*, BST (InterVarsity Press, 1985), 149–50; D. L. Bock, *Luke: 9:51–24:53*, BECNT (Baker Academic, 1996), 1055; D. A. Hagner, *Matthew 1–13*, WBC 33A (Word, 1998), 152. This would then signal a speech-act causal relationship rather than a mere cause-effect relationship between states of affairs. See further C. S. Locatell, "Causal Categories in Biblical Hebrew Discourse: A Cognitive Approach to Casual כִּ," *Journal of Northwest Semitic Languages* (2020).

108 One example which seems very difficult to take as anything except causal is Soph. Ajax 914, τί ποτε λέγεις, ὦ τέκνον; ὡς οὐ᾽ μανθάνω, "Whatever are you saying, O son? As/Because/For I do not understand." For additional similarly clear examples,

participle, rather than a finite verb, that ὡς is able to communicate causation.[109] This is common in the process grammaticalization. Extensions begin in certain contexts or constructions and slowly spread as they gain entrenchment. Furthermore, the more entrenched causal uses of ὅτι and διότι mitigated the extension of ὡς as a causal conjunction.[110] Thus, ὡς as a causal adverbial conjunction appears to still be emerging as a clearly semanticized use in the NT period. However, Robertson notes that this use did indeed gain ground "in certain contexts in later Greek."[111]

In light of the examples discussed above and the proposed processes involved in their extensions, I will now summarize the diachronic development and synchronic profile of these uses of ὡς in the NT and note some of the implications this perspective has for linguistic analysis of the Greek text.

4. SUMMARY OF ΩΣ IN THE GREEK NT AND CONCLUDING REMARKS

Based on converging evidence from crosslinguistically pervasive grammaticalization paths, inferential processes common to human cognition, and examples of ὡς from texts spanning its history, we can propose a semantic map. This semantic map presents its (partial) synchronic profile as found in the NT. However, because of the layering due to its various semantic and functional extensions, its synchronic profile also contains a diachronic dimension. This may be compared to taking a snapshot of a quickly moving object in which its past and future position can be seen by its blurry edges in the photo. Likewise, a synchronic snapshot of a polysemous form's usage profile will contain older uses which are fading, others which are more central at that point in its history, and emerging uses which are gaining strength. The semantic map of those uses discussed above can be visualized as in Figure 4.5 below.

---

see Montanari, *Dictionary of Ancient Greek*, 2426c. Cf. Acts 22:11 and LXX 1 Kgdms 13:13 where causal ὡς renders causal כ in the MT.

109 Jannaris, *Historical Grammar*, 408–09; Rijksbaron, *Temporal and Causal Conjunctions*, 150–58; BDAG, 1105.3aβ.

110 Jannaris, *Historical Grammar*, 408.

111 Robertson, *Grammar*, 963–64. Compare references in BDAG, 1105.3aβ.

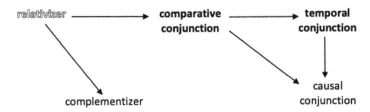

Figure 4.5: A (Partial) Semantic Map of ὡς

Synchronically, this representation says that it is the uses as a comparative and temporal conjunction that are most central (among those discussed here).[112] The older relative use, while having been fully semanticized and at one time the central use, has now drastically or perhaps completely fallen into disuse (as indicated by the faded label). The uses as a complementizer and causal conjunction are still emerging (indicated by their unbolded labels). Diachronically, this visualization presents the origin of ὡς as the ablative form of the relative pronoun in modally colored relative clauses. Through context induced reinterpretation it developed a comparative conjunction use. A tandem development seems to be its use as a complementizer, though with a lesser degree of entrenchment. Once sufficiently semanticized, its use as a comparative conjunction served as the locus of its own extension as a temporal conjunction. A subsequent causal use appears to have had a dual source. The gradually semanticized temporal use developed a causal implicature through the *post hoc ergo propter hoc* line of reasoning. The comparative use appears to have also developed a causal implicature. In a handful of cases noted above, a causal use appears to fulfill the criterion of semantic uniqueness. However, this use appears to have become widespread only at later stages of development.

Ideally, quantitative values from a representative corpus would be attached to each of these uses along with a behavioral profile analysis to determine how generalized they are across syntagmatic contexts.[113]

---

112 The comparative use indeed turns out to be the most prototypical in terms of frequency. Muraoka, "The Use of ὡς," 54.

113 For quantitative data on the uses of ὡς in various Koine texts, see Muraoka, "The Use of ὡς." For an explanation of a Behavioral-Profile analysis and an illustration

Each use would also be more thoroughly tested for semantic uniqueness to differentiate true polysemy from pragmatic polysemy. These steps would yield a more precise usage profile and more clearly reveal the semantic/pragmatic weight of each use relative to one another. And of course, a clearer picture would be yielded by an analysis of ὡς in all its uses and collocations.

Nonetheless, it is hoped that this selective study of some of its main uses illustrates the potential fruitfulness of grammaticalization theory in the study of the Greek NT. Some of the inferential processes proposed here as responsible for the development of ὡς in its various uses are clearer than others, and of course all can be challenged, especially in light of more data. However, what is clear is that scholars of Greek consistently trace ὡς back to an origin as the ablative case form of the relative pronoun from which extended a variety of other uses through a process of gradual change driven by inferential processes common to human cognition.

Finally, I will briefly note just two of the implications this perspective has for how we approach the study of the language of the NT.[114] One is that the processes of language change reveal that there cannot be a ridged and impermeable division between semantics and pragmatics. The fact that originally pragmatic extensions of meaning necessarily become progressively entrenched through Hebbian learning in neural activation means that it is instead better to see pragmatics and semantic as two poles of a continuum. Denniston expresses a similar perspective in his study of the Greek particles, writing, "It may be objected that the particle merely emphasizes, while the emotional nuance lies in the context. But the particle, from constant use in a particular kind of context, acquires a specific emotional tone."[115] What Dennison intuitively perceived is confirmed by the crosslinguistic observations of language change and the neural theory of language discussed above. Thus, words gradually travel toward the semantic pole

---

of how it can be applied to biblical languages, see J. Thompson and K. Lyle, "A Behavioral Profile Analysis of Biblical Hebrew פקד: Quantitative Explorations of Polysemy," in *Ancient Texts and Modern Readers: Studies in Ancient Hebrew Linguistics and Bible Translation*, ed. G. Kotzé, C. S. Locatell, and J. Messara, Studia Semitica Neerlandica 71 (Brill, 2019), 127–48.

114 Cf. Andrason and Locatell, "The Perfect Wave," 81–100.

115 Denniston, *The Greek Particles*, xxxviii, fn. 1.

through increased frequency of usage. This is the only way to account for the directly observable phenomenon that newer pragmatic meanings not only become semanticized, but even come to replace original meanings from which they arose. This is why we often observe that today's semantics is yesterday's pragmatics.

In light of this, a related implication is that our definitions of words must take into account that polysemy is their natural state.[116] Exegetically speaking, Black notes that ignoring polysemy has led to the fallacy of "illegitimate totality transfer" in which all meanings of a form are forced into every use.[117] Another extreme which shares some affinities with illegitimate totality transfer is the trend noted above to locate the "semantics" of a form in some proposed abstract core that is said to be distilled from every use and to relegate any other meaning to the realm of "pragmatics."[118] The cognitive processes described throughout this study as the driving mechanisms of language change reveal why this does not accurately reflect the way meaning actually works. Since pragmatic implicatures are continually being produced and undergoing entrenchment, a word's semantics is in a continually emerging process. Indeed, it is only in recognition of the emergent property of semantics that we can account for language change. As Bybee explains, "If each morpheme has only one fixed, abstract meaning that forms a system with other morphemes, then there is neither motivation nor mechanism for the system to change."[119] Similarly,

---

116 Compare the results of Kortmann's study from which he reports: "semantically polyfunctional subordinators out-number monofunctional ones; this is the situation in, for example, Classical Greek (60%:40%).... " Kortmann, *Adverbial Subordination*, 274.

117 D. A. Black, *Linguistics for Students of New Testament Greek: A Survey of Basic Concepts and Applications*, 2nd ed. (Baker Academic, 2000), 124–25. Cf. J. Barr, *The Semantics of Biblical Language* (Oxford University Press, 1961) 218–19.

118 See references in footnote 5 above.

119 J. Bybee, *Morphology: A Study of the Relation between Meaning and Form* (Benjamins, 1985), 5, quoted in Kortmann, *Adverbial Subordination*, 18. The necessity of recognizing polysemy in linguistic analysis is even more crucial in the study of ancient multi-author/multi-generational corpora like the NT, since they by definition contain multiple diachronic layers and therefore increase linguistic heterogeneity. C. S. Locatell, "Grammatical Polysemy and Grammaticalization in Cognitive and Generative Perspectives: Finding Common Ground in Inter-generational Corpora of Ancient Languages," *Stellenbosch Papers in Linguistics* 48 (2017): 239–53.

Traugott observes: "...without polysemy one cannot account for the fine-grained step-by-step developments that are attested by detailed study of texts and contexts over time."[120] Therefore, semantic maps such as the one proposed above with both diachronic and synchronic dimensions better approximate a word's real-world meaning.

To be sure, accounting for polysemy as presented here cannot be described as "simple." After all, on any account, language is a complex system. However, it is far simpler, both theoretically and exegetically, than denying polysemy. As Kortmann aptly observes, "there is little advantage in eliminating polysemy other than cleansing the sterile ideal of semantic theory from the messy reality of natural language. All that is achieved thereby is a far more complicated, because very abstract, monosemic lexical entry."[121]

With these considerations in mind, it is hoped that the main goal of this study has been achieved. Namely, to demonstrate that the heuristic application of cognitively motivated grammaticalization paths is a powerful tool on the Greek student's work bench. Of course, such work may not be pedagogically advisable for a first-year Greek student. Nevertheless, when approaching the expansive lists of uses of tense-forms, cases, and particles, even (and perhaps especially) the first-year Greek student would be greatly aided in being aware of the basic idea that such polysemy patterns are common to the languages of the world, that what are seemingly unrelated uses actually share a conceptual relationship, and that such conceptual relationships are what drive a word or form to develop extended uses in cognitively motivated and constrained ways. Even for those not actively engaged in linguistic sleuthing along these lines, it is hoped that approaching the study of Greek and the exegesis of NT texts with these concepts in mind will help alleviate the sense of aporia by understanding a little better the way meaning works.

---

120 E. C. Traugott, "Pragmatics and Language Change," in *The Cambridge Handbook of Pragmatics*, ed. K. Allan and K. Jaszczolt (Cambridge University Press, 2012), 551.

121 Kortmann, *Adverbial Subordination*, 18.

5

The Parting of the Ways of Old and New Testament Textual Criticism: Deconstructing a Disciplinary Division

Drew Longacre

INTRODUCTION

T HOSE WHO HAD THE OPPORTUNITY to study at the feet of Will Varner will undoubtedly recall his passionate commitment to original-language exegesis and linguistic analysis of the Greek Bible. In this paper I would like to explore another way in which his influence most profoundly directed my future academic course. It was in his New Testament (NT) Greek classes that I first encountered textual criticism (TC), which piqued my curiosity in ancient manuscripts and textual scholarship and led me ultimately to this field that has ever since captured my scholarly attention.

Since then, my research has focused almost entirely on the manuscripts and texts of the Hebrew Bible/Old Testament (OT), but I have never lost my interest in NTTC. Even while pursuing doctoral studies on the Dead Sea Scrolls (DSS), my formal text-critical training took place largely with NT textual scholars at the University of Birmingham. I make a point to keep abreast of current NT textual scholarship and incorporate relevant insights, methods, and tools in my work on the text of the OT. Thus, as a scholar with feet firmly planted in both worlds, I wanted to take this opportunity to address a long-standing disciplinary divide that my own experience substantially undermines.

In 1996 James Adair wrote a well-informed article for the electronic journal *TC: A Journal of Biblical Textual Criticism* addressing similarities and differences in OTTC and NTTC and encouraging greater collaboration.[1] In the more than two decades that have followed, there have been many significant developments in both fields, but the fundamental problem remains unchanged. Even informed scholars frequently stress the differences between OTTC and NTTC as if they were worlds apart. The consequence of such a mindset and practical division is that the guilds of OTTC and NTTC rarely engage each other at more than a superficial level, despite the great amount of overlap in both sources and methods. In this essay, I will suggest that this divide is—at least in principle—largely artificial and unnecessary and that OT and NT textual scholars have much to learn from each other in productive interdisciplinary dialogue. We can begin this deconstruction by considering the merits of some of the most commonly supposed distinguishing factors.

CORPORA

This is not the place to reconsider larger disciplinary divides between OT and NT studies, and it is clear that OT and NT scholars study different texts with different phenomena. But, of course, editors frequently encounter very different phenomena when creating critical editions of different OT texts, such as Genesis and Psalms. So also do those who are editing the gospels and those editing Paul's epistles. TC of John will look very different from TC of 2 Thessalonians, with quite different attestation and problems. Indeed, *every* work is unique in form and contents and should be treated in its own right, but we do not force impermeable disciplinary boundaries between each one. *Every* book is different in terms of attestation and problems that arise, but there are still similarities across corpora that allow productive dialogue. Comparisons between OTTC and NTTC often lump together the OT and NT into separate categories as wholes without realizing the diversity of challenges and opportunities faced by scholars within each field and the ways they are paralleled across disciplinary boundaries. When differences within each corpus are glossed over, it becomes easier to create false dichotomies across disciplines. The fact

---

1 James R. Adair, "Old and New in Textual Criticism: Similarities, Differences, and Prospects for Cooperation," *TC: A Journal of Biblical Textual Criticism* 1 (1996), http://jbtc.org/v01/Adair1996.html.

is, in at least some respects, certain OT and NT books more closely resemble each other than other books within their respective corpora (see below for examples).

Even more so, the interconnectedness of OTTC and NTTC is clearly evident in OT passages quoted in the NT. NT quotations are rightly considered part of the textual history of the OT by OT textual scholars, as well as part of the history of the NT text. Different forms of the OT text often inform text-critical decision making for the NT text, and NT citations sometimes influence the texts of manuscripts of the OT traditions the authors are citing. The boundaries between the two corpora are in many respects highly permeable.

Manuscript Attestation

The most frequent and superficially compelling argument I hear for the distinctiveness of OTTC and NTTC is the difference in manuscript attestation. The story goes something like this: "For the NT we have nearly 6000 Greek manuscripts and many more in other ancient languages dating all the way back to the centuries immediately after the books were written, making it the most well-attested corpus from the ancient world. On the other hand, the OT was carefully copied by a small, elite group of scribes who ensured that the text was transmitted accurately over thousands of years." As we shall see below, this argument falls apart upon critical reflection.

Embarrassment of Riches

The most commonly supposed distinguishing characteristic of NTTC is its embarrassment of riches. In response, we can note again the problem of treating the NT as a corpus, since the attestation is very uneven. The number of copies of John far exceeds the relatively sparse attestation of other books like Revelation, for instance. Furthermore, textual scholars almost unanimously agree that the sheer bulk of surviving numbers is largely irrelevant to the quality of transmission, especially since even for the NT the vast majority of manuscripts are medieval and attest to a relatively narrow part of the total tradition.

But if we insist on counting numbers as at least a practical difference between OTTC and NTTC, we here reveal our ignorance. To be fair, this is an ignorance of specialist and non-specialist alike, since even knowledgeable OT textual scholars cannot give reliable numbers of OT Hebrew manuscripts. This has nothing to do with actual differences in attestation, however, but only that nobody has ever bothered to count them. And little wonder. The Museum of the Bible alone has somewhere around 4000 handwritten Torah scrolls.

Even if we include only handwritten Hebrew codices and scrolls from the 15th century or earlier, the numbers are still impressive. Davis and Outhwaite catalogue over 24000 Bible fragments from the Cambridge University Library Cairo Genizah collections alone, which must have come from at least many hundreds of original manuscripts.[2] Yisrael Dubitsky of the National Library of Israel's (NLI) Institute of Microfilmed Hebrew Manuscripts kindly conducted a complicated search of their catalogue for me.[3] In total, his search yields

---

2 Malcolm C. Davis and Ben Outhwaite, *Hebrew Bible Manuscripts in the Cambridge Genizah Collections, Vol. 4: Taylor-Schechter Additional Series 32–255 with Addenda to Previous Volumes* (Cambridge University Press, 2003), ix, state that there are 24,326 separately-classified items in the four volumes of this catalogue of biblical fragments, plus many hundreds of minute biblical fragments which cannot be identified. Ben Outhwaite generously provided me with the relevant numbers and sources in personal communication, giving the sum total at around 24700. There are also hundreds of additional Bible fragments in the Mosseri Collection that are not included in this catalogue. Outhwaite further noted for reference that the large quantity of manuscripts publicly owned by the Cairo synagogues in the 11th–12th centuries is clearly indicated by several book lists preserved in the Genizah, for which see Nehemya Allony, *The Jewish Library in the Middle Ages: Book Lists from the Cairo Genizah*, ed. Miriam Frenkel and Haggai Ben-Shammai, Oriens Judaicus, Series I, vol. 3 (Ben-Zvi Institute, 2006), 295–307 (Hebrew). These lists do not include copies privately owned within the wider community, by synagogues other than the Palestinian (Ben Ezra) and Babylonian synagogues, or by Karaites.

3 The search excludes Samaritan manuscripts and Hebrew manuscripts written in other scripts. Meghillot and Torah scrolls are not consistently incorporated into the catalogue, but a good proportion of known "old" scrolls are included. Many of the entries provided are undated, but most of them are medieval. Dubitsky searched for the following labels within the main title field: תנ"ך, תורה, נביאים, כתובים, הפטרות, מגילות, ספר תורה, עשרת הדברות. Biblical passages (even if substantial) added to codices with different main titles (e.g., a Mahzor) were excluded. He ignored qualifying parentheses, which sometimes indicate more precisely the contents of incomplete manuscripts or special circumstances. Also, many Jewish manuscripts contain

10842 records of manuscripts and fragments, mostly *in addition to* the Cambridge Genizah fragments.[4] Compare these approximately 35000 manuscripts and separately catalogued fragments with the combined total of 5741 fragments, continuous-text manuscripts, and lectionaries currently catalogued in the online Institut für Neutestamentliche Textforschung (INTF) *Liste* for Greek NT manuscripts.[5]

With regard to the dating of the Hebrew manuscripts, Dubitsky's search yielded 233 records for תנ"ך without further qualification, usually meaning complete and (mostly) intact copies of the entire Hebrew Bible/OT, allowing for some inconsistencies in the cataloguing. Of these, all but 13 (which are undated in the catalogue) are dated from the 15th century or earlier. Compare these results with the fewer than 60 known manuscripts containing the entire Greek NT.[6]

If we divide the NLI catalogue results by section (see Table 1), we have about 750 complete medieval Jewish copies of the Torah in Hebrew,[7] plus around 5000 fragments (or otherwise qualified manuscripts) of the Torah. Furthermore, Alan Crown estimates a total of at least 750 complete Samaritan copies of the Pentateuch, of which

---

multiple texts, so when two or more of the searched categories occur in the main title, Dubitsky only included the manuscript in the category first mentioned in the title. This ensures that codices are not doubly counted, but also somewhat distorts the proportional representation of the different categories.

4 As Dubitsky and Ezra Chwat explained to me in personal communication, the NLI catalogue includes only one record for each box in the Cambridge collections. A handful of additional Cambridge fragments worthy of note are given their own independent catalogue entry (e.g., the famous Genesis fragment T-S NS 3.21), such that they are included in both the NLI and Davis and Outhwaite catalogues. The Mosseri collection fragments not included in Davis and Outhwaite's catalogue should be included in the NLI search results. The unsystematic inclusion of Genizah materials makes it difficult to say exactly how many of the fragments in the NLI catalogue are duplicates of those in that of Davis and Outhwaite, but they should usually have qualifying parentheses marking them as fragments. The NLI has plans to absorb the Friedberg Genizah Project database in the near future, which should facilitate a more precise counting and removal of duplicates.

5 http://ntvmr.uni-muenster.de/liste.

6 David C. Parker, *An Introduction to the New Testament Manuscripts and Their Texts* (Cambridge University Press, 2008), 71–74, 77–78.

7 The total numbers for this and subsequent sections must also include the number of complete Hebrew Bibles.

probably the majority are from the 16th century or earlier.[8] Thus, we have well over 1000 complete handwritten copies of the Hebrew Pentateuch from around the 16th century or earlier, plus many thousands of separately-catalogued fragments of varying size and from an unknown number of original manuscripts. For perspective, compare this with the comprehensive total of 2022 partial or complete continuous-text manuscripts of the Gospel of John cited in Bruce Morrill's 2012 dissertation (excluding lectionaries).[9]

Table 1 - NLI Catalogue Search by Contents

	Without qualifying parentheses	Total[10]
תנ"ך (Tanakh, complete Hebrew Bible/OT)	233	482
תורה (Torah, codices and fragments)	344	4081
נביאים (the Prophets)	83[11]	1793
כתובים (the Writings)	124	2376
הפטרות (Haftarot, collections of liturgical readings)	146	829

---

8 Alan D. Crown, *Samaritan Scribes and Manuscripts*, TSAJ 80 (Mohr Siebeck, 2001), 13–14. Of the estimated 750, Crown explicitly dates 162 to the 17th–20th centuries.

9 Michael Bruce Morrill, "A Complete Collation and Analysis of All Greek Manuscripts of John 18" (Ph.D. diss., University of Birmingham, 2012), 42.

10 Since few of these are from the Cambridge Genizah collections, the number of fragments should be supplemented for each section from the catalogue of Davis and Outhwaite. This would be more easily done for the Old Series (vol. 1 of the catalogue), since the fragments are there arranged roughly in order of their contents.

11 Eighty-three are simply recorded as the נביאים "Prophets". Of the records with qualifying parentheses indicating subsets of this section, 53 are labelled נביאים ראשונים "the Former Prophets", for a total of 136 copies of the Former Prophets. 56 are labelled נביאים אחרונים "the Latter Prophets", for a total of 139 copies of the Latter Prophets.

מגילות (Megillot, mostly of Esther)	747	849
ספר תורה (Torah scrolls)	154	421
עשרת הדברות (Ex 20 and/or Dt 5)	-	11

There are over 450 complete copies of the Prophets or Haftarot, plus more than 2600 fragments (or otherwise qualified manuscripts). There are over 350 complete copies of the Writings, plus over 2200 fragments and around 800 Megillot. Compare this with the nearly-exhaustive inclusion of 560 manuscripts containing the Epistle of Jude in the monograph of Tommy Wasserman (lectionaries selectively included).[12] According to the INTF *Liste*, there are only around 300 known manuscripts and fragments containing the book of Revelation in Greek.

These are only the original-language manuscripts, but the OT was also translated into other languages. The OT has a significant Jewish transmission history in the form of Aramaic targums in particular that are not paralleled in the Christian tradition. The OT was also translated into Greek (and subsequent Christian versions) and transmitted in parallel to the NT. Some of the most important Greek manuscripts contain both OT and NT text, requiring close interaction between OT and NT colleagues. The December 2012 online version of the *Verzeichnis* of the Göttingen Septuaginta-Unternehmen lists over 2000 Greek OT manuscripts and fragments.[13] There are more than 1200 listed Greek manuscripts with the Psalms and Odes, which in itself rivals the most well-represented NT books. In other words, the OT has perhaps half as many Greek manuscripts as the NT, but this is *in addition to* the large Hebrew tradition.

---

12 Tommy Wasserman, *The Epistle of Jude: Its Text and Transmission*, ConBNT 43 (Almquist & Wiksell, 2006), 105. Wasserman estimates that a total of around 200 lectionaries contain parts of Jude, of which he incorporates dozens.

13 http://hdl.handle.net/11858/00-001S-0000-0022-A30C-8.

While it remains impossible to give precise statements of the number of distinct Hebrew Bible/OT manuscripts in existence, the total number is certainly in a similar range as for Greek NT manuscripts. Thus, it becomes perfectly clear that the supposed distinction between OTTC and NTTC in terms of quantity of source materials is simply a myth that should be abandoned. Both fields study massive textual traditions, with all the opportunities and difficulties that entails.

Use of the Medieval Tradition

While there is essentially no meaningful difference in the quantity of source material between OTTC and NTTC, there are important differences in the ways that the majority of the evidence is handled. After Westcott and Hort (1881), NT textual critics almost universally came to consider the mass of Byzantine text(s) to be typologically late and its readings of little value for inclusion in critical texts. Virtually the entire Byzantine tradition could be treated as a homogenous unit (or represented by a handful of witnesses) and rejected *en bloc* as secondary. In recent years, however, NT textual critics have begun to find a new appreciation for the diversity and importance of the Byzantine texts.[14] The *Editio Critica Maior* series has moved towards the inclusion of far more minuscules than previous hand editions. The use of digital and statistical tools like full electronic transcriptions, semi-automated collation, and the Coherence-Based Genealogical Method (see below) has allowed NT textual critics to incorporate essentially all the Greek texts of certain books. In this process, the full (and to some extent diverse) medieval evidence takes on a significance of its own and sometimes shines new light on the earlier transmission of the NT text.

OTTC, in stark contrast, lags at least a generation or two behind the recent progress in NTTC towards consideration of the totality of the evidence. Since the collations of Kennicott (1776–1780) and De Rossi (1784–1788), the entire medieval Jewish tradition has come to be

---

14 Cf. Gregory R. Lanier, "Taking Inventory on the 'Age of the Minuscules': Later Manuscripts and the Byzantine Tradition within the Field of Textual Criticism," *CurBR* 16, no. 3 (2018): 263–308.

treated by most textual critics as essentially homogenous and of little interest for earlier textual history.[15] The abundance of fresh early materials with the discovery of the DSS has further reduced interest in the medieval Hebrew tradition within the field. Thus, most OT textual critics today do little more than collate one medieval manuscript (or at most a handful) selected for its supposed significance and authoritativeness, sometimes with occasional spot-checking of Kennicott, De Rossi, or other editions. While a few scholars have attempted to revive text-critical interest in the medieval Jewish manuscripts,[16] even these ambitious projects fall short of the comprehensive and nearly exhaustive approaches to incorporating the entire tradition that are currently in vogue in NTTC. The creation of substantial digital transcriptions, collations, and analytical tools are not even on the horizon for most OT textual critics.[17] Most of the mass of medieval Jewish evidence seems likely to be simply ignored for many years to come, and I would suggest that OT textual critics should be inspired by the vision of NT colleagues. The results of studying it may not be spectacular for reconstructing the earliest history of the text, but the medieval tradition is worthy of study in its own right and may yet yield new insights relevant for the earlier periods.

The general disregard for the medieval Jewish tradition is all the more striking, since the Masoretic text (MT) is frequently considered to be the "best" and "earliest" text, in contrast to the usual analysis of the Byzantine NT texts. While most NT textual critics recognize the relative lateness of the Byzantine texts, many (sometimes even skilled scholars) seem to think that the Masoretic text reflects such a careful and controlled transmission that we can essentially take a single

---

15 For a classic statement of this position, see Goshen-Gottstein, "Hebrew Biblical Manuscripts," *Bib* 48, no. 2 (1967): 243–90.

16 See, for example, Gary A. Rendsburg, "The Book of Samuel in the Cairo Genizah: An Interim and Introductory Report," *Textus* 27 (2018): 111–21. So also the work of Kim Phillips and Samuel Blapp on the Genizah manuscripts of Exodus. The Hebrew University Bible Project also incorporates some of the more important medieval manuscripts.

17 As an intermediate goal, I have long dreamed of a project to digitize and convert into full transcriptions the data of Kennicott, De Rossi, and other printed editions as a basic (if far from perfect) starting point, supplemented by original transcriptions of some of the most significant older manuscripts.

witness ("the best manuscript") as representative and assume that it reflects a very early (almost pristine) state of the text. The discovery of the DSS has revealed that supposition to be at best a half-truth, and at worst grossly misleading. The truth is far more complicated, differing on a case-by-case basis. The quality of the Masoretic text varies greatly, from a relatively (but not absolutely) conservative Pentateuch, to an expansionist Jeremiah, and a badly corrupted Samuel.[18] A more realistic appraisal depends on both treatment of the medieval tradition on its own terms, as well as approaching the Masoretic text on the basis of critical evaluation, rather than comfortable assumption.

Proximity to Originals

A further popular distinction between OTTC and NTTC regards the antiquity of the evidence. Apologists in particular frequently stress the antiquity of the NT manuscript evidence and the manuscripts' proximity to the originals. Recent years have seen intense debate about the dating of the NT papyri in particular, with some paleographers accusing certain scholars of an ideologically-motivated tendency to date NT manuscripts earlier and more precisely than paleographic methods can reasonably be expected to warrant.[19] But even the most optimistic of scholars must admit the almost complete dearth of manuscript evidence from the first two Christian centuries.[20] Manuscripts like P. Ryl. Gk. 457 (aka P52)—that may (or may not) have been written within a few generations of the composition of

---

18 See Emanuel Tov, *Textual Criticism of the Hebrew Bible*, 3rd rev. and expanded ed. (Fortress, 2012) for details.

19 Cf. Pasquale Orsini and Willy Clarysse, "Early New Testament Manuscripts and Their Dates: A Critique of Theological Palaeography," *ETL* 88, no. 4 (2012): 443–74; Brent Nongbri, *God's Library: The Archaeology of the Earliest Christian Manuscripts* (Yale University Press, 2018). While less polemical, the degree of precision that can be expected in the paleographic dating of Hebrew manuscripts also remains an open discussion. For a recent example, see Drew Longacre, "Reconsidering the Date of the En-Gedi Leviticus Scroll (EGLev): Exploring the Limitations of the Comparative-Typological Paleographic Method," *Textus* 27 (2018): 44–84.

20 Cf. Eldon Jay Epp, "Are Early New Testament Manuscripts Truly Abundant?," in *Israel's God and Rebecca's Children: Christology and Community in Early Judaism and Christianity. Essays in Honor of Larry W. Hurtado and Alan F. Segal*, ed. David B. Capes et al. (Baylor University Press, 2007), 77–117.

Gospel of John—are quickly touted for apologetic advantage without recognizing both the complicated and ambiguous nature of dating ancient literary papyri paleographically and the exceptionalness of such cases.

That is not, of course, cause to despair of the whole text-critical enterprise. The discoveries of the great majuscules and over 120 Greek NT papyri have created a real treasure trove of material that sheds much light on earlier stages in the tradition. Compared to much of ancient literature, textual scholars studying the NT are indeed in an enviable position. But in this they are not alone.[21] Again, the Göttingen *Verzeichnis* lists around 400 early LXX fragments (parchment and papyri).[22] And fragments of over 200 Hebrew "biblical" scrolls were discovered in the caves of the Judean Desert, which have fundamentally reshaped the scholarly study of the OT text.[23] Thus, numerically, the "early" or "ancient" text of the OT is at least as well documented as that of the NT.

Nor is the chronological gap between "original" and copy necessarily drastically different between the two corpora of OT and NT, as is commonly supposed. Several Greek OT papyri were probably written within two centuries of the original translations (e.g., P. Ryl. Gk. 458 = Ra 957 and several Greek scrolls from the Judean Desert). Though the dates of composition for many of the OT books are highly

---

21 As a side note, to push back against some apologists' claims about the uniqueness of the attestation of the NT in early papyri, large numbers of papyri have also been found from other classical and Hellenistic authors. Though biblical texts clearly predominate in the Byzantine manuscripts, there are now far more papyri of Homer than the NT. Martin L. West, *Homerus, Odyssea*, BSGRT 2026 (de Gruyter, 2017), xxvii–xlii, incorporates about twice as many early fragments of Homer's Odyssey (557) into his edition as the total number of Greek manuscripts in existence for lesser attested books like the pastoral epistles and Revelation (just over 300 each).

22 A recent announcement by the Egypt Exploration Society indicates the pending publication of over 80 new LXX and related texts from Oxyrhynchus, in addition to around 20 new NT papyri; see https://www.ees.ac.uk/news/unpublished-ees-biblical-papyri.

23 Indeed, it could be argued that the DSS have had a much more important effect on scholars' understanding of the early Hebrew textual tradition than the Greek papyri have had for the text of the NT; cf. Eldon Jay Epp, "The Papyrus Manuscripts of the New Testament," in *The Text of the New Testament in Contemporary Research: Essays on the* Status Quaestionis, ed. Bart D. Ehrman and Michael W. Holmes (Eerdmans, 1995), 3–21, here 13–14.

controversial, the DSS also close the gap between composition and copy more than is often realized. The combined books of Samuel–Kings—which are generally considered a continuous and literarily unified record of Israel's monarchic history—include the exile of Judah to Babylon, which requires a post-exilic date for their "final" form that cannot have been more than about 300 years earlier than 4QSam[b] (probably 3rd century BCE). If we agree that the Pentateuch as known in the major versions reflects post-exilic editorial work, then the same can also be said of 4QExod-Lev[f] (probably 3rd century BCE). Likewise 4QJer[a] documents the expanded proto-Masoretic version of Jeremiah (which records events after the exile) as early as the late 3rd or early 2rd century BCE. 4QDan[c], 4QQoh[a], and 4QPs[a] are all roughly contemporary with commonly supposed "final" editorial stages of those respective books (i.e., 2rd century BCE). In fact, some scholars propose very late dates for the final editing of some books (e.g., the final editing of the psalter in the 1st century CE), which would mean that we actually have psalms manuscripts older than the book of Psalms itself. Thus, depending on how we define the "original" or "final form" (see below), one might even be tempted to suggest (tongue-in-cheek) that some of the copies among the DSS pre-date their originals! While ongoing debates about the composition and dating of the OT books and the precision of paleographic dating greatly complicate the discussion, it seems clear that both OTTC and NTTC are at least comparable in regard to their ancient, as well as medieval, attestation.

Use of Versions

One major difference between OTTC and NTTC as presently practiced is the significance of the role of ancient translations, which is not necessarily to say that there *should be* such a difference. In OTTC, the use of ancient versions typically plays a much more important role in reconstructing the Hebrew and Greek OT texts than is the case in NTTC. The reinvigorated field of Septuagint (LXX) Studies in particular has produced a wealth of new investigations into textual history, translation technique, interpretation, and linguistics. Nearly all scholars today recognize the central importance of the Septuagint in OTTC as reflecting an early Hebrew text that at times differed from now surviving Hebrew texts. The Septuagint is typically systematical-ly included in text-critical work, even in the (re)construction of text types and variant Hebrew *Vorlagen*. While debates continue to rage over how best to use the Septuagint in textual criticism, there can be little doubt that the versional evidence plays a much more important role than in NTTC.

In NTTC, the versions tend to be understudied and undervalued. I do not want to give the impression that NT textual critics are com-pletely negligent in this regard. Most ancient languages have com-petent professionals working on their respective versions, collecting and analyzing the relevant data.[24] But this research remains largely in the domain of specialist knowledge with limited dissemination and is only inconsistently incorporated into critical decision making. In the Coherence-Based Genealogical Method, for example, versions can be spot-checked for help in initially evaluating particular variation units, but they are not systematically incorporated into the iterative process or reconstructed textual history in the same way the Greek manuscripts are. There may indeed be legitimate pragmatic reasons for temporarily excluding versional evidence in this way, but schol-ars also miss out on important and interesting parts of the tradition. Some scholars assume that the versions are of little value for the NT tradition, given the wealth of Greek material. But the NT versions are valuable in their own right, filling in the picture of the textual histo-ry and potentially even providing evidence for now-lost Greek texts. Only when these traditions are more thoroughly studied and with methodological rigor will we really be able to make definitive state-ments on the value of the versions. I cannot promise that the results will be as spectacular as is frequently the case with the Septuagint, but they will be important and deserve rigorous treatment regardless. The 2019 Birmingham colloquium on the textual criticism of the New Testament had the theme "At One Remove: Versions and Other Indi-rect Evidence for the New Testament," which is a promising develop-ment in this regard. I would suggest that NT textual critics could learn

---

24 For example, Hugh Houghton and his Birmingham team on the Latin tradi-tion and Christian Askeland on the Coptic versions, among many others too numer-ous to list.

much from the example of and substantial scholarship on the Septuagint and its role in OTTC.

An even more obvious continuity between OTTC and NTTC is that the OT was translated (usually via the Greek) into the same languages as the NT (e.g., Latin, Syriac, Coptic, Ethiopic, Armenian, Georgian, Old Church Slavonic, Arabic, etc.). Thus, specialists in these versions have much to contribute to discussions in both fields, and in such small subfields it obviously makes little sense to maintain strict disciplinary boundaries between corpora.

Scribal Practices

Approaches to scribal practices in OTTC and NTTC are sometimes also suggested as differences between the fields. The early period of transmission of the NT texts is frequently (if perhaps tendentially) thought to have been fluid and chaotic, unprofessional and uncontrolled at best, and "wild" at worst. In contrast, we have the common myth of a pristine Hebrew text that we have already dispelled above. The reality in each case, however, is far more complex and belies simplistic caricatures. The overall homogeneity of the NT textual traditions should not be underestimated, even in the earliest papyri.[25] And the texts of the OT outside of the Masoretic tradition (DSS, LXX, Samaritan Pentateuch) reveal many large differences of an editorial nature in the early transmission of the Hebrew texts.[26] While every book is to some extent unique in the particular problems encountered by textual critics, there are many parallels in the transmission of the OT and NT that invite dialogue across disciplinary boundaries.

The use of so-called "singular readings" is a particular approach to scribal practices that has become popular in NTTC in recent years, based on the assumption that unique readings are most likely to have been the creations of the scribes who produced the manuscripts in

---

25 Cf. Lonnie D. Bell, *The Early Textual Transmission of John: Stability and Fluidity in Its Second and Third Century Greek Manuscripts*, NTTSD 54 (Brill, 2018).

26 For overviews of some of the major differences, see Tov, *Textual Criticism*; Eugene Ulrich, *The Dead Sea Scrolls and the Developmental Composition of the Bible*, VTSup 169 (Brill, 2015).

which they are found.[27] The use of singular readings for delineating scribal practices is not unique to NTTC, however, and several scholars have explicitly used them as a criterion for OT texts.[28] In my opinion, the basic assumption of the method is problematic when studying the NT papyri in a period of the textual history with so many missing links, but it is especially so when applied to the early Hebrew texts, some of which may even uniquely preserve the earliest recoverable readings. In my treatment of the topic with regard to the DSS containing Exodus, I propose the rather more modest goal of using unique readings to illuminate the dynamics of the layered textual traditions after they branched off from other known traditions on the assumption that the large majority are likely to be secondary.[29] Thus, singular readings present an interesting case for interdisciplinary methodological discussions, and I would caution against the optimism of some NT colleagues in this regard.

LANGUAGE OBSCURITY AND CONJECTURAL EMENDATIONS

One real difference between OTTC and NTTC is that the Greek language of the NT is much more well-documented and understood than the Hebrew of the OT. In many cases, OT textual critics vigorously debate whether difficult texts are the non-sensical results of scribal errors or sensible ancient Hebrew forms, usually heavily informed by evidence from cognate languages. The same degree of uncertainty about basic linguistic phenomena is not usually the case in Greek. Nevertheless, this difference is only relative. While it may be true that OT textual critics frequently entertain greater doubts about the basic

---

27 This approach was popularized by James R. Royse, *Scribal Habits in Early Greek New Testament Papyri*, NTTSD 36 (Brill, 2008), and has been subsequently applied by numerous scholars.

28 Donald W. Parry, "Unique Readings in 4QSam[a]," in *The Bible as Book: The Hebrew Bible and the Judaean Desert Discoveries*, ed. Edward D. Herbert and Emanuel Tov (British Library, 2002), 209–19; Frank Moore Cross and Richard J. Saley, "Singular Readings in 4QSamuel[a] and the Question of Rewritten Scripture," *DSD* 20, no. 1 (2013): 1–16.

29 Drew Longacre, "A Contextualized Approach to the Hebrew Dead Sea Scrolls Containing Exodus" (Ph.D. diss., University of Birmingham, 2015), 167–76.

linguistic meaning of the preserved texts, these vary from book to book and are not completely absent in the Greek NT.

The difficulty of understanding many Hebrew texts led to the proliferation of implausible conjectures in past generations, and most current scholars have taken a much more cautious stance towards conjectural emendation. Nevertheless, virtually all OT textual critics still agree on the presence of primitive corruptions, such that the earliest texts have now been completely lost in the documented textual tradition. Conjectural emendation thus continues to play an important role in OTTC.

The trend in contemporary NTTC has generally been in a similar direction away from the wanton conjectures of the past, and many NT textual critics today feel safe in concluding that conjectural emendation is rarely if ever necessary. The large manuscript tradition and general comprehensibility of the earliest recoverable texts, however, do not necessarily warrant this confidence. The earliest history of the text remains largely unknown,[30] and primitive corruption is just as likely to create sense as nonsense. In light of this, Ryan Wettlaufer has recently called for a reappreciation of the method of emendation and its application to NT texts.[31] Jan Krans has also collected all known proposed emendations to the text of the Greek NT in the large Amsterdam Database of New Testament Conjectural Emendation.[32] Only time will tell where the field will move in the future. But while OT textual critics are typically more ready to accept conjectural

---

30 E.g., many scholars have plausibly argued that the entire documented tradition of Mark is descended from a single damaged manuscript without the original ending of the book; cf. N. Clayton Croy, *The Mutilation of Mark's Gospel* (Abingdon, 2003). If scholars can imagine such a scenario in one case (a gospel no less), it would hardly be surprising occasionally to encounter scribal errors already in the earliest text recoverable by comparison of textual witnesses.

31 Ryan Donald Wettlaufer, *No Longer Written: The Use of Conjectural Emendation in the Restoration of the Text of the New Testament, the Epistle of James as a Case Study*, NTTSD 44 (Brill, 2013).

32 Cf. also Jan Krans, "Conjectural Emendation and the Text of the New Testament," in *The Text of the New Testament in Contemporary Research: Essays on the Status Quaestionis, Second Edition*, ed. Bart D. Ehrman and Michael W. Holmes, NTTSD 42 (Brill, 2013), 613–35. For further historical discussion, see Bart L.F. Kamphuis, *New Testament Conjectural Emendation in the Nineteenth Century: Jan Hendrik Holwerda as a Pioneer of Method*, NTTSD 56 (Brill, 2018).

emendations, this tendency cannot be considered a fundamental difference between the two fields.

ORIGINAL TEXTS AND GOALS

One clear area of parallel development in OTTC and NTTC is the problematization of the concept of an original text. While earlier generations of scholars tended to assume that a single original once existed and could be reconstructed, both presuppositions have recently come under attack. The long editorial histories of many OT books and continuing editorial changes evident in the textual witnesses have made it increasingly difficult to identify a particular editorial stage in this process that can justifiably be singled out as uniquely "original" or "final." For instance, books like the Pentateuch and the Psalter seem to reflect multiple stages of editing before they came to be in the forms we now know them, so it makes little sense to call one of the latest (perhaps minimally innovative) stages of editing "original" in contrast to the earlier stages. At the same time, it makes little sense to call it the "final" form of the text, when the DSS document that both the Pentateuch and the Psalter continued to be revised even after the earliest editorial stages preserved for us in different manuscripts. Thus, Emanuel Tov states that "now more than ever it seems to me that there never was an 'archetype' or 'original text' of most scripture books."[33] Ronald Hendel bypasses the question of an original text and contents himself with aiming to reconstruct a "corrected archetype" (i.e., the earliest recoverable text, with obvious scribal errors corrected),[34] but even here many scholars stress pragmatic limitations. To some extent, the early OT text appears to be a rolling corpus, accumulating ever more traditions as it advances.[35]

---

33 Emanuel Tov, "Modern Editions of the Hebrew Bible," in *The New Cambridge History of the Bible, Volume 1: From the Beginnings to 600*, ed. J. C. Paget and J. Schaper (Cambridge University Press, 2013) 365–85, here 380.

34 Ronald Hendel, *Steps to a New Edition of the Hebrew Bible*, TCSt 10 (SBL Press, 2016), 23.

35 For my own methodological approach to "unrolling" this tradition, see Drew Longacre, "Multilinear Genealogical Networks: Expanding the Scope of Textual History" in *From Scribal Error to Rewriting: How Ancient Texts Could and Could Not Be Changed*, ed. Anneli Aejmelaeus, Drew Longacre, and Natia Mirotadze, De Septuaginta Investigationes 12 (Vandenhoeck & Ruprecht, 2020), 181–98. For another

Similar discussions have gained prominence in NTTC as well in recent decades.[36] While the NT books do not have such long editorial (pre-)histories, their composition processes were undoubtedly complex. The dynamic interrelationships between the synoptic gospels and oral traditions in particular led David Parker famously to refer to "the living text of the gospels," a proposal which still provokes much controversy.[37] The epistles as well, which once seemed to be simple examples of works with single originals, have been problematized in recent years with regard to the use of secretaries, the retention and re-publication of author's copies, circular letters, etc.[38] But even among those who still suppose a single original, scholars continue to debate the feasibility of reconstructing this hypothetical text. The use of the term "initial text"—currently in vogue and similar in meaning to Hendel's "corrected archetype"—is a good pragmatic compromise, focusing on explaining the documented evidence while still allowing scholars to speculate about the relationship between this initial text and a supposed original if they wish to do so. My point here is not to take a position on these controversial questions, but merely to show the similarities in ongoing theoretical discussions between OTTC and NTTC.

Within both OTTC and NTTC, there are also parallel discussions on expanding the goals of textual criticism. It is safe to say that the horizons of textual critics in these fields have broadened considerably in scope to incorporate much of what might be considered reception history. There are few today in either discipline who would support the single-minded attempts of the 19th–20th centuries at

---

theological attempt to account for editing in the OT, see Michael A. Grisanti, "Inspiration, Inerrancy, and the OT Canon: The Place of Textual Updating in an Inerrant View of Scripture," *JETS* 44, no. 4 (2001): 577–98.

36 For a foundational article on the topic, see Eldon Jay Epp, "The Multivalence of the Term 'Original Text' in New Testament Textual Criticism," *HTR* 92, no. 3 (1999): 245–81. For a survey of recent discussion, see Michael W. Holmes, "From 'Original Text' to 'Initial Text': The Traditional Goal of New Testament Textual Criticism in Contemporary Discussion," in *The Text of the New Testament in Contemporary Research: Essays on the* Status Quaestionis, *Second Edition*, ed. Ehrman and Holmes, 637–88.

37 David C. Parker, *The Living Text of the Gospels* (Cambridge University Press, 1997).

38 For a recent discussion, see Timothy N. Mitchell, "What Are the NT Autographs? An Examination of the Doctrine of Inspiration and Inerrancy in Light of Greco-Roman Publication," *JETS* 59, no. 2 (2016): 287–308.

reconstruction of the original to the neglect of the larger tradition and reception of the texts. At the very least, textual critics of both disciplines now pay closer attention to questions of reception history than many of their predecessors. Furthermore, under the influence of the New (or Material) Philology, even those still intent on reconstructing earlier texts now frequently laud the study of particular manuscripts as textual artifacts worthy of study and contextualization in their own right. Another, perhaps more controversial, development can be seen in the increasing use of variant readings for drawing out socio-historical data from the textual tradition. While there is a long history of scholars' attributing theological, partisan, or polemical motives to the creation of variant readings, NT scholars like Eldon Epp, Bart Ehrman, and David Parker in particular have recently stressed the historical value of these readings.[39] There is no shortage of similar attempts by OT scholars, continuing a long tradition.[40] These attempts are by no means uncontroversial (or unproblematic), but they reflect clearly parallel discussions in both OTTC and NTTC.

Text-Critical Methodology

Eclecticism in text-critical methodology remains a contentious discussion in both OTTC and NTTC. In OTTC, some recent scholars have suggested schematic text-historical reconstructions, but these largely reflect the synthesis and end results of text-critical inquiry, rather than being a functional tool for making text-critical decisions.[41] Emanuel Tov, on the other hand, explicitly rejects the reliance on external evi-

---

39 E.g., Bart D. Ehrman, "The Text as Window: New Testament Manuscripts and the Social History of Early Christianity," in *The Text of the New Testament in Contemporary Research: Essays on the* Status Quaestionis, *Second Edition*, ed. Ehrman and Holmes, 803–30.

40 For a good review of previous scholarship and innovative contributions in this regard, see David Andrew Teeter, *Scribal Laws: Exegetical Variation in the Textual Transmission of Biblical Law in the Late Second Temple Period*, FAT 92 (Mohr Siebeck, 2014).

41 E.g., Ronald S. Hendel, "Assessing the Text-Critical Theories of the Hebrew Bible," in *The Oxford Handbook of the Dead Sea Scrolls*, ed. Timothy H. Lim and John J. Collins (Oxford University Press, 2010), 281–302; Eugene Ulrich, "The Evolutionary Production and Transmission of the Scriptural Books," in *Changes in Scripture: Rewriting and Interpreting Authoritative Traditions in the Second Temple Period*, ed.

dence and established rules for making text-critical decisions, staking out a position with striking similarities to the "thoroughgoing eclectics" in NTTC.[42] Most OT textual critics are not as clear in their methodological formulations, but many today would be sympathetic, only rarely drawing on reconstructions of textual history of the Hebrew books and the relations between manuscripts to help make text-critical decisions.[43] Variants are typically preferred almost exclusively on the basis of the merits of the readings themselves without regard for which manuscripts attest them and how they are related to each other.[44]

In stark contrast, with few exceptions (e.g., Keith Elliot), NT textual critics have tended towards more "reasoned eclectic" approaches, giving external evidence a much more prominent place in decision-making processes alongside internal indications favoring the given readings. In the Coherence-Based Genealogical Method, traditional approaches to grouping manuscripts and reconciling internal and external evidence have morphed into a more comprehensive and rigorous attempt to ensure the coherence of text-critical decisions.[45] Thus, textual history, even if not exactly of a traditional stemmatological kind, continues to play an important role in most work in NTTC. Textual history not only reflects scholars' conclusions on numerous variation units, but also serves as a guide in resolving difficult cases and a control on arbitrary decision making in an iterative process.

As scholars in both disciplines have increasingly come to realize that both the OT and NT traditions were "open" to the mixture

---

Hanne von Weissenberg, Juha Pakkala, and Marko Marttila, BZAW 419 (de Gruyter, 2011), 47–64.

42 Emanuel Tov, "The Relevance of Textual Theories for the Praxis of Textual Criticism," in *A Teacher for All Generations: Essays in Honor of James C. VanderKam*, ed. E. F. Mason, JSJSup 153 (Brill, 2012), 23–35.

43 This is not the case for Septuagint studies, however, where textual history and manuscript relationships still play a crucial role in reconstructing the Old Greek translations.

44 Of course, even today there are some scholars who give special weight to readings attested in particular favored traditions, such as the MT or LXX, but this approach is not well regarded in most methodological discussions.

45 For a simple introduction to the method, see Tommy Wasserman and Peter J. Gurry, *A New Approach to Textual Criticism: An Introduction to the Coherence-Based Genealogical Method*, RBS 80 (SBL Press, 2017).

of various texts, this methodological discussion is ever more urgent. Septuagint scholars have developed finely tuned tools for recognizing contamination at the micro-level, aided by a thorough knowledge of the texts of the ancient revisions and the processes by which they entered the mainstream textual tradition. On the other hand, in lieu of rigorous tools for dealing with complex and sometimes conflicting patterns of agreement and disagreement, most Hebrew Bible/OT textual scholars have adopted a rather eclectic methodology, often without due regard for the coherence of their many textual decisions. Against this historical pessimism, the example of NT textual scholars of the systematic study of all the complex evidence in a methodologically controlled way offers better prospects for future research. In my dissertation, I stressed the need for and potential usefulness of a systematic and iterative approach to the relationship between textual history and the adjudication of variant readings,[46] and I am convinced that OT colleagues can learn much from NT scholars in this regard.

EDITORIAL PHILOSOPHY

Editorial philosophy has traditionally been one of the largest gaps between OTTC and NTTC, but this division too is quickly eroding. The construction of eclectic texts and editions has become standard practice among NT textual scholars, a situation which shows no signs of changing any time soon. With the *Editio Critica Maior* the apparatuses have grown exponentially beyond the standard Nestle-Aland and United Bible Societies hand editions, but the shared base text remains an eclectic reconstruction. The same is also true of the recent Society of Biblical Literature and Tyndale House Greek New Testaments, though the latter aims at more closely representing the documented tradition in some respects. The recent suggestion by Stanley Porter and Andrew Pitts that Codex Sinaiticus could be used as a base text is the sole (and, in my opinion, unfortunate) exception that I am aware of, based on the parallel situation in OTTC.[47]

---

46 Longacre, "Contextualized Approach," 93–97, 251–52.

47 Stanley E. Porter and Andrew W. Pitts, *Fundamentals of New Testament Textual Criticism* (Eerdmans, 2015), 95–96.

In contrast, the current standard critical edition of the Hebrew Bible/OT is *Biblia Hebraica Stuttgartensia*, which provides a transcription of the famous St. Petersburg (i.e., Leningrad) Codex as its base text. The inadequacies of this edition have been frequently lamented, such as the lack of most evidence from the Dead Sea Scrolls, uncritical use of versional evidence, and frequent baseless conjectures. In essence, the non-specialist is left with only a transcription of a single late manuscript and a limited number of frequently unreliable footnotes, which is hardly a sufficient foundation for critical engagement with the texts of the Hebrew Bible/OT. Current editorial projects like *Biblia Hebraica Quinta* and the Hebrew University Bible Project seek to remedy these deficiencies with improved apparatuses and textual commentaries, but continue to provide diplomatic transcriptions of individual manuscripts as their base texts (the St. Petersburg and Aleppo Codices, respectively). The same is also true of the ongoing *editio maior* of the Samaritan Pentateuch directed by Stefan Schorch. While this editorial philosophy has dominated the field of OTTC for generations and remains well-represented among specialists, the situation in OTTC has changed rapidly in recent years.[48] The *Biblia Qumranica* project aims rather to reproduce the multiple texts of the MT, LXX, and DSS in parallel in a synoptic format similar to the old polyglots. And in an even more dramatic shift from the traditional diplomatic edition, the editors of *The Hebrew Bible: A Critical Edition* project headed by Ronald Hendel intend to construct eclectic, critical texts for each book of the Hebrew Bible/OT. Sharp disagreements about the feasibility and desirability of eclectic editions have finally brought editorial philosophy to the forefront of the discussion in OTTC, infusing new vigor into the field. I, for one, see these developments as very beneficial for the field, and I welcome attempts to bring critical awareness and more helpful tools to non-specialist readers in the form of eclectic editions. In doing so, OT textual scholars are now walking in paths long since trodden by NT (and LXX) colleagues, and they have much to learn from past and current discussions in related fields. Wherever the dust may settle in the area of Hebrew Bible/OT

---

48 For a series of articles surveying current developments in critical editing, see the thematic issue of *HBAI* 2 (2013).

critical editions, it is clear that editorial philosophy can no longer be viewed as a fundamental divide between OTTC and NTTC.

DIGITAL TOOLS

Recent years have seen a proliferation of digital tools for OTTC and NTTC. The availability of online digital images of manuscripts has dramatically democratized access to the primary source materials in both fields. The INTF's Virtual Manuscript Room (VMR) now makes images of a large number of Greek and Coptic NT manuscripts freely available online to registered users, along with an up-to-date version of the *Liste* and electronic transcriptions for a number of manuscripts.[49] The Center for the Study of New Testament Manuscripts led by Daniel Wallace also provides quality digital images of a selection of manuscripts, including some Septuagint codices.[50] High-quality images of most of the DSS are now freely available on the Leon Levy Dead Sea Scrolls Digital Library.[51] The National Library of Israel also provides images or links to many medieval manuscripts.[52] Some individual important manuscripts now have websites dedicated to them, and many are published online by host institutions.[53] On my blog I have created a webpage collecting links to many of the most important OT manuscripts, editions, and resources available online.[54] Thus, both OTTC and NTTC share the revolutionary increase in access to primary materials, which will undoubtedly continue to advance for the near future.

But the digital revolution entails more than simply easier access to better pictures. It is quickly becoming standard for NT textual critics to work in digital workspaces, like the INTF VMR, which facilitates ongoing indexing and transcription projects, provides access to the

---

49 http://ntvmr.uni-muenster.de.

50 http://www.csntm.org.

51 https://www.deadseascrolls.org.il/home.

52 http://web.nli.org.il/sites/NLIS/en/ManuScript/.

53 E.g., Codex Vaticanus (https://digi.vatlib.it/view/MSS_Vat.gr.1209), Codex Sinaiticus (http://www.codexsinaiticus.org/en/), Codex Bezae (https://cudl.lib.cam.ac.uk/view/MS-NN-00002-00041/1), the Aleppo Codex (http://www.aleppocodex.org), and 1QIsaᵃ (http://dss.collections.imj.org.il/isaiah).

54 http://oldtestamenttextualcriticism.blogspot.com/p/online-digital-images.html.

Amsterdam database on conjectural emendations, and permits easy access to photographs and information about many manuscripts. The regular use of complete electronic transcriptions, semi-automated collation and regularization, and advanced quantitative analyses like the Coherence-Based Genealogical Method means that much of the work in NTTC is now thoroughly integrated into the digital humanities.

OT textual critics are behind their NT colleagues in this regard, but they too have started to move in the same direction. A particularly ambitious project is the ERC project "The Hands that Wrote the Bible: Digital Palaeography and Scribal Culture of the Dead Sea Scrolls" led by Mladen Popović of the University of Groningen, which aims to reassess the current model for paleographic dating of the DSS through the interaction of new radiocarbon dates, Artificial Intelligence, and traditional paleography. The Friedberg Jewish Manuscript Society provides digital images and a useful workspace for the Cairo Genizah manuscripts, including tools for creating transcriptions and synopses.[55] The cooperative project Scripta Qumranica Electronica (Universities of Göttingen, Haifa, and Tel Aviv) is also developing a workspace for research on the DSS and the creation of electronic editions.[56] Tuukka Kauhanen has developed a digital platform for his work on the Göttingen Septuagint edition of 2 Samuel based on the handwritten collation books. Ronald Hendel speaks of developing an electronic version of *The Hebrew Bible: A Critical Edition*, including all the printed material, full source texts, and photographs of important manuscripts.[57] These positive movements in OTTC bode well for the future of the discipline, though they have yet to materialize into fully integrated digital platforms and analytical tools like in NTTC.

CONCLUSION

James Adair was right in 1996 when he stressed that OT and NT textual critics have much to learn from each other, and the decades since have only made that even clearer. Popularly supposed distinctions

---

55 https://fjms.genizah.org.
56 https://www.qumranica.org/blog/.
57 http://hbceonline.org.

between OTTC and NTTC have almost all turned out to be the results of misinformation and/or premature methodological decisions. Of course, in one sense, every text is unique. But the extensive (at least potential) parallels in both data and methods between the two fields invites productive interdisciplinary dialogue, which nevertheless remains hindered by increasing specialization. If we are willing to reach across the largely arbitrary disciplinary boundaries that divide us, we have much to learn from each other.

6

Circumcising the Heart: Man's Role or God's (Deut 10:16 and 30:6)?

Michael Grisanti[1]

THE INTERRELATIONSHIP OF GOD'S ACTIVITY on behalf of His children (what He has done) and what He commands them to do (what He expects) always presents interesting and significant issues for the biblical interpreter. How does what God promises to do relate to the things He requires of His children? This paper will deal with those two sides of the coin as depicted in Deuteronomy 10:16 and 30:6. In Deuteronomy 10:16 Yahweh *commands His children* "to circumcise" their hearts. Later, however, addressing a future audience who are depicted as having been languishing in exile, the Lord *promises that He Himself will* "circumcise" their hearts (30:6). How should a student of the Word resolve the interpretive tension that exists between these two passages?

The issue at hand concerns the very heart of Israel's relationship with Yahweh. After beginning that relationship with the descendants of Abraham (by means of the Abrahamic covenant, Gen 12:1–3), the Lord makes that relationship more concrete by giving the Israelites His Law in the form of a covenant. He clearly sets before them His expectations of them, first in the Ten Commandments and then in

---

1 Soon after I began teaching at TMS in Fall 1997, I had the joy of meeting Dr. Varner as one of my colleagues at TMC. We soon discovered that we shared a love for the connection of Scripture with the land of the Bible. He opened the way for me to begin leading the college's 10-day Israel trip, which led to my current expanded involvement in that endeavor. Dr. Varner is one of those people who is quite skilled in several realms of biblical study. I am so grateful for his ministry in my life and for this chance to offer this essay as a token of my gratitude for him.

the detailed legislation that followed. Israel's continued existence as a nation and their ability to accomplish God's worldwide intentions for them was dependent on their obedience to the covenant stipulations found in that covenant or Law (cf. Exod 19:5–6; Deut 4:13–14; 2 Kings 17:15).[2] Did Yahweh set before His people an impossible task? When He demanded their wholehearted love (Deut 6:4–5) and required that they circumcise their hearts (Deut 10:16), did He ask of them something they were able to do or not?

This essay will deal with the basic meaning of physical circumcision, the broad question of what "circumcising" the heart signifies, and will offer an attempt to demonstrate the interrelationship of God's requirement that the Israelites circumcise their hearts and His promise that He will do just that in the future.

PHYSICAL CIRCUMCISION: THE CONCEPTUAL BACKDROP

The verb, מוּל, occurs 32 times[3] in the OT and means "to circumcise" (Qal),[4] or "to circumcise oneself," or "to be circumcised" (Niphal).[5] The object of this verb can be the person himself (Gen 17:10, 12, 13, 26, 27; 21:4; 34:15, 22, 24; Exod 12:44, 48; Josh 5:2, 3, 4, 5, 7), "the flesh of the foreskin" (בְּשַׂר עָרְלָה—Gen 17:11, 14, 23, 24, 25; Lev 12:3), the "foreskin" (עָרְלָה—Jer 9:25 [Heb. 9:24]), "the flesh of your heart" (עָרְלַת לְבַבְכֶם—Deut 10:16; Jer 4:4), or "the heart" (אֶת־לְבָבְךָ—Deut 30:6). In all but three passages (Deut 10:16; 30:6; Jer 4:4),[6] the verb describes the physical act of circumcision.

---

2 R. Clements, *Old Testament Theology: A Fresh Approach* (John Knox Press, 1975), 101.

3 The lexical works disagree on whether the occurrences of מוּל in Psalm 118 (vv. 10, 11, 12) are from the same verb (e.g., E. Carpenter, "מוּל," *NIDOTTE*, 2:869) or from a homonym (מוּל II "to cut off"—*HALOT*, 2:556; *DCH*, 5:173; G. Mayer, "מוּל," *TDOT*, 8:160).

4 13 times: Gen 17:23; 21:4; Exod 12:44; Deut 10:16; 30:6; Josh 5:2, 3, 4, 5 [2x], 7 [2x]; Jer 9:25 [Heb. 9:25].

5 19 times: Gen 17:10, 11, 12, 13 [2x], 14, 24, 25, 26, 27; 34:15, 17, 22 [2x], 24; Exod 12:48; Lev 12:3; Josh 5:8; Jer 4:4.

6 In Jeremiah 9:25–26 [Heb. 9:24–25] the Lord describes a future time when those who are only physically circumcised (but are spiritually uncircumcised) will experience divine judgment.

Although it was practiced by other peoples in the biblical world,[7] the circumcision God demanded of Israel was distinct from those ANE practices in both function and timing. In Genesis 12:1–3, Yahweh established a covenant with Abraham and his descendants in which He promised to make them a great nation, bless them, and make them a blessing to other nations. He first mentioned the issue of circumcision when He confirmed His covenant with Abraham in Genesis 17. According to that passage (where the verb "to circumcise" occurs 10 times), every Israelite male was to be circumcised on the eighth day after birth (Gen 17:12). Consequently, circumcision did not serve as a puberty right for Israelites but had religious or spiritual significance.[8] The acceptance of circumcision would have signified the appropriation of the covenant (Gen 17:10).[9] Eventually, slaves and foreigners were included in this requirement (Gen 17:12b, 13a; Exod 12:43–50).[10]

---

7 The prophet Jeremiah (9:25–26 [Heb. 9:24–25]; cf. Ezek 32:19, 28, 32) mentions that the Egyptians, Edomites, Ammonites, Moabites, and Arabs were peoples that practiced circumcision (for further documentation on the Egyptian practice, cf. J. Sasson, "Circumcision in the Ancient Near East," *JBL* 85, no. 4 (December 1966), 474; Hans Bonnet, "Beschneidung," *Reallexikon der ägyptischen Religionsgeschichte*, 3 rd ed. (de Gruyter, 2000), 109–11. In general, circumcision was performed on young men by the time they reached the age of puberty (ca. 13 years old) (M. V. Fox, "The Sign of the Covenant," *RB* 81, no. 4 [October 1974], 591). It may have been a rite of initiation for manhood and marriage (Gen 34:15–16; L. Allen, "Circumcision," in *NIDOTTE*, 4:474). For an overview of the ANE practice of circumcision, see C. Westermann, *Genesis 12–36* (Augsburg, 1985), 265; J. Morgenstern, *Rites of Birth, Marriage, Death and Kindred Occasions among the Semites* (Hebrew Union College Press, 1966), 48–66. Eventually, only priests were circumcised (G. Mayer, "מוּל," *TDOT*, 8:160).

8 Although modern scholars (O. Abolaji, "Preventive Medicine: God's Original Method and Implications for the Church, *Ogbomoso Journal of Theology* 18, no. 3 [2013]: 99–100) discuss the hygienic benefits of circumcision (and ancient—Philo, *Spec. Leg.* [I.1–11]), that issue has no clear relevance to the OT practice of circumcision. Some have argued that since human sinfulness has concentrated itself in the sexual organs, the removal of the foreskin from the male sex organ represents the purification of "the organ of generation, by which life is propagated" (e.g., C. F. Keil, *The Pentateuch*, Commentary on the OT [reprint, Eerdmans, 1981], 1:227). Since the biblical text does not draw attention to these realities, one needs to be cautious about making these kinds of interpretive suggestions.

9 Since an eight-day old child was involved, the decision to circumcise a child evidences their parents' acceptance of this covenantal demand.

10 L. Allen calls circumcision "God's indispensable branding of his people" ("Circumcision," in *NIDOTTE*, 4:474).

Although Jacob's children treat circumcision as a mark of ethnic identity in their dealings with the Shechemites (Gen 34:15, 17, 22, 24),[11] the Lord identifies it as a "sign" (לְאוֹת) of the covenant He had established with Abraham and his descendants (Gen 17:11).[12] He goes on to say: "So shall my covenant be in your flesh an everlasting covenant" (HCSB, i.e., as a permanent reminder; Gen 17:13). Hence, circumcision served as a tangible evidence of Israel's elect, holy status before God and in the world.[13]

The fact that an Israelite's refusal to be circumcised occasioned his eviction from the people of Israel (Gen 17:14) highlights the importance of this practice. It was an integral part of the Israelite identity of a male descendant[14] of Abraham. It also implies that the acceptance of circumcision evidenced that person's membership in the covenant community.

Physical circumcision was also a prerequisite for God's people to celebrate the Passover. At the time of the first Passover (Exod 12:44, 48) and right before God's people began the Conquest of Canaan (Josh 5:6, 11–12), God demanded that all Israelites be circumcised. In

---

11 Besides the fact that Jacob's sons required that the Shechemites be circumcised as part of their deception, it may indicate that circumcision represented membership as part of the descendants of Abraham.

12 Although the text of Genesis explicitly presents circumcision as a sign or demonstration of the covenant, various scholars have suggested it served as a purification ritual, a sacrifice for redemption, or an act of consecration (cf. H.-J. Fabry, "לֵב," in *TDOT*, 7:433). Von Rad contends that since heart circumcision signifies internal purity, the external/physical circumcision must have been an implicit act of bodily purification and dedication. G. Von Rad, *Genesis: A Commentary*, OTL (Westminster, 1972), 201.

13 J. G. McConville, *Deuteronomy* (InterVarsity Press, 2002), 200. Moses later presents the Sabbath as the "sign" of the Mosaic Covenant, reminding God's people that Yahweh is the one who makes them holy (just as He made the Sabbath holy) (Exod 31:12). In a similar fashion, circumcision would serve as a reminder to all Israelites of their distinctive status as participants in this special covenant relationship.

14 Various scholars have questioned or wondered about the gender-exclusiveness of biblical circumcision. Although he does not resolve the debate, Goldingay summarizes some of the comments critiquing this reality (John Goldingay, "The Significance of Circumcision," *JSOT* 88 [2000]: 4–5, 15–16). Since the biblical text offers no rationale for this "gender-exclusivity," it would seem to be connected to the leadership role of Israelite men in families, national leadership, worship, and military service.

Joshua 5, a number of Israelites born during the time of Israel's wilderness wandering had not been circumcised. Their acceptance of circumcision at Gilgal signified a break with the past (the reproach of Egypt—5:9), an act of obedience, and a step of dedication to God.

Physical circumcision, however, never served as an indication of the internal or spiritual state of the person involved. It was a marker of the person's ethnicity or membership in the covenant nation, but provided no clear evidence of their standing before God individually.[15]

WHAT DOES "CIRCUMCISION OF THE HEART" MEAN?

Before we give attention to the two key passages (Deut 10:16 and 30:6), we will briefly consider a few other passages that address the concept of heart circumcision.[16] These preliminary passages refer to an uncircumcised heart by itself or contrast an uncircumcised heart with a circumcised one. The contrast between those who are circumcised (מוּל) and not circumcised (עָרֵל) helps clarify the meaning or significance of circumcision for an Israelite. The adjective "uncircumcised" (עָרֵל) occurs 32 times in the OT and most frequently signifies ethnic identity (a non-Israelite because they are not circumcised—Exod 12:48; Judg 14:3; 15:18; 1 Sam 14:6) or refers to the absence of heart circumcision (Lev 26:41; Jer 9:26 [Heb. 9:25]; Ezek 44:7, 9).[17]

---

15 Goldingay overstates the message of men (and not women) being circumcised. Because he regards heart circumcision as a Priestly innovation (later in the development of the Pentateuch), he suggests that the "very fact that it is the males who bear this sign means that it is the males who embody spiritual and mental unfitness to the people of promise" ("The Significance of Circumcision," 16).

16 *The Manual of Discipline* (1QS 5:5) and the *Habakkuk Pesher* (1QP *Hab* 11:13) also refer to the circumcision of the mind or heart. The former also connects the circumcision of the mind with the circumcision of the stiff neck.

17 In addition to these primary uses of עָרֵל, it modifies trees, lips, and ears. Leviticus 19:23–25 demands that any fruit produced by a tree in its first three years must be treated like "foreskins" (19:23). In other words, the Israelites were not to eat that fruit. The point of this requirement appears to be that the fruit is to be left in place just as a foreskin is left in place. In the same way that the uncircumcised cannot worship at the Tabernacle, this fruit could not be eaten (G. Mayer, "עָרֵל," in *TDOT*, 11:360). Moses objects to God's commissioning as a messenger to stand before the Egyptian pharaoh on the grounds that he had "uncircumcised lips" (Exod 6:12, 30). Although some scholars regard this as a reference to some difficulty Moses had with speaking (Mayer, 11:360; S. R. Driver, *A Critical and Exegetical Commentary on Deuteronomy*,

Leviticus 26:40–42

This passage occurs in the midst of the epilogue of the Holiness Code (Lev 26:3–46). Verses 3–13 provide a description of the blessings that Israel's faithfulness to the covenant would occasion. The largest section concerns the consequences of covenant treachery (vv. 14–45) and verse 46 concludes the epilogue.[18] Verses 40–42 read as follows:

> [40] But if they will confess their sin and the sin of their fathers— their unfaithfulness that they practiced against Me, and how they acted with hostility toward Me, [41] and I acted with hostility toward them and brought them into the land of their enemies—and if their *uncircumcised hearts* will be humbled, and if they will pay the penalty for their sin, [42] then I will remember My covenant with Jacob. I will also remember My covenant with Isaac and My covenant with Abraham, and I will remember the land.

Verse 40 envisions a future time when surviving Israelite exiles will repent of their covenant treachery. Verse 41 states a fact, i.e., the spiritual reality indicated by their repentance. Their repentance comes as a consequence of the divine humbling of their "uncircumcised hearts". This humbling of their uncircumcised hearts will occasion their reinstatement to a proper covenant relationship with Yahweh. In summary, the uncircumcised hearts of many Israelites represented the opposite of God's demands of them and stood in the way of their functioning as His servant nation.

ICC [T&T Clark, 1895], 125; Lemke, "Circumcision of the Heart," 305, n. 13) or to his lack of maturity in this area (I. Cairns, *Word and Presence: A Commentary on Deuteronomy*, ITC [Grand Rapids: Eerdmans, 1992], 111), he is probably saying that his lips are unfit for cultic use (cf. Lev 19:23; Isa 6:5; 52:1; L. Allen, "עָרֵל," in *NIDOTTE*, 3:538; J. Currid, *Exodus* [Evangelical Press, 2000], 143). When Jeremiah affirms that Israel's ear is uncircumcised, he was emphasizing Israel's unresponsiveness to God's call for repentance (Jer 6:10; cf. Mayer, 11:360; Allen, "עָרֵל," in *NIDOTTE*, 3:538; M. Weinfeld, *Deuteronomy 1–11*, AB [Doubleday, 1991], 438). Lemke, "Circumcision of the Heart," 305, concludes that the Israelites were "incapable of listening to God's prophetic word."

18 This passage is quite similar to the blessing and cursing sections of various ANE suzerain-vassal treaties as well as Deut 28.

Jeremiah 4:4

After his introductory visions (1:4–19), the prophet Jeremiah indicts Israel for her sinful rebellion against Yahweh (2:1–28). It is absolutely clear that Israel deserves the judgment that God promised His chosen nation through His prophet (2:29–37). In 3:1–4:4 Jeremiah pleads for Israel to repent of her covenant treachery. After drawing attention to the nation's spiritual adultery (3:1–11), the prophet summons Israel to repent and weaves together references to Israel's guilt, God's promise of forgiveness and restoration, and Israel's need to return to a vibrant covenant relationship. At the end of this section the prophet calls Israel to repentance once again. Verse 3 utilizes an agricultural metaphor while verse 4 alludes to Israel's covenant with Yahweh:

> ³ For this is what the LORD says to the men of Judah and Jerusalem: Break up the unplowed ground; do not sow among the thorns.
> ⁴ Circumcise yourselves to the LORD[19]; remove the foreskin of your

---

19 R. Althann ("*mwl*, 'Circumcise' with the *lamedh* of Agency," *Bib* 62 [1981]: 239–40) has suggested that the *lamed* preposition prefixed to Yahweh (לַיהוָֹה) should be regarded as a *lamed* of agency, designating Yahweh as the one who accomplishes this circumcision: "be circumcised by the Lord" (much like Deut 30:6) (cf. P. Craigie, P. Kelley, J. Drinkard, *Jeremiah 1–25*, WBC [Word Books, 1991], 67). However, this requires giving the verb a passive significance rather than a reflexive nuance. Althann surveys five other passages where the verb מוּל is followed by the preposition lamed (Gen 17:10, 12; 34:15, 22; Exod 12:48). In each case he translates the preposition with idea of agency, pointing to the one who must perform the circumcision (e.g., Exod 12:48—"let every male be circumcised by him"; cf. C. Houtman, *Exodus*, HCOT [KOK, 1996], 2:209). In each case, however, the *lamed* preposition seems to function in a possessive sense (as is common in biblical and modern Hebrew, referring to all who "belong" to the person being addressed (e.g., Exod 12:48—"when every male of his family is circumcised"; J. Durham, *Exodus*, WBC [Word Books, 1987], 169; P. Joüon, *A Grammar of Biblical Hebrew*, trans. T. Muraoka [Editrice Pontificio Istituto Biblio, 1993], 476–77, §130g). Also, every other instance of the verb מוּל as a command carries the active (Qal) and not passive notion (cf. Deut 10:16; 30:6; Josh 5:2). Most English translations translate Jeremiah 4:4 with the reflexive idea, e.g., "circumcise yourselves." Finally, the use of "foreskin of the heart" in this passage parallels its occurrence in Deut 10:16, which is a command for the Israelites to circumcise their hearts (not be circumcised). It appears best to regard Yahweh as the goal or object of the action rather than the agent of the action.

hearts,[20] men of Judah and residents of Jerusalem. Otherwise, My wrath will break out like fire and burn with no one to extinguish it because of your evil deeds.

If Israel is to fulfill God's intended role for her and avoid the experience of covenant curse, God's chosen nation must heed these two commands. God's people must give attention to internal spiritual realities, i.e., they must repent of their sin and renew their commitment to Yahweh's covenant demands. Although many nations may practice circumcision (cf. Jer 9:25–26 [Heb. 9:24–25]), "Israel is to do it for Yahweh, so that her heart, which is the center of planning and decision making, of action as well as emotion and thought, may be conformable to His will."[21]

Jeremiah 9:25–26 [Heb. 9:24–25]

As far as the prophet Jeremiah was concerned, Israelites who were unrepentant and sinful, i.e., uncircumcised in heart, were just like Gentile pagans who were also circumcised in the flesh *alone* (Jer 9:25–26 [Heb. 9:24–25])!

> [25] The days are coming"—the LORD's declaration—"when I will punish all the circumcised yet uncircumcised[22]: [26] Egypt, Judah, Edom, the Ammonites, Moab, and all the inhabitants of the desert who clip the hair on their temples. All these nations are uncircumcised, and the whole house of Israel is uncircumcised in heart."[23]

---

20 For emphasis, the NET Bible provides a more expansive translation of the first two verb clauses of verse 4: "Just as ritual circumcision cuts away the foreskin as an external symbol of dedicated covenant commitment, you must genuinely dedicate yourselves to the Lord and get rid of everything that hinders your commitment to me."

21 W. Holladay, *Jeremiah 1*, Herm (Fortress Press, 1986), 1:130.

22 This could be translated "all who are circumcised in the flesh." Literally, it could be rendered, "all who are circumcised with a foreskin" (כָּל־מוּל בְּעָרְלָה).

23 At the end of the next verse, the Aramaic Targumim (Onqelos and Pseudo-Jonathan) paraphrase this verse by replacing "circumcise the foreskin of your heart" with "remove the obduracy of your heart." Targum Neofiti has "circumcise the foreskin of the obduracy of your heart"; B. Grossfeld, *The Targum Onqelos to Deuteronomy*, the

God declares that various nations around Israel may have been physically circumcised, but in His estimation His chosen people *were also uncircumcised.* These spiritually uncircumcised nations will experience divine judgment just like all other pagan nations. Jeremiah points out the sad reality that Israel, God's chosen nation who God expected to have circumcised their hearts (Deut 10:16), was just like these pagan nations. The Israelites were uncircumcised in heart and were more deserving of divine judgment because they were rebelling against God's clear demands.

Ezekiel 44:6–9

The larger pericope (44:4–31) details legislation pertaining to Temple personnel and delineates who can carry out priestly duties relating to service in the Temple (priests [vv. 15–31], Levites [vv. 10–14], but not foreigners [vv. 6–9]). In direct violation of those parameters, Israel (v. 6, "the rebellious people") had allowed foreigners, those who were "uncircumcised in heart and flesh" (v. 7), to discharge priestly duties in the Temple. These foreigners were not only physically uncircumcised but were spiritually uncircumcised as well. God's chosen people, who Yahweh expected to be physically and spiritually circumcised, were acting like the pagans by facilitating this covenant treachery.

Deuteronomy 10:16[24]

This verse belongs to a section in which the Lord affirms His singular requirement of His chosen people: wholehearted and undiluted

---

Aramaic Bible (Michael Glazier, 1988), 43. Weinfeld suggests that the omission of "circumcise" and "foreskin" by Onqelos and Pseudo-Jonathan manifests opposition to the contrast between circumcision of the heart and physical circumcision (Weinfeld, *Deuteronomy*, 437). See also Jason S. DeRouchie, "Circumcision in the Hebrew Bible and Targums: Theology, Rhetoric, and the Handling of Metaphor," *BBR* 14, no.2 (2004): 190–203.

24 Some scholars resolve any tension between Deut 10:16 and 30:6 by regarding both as later insertions in the compositional development of Deuteronomy, likely drawing on Jeremiah's use of "circumcision" in his message"—e.g., W. Lemke, "Circumcision of the Heart: The Journey of a Biblical Metaphor," in *A God So Near: Essays on Old Testament Theology in Honor of Patrick D. Miller*, eds. B. Strawn and N.

allegiance to Him (10:12–22). In the immediately preceding section (9:1–10:11), Moses warned Israel to avoid the feeling of self-righteousness and the practice of rebellion that might arise from their imminent dispossession of the Canaanite nations. He first sought to convince Israel that their future conquest of Canaan would not be the fruit of their righteousness but would be the result of the Lord's holiness (which demands He judge sin) and faithfulness (to His covenant made with their forefathers) (9:1–6). He then warned Israel about the dangers of rebelling by reminding them of the "golden calf" rebellion at the time of His giving His Law to His servant nation through Moses (9:7–10:11).

As Wright points out concerning 10:12–22:

> These verses begin the buildup toward the climax of the opening exhortation of the book in chapter 11. Deuteronomy 10:12–22 is unquestionably one of the richest texts in the Hebrew Bible, exalted and poetic in its language, comprehensive and challenging in its message. It purposely tries to "boil down" the whole theological and ethical content of the book into memorable phraseology, packed and pregnant, rich and resonant of all the surrounding preaching. Indeed, there are not many dimensions of "OT theology," that are not directly expressed or indirectly echoed in this mini-symphony of faith and life.[25]

This passage (10:12–22) appears to have an envelope structure with vv. 12–13 and vv. 20–22 serving as the boundary elements of the paragraph. Both sections of verses emphasize the "what" and the "why": Obey Yahweh wholeheartedly because of who He is and what He does. This envelope structure (10:12–13, 20–22) bounds a central section (10:14–19) in which Moses grounds His exhortation for God's people on the high and lofty character and conduct of Yahweh. Because of this reality, they need to live in genuine submission to His expectations and demands (10:16) and live out His character before others, especially before those of whom it would be easy to take advantage

---

Bowen (Eisenbrauns, 2003), 301–3, 308–9. This approach represents an unfortunate side-stepping of a key interpretive issue.

25 C. Wright, *Deuteronomy*, NIBC (Hendrickson, 1996), 144.

(10:19). Both of these sections serve as repetitive triplets, founding the exhortation squarely on God Himself: Yahweh's marvelous (superlative) character (10:14, 17), Yahweh's unique conduct (10:15, 18), and Yahweh's covenantal demand (10:16, 19).

The section (10:12–22) begins with וְעַתָּה ("and now"), which marks a transition from narrative to exhortation, from history to application.[26] Moses' recitation of Israel's repeated acts of rebellion make quite evident that Israel must deal with her rebellious spirit if the nation would be able to carry out God's intentions for them. The look back at Israel's rebellion with the golden calf should have also motivated Israelite to genuinely pursue covenant loyalty in light of their receiving God's abundant mercy and grace through forgiveness.

Moses' reference to Israel's ancestors, God's choice of them as a people and their ancestry in Abraham in verse 15 evidences clear connections between this passage with the Abrahamic covenant. Circumcision was a mark or evidence of the covenant Yahweh made with Abraham and his seed.[27] By commanding His people to circumcise their hearts, Yahweh required that they make their identity as His covenant people an *internal reality*. The point appears to be that unless the physical sign of circumcision reflected an inner reality (of covenant conformity), it was of limited value in generating the kind of relationship Yahweh desired to have with His chosen people (Deut 10:16).[28]

26　Paul A. Barker, *The Triumph of Grace in Deuteronomy: Faithless Israel, Faithful Yahweh in Deuteronomy* (Paternoster, 2004), 103. A. Niccacci (*The Syntax of the Verb in Classical Hebrew Prose* [Sheffield Academic Press, 1990], 101) points out that in narrative speech, this expression "introduces the result arising or the conclusion to be drawn concerning the present action from an event or topic dealt with beforehand." This construction indicates a contrast between then and now "when one reflects on past events and commits to present or future action" (Bill T. Arnold and Arnold H. Choi, *A Guide to Biblical Hebrew Syntax*, 2 nd ed. [Cambridge University Press, 2018], 151, §4.2.14b; cf. C. van der Merwe, J. Naudé, and J. Kroeze, *A Biblical Hebrew Reference Grammar* [Sheffield Academic Press, 1999], 454, §40.39, [2]); B. Waltke and M. O'Connor, *An Introduction to Biblical Hebrew Syntax* [Eisenbrauns, 1990], 667, §39.3.4f).

27　Merrill ("Deuteronomy," in *BKKWS* [Victor Books, 2003], 476) suggests that Moses incorporated circumcision into the Law in order to make an explicit connection between the Abrahamic and the Sinaitic covenants, thereby highlighting their continuity (Exod 12:43–51).

28　G. Hall, *Deuteronomy* (College Press, 2000), 199.

Possible Meanings for Spiritual Circumcision

Various English translations have offered different alternatives for the meaning of heart circumcision (see Figure 6.1 at the end of the essay). Although some have referred to it as "the deepest spiritual reality of the Hebrew religion"[29] or as a "call to walk before the Lord,"[30] most suggestions focus on the removal of something, the idea of sensitivity to God, or an internal motivation to obey God's covenant expectations.[31] Understanding the meaning of heart circumcision impacts our understanding of what Moses means by referring to it in 10:16 and 30:6.

Removal

Drawing on the removal of the foreskin that takes place in physical circumcision, various scholars have focused on the idea of spiritual circumcision removing something that represents an obstacle to obeying Yahweh. Some have suggested that spiritual circumcision signifies the removal of one's sinful disposition or general hindrances to obedience, or a mental block that has made Israel stubborn.[32] Ridderbos suggests that the "foreskin" can symbolize uncleanness or the profane (that which has not been devoted to God). Hence the foreskin of the heart would refer to the worldly disposition that turns a person away from God. Circumcision represents putting aside that rebellious disposition. They must no longer be stiff-necked (Deut 9:6, 13, 22–24).[33] The NET Bible's translation of "cleansing" seems to suggest

---

29 E. Smick, "מול," TWOT, 1:495.

30 E. Carpenter, "מול," NIDOTTE, 2:869. In his entry Carpenter suggests that this call came to Israel before Yahweh brings about the internal changes (30:6) that make it possible for God's people to actually obey this call (see discussion below). In other words, Carpenter affirms that God's people would not be able to obey the command in 10:16 until the future day when God circumcised the Israelites' hearts (30:6).

31 Although the second and third categories overlap, they also have distinctives. The third option is more concrete than the second—starting in the heart and including obedience.

32 J. Tigay, *Deuteronomy*, JPS (Jewish Publication Society, 1996), 108; D. Christensen, *Deuteronomy 1:1–21:9*, WBC (Thomas Nelson, 2001), 1:204; Christensen, *Deuteronomy 21:10–34:12*, WBC (Thomas Nelson, 2002), 2:739.

33 J. Ridderbos, *Deuteronomy* (Zondervan, 1984), 142, cf. 270. See Keil, *The Pentateuch*, 1:344, who suggests that the foreskin of the heart refers to whatever interferes

the idea of the removal of sin as well.[34] The NJPS translation focuses on the removal of hindrances in its translation, "cut away the thickening about your hearts." In this regard, circumcision of the heart takes place "in order to remove impediments or blockages to obedience ... free yourselves from all hindrances in thought and will and make yourselves open to obedience (cf. Exod 6:12, 30; Jer 6:10)."[35]

Sensitivity to God

The conduct of Israel during the time of Moses and Joshua makes it clear that physical birth and the sign of circumcision (Josh 5:1–9) did not guarantee sensitivity to God. Rather, the nation of Israel involved a seed within the seed, a people within the people, and the circumcised of heart within the uncircumcised of heart.[36] Driver suggests that it means being "receptive to godlike affections."[37] Thomp-

---

with the expression of genuine love for Yahweh.

34 NET Bible note on 10:16 affirms that reference "to the Abrahamic covenant prompts Moses to recall the sign of that covenant, namely, physical circumcision (Gen 17:9–14). Just as that act signified total covenant obedience, so spiritual circumcision (cleansing of the heart) signifies more internally a commitment to be pliable and obedient to the will of God (cf. Deut 30:6; Jer 4:4; 9:26)." It is interesting to note that even though the translation highlights the idea of the removal of sin (hence cleansing), the note highlights the notion of internal pliability (see below meaning option). G. Oehler (*Theology of the Old Testament* [T&T Clark, 1873; reprint, Klock & Klock Christian Publishers, 1978], 194) affirms that circumcision of the heart functions as a "symbol of the renewal and purification of the heart." A. Phillips (*Deuteronomy* [Cambridge University Press, 1973], 76) develops the idea of "cleansing" by connecting the biblical practice of circumcision with ANE practices. Since circumcision in the ANE took place at the age of puberty and constituted an act of purification and dedication by the young man passing into adulthood, biblical circumcision signifies the idea of purification as well. Unfortunately, part of Phillips' grounds for this conclusion is his suggestion that the Priestly legislators (P) adapted the original account of Yahweh's covenant with Abraham to include this concept of circumcision.

35 R. Nelson, *Deuteronomy*, OTL (Westminster John Knox Press, 2002), 137. Jack R. Lundbom, *Deuteronomy: A Commentary* (Eerdmans, 2013), 391. He also sees this as a flawed human effort, "In 10:16 people are told to bring about a change of heart themselves (Lundbom, *Deuteronomy*, 818). He points to Jer 6:10 as a key meaning analogy: Uncircumcised ears "need to be opened up for hearing to take place" (Lundbom, *Deuteronomy*, 819).

36 W. VanGemeren, *The Progress of Redemption* (Zondervan, 1988), 173.

37 Driver, *Deuteronomy*, 125.

son writes that if whatever hinders is cut off, "then the circumcised heart becomes open and, being freed from hindering obstructions, it can become pliable and amenable to the direction of God. The result of such a circumcision will be submission to the will of God and the end of stubbornness."[38] Cairns contends that the circumcised heart is "aware and receptive of God's grace, sensitive to the privilege of membership in God's people, and 'fruitful' in the God-like qualities of compassion which that membership involves."[39]

Internal Motivation for Obedience

In the book of Deuteronomy in particular (as a book dealing with "covenant renewal"), the imagery of heart circumcision appears to highlight Israel's need to demonstrate the genuine internal conformity to Yahweh's covenant demands that physical circumcision allegedly evidenced (on the part of the parents). An "internalization" of the Law (God's covenant expectations) would occasion covenant allegiance/loyalty. For those camped on the plains of Moab (and every generation after that), the external sign of the covenant was meaningless without the proper inner attitude of those who were renewing their allegiance to their covenant Lord. In this regard, Craigie explains heart circumcision as follows:

> The metaphor thus aptly employs an act symbolizing the covenant relationship, but applies it to the present moment in a spiritual sense. God's requirement was that his people *love Him* (10:12), but to do this, they required a particular attitude of heart and mind, which—like circumcision—involved decision and action symbolizing allegiance. Thus to circumcise the heart is to take an attitude to God which is the opposite of being *stubborn* (or stiff-necked).[40]

---

38 J. Thompson, *Deuteronomy: An Introduction and Commentary*, TOTC (Inter-Varsity, 1974), 149. According to Lundbom (*Deuteronomy*, 391, 819), Moses calls God's people to "open up" their own hearts.

39 Cairns, *Word and Presence*, 111.

40 P. Craigie, *Deuteronomy*, NICOT (Eerdmans, 1976), 205; cf. Fabry, "לֵב," in *TDOT*, 7:434. C. Wright (*Deuteronomy*, 151) affirms that heart circumcision "indicates an inner commitment to obedience that lives out the meaning of the physical sign

In this regard, some have highlighted the idea of repentance, covenant renewal, or a renewal of one's allegiance to God. As a term that highlights the recipient's wholehearted submission to God's expectations, it can be a phrase that depicts an Israelite as "regenerate" (cf. Rom 2:28–29; 4:1–2; Col 2:11).[41]

In its broadest sense, circumcision of the heart may connote an inner spiritual conformity to God's expectations (cf. Jer 4:4).[42] If physical circumcision demonstrated external conformity to the covenant ideal (on the part of the parents but experienced by the infant), circumcision of the heart would signify an inner conformity to Yahweh's covenantal demands (Jer 4:4; Rom 2:28–29) that would show up in external obedience.[43] By making this connection with the Abrahamic covenant in Deuteronomy 10, Moses declared to God's servant nation that Yahweh, their awesome God, demanded that the descendants of Abraham, Isaac, and Jacob enjoy this covenant relationship *as an inner reality*. Being heart circumcised represented a wholehearted commitment to the covenant (and a relationship with Yahweh). In light of the preceding delineation of the golden calf incident as well as other instances of Israelite rebellion against Yahweh (Deut 9:1–10:11) and the exhortation "do not be stubborn again" (Deut 9:6), this command for Israelites to circumcise their hearts focuses on the covenantal status of their hearts: in conformity with God's demands or in treacherous rebellion against them. God's people must

---

in the flesh." Nelson (*Deuteronomy*, 348) suggests that heart circumcision "is a metaphor for a radical, interior renewal that makes love and obedience fully possible (cf. Jer 4:4); cf. R. Le Déaut, "Le theme de la circoncision du coeur (Dt. XXX 6; Jér. IV 4) dans les versions anciennes (LXX et Targum) et à Qumran," in *Congress Volume*, ed. J. Emerton, VTSup 32 (Brill, 1981), 181.

41 VanGemeren, *The Progress of Redemption*, 167; Eugene H. Merrill, *Deuteronomy*, NAC (Broadman & Holman, 1994), 388; Le Déaut, "Le theme de la circoncision du coeur," 180. Merrill (*Deuteronomy*, 388) writes: "Just as circumcision of the flesh symbolized outward identification with the Lord and the covenant community (cf. Gen 17:10, 23; Lev 12:3; Josh 5:2), so circumcision of the heart … speaks of internal identification with Him in what might be called regeneration in Christian theology."

42 McConville, *Deuteronomy*, 200.

43 Merrill, *Deuteronomy*, 203. According to Thompson (*Deuteronomy: An Introduction and Commentary*, 149), a circumcised heart is one that is "pliable and amenable to the direction of God." Cf. Driver, *Deuteronomy*, 125; H. W. Wolff, *Anthropology of the Old Testament* (Fortress Press, 1974), 52.

choose between remaining stubborn and rebellious or being circumcised of heart.[44]

The reality of Israel's spiritual condition (continued rebellion) after Moses gave this exhortation, and an understanding of mankind's
depravity, occasions the question, "Was this kind of heart change even
possible without divine assistance?" Was Israel able but unwilling to
keep the covenant requirements or, rather, both unable and unwilling
to do so?[45]

Yahweh's Promise to Circumcise the Israelite Hearts (30:6)

Having set God's covenantal expectations (chs. 5–11—general stipulations; chs. 12–26—specific stipulations) before his fellow Israelites
and having clearly delineated the far-reaching consequences of their
choice to obey or disobey (blessing or cursing respectively, ch. 28),
Moses exhorts the Israelites to renew their commitment to this covenant relationship (chs. 29–30).

The pericope at hand (30:1–10) begins and ends with a focus on
Israel's need to repent of their covenant rebellion and pursue a life
of heartfelt covenant loyalty. These verses entail an extended "when
… then" sequence and is organized around the idea of returning or
repenting (שׁוּב).[46] In 30:1–2 and 30:10, wholehearted repentance for
their rebellion and genuine obedience to Yahweh provide the grounds
for God's restoration of His covenant people.[47] This restoration brings

---

44 It would also seem that this call for heart circumcision could represent a call
to "salvation" as well as an exhortation to believing Israelites to pursue a life characterized by heart circumcision.

45 Barker, *The Triumph of Grace in Deuteronomy*, 106.

46 This verb occurs 7 times in these verses (vv. 1, 2, 3 [2x], 8, 9, 10). Israel will
"take to heart" (cause them to return to the heart) the blessing and cursing they experienced (v. 1) and will return to Yahweh (vv. 2, 8, 10). Yahweh will restore his people
(v. 3a) and will turn and gather (v. 3b) and will again delight over (v. 9) his people.

47 The passage begins and ends with the protasis or "if" statement (vv. 1–2, 10).
A long (vv. 4b–7) and a brief apodosis (v. 9) frame the central/climactic exhortation
(v. 8—"Israel will again heed the Lord and obey all his commandments"). The chain
of waw consecutive + perfect forms that ends in v. 7 and the presence of "and you"
(וְאַתָּה) at the beginning of v. 8 evidences a clear syntactical break between those
two verses. The structure of 30:1–10 is as follows (see McConville, *Deuteronomy*, 424):

A   Protasis (1–2): Israel's Repentance

clarity to the conundrum occasioned by Moses' description of Israel's experience of covenant curse. At the end of chapter 29, one could wonder how Israel's eviction from the land of promise and their languishing under the oppressive rule of pagan nations cohered with God's promise that Israel would yet function as His servant nation before the other nations of the world. As Merrill points out, "What the nations could not understand on the basis of empirical historical evidence Israel could understand on the basis of God's covenant promises."[48]

Verses 3–7 delineate what God will do to and for Israel in the wake of their repentance. He will bring an end to their exile and regather them from the various regions in which He had scattered them (vv. 3–4). He will restore them to the land of promise and to a position of abundant blessing and prosperity (v. 5). He will also transform them, i.e., "circumcise their hearts," so that they would be able to love Him with all their being (v. 6).[49] Even though the section of verses references God's circumcising their hearts after it addresses Israel's restoration to the land and prosperity, it is doubtless that God's activity would precede and make possible the promised restoration.[50] The repetition of the key phrase "with all your heart and soul" (vv. 2, 10), and the promise that God will "circumcise their hearts" (v. 6) emphasize that this repentance (i.e., internal transformation) of the nation of Israel cannot happen without God's intervention, i.e., His circumcision of their heart. This heart circumcision will enable Israel (as a nation) to do what God had always demanded His people do throughout their history: love Him with their entire being.[51]

B Apodosis (3–7): Yahweh's Restoration of Israel
   C Central Exhortation (8): Wholehearted Obedience
B′ Apodosis (9): Yahweh's Restoration of Israel
A′ Protasis (10): Israel's Repentance

48 Merrill, *Deuteronomy*, 387.

49 Thompson (*Deuteronomy: An Introduction and Commentary*, 285) explains that Yahweh "will reconstitute Israel."

50 OT writers were not always concerned with exact chronological sequence, esp. when they are addressing thematic concerns. For example, the difference in the way Exodus 32 and Deuteronomy 9 present the events of the golden calf incident does not indicate that they are divergent accounts but have different thematic concerns.

51 "Love" makes an obvious allusion to the demands of the Shema (Deut 6:4–5). Merrill (*Deuteronomy*, 388) affirms: "This impossible standard was always understood

Finally, Yahweh will cause the punishment He had delivered against Israel to fall upon those nations that had persecuted His people (v. 7). The central exhortation of this pericope occurs in verse 8: "And you shall again obey the voice of the Lord and keep all His commandments that I command you today." Israel's repentance, God's restoration of the nation to the land of promise, and His circumcision of their heart will occasion their ability to, for once, conduct themselves *as the servant nation* God had always intended them to be. As a nation, they would live in genuine, wholehearted conformity to the covenant. Verses 9–10 conclude the paragraph by reversing the protasis and apodosis, forming a chiastic inclusio for verses 1–2. God will make His chosen people prosperous and numerous once again (v. 9) when they obey their covenant lord with their entire being (v. 10).

Israel's history up until this point had clearly demonstrated the *nation* of Israel's inability to live in accordance with Yahweh's demands for absolute allegiance. Israel, His chosen people, had no hope without God's gift of a heart to know and obey (cf. Deut 29:4 [Heb. 29:3]).[52] When Yahweh causes His *chosen nation* to return to their homeland, He will circumcise their hearts with the result that they will genuinely love Him with their entire being ("with all your heart and with all your soul"). Unlike God's demand that His covenant people circumcise their hearts (Deut 10:16)[53], in 30:6 He promises to circumcise their heart. By circumcising their hearts, Yahweh makes possible the love that He required of them.[54] He will create in His people a new spirit of obedience within every Israelite (at a national level). In that eschatological setting, Yahweh promises to provide His covenant nation the

---

as the ideal of covenant behavior, one to be sought but never fully achieved (c.f. [sic] Matt 22:40; Mark 12:33)." He adds: "People can love God with all their heart only after the heart itself has been radically changed to a Godward direction. When that happens, not only is obedience possible but so is life (v. 6)." Wright (*Deuteronomy*, 290) posits that "the fundamental demand of the law (to love God with all one's heart and soul) is presented as the ultimate fruit of God's grace in the human heart."

52 See my attempt to explain that difficult passage here: Michael A. Grisanti, "Was Israel Unable to Respond to God? A Study of Deuteronomy 29:2–4," *BSac* 163 (April-June 2006): 176–96.

53 This command was only embraced by the remnant (believing Israelites) during Israel's history and not by the entire nation of Israel.

54 Cairns, *Word and Presence*, 264.

willingness and power to obey.[55]

When God "operated" on Israel's heart, His people would be able to love Him wholeheartedly and live (30:6). In this future juncture, they would see their enemies and former persecutors experience the curses under which they had suffered (30:7). They would once again experience God's covenant blessings (30:8–9). Even then, this experience of blessing was not a guarantee without their submission to Yahweh's directives (30:10).[56]

The Tension between the Command (10:16) and the Promise (30:6)

In the preceding pages, this author has sought to explain the basic significance of physical and spiritual (heart) circumcision as well as provide a brief exposition of the two passages that many regard as "at odds". The one passage presents a present exhortation to God's chosen people and the other passage explains God's future action of circumcising the hearts of His people.

How then should one explain the "tension" between Yahweh's demand that Israel circumcise their hearts (in the time frame of Deut 10:16) and His promise to circumcise their hearts at some future time (Deut 30:6)? The fact that Israel's "story" is one in which the nation perpetually fails to live in accordance with God's covenantal expectations[57] contributes to this question. The Old Testament teaches and demonstrates that Israel would be rebellious against God for a large segment of her history. As a whole (at a national level), Israel remains unregenerate until the last part of redemptive history (Jer 31:31–34; Ezek 36:22–28; 37:14).[58] In contrast to the command in 10:16, Deuteronomy 30:6 "speaks of circumcision of the heart as something that would be done by Yahweh in order to restore Israel."[59] How does this

---

55 R. Clements, "The Book of Deuteronomy," in *The New Interpreter's Bible*, ed. L. Keck and others (Abingdon, 1998), 2:513.

56 Craigie, *Deuteronomy*, 364.

57 J. McConville, *Grace in the End: A Study in Deuteronomic Theology* (Zondervan, 1993), 133. This penchant for rebellion is epitomized by Israel's rebellion at Kadesh Barnea (Deut 1:26–46) and the golden calf incident (Deut 9–10).

58 D. Fuller, "The Importance of a Unity of the Bible," in *Studies in Old Testament Theology*, eds. R. Hubbard, Jr., R. Johnston, and R. Meye (Word Publishing, 1992), 68.

59 Nelson, *Deuteronomy*, 137.

promise of a future reality relate to God's demand that Israelites in Moses' day circumcise their hearts? There is no doubt that Deuteronomy 30:1–10 envisions a future day when God will restore His people and enable them to worship him. For example, Allen writes that Deuteronomy 30:6 "promises that when Israel was restored to the land after repenting in exile, God would inaugurate a new era marked by His own circumcision of their hearts so that they would love 'with all their heart' (contrast 29:4)."[60] On the one hand, is heart circumcision *an entirely future reality*? If so, what does this say about Israel's *spiritual existence or capacity* in Moses' day and in the centuries after that time? On the other hand, if this promised circumcision is not entirely or exclusively future, how can one explain the future orientation of this promise, especially in comparison with the command found in Deuteronomy 10:16?

Over the years, scholars have offered various suggestions that can be categorized in three ways. The below categories do not include any resolution of the interpretive tension by appealing to later interpolations by other authors, which allegedly resolves this tension between these passages. This author finds these suggestions unsatisfactory and will offer his resolution in a following section.

Israel's Relationship with God had been Totally External

Lemke suggests that Jeremiah 31:31–34 envisages an internalization of the relationship between God and His people. He writes: "The renewal of the covenant relationship between God and Israel would be entirely the result of God's unilateral redemptive and forgiving activity, rather than by human effort or deserving."[61] The confusion caused by the above quotation draws on the suggestion that Israel's relationship with God *was ever the result of human effort or worth*. The Bible never depicts human merit or effort as having any redemptive significance in God's estimation. Beyond that, a number of Old Testament pas-

---

60 Allen, "Circumcision," in *NIDOTTE*, 4:475. God will replace Israel's failure to obey the law with both the will and ability to obey Him (E. Nicholson, *Preaching to the Exiles: A Study in the Prose Tradition in the Book of Jeremiah* [Schocken Books, 1971], 83).

61 Lemke, "Circumcision of the Heart," 313.

sages demonstrate that ritualistic obedience to God's expectations was nothing less than something despised, i.e., an abomination (Isa 1:11–15; 1 Sam 15:22; Hos 6:4–6; Amos 5:21–25; Micah 6:6–8; Jer 7:4–7, 21–23; Ps 50:8–20).

Israel's Circumcision was Ineffective

In his *NIDOTTE* entry on the verb "to circumcise" (מול), Eugene Carpenter contends that the call for Israel to circumcise their heart was a call for them to walk before the Lord. However, since this circumcision did not create a change in the persons involved, it was "ineffective" or weak.[62] In other words, in Deuteronomy 10:16, Yahweh demanded that Israel change their inner or heart attitude and render service to him. Because this appeal does not bear abundant "fruit" and is clearly "ineffective," God Himself must circumcise the hearts of Israelites in some distant future setting (Deut 30:6). However, the fact that God's commands do not always generate the desired lifestyle for all Israelites does not signify that human failure demonstrates or implies any ineffectiveness in that divine expectation.[63]

What God Asked of Israel was Impossible

Various commentators describe Deuteronomy 10:16 and 30:6 as referring to what Israel was, and what God wanted Israel to be, respectively.[64] In other words, these verses depict the Israel of the past and the Israel of the future. Scholars who take this view normally point to the New Covenant that promises that the Torah would be inscribed on the heart of every participant in that covenant (Jer 31:31–34). Ezekiel promises that God would give His people a new heart, i.e., a responsive heart (replacing a heart of stone—Ezek 11:19; 36:26).

---

62 E. Carpenter, "מול," *NIDOTTE*, 2:869.

63 It is correct to notice that the nation of Israel was not characterized by conduct expected of a "circumcised" heart in the centuries following Deut 10. That in itself does not negate the potential "effectiveness" of the command in Deut 10:16. Toward the end of this essay I point to the consistent presence of an Israelite remnant in OT history.

64 Hall, *Deuteronomy*, 200.

P. Barker writes that Deuteronomy provides "no indication at all that Israel will be willing or able to keep the covenant."[65] He contends that Deuteronomy only presents a hope for Israel that is entirely dependent on Yahweh's grace since Israel cannot pursue the relationship with Yahweh and the covenant obedience set before them. Doubtless, the right response to God's call for obedience, as seen before, is to stem from the heart, combining attitude and action. He rejects the suggestion that Israel genuinely living out the verbs of Deuteronomy 10:12–13 is a "practical possibility".[66]

All three of these potential resolutions for the interpretive tension between 10:16 and 30:6 either misunderstand the core idea of God's expectations of His covenant people in the past or regards the command in 10:16 as an empty command. Is there a better way to deal with this *crux interpretum*?

A Resolution of the Tension between the Command (10:16) and the Promise (30:6)

If one regards heart circumcision as something that never actually happened in Israel's history, but was an entirely and exclusively future reality and something only God could do, how can interpreters actually resolve the tension that exists between a command for Israel to circumcise their hearts that historically precedes (by hundreds of years at least) the future experience of the divine promise to bring to pass that needed heart circumcision? Several lines of argument offer some relief to this understandable tension.

---

65 Paul A. Barker, *The Triumph of Grace in Deuteronomy: Faithless Israel, Faithful Yahweh in Deuteronomy* (Paternoster, 2004), 104. According to J. Lundbom (*Deuteronomy: A Commentary*, 819), "In Jeremiah (Jer 31:33; 32:39) and Ezekiel (Ezek 36:26–28), as also here, Yahweh must bring about the change; the people cannot do it themselves."

66 Barker, *The Triumph of Grace in Deuteronomy*, 103, citing the affirmation of Cairns, *Word and Presence*, 110. Barker wrestles with these options: was Israel able but unwilling to keep the covenant requirements or unable and unwilling to do so. He concludes that without divine intervention (Deut 30:6), Israel is both unable and unwilling to do what Yahweh demands. It is impossible for them to obey Yahweh's demand for heart circumcision (Barker, *The Triumph of Grace in Deuteronomy*, 104–6).

The Concept of a Remnant

The Hebrew terms used to point to a "remnant" in the OT[67] can carry a negative idea of total annihilation (none left—2 Kings 21:13–15; Isa 17:4–6; Jer 8:3; Ezek 15:1–8) or the positive notion of the survival of a remnant (some left—Gen 8:15–19; 45:7; 1 Kings 19:18; Isa 1:25–26; 28:5–6; Jer 23:3–4)).[68] For example, in the book of Deuteronomy, the verb שָׁאַר occurs nine times to refer to the total absence of enemy survivors in Israel's conquest of the Transjordan region (2:34; 3:3) or to a very small group of survivors (3:11; 7:20). When writing about the potential impact of covenant curses, Moses points out that in the event that Yahweh sends covenant judgment upon Israel by means of attacking pagan nations, these nations will not *leave behind* any "grain, new wine or oil, nor any calves of your herds or lambs of your flocks" (28:51; cf. v. 55). Finally, the verb also describes the Israelites who survive Israel's experience of covenant curses (4:27; 28:62).[69] As Hasel pointed out, when this verb describes human survivors, "the fragmentary nature of the residual part nor the painful loss of the other part is of greatest importance. Rather the surviving or escaping remnant is itself a new whole which possesses all potentialities of renewal and regeneration."[70]

---

67 The main verbal root, שָׁאַר (235x, "to leave behind"), is often combined with several other near synonyms: יָתַר, be left (235x), פָּלַט (80x), and שָׂרַד (27×): e.g., שָׁאַר, שָׂרַד, and פָּלַט (Josh 8:22); שָׁאַר. פָּלַט, and יָתַר (Isa 4:2–3); יָתַר and שָׂרַד (Isa 1:9); פָּלַט, escape, שָׂרַד, survive, and שָׁאַר, remain, (Jer 44:14). These verbs and their derived nouns can carry the idea of someone or something "left over" or "left behind." The main verb and its derived forms occur most frequently with the nuance of surviving or being left behind. See Sang Hoon Park, "שָׁאַר," in the *New International Dictionary of Old Testament Theology & Exegesis*, ed. W. VanGemeren (Zondervan, 1997), 4:11–17.

68 G. Hasel, *The Remnant: The History and Theology of the Remnant Idea from Genesis to Isaiah*, 3 rd ed. (Andrews University Press, 1980), 387. Hasel also points out that this concept describes three types of groups: a *historical remnant* (survivors of a catastrophe), a *faithful remnant* (characterized by genuine spirituality and the carrier of all divine election promises), and an *eschatological remnant* (those who survive end time judgments and enter the everlasting kingdom) (G. Hasel, "Remnant," in *ISBE*, rev. ed., ed. by G. Bromiley [Eerdmans, 1988], 4:130).

69 The verb שָׁאַר occurs once simply to refer to the "rest" of the Israelites who will hear about a legal decision (Deut 19:20).

70 Hasel, *The Remnant*, 388.

In Isaiah 6:9–10 Yahweh told the prophet: "He said, 'Go and tell this people: "Be ever hearing, but never understanding; be ever seeing, but never perceiving." Make the heart of this people calloused; make their ears dull and close their eyes. Otherwise they might see with their eyes, hear with their ears, understand with their hearts, and turn and be healed.'" Even in the "bad news" scenario described for Isaiah's ministry, a time characterized by widespread hard-heartedness, there would be a "stump" left behind, i.e., a small remnant (Isa 10:33–11:1).

Although the concept of the remnant receives more detailed attention and gains more eschatological focus later in the OT (especially in Isaiah), when used with regard to Israel, this concept consistently points to God's continuing plans for His chosen nation.[71] Those continuing plans of Yahweh include His intention to bring himself glory through His servant nation that would include believing Israelites (i.e., heart-circumcised Israelites). Do those continuing plans of Yahweh for His chosen nation wait until the eschaton for *any realization*? Could it be that the existence of a remnant at various points in OT history signifies the presence of regenerated individuals in Israel during their ancient history? Regenerated Israelites would entail individuals who are redeemed and able to live in accordance with Yahweh's expectations (though imperfectly). The only way for this remnant to live in accordance with God's covenantal demands would have been for them to have enjoyed God's enablement, intervention, or heart circumcision. As Merrill points out: "for though the nation as a whole might reject his overtures of grace, a remnant would believe, and that would be the nucleus of his salvific purposes (Isa 10:20–23; Rom 9:27–28; 11:1–7)."[72]

The National or Corporate Perspective of 30:1–10

Although the whole book of Deuteronomy addresses the entire nation of Israel, that focus is especially evident in chapters 28–30. The

---

71 Hasel ("Remnant," *ISBE*, 4:131) writes: "the escape of a remnant from a mortal threat reveals the immense future potentiality for life and continued existence, regardless of the size of that surviving remnant."

72 Merrill, *Deuteronomy*, 376.

threat of covenant blessing or curse was not an individual issue but *a national one*. As the nation was characterized by covenant conformity or treachery, the nation would experience covenant blessing or curse. The exilic fate that Moses refers to in chapter 29 as a likely scenario views the nation as the recipient of that judgment. In the wake of that likely covenant judgment, chapter 30 delineates God's restoration of the nation to the place of blessing and prominence that God had always wanted them to occupy. Merrill points out that "in terms of Israel as an elect people in a collective, national sense, the circumcision described here ... lies in the future."[73] He adds: "As far as the radical work of regeneration described here as circumcision of the heart, that clearly awaits a day yet to come *as far as the covenant nation as a whole is concerned*" (emphasis mine).[74] Deuteronomy 30:6 rightly affirms that *all Israel's* experience of heart circumcision waits for a future day. It does not necessarily mean that God left *individual Israelites* without any hope of heart circumcision until that future time.

The Following Context of Deuteronomy 30:6 (30:11–14)

The immediately following verses belabor the point that what God asked of Israel (in the Mosaic timeframe[75]) was not beyond their God-given ability. Chris Wright states:

---

73 Merrill, *Deuteronomy*, 388.

74 Merrill, *Deuteronomy*, 388.

75 Several scholars conclude that the time frame described by 30:11–14 is the future New Covenant age. Cf. Steven R. Coxhead, "Deuteronomy 30:11–14 as a Prophecy of the New Covenant in Christ," *WTJ* 68 (2006): 305–20; Bryan D. Estelle, "Leviticus 18:5 and Deuteronomy 30:11–14 in Biblical Theological Development: Entitlement to Heaven Foreclosed and Proferred," in *The Law Is Not of Faith: Essays on Works and Grace in the Mosaic Covenant*, eds. B. D. Estelle, J. V. Fesko, and David VanDrunen (P & R, 2009), 122–46 (and various commentators). Regardless, although 29:19–21 [Heb. 18–20] address Israel's near future (individual judgment) and 29:22–28 [Heb. 21–27] point to quite distant national judgment, and 30:1–10 delineates a divine intervention in human history that involved heart circumcision performed by Him, 30:11–14 brings the focus back to Moses' present audience. 30:11 opens with the statement: "For this commandment that I command you today." 30:15–20 presents the sobering choice faced by Israel—obedience for life or disobedience for curse. Moses' call to covenant renewal was meant for his current audience. He called them to pursue lives of wholehearted covenant loyalty in the centuries to follow their encampment on the Plains of Moab.

The idea that God deliberately made the law so exacting that nobody would ever be able to live by it belongs to a distorted theology that tries unnecessarily to gild the gospels by denigrating the law. The frequent claims by various psalmists to have lived according to God's law are neither exaggerated nor exceptional. They arise from the natural assumption that ordinary people can indeed live in a way that is broadly pleasing to God and faithful to God's law, and that they can do so as a matter of joy and delight. This is neither self-righteousness nor a claim to sinless perfection, for the same psalmists are equally quick to confess their sin and failings, fully realizing that only the grace that could forgive and cleanse them would likewise enable them to live again in covenant obedience. Obedience to the law in the OT ... was not the means of achieving salvation but the response to a salvation that was already achieved.[76]

God did not doom Israel to utter and total spiritual failure throughout her long existence as a nation. God did not ask Israel to do or be something that it was impossible for them to do or be in any fashion. Although *the nation* was never characterized by genuine submission to Yahweh's covenantal demands, throughout Israel's existence there were Israelites (though relatively small in number) who enjoyed God's circumcision of their hearts and who could heed His command to circumcise their hearts.

The Future Emphasis Has Present Implications in 30:1–10

What God promised to do in the future was not unrelated to Israel's OT existence (i.e., time of Deut 10:16). Craigie points out that this material (Deut 29–30) is not "primarily prophetic." He goes on to affirm that Moses "employs both the experience of the past and his notion of the potential future to force home upon the Israelites the need for obedience in the present. Before they have even entered the land, He warns of their being driven out again and scattered, and then brought back in."[77]

76　Wright, *Deuteronomy,* 290.

77　Craigie, *Deuteronomy,* 364. As with all predictions presented against the

The chart in Figure 6.2 attempts to put the events described in Deuteronomy 29–30 on a timeline. Israel's rebellion against their covenant with Yahweh (envisioned by Moses in chapter 29) leads to the nation's experience of covenant cursing. This traumatic experience of divine judgment includes the eviction of God's people from the land of promise and leaves His people scattered in exile among various Gentile nations.

The future national repentance and restoration described in Deuteronomy 30:1–10 does not happen primarily as a consequence of human initiative. God's intervention in their midst by "circumcising their hearts" triggers Israel's repentance of their hard-heartedness and rebellion. The reality of "all Israel" being saved (Rom 11:26) takes place before their restoration (30:2 occasions 30:3). The account in Deuteronomy 30 ends with Israel's enemies experiencing divine punishment in light of their rejection of Israel's God. Moses' ultimate point in this set of totally likely future events is that God's internal work will be a prerequisite if Israel (as a nation, not just individual Israelites) will be able to genuinely and wholeheartedly love Yahweh. Also, keep in mind that Moses was addressing Israelites who were camped in the plains of Moab, preparing for their conquest of Canaan. This "new generation" of Israelites involved the descendants of those who rebelled against God's plan to bring His people into the land of promise almost 40 years earlier. On their own, they were no more prepared to successfully conquer the Canaanite peoples, let alone able to live in such a fashion that they could function as God's servant nation. In the same way that God will in some distant future setting provide *the only*

---

backdrop of the Mosaic Covenant (cf. Jer 17), there was an "if-then" aspect to those predictions. Moses is not saying to God's people that Israel's failure is a done deal, so you might as well just give up. Don't bother pursuing a life of covenant loyalty. As God says in Jer 17, after the potter and clay analogy, God will take back any promise of judgment if the condemned people repent and will revoke any promise of blessing if the recipients of that promise turn their backs on God. The future presentation of divine judgment in the near term and far term as a totally likely set of events gives seriousness to the divine threat/promise. As with several other passages (see 30:11–15), the Lord sets before His people the fate before them if they pursue a life of covenant treachery. That potential should have gripped the heart of God's people and motivated them to obey their unparalleled God. Sadly, it did not impact the majority of the nation, but it did grab the hearts of those Israelites who became part of the believing remnant.

means for national restoration and genuine obedience in the wake of covenant judgment, God's intervention in the hearts of the Israelites of Moses' day represents *the only way* for those Israelites to carry out God's expectations for them as well.

The "Nature" of the Mosaic ("Old") and New Covenants

Yahweh established the Mosaic Covenant[78] with the nation of Israel after their departure from Egypt. This covenant begins with the Ten Commandments (Exod 20:1–17) and also involves numerous rules that deal with various aspects of Israelite life (their relationship with God and with others). Although Yahweh established this covenant with the entire nation of Israel (Exod 19:7–8), not all the Israelites who made up that nation were believers. After the original establishment of this covenant, each new generation of Israelites automatically became participants in it by virtue of their physical birth and external circumcision.[79] Because the majority of Israelites were unregenerate, "they were enslaved by their confirmed, sinful dispositions of enmity against God."[80] Consequently, not only did they fail to live in accordance with Yahweh's covenantal expectations, but they (as unbelievers) were absolutely unable to do this (Rom 8:7). Jeremiah wrote with great emphasis: "Judah's sin is engraved with an iron tool, inscribed with a flint point, on the tablets of their hearts" (Jer 17:1). As Huey points out, "Judah's sin was so deeply ingrained that it was as though its sin had been engraved with an 'iron tool' (cf. Job 19:24), with a 'flint point,' an instrument used to carve inscriptions on stone."[81] Only when Yahweh wrote His law on their heart (i.e., "radical surgery"[82] on a national level in the future) would Israel, as a nation, be able to avoid rebellion and live in genuine submission to His demands. The promise of the New Covenant later in Jeremiah looks forward to that

---

78 Although this name is probably too firmly entrenched to change it, it would be preferable to refer to it as the Israelite covenant since it was made with the entire nation of Israel and not with Moses (like the Noahic, Abrahamic, and Davidic covenants).

79 R. Showers, *The New Nature* (Loizeaux Brothers, 1986), 33.

80 Showers, *The New Nature*, 33.

81 F. Huey, *Jeremiah, Lamentations*, NAC (Broadman & Holman, 1993), 171.

82 F. Huey, *Jeremiah, Lamentations*, 171.

very phenomenon (Jer 31:31–34). Although Judah's sin is written on
the heart of God's chosen nation in general, God's law will be written
on their heart *at a national level* (= heart circumcision).

In this regard, it is essential to notice a key difference between the
nature of the Mosaic Covenant and the New Covenant. Since the Mosaic Covenant included believing and unbelieving Israelites, participating in that covenant did not *necessarily* include an internal conformity to Yahweh's requirements. God's law was not written on the
heart of an Israelite *as a necessary or automatic part* of participating
in the Mosaic Covenant. Israel's perpetual hard-heartedness (Ps 95:8;
Ezek 3:7; Zech 7:12), stiffened neck (Deut 9:6, 13; 10:16; 31:27; 2 Kings
17:14; Jer 7:26; 17:23; 19:15), and stubbornness (Neh 9:29; Isa 30:1; 65:2;
Jer 6:28; Hos 4:16; 9:15; Zech 7:11) make this reality abundantly clear.

Although the Mosaic Covenant was external in *nature*, it would
be incorrect to conclude that it had nothing to do with an Israelite's
internal disposition. After giving the Ten Commandments to Moses,
Yahweh declares: "Oh, that their hearts would be inclined to fear me
and keep all my commands always, so that it might go well with them
and their children forever!" (Deut 5:29). Biblical spokesmen reminded
God's people that God looks on the heart (1 Sam 16:7), the law must be
kept with the heart (Prov 3:1), the heart determines the issues of life
(Prov 4:23), and that having the law in one's heart occasions delight in
God's will (Ps 40:8 [Heb. 9]).[83]

Throughout the OT, Yahweh places great value on a pure heart
(Ps 51:10 [Heb. 12]; Prov 22:11) and a contrite heart (Ps 51:17 [Heb. 19];
Isa 57:15). He equated those who know righteousness with people in
whose heart is His Law (Ps 51:7). The psalmists (and numerous other
Old Testament individuals) longed to observe God's Law with their
entire being (119:34). The psalmists also declared that God's Law was
in the hearts of His children (37:31). The psalmist delighted in God's
statutes (119:16, 47), longed for His precepts (v. 40), loved His commands (v. 48), took comfort in His ordinances (v. 52),[84] and found
them the joy of his heart (19:8). Jeremiah 3:10 refers to a return to Yahweh as a change of heart (nationally). Jeremiah said repentance was
an inner circumcision (4:4; 9:25–26). Doing anything with "all your

---

83 Showers, *The New Nature*, 34.
84 John Goldingay, *Old Testament Theology* (InterVarsity, 2003), 1:380.

heart and all your soul" required something more than external conformity (Deut 4:29; 6:5; 10:12; 11:13; 13:3; 26:16; Josh 22:5; 1 Sam 12:20, 24).
After giving the great Shema and the command for all Israel to love
Yahweh wholeheartedly (Deut 6:4–5), Moses exhorted his fellow Israelites, "These words, which I am commanding you today, shall be on
your heart" (v. 6).

Clarification on the "Newness" of the New Covenant

The wording of Deuteronomy 30:6 automatically directs one's attention to the language of the New Covenant (Jer 31:31–34; 32:39–41; Ezek
11:19–20; 36:24–27). The prophet Jeremiah, looking forward to a future
day, affirms that Yahweh will imprint His will directly on the heart of
people who participate in this covenant as part of the work of God in
the New Covenant (Jer 31:31–34).[85]

In general, what appears to be new in all these passages is the *comprehensive "interiorization"* of Israel's conduct and worship.[86] At this
point, it is essential to notice a very important distinction. The Old
Testament abundantly evidences the concept of "internal" obedience
long before the introduction of the New Covenant. Doing anything
with "all your heart and all your soul" required something more than
external conformity (Deut 4:29; 6:5; 10:12; 11:13; 3:3; 26:16; Josh 22:5; 1
Sam 12:20, 24). After the great Shema and the command for all Israel
to love Yahweh wholeheartedly (Deut 6:4–5), Moses exhorts his fellow
Israelites: "These commandments that I give you today are to be upon
your hearts" (Deut 6:6). The psalmists claim that this was so for them
(Pss 37:31; 40:8 [Heb. 40:9]). The prophet Isaiah equates those who
know righteousness with people in whose heart is God's law (Isa 51:7).

Walter Kaiser contends that the Mosaic and New Covenants share
at least five features: the same covenant-making God, the same law,
the same divine fellowship ("I will be your God"—Lev 20:7), the same
seed or people, and the same forgiveness.[87] With regard to the last feature, a hymnic statement describing God's character and the manner in which He relates to His people refers to the potential of Israel

---

85 Le Déaut, "Le theme de la circoncision du coeur," 182, n. 16.

86 Le Déaut, "Le theme de la circoncision du coeur," 181.

87 Kaiser, *Toward an Old Testament Theology* (Zondervan, 1991), 233.

experiencing divine forgiveness. For example, Exodus 34:6–7 affirms: "6 Then the Lord passed in front of him and proclaimed: 'Yahweh— Yahweh is a compassionate and gracious God, slow to anger and rich in faithful love and truth, 7 maintaining faithful love to a thousand generations, *forgiving wrongdoing, rebellion, and sin.* But He will not leave the guilty unpunished, bringing the consequences of the fathers' wrongdoing on the children and grandchildren to the third and fourth generation'" (cf. Num 14:18; Deut 5:9–10; Neh 9:17, 31; Pss 86:15; 103:8–12; Joel 2:13; Jonah 4:2). Because of these elements of continuity between the Mosaic and New Covenants, some scholars have referred to the New Covenant as the "Renewed" or "Enlarged" Covenant (see Figure 6.3).[88]

The above emphasis on the continuity between the Mosaic and New Covenants does not disregard the fact that the New Covenant may represent relational issues that were more comprehensive, more effective, more spiritual, and even more glorious than those described by the old covenant.[89] The salient point, however, as it relates to the newness of the features or provisions of the New Covenant, is that not all those features are *entirely new*. One need not regard these internal features of the New Covenant as having had no existence among God's people before the establishment of the New Covenant. In the same fashion, the circumcision of the heart accomplished by Yahweh in the Israelites as a nation in the eschaton does not preclude heart circumcision from having taken place in godly Israelite believers during Israel's historical existence.

Conclusion

Scholars have often debated questions that deal with the nature of Israel's salvation during the Old Testament. The present two passages allow us as Old Testament readers a glimpse of one aspect of that discussion. When Yahweh demanded that Israel conform to His covenantal demands internally (through heart circumcision—Deut 10:16) as well as externally (through physical circumcision—Gen 17), was He

---

88 Kaiser, *Toward an Old Testament Theology*, 234; Clements, *Old Testament Theology*, 103.

89 Kaiser, *Toward an Old Testament Theology*, 234.

asking them to do something for which He had not enabled them? Was the potential for Israel to actually experience heart circumcision from the time of Moses on something that actually awaited the establishment or inauguration of the New Covenant in the distant future? Was God's promise to circumcise Israel's heart (Deut 30:6), a promise given in the wake of Moses' envisioned exile of Israel from the land of promise, an *exclusively future hope*?

This paper suggests that Deuteronomy 30:6 correctly affirms that God's intervention in Israel, bringing about the circumcision of their heart *at a national level* (as part of His restoration of the nation to the land of promise), describes the manner in which God will enable His chosen people, at long last, to conduct themselves as His *servant nation*, directing the attention of each other and the world around them to their God's surpassing glory and greatness. What God will do on a comprehensive or national scale in the future, however, does not preclude Him from enabling His chosen nation from living in genuine conformity to His expectations during their historical existence. By recognizing the existence of a godly remnant, understanding the distinctive nature of the Mosaic and New Covenants, and by giving attention to Moses' intent to impact the generation of Israelites alive in his time, one need not insert a great gulf between God's command for the Israelites to circumcise their hearts (Deut 10:16) and His promise to circumcise their hearts in the eschaton (Deut 30:6).

Figure 6.1: Translation Overview: Deut 10:16

ESV/NKJV/NRSV

Circumcise therefore the foreskin of your heart, and be no longer stubborn.

NASB/NIV

So circumcise your heart, and stiffen your neck no longer.

The Message

So cut away the thick calluses from your heart and stop being so willfully hardheaded.

NCV

Give yourselves completely to serving him, and do not be stubborn any longer.

NJPS

Cut away, therefore, the thickening about your hearts and stiffen your necks no more.

NET/NLT

Therefore, cleanse your heart and stop being so stubborn!

Translation Overview: Deut 30:6

ESV/NASB/NIV/NKJV/NRSV

And the Lord your God will circumcise your heart and the heart of your offspring, so that you will love the Lord your God with all your heart and with all your soul, that you may live.

NCV

The Lord your God will prepare you and your descendants to love Him with your whole being so that you will live.

The Message

God, your God, will cut away the thick calluses on your heart and your children's hearts, freeing you to love God, your God, with your whole heart and soul and live, really live.

NET/NLT

The Lord your God will also cleanse your heart and the hearts of your descendants so that you may love Him with all your mind and being, in order to live.

NJPS

Then the Lord your God will open up your heart and the hearts of your offspring to love the Lord your God with all your heart and soul, in order that you may live.

Figure 6.2: The Present Relevance of Future Events (cf. Deut 30:6)

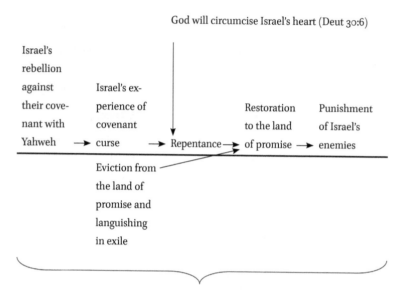

In this set of likely future events**, God's
internal work is a prerequisite if Israel as a
people will be able to genuinely love Yahweh.

** This essay does not develop this nuance. Deuteronomy 29 presents two scenarios, one near and one far, each with a clear, expected set of results. These sections are not purely predictive, but totally expected. In the far-term set of events (29:22–28; Heb. 21–27), Israel's experience of covenant curse will result in the devastation of the land of promise and the eviction of God's people of promise from that land. Chapter 30 presents what will happen after Israel would experience covenant curse, including eviction from the land of promise. If Yahweh brings the devastation of covenant curse on His servant nation, the divine intervention depicted in Deuteronomy 30 will also assuredly take place.

Point of Deuteronomy 30: In the same way that God will provide the only means for restoration and genuine obedience in the wake of covenant judgment, God's intervention in the hearts of the Israelites of Moses' day represents the only way for those Israelites to carry out God's expectations for them as well.

Figure 6.3: What is New in the New Covenant (for Israel)?

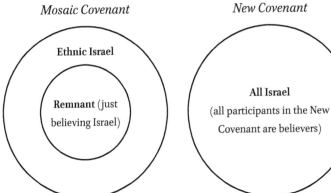

| **Mosaic Covenant** | **New Covenant** |

Nature of Covenant: External Reality (since it included unbelievers)- not necessarily internal in impact

All Israel (Ethnic)- Every member of the nation of Israel was a participant in the Mosaic Covenant. However, not every member of God's chosen people enjoyed OT salvation.

Remnant (Spiritual Israel)- Only those members of the nation of Israel who enjoyed a faith relationship with Yahweh had God's law written on their heart and had the ability to bring any glory to God.

Point: Not all Israelites had the Law of God written on their heart since not all Israelites enjoyed salvation

Nature of Covenant: Internal Reality (since it only included believers) (no insiders and outsiders).

Every New Covenant Participant- Everyone who participated in the New Covenant would have God's Law written on their heart and have the ability to bring glory to His name (imperfectly since man-kind still possesses a sinful nature).

Point: All Israelites would have the Law of God written on their heart since all Israelites at that time will enjoy salvation (Rom 11:26- "all Israel will be saved"

7

Where Did David Go?: David's Wilderness Wanderings and the Testing of God's Son

Abner Chou

D R. VARNER HAS MENTORED ME both as a student and as a colleague. I owe much of my learning, teaching style, ministry philosophy, and academic career to him. This essay intends to honor him by perusing a convergence of his interests in discourse analysis (an examination of large portions within a book), intertextuality,[1] and the Messiah in the OT.

In a lot of ways, "connect the dots" sums up the task of biblical theology. In connect the dots, we know that the dots on the page are not random but link together to create a picture. We know then that each dot matters; each dot plays an important role in light of the whole. Furthermore, we also know that the more dots we connect, the more complete the picture is. These principles apply to biblical theology. In biblical theology, we endeavor to connect the dots (or passages) of Scripture to form the grander scheme of God's plan. This larger picture helps to show the value of each passage even as each passage helps to construct the whole. Moreover, the more passages we collate, the clearer the larger biblical theological picture becomes.

All of this is illustrated in our Lord's temptations in Matthew 4. The text has plenty of allusions. Jesus quotes from Deuteronomy. His

---

1 In certain circles, intertextuality refers to deconstructionism. However, the usage here refers to the literary phenomenon that is deemed by some as "traditional intertextuality" which stresses authorial intent. See Heinrich F. Plett, "Intertextualities," in *Intertextuality*, ed. Heinrich F. Plett (de Gruyter, 1991), 3–7.

sojourn parallels Israel's wilderness wanderings.[2] His fasting for "forty days and nights" resembles Moses (cf. Exod 24:18) and perhaps Elijah (1 Kgs 19:8).[3] To be sure, our Lord's trials do not happen in a vacuum. By connecting these dots, we can better understand the significance of this moment. Jesus' temptations are not merely a lesson on how to handle our own trials. Rather, Matthew's rich intertextual tapestry presents Jesus as the culmination of Israel, Moses and Elijah. They failed but He will overcome and complete their work. Allison has aptly advanced this thesis.[4]

Having observed this, I would say that this picture is valid yet incomplete. We are missing a dot that could provide us with a more holistic picture of what is happening in Matthew. That dot is David. After all, the issue of David is central in Matthew's gospel (Matt 1:1). Davidic kingship is even critical within the temptation narrative. Satan asks if Jesus is the "Son of God," which is a title for the Davidic ruler (2 Sam 7:13–14; Ps 2:7). Even more, David has his own wilderness sojourn just like Moses, Israel, and Elijah (1 Sam 21:1–26:25). Could David not serve as part of the backdrop of Jesus' wilderness sojourn as well?

That is what I would like to explore in this essay. To do this, we first need to ascertain that Matthew does in fact allude back to David's wanderings. Having established such a connection, we then need to interpret it. That requires us to go back and observe the biblical theological significance of David's time in the wilderness. Within this, I contend that David's wilderness journey brings together a biblical theology of the wilderness. His sojourn connects back with the journeys of Israel and Moses. His sojourn also sets up for a new David who too will come forth from wilderness (Mic 1:15) to deliver His people from their own wilderness of exile (cf. Isa 40:3). Thus, the wilderness scenes are not random events but a tightly bound theme in God's plan. This explains why Matthew makes so many allusions in

---

2 J. Nolland, *The Gospel of Matthew*, NIGTC (Eerdmans, 2005), 162; Donald Hagner, *Matthew 1–13*, WBC (Word Books, 1993), 61.

3 Dale C. Allison, *The New Moses: A Matthean Typology* (Fortress Press, 1993), 168–70. See also, I. Howard Marshall, *Gospel of Luke*, NIGTC (Eerdmans, 1978), 168. If one widens the discussion to Luke's account, then Adam is also involved in the background of this narrative, especially since Luke in context presents a genealogy that traces back to him.

4 Allison, *The New Moses*, 168–70.

his account of Jesus' wilderness trials. They are not arbitrary. Rather, the gospel writer draws on a singular thread bound together in David. Matthew follows the logic of the biblical theology of the wilderness.

In light of this, the title of my essay, "Where did David go," is a little bit of double entendre. Initially, we may ask that question as we ponder why David is missing from the discussion of Matt 4. We then ask the question again as we investigate David's own wilderness sojourn only to discover that his experience ties together an entire biblical theological theme from OT to NT. Where did David go is indeed an apt question.[5]

Nevertheless, the point of all this is not only to muse on the interconnectedness of Scripture. To the contrary, this entire discussion sharpens our grasp of the theological significance of Matthew 4. The passage does not merely talk about Jesus being better than past OT figures as scholars have observed (see above). It does so in a particular way. As we will see, Matthew's point is that the wilderness trials prove that Jesus fulfills a specific role, anticipation, and theology established in the compounding wilderness plotline of the OT. Namely, Jesus is the one destined to raise up the tattered ashes of the Davidic dynasty from the wilderness and thereby fulfill the climatic role of all Israel's past leaders to deliver God's people from their own wilderness. Jesus is the new and final David. The "missing dot" of David's wanderings provides us a more complete biblical theological picture about the Messiah.

DAVID'S WANDERINGS AND JESUS' TEMPTATIONS

Is there a legitimate connection between Jesus' wilderness trials and David's wanderings? Put differently, is David's wilderness time really a "dot" in Matthew's biblical theological backdrop? If not, then the rest of this essay is moot.

Hence, the goal of the following discussion is to make the case that David is in the background of Jesus' trials.[6] To be clear, I am not argu-

---

5 In fact, one could argue that Israel (particularly, post-exilic Israel) might ask the question "where did David go" in light of their expectation for the new Davidic king. The question is indeed fitting.

6 We could make some initial observations to this end that even fulfill Hays' criteria for an echo (see Richard B. Hays, *Echoes of Scripture in the Letters of Paul* (Yale

ing that everything in Matthew 4 alludes to David's wilderness journey. Rather, my point is David's sojourn serves as part of the substructure to Matthew's narration of Jesus' experience in the wilderness. It is a critical component of what grounds that occasion and has key points of contact in Matthew's story.

Proof 1: The Intertextuality of Discourse Analysis

One of the most major evidences of a connection between Jesus and David is not a word or phrase but the very structure of their trials. The way their wilderness wanderings are organized contain fundamental striking similarities which show they are indeed parallel.

To see this, we need to ascertain the structure of David's wilderness wanderings in 1 Sam 21–26.[7] Within this, we can initially observe that 1 Sam 21–22 are a unit. Chapter 21 begins with David lying for bread and chapter 22 ends with the priests being killed because of that lie. This inclusio ties these two chapters together. Thus, 1 Sam 21–22 is the first unit of David's sojourn in the wilderness.

How do we think through the rest of David's wanderings in 1 Sam 23–26? In answering this question, 1 Sam 24 and 26 are critical. They both record a highly similar event where David could have killed Saul but refrains. Some scholars argue that these events are one and the

---

University Press, 1989), 17–24.). As noted, the language of "Son of God" also alludes back to David himself (Matt 4:3; cf. Ps 2:7), which is significant given that Davidic kingship is the theme of the book (cf. Matt 1:1). This begins to address both Hays' criteria of volume and thematic coherence. In addition, since 1 Samuel precedes Matthew and is alluded to elsewhere in the book (Matt 12:3), we can meet the criteria of availability and recurrence. Even more, the intertextual nature of the temptation narrative (e.g., note quotations of Deuteronomy and allusions to Israel) is also a form of recurrence. It demonstrates the gospel writers were thinking of a variety of texts in the background of this passage. That makes it far more likely Matthew included David's wanderings into this matrix. These observations already indicate it is not unreasonable for us to detect allusions to David in Matthew. That theme is dominant in the gospel and even in the particular narrative, Matthew indicates he is thinking intertextually and within that, even uses certain terms to trigger a connection with David. Nevertheless, this is all preliminary and is nice supplementary (or even introductory) evidence to what I will present below.

7 Christo H. J. Van der Merwe, "A Critical Analysis of Narrative Syntactic Approaches, with Special Attention to Their Relationship to Discourse," in *Narrative Syntax and the Hebrew Bible*, ed. E. J. van Wolde (Brill, 2002), 136–43.

same but that is incorrect.[8] Nevertheless, one must still account for why the author records such similar events. Like in other instances (cf. Gen 12:10–20; 20:1–18), these parallels create symmetry in the plotline.[9] Accordingly, these chapters help structure David's time in the wilderness.

We have two options for how these chapters could structure David's wanderings. They could be an inclusio such that chapters 24–26 are one unit. If so, David's encounter with Saul at En Gedi (1 Sam 24) would begin a section which concludes with his reengagement with Saul in the wilderness of Ziph (1 Sam 26). Alternatively, chapters 24 and 26 could be parallel, each serving as the conclusions to certain sections of the narrative. In that case, David's time at En Gedi would finish the section beginning in 1 Sam 23 (structural unit: 1 Sam 23–24). Likewise, 1 Sam 26 would conclude the next section (structural unit: 1 Sam 25–26).

The latter view is best for the following reasons:

1. The endings of both 1 Sam 24 and 26 indicate a hard break from what happens in their respective next chapters. Commentators agree that 1 Sam 26 is separate from chapter 27.[10] However, 1 Sam 24 and 26 share essentially identical endings in grammar and content. They both contrast David's and Saul's departures to different places:

	Disjunctive clause + preposition	*Wayyiqtol* + preposition
1 Sam 24:23	וְדָוִד וַאֲנָשָׁיו עָלוּ עַל־הַמְּצוּדָה	וַיֵּלֶךְ שָׁאוּל אֶל־בֵּיתוֹ
1 Sam 26:25	וְשָׁאוּל שָׁב לִמְקוֹמוֹ	וַיֵּלֶךְ דָּוִד לְדַרְכּוֹ

---

8 Gordon observes that one may play the comparisons between the two far too greatly. See Robert P. Gordon, "David's Rise and Saul's Demise: Narrative Analogy in 1 Samuel 24–26," *TynBul* 31 (1980): 40–42. Differences of locations and details of plot lend credence that they are actually two distinct events. See also, David T. Tsumura, *The First Book of Samuel*, NICOT (Eerdmans, 2007), 594–95.

9 See discussion in K. A. Matthews, *Genesis 11:27–50:26*, NAC (Broadman and Holman, 2005), 248.

10 Ralph W. Klein, *1 Samuel*, WBC (Word Books, 1983), 262; Tsumura, *The First Book of Samuel*, 607.

Consistently, if the ending of chapter 26 structurally separates it from the next chapter, so the identical ending of chapter 24 should do the same. This eliminates the inclusio view. First Sam 24–26 cannot be a unit when 1 Sam 24 does not grammatically connect with chapter 25. Instead, the grammar indicates both serve as conclusions to their respective sections (1 Sam 23–24; 25–26).

2. The proposed units fit well together. First Samuel 23–24 cohere together. We can observe this in numerous ways. Both chapters heavily use the term "hand" (יָד). In fact, 1 Sam 23–24 use the term twice as many times as 1 Sam 25–26.[11] The repeated usage plays into a major theme of the chapters. In context, the word is used often in the question of whether God gives a certain person/group (e.g., David, Philistines, Saul) into the *hand* of another. Thus, the unique frequency of this word binds these chapters together both linguistically and thematically. A literary perspective reinforces this connection. 1 Sam 24 picks up right where 1 Sam 23 leaves off. At the end of 1 Sam 23, Saul calls off his hunt for David to confront the Philistines (vv. 27–28). In 1 Sam 24:2, the author discusses how when Saul finished with the Philistines, he returned to pursuing David. Furthermore, 1 Sam 23 and 24 are connected from a geographical perspective. The ending of 1 Sam 23 speaks of David's flight to En Gedi (v. 29).[12] This is the location of 1 Sam 24. The fact that 1 Sam 24 references and continues the plotline and location of 1 Sam 23 shows they are an integrated unit. These observations indicate the interconnectedness between chapters 23 and 24.

3. Not only do chapters 23–24 cohere together, 1 Sam 25 and 26 do so as well. One significant piece of overlap is the use of the root נגף (smite). First Samuel rarely uses this word, but it is found in 1 Sam 25:38 and 26:10.[13] God smites (נגף) Nabal, David's enemy in 1 Sam 25:38 and then David replies to Abishai that the Lord will smite his enemies in 1 Sam 26:10. As will be discussed, this becomes a major thematic element in chapters 25–26. Such word play demands that

---

11   Cf. 1 Sam 23:4, 7, 11, 12, 14, 17, 20; 24:4, 6, 10, 11, 12, 13, 15, 18, 20.

12   John I. Durham, *Exodus*, WBC (Thomas Nelson, 1987), 229.

13   Other instances found in 1 Sam 4:2, 3, 10; 7:10. All of these passages are remote from the David's wanderings in chapters 21–26. This further evidences that נגף could tie chapters 25 and 26 together.

chapters 25–26 are bound together. It shows that the author designed these chapters to fit together.

In light of this analysis, David's wilderness wanderings in 1 Sam 21–26 breaks down into three units. First, we have 1 Sam 21–22 which revolves around David's lie about bread. Second, we have a narrative ending with David's confrontation of Saul at En Gedi (1 Sam 23–24). Third, we also have a section ending with a second confrontation at Ziph (1 Sam 25–26). *In sum, the author of Samuel organizes David's time in the wilderness around three major sections or trials and the first of these deals with bread.*

At this point, we should ask who else is tested three times in the wilderness with the first of those trials dealing with bread? Answer: Jesus. The very setting and structure of Jesus' wilderness experience is designed to give the reader textual déjà vu with what David experienced. This itself is strong evidence that David is part of the narrative substructure of Matthew 4. David's wanderings explain the very way the event is organized in God's providence.

Proof 2: Parallels Between the First Test of David and Jesus

If David's and Jesus' sojourn parallel each other in their overarching structure, could their details parallel each other as well? We can begin answering this by examining the first tests of David and Jesus.

The above discussion has already brought out a key linguistic connection between their first temptations. Both share the term "bread." This is significant given how the word functions in both contexts. It is not only the focus of David's and Jesus' test (1 Sam 21:1–9; 22:6–23; Matt 4:4), but it is also the *first* of those temptations. Such an exact use of "bread" can hardly be coincidental. It evidences that Jesus' and David's first wilderness tests are parallel.

Based upon this, we can further observe some fundamental thematic parallels between the two stories as well. Both Jesus' and David's first test allude back to Israel. Jesus cites Deut 8:3, drawing upon Israel's wilderness sojourn. As will be later discussed, David's trial about bread parallels Israel's own struggle about bread in the wilderness.[14]

---

14 See below. See discussion in Robert D. Bergen, *1, 2 Samuel*, NAC (Broadman and Holman, 1996), 220.

Hence, both trials share the same textual base. Moreover, both Jesus' and David's temptation around bread deal with obedience to God's Word. Jesus puts it plainly. Per Deut 8:3, man should not live by bread alone but obey God's Word.[15] David's first test deals with this too. Throughout 1 Sam 21–22, David's lack of trust in God for bread (1 Sam 21:1–9) is contrasted with his reliance upon God's revelation for various situations (cf. 1 Sam 21:10–15; 1 Sam 22:1–5). Bergen puts it well:

> In obeying the Torah—even though it meant leaving a stronghold built by human hands, David would find himself in a far safer stronghold, Yahweh himself (cf. 2 Sam 23:14; Ps 18:2 [Hb. v. 3]; 31:3 [Hb. v. 4]; 144:2).[16]

Thus, David's and Jesus' first trial have linguistic and thematic overlap. They are tested over the same object (bread) concerning the same principle (dependence upon God's Word).

Proof 3: Parallels Between the Second Test of David and Jesus

Do the parallels continue in the second temptation of both David and Jesus? Certain linguistic parallels initially indicate an association. One might observe the usage of the term "hand" found in both accounts (יָד, χείρ), but the link is not strong.[17] A better potential connection is the use of the term "pinnacle" (πτερύγιον) in both texts.

---

15 See Peter C. Craigie, *The Book of Deuteronomy*, NICOT (Eerdmans, 1976), 185.

16 Bergen, *1, 2 Samuel*, 226. Bergen argues that Gad's command was based upon the Mosaic law that Israel was not to make treaties with Moab (cf. Deut 23:2–6). If the "stronghold" is in Moab, this makes sense; however, that is not a certain fact especially since David departs from the king of Moab. Nonetheless, the principle of what Bergen observes is true. David lies and violates God's Word before but now learns that obedience is far better and far safer. The next pericope of the slaughter of the priests illustrates this very reality.

17 As mentioned, the term "hand" is a keyword which links 1 Sam 23–24 together. Interestingly enough, the term is mentioned as Satan tempts Jesus. He says that the angels will carry Jesus by the hand (Matt 4:6). Some may object that the term "hand" is only here because of an OT quotation. At the same time, the OT quotation is modified to give the phrase "upon their hand they will bear you up" prominence. The quotation is from Ps 91:11–12. However, the latter part of Ps 91:11 is omitted to front v. 12a which mentions hand. However, this may be explained in alternative ways. For example, Satan omits v. 11b in order to discuss the issue of the angels *bearing* Jesus up

Jesus is tested at the temple pinnacle (Matt 4:5) and David cuts the "tip" or "pinnacle" of Saul's robe (1 Sam 24:6, 12). Several factors suggest that Matthew deliberately chose this word to point back to part of David's second test. Scholars note that the use of πτερύγιον is baffling because it has not been used in other literature to designate a specific place within the temple. For certain locations, other terms would be far more appropriate (ὑπέρθυρον).[18] Nevertheless, Matthew uses πτερύγιον, a word that is not only rare in biblical usage but also used primarily to describe clothing as opposed to buildings (Num 15:38; Ruth 3:9; 1 Sam 15:27).[19] Hence, by using πτερύγιον, Matthew uses a term that is rare and perhaps not as fitting for the context.[20] So why does Matthew use this word? The very question asked by commentators is indicative of the potential linguistic distinctiveness of the word. Such unusual word choice would grab the reader's attention. Given the already present associations between Matthew and 1 Samuel, this would direct them back to David.[21] Matthew's unusual word choice gives further "volume" (to use Hays' terminology) to the association between David's and Jesus' second test in their respective wilderness wanderings.

Consistently, their second trials also contain significant thematic overlap. These second trials revolve around whether people will misuse God's revelation to act recklessly. Jesus' test explicitly portrays this. Satan misuses Ps 91:11–12 to tempt Jesus to perform a public stunt and test God. David's trial has a similar logic. This is brought out by word play. At En Gedi, David's men encourage him to strike Saul down because God gave Saul into David's *hand* (1 Sam 24:4). The use of "hand" recalls earlier instances when God gave David's enemies into his *hand* (1 Sam 23:2, 4, 11–12). However, in this context, God never made such a

---

which is appropriate in the situation of Jesus leaping from the pinnacle of the temple. Hence, this evidence is not absolutely compelling.

18 See BDAG, 895. See also, Hagner, *Matthew 1–13*, 66.

19 The word only occurs in the gospels in this event and seventeen times in Greek translations of the OT. See BDAG, 895.

20 The term is not extant in other literature of describing a designated point of the temple.

21 Alternative is the suggestion that this refers to Ps 91:4 and angels carrying someone on their wings. This could be a connection as well given the usage of Ps 91 in context. However, that part is not quoted in Satan's statement of Ps 91 and the term is slightly different (wing, πτέρυγας, instead of pinnacle, πτερύγιον).

promise about Saul. David's friends have twisted God's words akin to what Satan will do to Jesus. Alter observes:

> David's eager men exhibit a certain theological presumptuousness. They surely know that their leader has been secretly anointed to be king, but nothing in the preceding narrative indicates a divine promise that God would deliver Saul into David's hands.[22]

So, when David cuts Saul's robe, he acts independently and recklessly. For this reason, he is convicted of stretching out his *hand* against the Lord's anointed (1 Sam 24:6). David acted irresponsibly because of a distorted understanding of God's Word.

With that, the second set of trials share thematic overlap not only on a general level but even in the precise mechanism (misuse of divine revelation) by which this takes place. While the situations may differ, the second test of David and Jesus revolve around the same issue and have linguistic ties to bind them together.

Proof 4: Parallels Between the Third Test of David and Jesus

The parallels between Jesus and David continue into their respective third and final tests. We can observe this linguistically. Both tests (1 Sam 25–26; Matt 4:10) mention "falling down" (πίπτω) and "worshipping" (προσκυνέω) (1 Sam 26:19; Matt 4:10). Both also reference not worshipping other gods (1 Sam 26:19; Matt 4:10). Both even allude to the same base texts. In Matthew, Jesus quotes from Deut 6:13 to refute Satan. In 1 Samuel, David's reference to serving other gods goes back to Deut 6:14 (see also Deut 7:14; 8:19). Substantial linguistic associations exist between Jesus and David on this front.

This spills over into the thematic association between their tests. Both David's and Jesus' trials revolve around whether they will wait on the Lord or seize the kingdom prematurely. Once again, Jesus' test displays this succinctly. Will He obtain the kingdom by bowing to Satan or go through the path God has set for Him (Matt 4:8–11)?[23]

---

22 Robert Alter, *The David Story: A Translation and Commentary with 1 and 2 Samuel* (W. W. Norton & Company, 1999), 147.

23 L. Morris, *The Gospel According to Matthew*, PNTC (Eerdmans, 2000), 77.

We can observe a similar issue for David in his interaction with Nabal.[24] In response to Nabal's insolence, David sets his heart to kill the man (25:13). By taking matters into his own hands, he prematurely becomes judge, executioner, and king.[25] Abigail points out this folly to David (1 Sam 25:30–31). She reminds him that when he actually becomes king, any act against Nabal would be considered shameful because David did it as personal vengeance and not as a ruler. David should not act presumptively, and he learns his lesson. When the opportunity to kill Saul again arises, David refrains. Instead, he states that the Lord will strike him down in His own timing (26:10). The word "to strike" (נגף) is the same word Abigail used to remind David that God would deal with his foes. By this word play, David shows he has learned not to do things his own way but rather the way God has set for him.[26] David's final test concerns not usurping authority but doing things the Lord's way and in His timing.

With that, the third trial of both David and Jesus overlaps significantly. Both share the same language surrounding the temptation and the response. Both share the same underlying principle. In fact, both

---

24 In 1 Sam 25–26, Nabal on a literary level assumes the role of Saul. John Van Seters, "Two Stories of David Sparing Saul's Life in 1 Samuel 24 and 26: A Question of Priority," *SJOT* 25, no. 1 (2011): 93–104; W Lee Humphreys, "The Tragedy of King Saul: A Study of the Structure of 1 Samuel 9–31," *Journal for the Study of the Old Testament* 6 (1978): 18–21; W Lee Humphreys, "From Tragic Hero to Villain: A Study of the Figure of Saul and the Development of 1 Samuel," *JSOT* 22 (1982): 97–100; W Lee Humphreys, "The Rise and Fall of King Saul: A Study of an Ancient Narrative Stratum in 1 Samuel," *JSOT* 18 (1980): 74–80.a constructive scene (10:17–11:15; 16:14–19:10 See also, Gordon, "David's Rise and Saul's Demise," 49–52. Similarities between the two include their status as prominent men (cf. 1 Sam 25:2), their antipathy toward David (cf. the language of Nabal and Saul in 1 Sam 25:10 with 20:27, 30), their absolute folly (cf. name of Nabal with Saul playing the fool in 1 Sam 26:21) and how David addresses both of them (cf. the language of sonship in 1 Sam 25:8 with 26:17, 21, 15. See also Alter, *The David Story*, 154–55.

25 This becomes more poignant in light of the kingly way David acts. David offers protection (1 Sam 25:14–19) and requests aid *in his name* (1 Sam 25:3–6). These are actions of a king. The test of whether David will act upon his assertions of royal authority is provoked by Nabal's response. Nabal regards David as a runaway slave (1 Sam 25:8).

26 This is why David appeals to Saul to allow him to return, for he does not want to serve other gods (1 Sam 26:19–20) but the one true God. This of course has parallels with Jesus' response that one must worship and serve God alone.

allude to the same passages in Deuteronomy as the foundation for their respective discussions. This further demonstrates how David's trials are the substructure for Jesus'.

Synthesis

Does Matthew draw from David's wilderness wanderings? If we synthesize what we observed above, the evidence is compelling. At every juncture of the narrative, Matthew establishes links that anchor Jesus' wanderings into David's. The structure of Matthew's narrative parallels David. Each respective trial contains word choices that uniquely hook into David's narrative. Matthew even presents the mechanism of the trials in a way that shows David and Jesus are tempted about the same issues conceptually.

All of these factors cannot be coincidental, especially since Matthew already explicitly states he is focused upon David in context (cf. Matt 1:1). To be sure, one could argue that God in His providence set up these parallels. That is true. However, we can also observe Matthew did not have to recount the wilderness wanderings the way he does. Mark and Luke have alternative orders and presentations of this episode. That brings out how Matthew's wording and structure are not because of "tradition" but rather stem from his deliberate choices. In light of the above observations, part of those choices are driven by a desire to highlight the resonance of Jesus' trials with David's. Matthew intends to show that our Lord's experience recapitulates David.

To be clear, Matthew is not exclusively drawing from 1 Samuel nor does everything in his narrative tie with David's sojourn. As noted, a variety of allusions occur (e.g., Moses, Israel, and Elijah). Nevertheless, the above evidence shows that David is a missing "dot" in all of that.

David's Wanderings in the Plotline of Scripture

Having said this, we should now ask why Matthew alludes to David. For that matter, why does Matthew also allude to Moses, Israel, and Elijah? Is there any reason to connect them all together? These questions prompt us to further contemplate David's wanderings. As we will see, David's time in the wilderness is not random. Rather, it is designed to recapitulate the experiences of David's predecessors and thereby define what it means to be king. This episode draws together a biblical theological theme of the wilderness running through the OT.

The Intertextual Nature of Wilderness

One of the foundational bridges between David and past revelation deals with the very term "wilderness" (מִדְבָּר). Although we might think the word is common in the OT, the chart below shows how often מִדְבָּר appears in a book in comparison with how many times the word occurs in the OT. In light of this, only a select number of books (those above five percent) establish the dominant usage of the word and thereby provide its major connotations.[27]

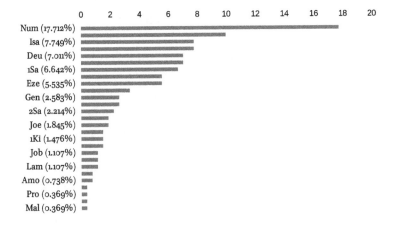

In the books where "wilderness" is used frequently, it refers only to Israel's wilderness wanderings, David's wanderings in the wilderness (especially in Psalms), or the exile of Israel (in Isaiah and Jeremiah). Accordingly, contrary to what we might think, the term "wilderness"

---

27 One might wonder if such analysis changes if one compares how often מִדְבָּר occurs within a book with how many words there are in a book. After all, perhaps certain books have a greater number of usages just because they are larger books while a smaller book might actually use the word more frequently relative to its size. In running this analysis, the only substantive difference would be the book of Joel. However, even there, the term "wilderness" seems to allude to Israel's judgment and culmination of exile. Duane A. Garrett, *Hosea, Joel*, NAC (Broadman & Holman Publishers, 1997), 330. This too establishes the above analysis.

does not describe just any event but is reserved for a very tight cluster of events. It essentially serves as a technical descriptor of these moments. For this reason, as we will see, the term helps to establish a foundation for an entire biblical theology of wilderness in the OT.

Nevertheless, at this point of the discussion, the use of "wilderness" in 1 Samuel triggers us to think back to Exodus and Numbers; i.e., Israel's wilderness wanderings and even Moses' own wilderness sojourn. By situating David in the same setting, the author of 1 Samuel begins to put him in parallel with those before him. Let us examine how David links with both Israel and Moses.

David's Wanderings and Israel

While the word "wilderness" in David's sojourn alludes back to Israel, the connections do not end there. Rather, the term merely gets us started to see how thoroughly David's wilderness wanderings link with Israel's. Bergen has done tremendous work showing compounding factors that present David as a recapitulation of Israel.[28] For example, both David and Israel desire to eat bread (1 Sam 21:3; Exod 16:3–4). Even more, the incident of bread happens early on in both of their sojourns. Not only are the events parallel but the timing of them is parallel as well. This does not appear to be coincidence.

The list continues. Both Israel and David run away from hostile kings. Both do so before they possess their inheritance. Both have a stay in Moab where God protects them (cf. Num 11:11–26; 1 Sam 22:3–4). Both have conflict with the Amalekites (cf. Exod 17:15–16; Deut 25:17–19; 1 Sam 30:1–31). This latter parallel is particularly significant. In Israel's wanderings, God decrees that Amalek should be wiped out (Exod 17:16). David's wanderings work to accomplish that purpose (see 1 Sam 30:1–31; contra Saul in 1 Sam 15:1–3). This poses David as the one who continues Israel's mandate begun in the wilderness.[29] There appears to be continuity (even climax) between Israel as a nation and David, and all of that is formulated in their wilderness sojourns.

We can make one final observation that ties David and Israel together. After Samuel's death, David flees to the wilderness of Paran

---

28 Bergen, 1, 2 Samuel, 220–26.

29 Bergen, 1, 2 Samuel, 168, 273–74.

(1 Sam 25:1). The mention of this geographical location is somewhat strange since David's activity will end up elsewhere (Maon, v. 2). It is also far away from all of David's other activities in the wilderness. For these reasons, the Greek translations changes the word Paran to Maon. Nevertheless, the MT is to be preferred.[30] Why does the author go out of his way to include this unusual fact?[31] Arguably, since Israel wandered in Paran, so the author mentions this to remind all that David is recapitulating Israel. Bergen puts it well:

> Favoring the Paran location is the fact that David's life is deliberately presented as a parallel to the history of Israel; this portion of David's life is more closely parallel with Israel if he, like Israel, spent time in the Desert of Paran (cf. Num 10:12ff.). Furthermore, the Desert of Paran, which included Kadesh Barnea, was situated on the southern border of tribal territories allotted to Judah (cf. Josh 15:3) and thus provided the most isolated location within David's homeland for hiding from Saul.[32]

Overall, the author of 1 Samuel has paralleled David's wanderings with Israel's in numerous ways. Repeatedly, David's and Israel's experiences share the same terminology, geography, and even kinds of events. When given the opportunity, the narrator casts David's wilderness sojourn in light of Israel's experience.

David's Wanderings and Moses

The author of Samuel not only casts David as Israel but also as Moses. To prove this, we can initially make some broad parallels between the two and then zero in on some similarities within David's wilderness wanderings.

On a general level, scholars have noted quite a few substantial parallels between the two. Both David and Moses are shepherds (Exod 3:1; 1 Sam 16:11), have the title "man of God" (Deut 33:1; 2 Chron 8:14),

---

30 Bergen, *1, 2 Samuel*, 243; Tsumura, *The First Book of Samuel*, 575.

31 There is a textual critical issue of Paran. Arguably though, the Paran reading is the *lectio difficilior*. The LXX reads τὴν ἔρημον Μααν most likely because Maon is closer in proximity.

32 Bergen, *1, 2 Samuel*, 263.

commission the building of God's house (Exod 25:1–31:18; 2 Sam 7:1–3), and must pass on the completion of their work to another man (e.g., Joshua and Solomon).[33] These parallels are not merely conceptual but linguistic. For example, both Moses and David say, "Be strong and courageous" (חֲזַק וֶאֱמָץ) (Deut 31:23; 1 Kgs 2:2; 1 Chron 22:13). David also gives the exact same exhortations Moses did to Israel (Ps 27:14; 31:24; cf. Deut 31:6). In addition, David uses the same terminology for the pattern of the tabernacle (תַּבְנִית, cf. Exod 25:9) in his instructions for the temple (1 Chron 28:11). Traditionally, the rabbis believed that David took on the role and mantle of Moses.[34] These examples confirm such an idea. Moses and David share a fundamental connection.

These overarching associations extend into the wilderness account in 1 Samuel. During that time, David possesses the same title as Moses. Both are called prince (שַׂר; 1 Sam 22:2; Exod 2:14). In addition, we can observe a parallel at the beginning of their wanderings. Both encounter bitterness from the start of their sojourn (מַר), whether that be at Marah (Exod 15:23) or in personal experience (1 Sam 22:2). Just as Moses was a prince who led a bitter people, so David also leads a band of men who are equally bitter. We can also observe a parallel at the end of their wanderings. At the conclusion of David's wanderings, he makes a regulation concerning the spoils of war (1 Sam 30:25). The narrator declares that his words are לְחֹק וּלְמִשְׁפָּט לְיִשְׂרָאֵל. Such phraseology is significant. So far in Scripture, the collocation of חֹק and מִשְׁפָּט only refers to the law given by Moses.[35] By applying this distinctive phrase to David, the author makes his point: David's word is equal to Moses'. At the conclusion of the wilderness time, David emerges as a continuation of Moses.

With that, David's wanderings are rooted in Moses. He parallels Moses at the beginning and at the end of his sojourn. Even the *telos* of the wilderness journey involves raising up David to be like Moses. For the author of 1 Samuel, the connection with Moses is a key theological point within David's time in the wilderness.

---

33 Allison, *The New Moses*, 35–37.

34 Allison, *The New Moses*, 35–37.

35 See Exod 15:25; Lev 26:46; Deut 4:1, 5, 8, 14, 45; 5:1, 31; 6:1, 20; 7:11; Josh 24:25. Even in Josh 24:25, Joshua reaffirms the Mosaic covenant with the people of Israel using the terms.

Biblical Theological Significance of David, Israel, and Moses

We have noted some associations between the wilderness sojourns of David, Israel, and Moses. What is the significance of all of this? Bergen both sums up the parallels and hints at their contribution:

> These nine chapters depict David's "wilderness experience." As Israel's wilderness experience followed an exodus from a foreign king, so David's followed an exodus from a king "such as all the other nations have." And as the wilderness for Israel preceded possession of the Promised Land, so for David it preceded possession of a promised kingdom. Furthermore, during this wilderness period David experienced events that in crucial ways paralleled those of the Israelites following their expulsion from Egypt—pursuit by the armed forces of the king they were fleeing, a hostile encounter with the Midianites, an attempted foray into Moab, and yet the Lord's protection against all human foes.
>
> These connections between David's life and the Israelites' experiences recorded in the Torah not only magnify the story of David to one of epic proportions, but they also create the expectation that the Lord would ultimately give David the fulfillment of all the good promises made to him.[36]

Bergen's comment about "epic proportions" helps to establish the significance of these connections. David does not merely recapitulate Israel and Moses for the sake of literary artistry. He does so because of a driving biblical theological theme of the wilderness. God refined Israel in the wilderness, and so He also raised up Moses from the wilderness to be their representative and lead them. This logic extends to David, who bears the story of Israel upon himself in order to represent Israel and bring his people to the end of their sojourn. He is the continuation of what Moses was doing in the wilderness. Hence, this wilderness experience becomes a key part of what God does to formulate leaders and specifically, Israel's king.

---

36 Bergen, *1, 2 Samuel,* 220. See also, James M. Hamilton, "Was Joseph a Type of the Messiah? Tracing the Typological Identification between Joseph, David, and Jesus," *SBJT* 12 (2008): 52–77.

From David to New David

The wilderness plotline does not end with David. Subsequent prophets pick up on the wilderness motif. Some confirm the connections made so far between David, Moses, Israel, and the wilderness. Psalm 23 is a good example. In that psalm, David applies language used of how God guided (Ps 23:2; cf. Exod 15:13)[37] and provided for His people (Ps 23:5; cf. Ps 78:19) to himself. Accordingly, David himself believes that his own sojourn is a microcosm of Israel's time in the wilderness.[38]

While some confirm these associations, others build upon them. Asaph, in Psalm 78, does so. Asaph recounts Israel's wilderness wanderings as the backdrop for God's choice of David and his rise to power (cf. Ps 78:1–69).[39] However, in the flow of thought, Asaph asserts that the Davidic dynasty arises in connection with Israel's wilderness wandering to end it.[40] This highlights an important paradigm: the king emerges from the wilderness to bring his people out of the wilderness.

That framework of the "arising in the wilderness to end it," becomes critical for the rest of the wilderness plotline of the OT. To be clear, the wilderness theme does not stop at Moses, Israel, or David. Rather, the prophets develop the storyline from there toward the NT and what we have observed so far will help us understand the trajectory of this theme.

The first part of tracing the ongoing plotline is to see that Israel will return to the wilderness. We can actually see the beginnings of this in David's own wilderness journey. While David's sojourn is formative for him as Israel's king, he by no means is successful within that. In each of the three segments discussed above, David in some way fails. He lies resulting in the death of the priests (1 Sam 22:6–23). He cuts Saul's robe, which he later regrets (24:5). He intends to kill

---

37 The language of "guiding" (נהל) and "green pastures" (נוה) are found concerning Israel in Exod 15:13.

38 Peter C. Craigie, *Psalms 1–50*, WBC (Thomas Nelson, 2004), 207.

39 Marvin Tate, *Psalms 51–100*, WBC (Word Books, 1990), 295.

40 Marvin Tate, *Psalms 51–100*, 295; Erich Hossfeld, Frank-Lothar; Zenger, *Psalms 2: A Commentary on Psalms 51–100*, ed. Klaus Baltzer, trans. Linda M. Maloney (Fortress Press, 2005), 299–300.

Nabal only to be stopped by Abigail (25:13, 21–22). While God refines David in each of these tests, this takes place through his sin.

These failures set up for later failures. For instance, some have observed that David's sin in the Nabal/Abigail incident foreshadow what happens with Bathsheba.[41] David's fiery temper and his marriage to multiple women described in 1 Sam 25 highlight some character issues that set up for his subsequent sins.[42] In response to those crimes, Nathan proclaims that the sword will not leave David's house (2 Sam 12:10). In this way, David's wilderness episode sets redemptive history on a trajectory to the downfall of the Davidic dynasty.

The book of Kings details such a downfall. The Davidic dynasty reaches a point where the kings no longer truly rule Israel/Judah. Accordingly, God raises up prophets, like Elijah, to uphold His Word and hold His people accountable like Moses (1 Kgs 18). Elijah acts as a surrogate king at this time.[43] For this reason, God raises up Elijah in the wilderness like his predecessors. Just as Israel's and David's journey dealt with bread, so does Elijah (1 Kgs 19:6).[44] Just as Moses spent forty days on Mount Sinai (Deut 9:11), so Elijah also has a forty day period revolving around Sinai (1 Kgs 19:8). Even more, just as Moses stood before God's glory on that mountain, so Elijah encounters God's presence (cf. Deut 34:6–8; 1 Kgs 19:11–13).[45] The wilderness plotline continues through Elijah.

However, raising Elijah up in the wilderness does not lead Israel out of the wilderness. In context, Elijah's episode at Sinai solidifies

---

41 Gordon, "David's Rise and Saul's Demise," 52–53.

42 Alter, *The David Story: A Translation and Commentary with 1 and 2 Samuel*, 160–61; Peter D. Quinn-Miscall, *1 Samuel: A Literary Reading* (Indiana University Press, 1986), 156.

43 Paul R. House, *Old Testament Theology* (InterVarsity Press, 1998), 259–61. House presents that God rules through Elijah to demonstrate His supremacy over Baal and Ahab.

44 Note that the term עֻגָה is not commonly used in the OT (only seven times) and the major usages are in the Elijah story (1 Kgs 17:13; 19:6) and Israel's Exodus/wilderness wanderings (Exod 12:39; Num 11:8). David's and Elijah's are associated in their common rootedness in Israel's sojourn.

45 Craig C. Broyles, "Traditions, Intertextuality, and Canon," in *Interpreting the Old Testament: A Guide for Exegesis*, ed. Craig C. Broyles (Baker Books, 2001), 160–65.

Israel's condemnation (1 Kgs 19:14–17).[46] At this point, Israel's history takes a sharp turn in heading to the wilderness. Because of their disobedience, Israel will be put under covenant curse. Per Deuteronomy, those curses will reduce Israel back to the time of their Egyptian and wilderness sojourn (cf. Deut 28:68; see also vv. 27, 46, 60). The failure of the Davidic dynasty and Israel itself will take them back to the wilderness.

This is not merely a logical deduction but the prophets' own viewpoint. Isaiah explicitly describes the exile as a new era in the wilderness. After all, he talks of a "voice crying from the wilderness" (Isa 40:3) and how God will lead Israel out of exile by making a "way in the wilderness" (Isa 43:19). Other prophets parallel Israel's exile with their earlier time in Egypt and the wilderness (Hos 11:1–14; 13:4).[47] The wilderness is not merely indicative of their past but their future.[48]

However, Israel is not just plunged into the wilderness to their doom. Just as God delivered Israel before from the wilderness, so He will be faithful to do again. In Hos 11:1–11, the prophet states that God's love in the first Exodus drives a second Exodus from Israel's exile.[49] Isaiah states that God will make a roadway through the sea and the wilderness (Isa 43:16–20) highlighting a new Exodus and deliverance from the wilderness. The prophets continue the wilderness theme to point to an eschatological and final deliverance from the wilderness.

Like before, such a deliverance requires a leader. In discussing the new Exodus, Hosea speaks of one new leader who will lead the

---

46 Simon J. DeVries, *1 Kings*, 2nd ed., WBC (Word, 2004), 236.

47 Those in Nehemiah's day acknowledge that they are still slaves in their land akin the slavery in Egypt (Neh 9:36). Paul R. House, "Examining the Narratives of Old Testament Narrative: An Exploration in Biblical Theology," *WTJ* 67 (2005): 243–45. Hosea also describes Israel's exile to Assyria as their going down to Egypt once again (7:11, 16; 8:13; 9:3). Zechariah parallels Israel's deliverance from exile with the Feast of Booths (Zech 14:16–19). The logic is that just as God was faithful to Israel in the wilderness (the original purpose of the feast), so He will deliver them from exile. See George L. Klein, *Zechariah*, NAC (B&H Publishing Group, 2008), 423.

48 As noted, the term "wilderness" is a distinctive term used primarily for the wanderings of Israel and David. Isaiah's use of the word ties Israel's exile with that. This makes for an intentional and linguistically distinct connection between the earlier wilderness epochs and Israel's exile.

49 Abner Chou, *The Hermeneutics of the Biblical Writers: Learning Interpretation from the Prophets and Apostles* (Kregel, 2018), 105–10.

second Exodus through the wilderness (1:11; 2:14–23). Hosea antici-
pates a new Moses. Furthermore, he declares that this new Moses is
"David their king" (3:1–5). Isaiah follows suit. The Servant certainly is
characterized as being a Davidic king (cf. Isa 42:1; 7:14; 9:6) but at the
same time the One who leads God's people through the wilderness
(43:2) to the point where His deliverance eclipses the original Exodus
(43:16, 18–19).[50] Like Hosea, Isaiah declares the Messiah is both new
David and new Moses. Even more, Isaiah also calls the Servant Israel
(49:3) for like Moses and David, He must represent Israel as well. With
that, the prophets anticipate a new era of wilderness wanderings, a
new Exodus, and thereby a new David and Moses.

This is where the paradigm of "arising in the wilderness to end it"
(see above) comes back into play. Based upon previous pattern, we
would expect that this new David would arise from the wilderness. After all, Moses, David, and Elijah all experienced this. And Micah confirms that the second David will experience this too. He notes that
Israel is not the only entity back in the wilderness. Micah also states
that the glory of Israel, the Davidic dynasty, has returned to Adullam
(Mic 1:15). Adullam is the location where David began his wilderness
sojourn (1 Sam 22:1). The exile has reduced not only Israel back to
their humble beginning but also the Davidic dynasty. For this reason,
Micah reveals that the new king must be born in Bethlehem (5:2) and
emerge from the wilderness (1:15) —precisely like David—in order to
deliver God's people a second Exodus (7:14–15).[51] Thus, the pattern we
have observed about the wilderness is confirmed. The second and final David must take on the wilderness experience of his predecessors
to fulfill them once and for all.

---

50 John N. Oswalt, *The Book of Isaiah Chapters 40–66*, NICOT (Eerdmans, 1998),
155; A. Motyer, *The Prophecy of Isaiah: An Introduction and Commentary* (InterVarsity
Press, 1993), 337.

51 Cf. Mic 6:4; Kenneth L. Barker, *Micah, Nahum, Habakkuk, Zephaniah*, NAC
(Broadman & Holman Publishers, 1999), 100, 131. Barker and Bailey claim that God
responds with an "exodus theology" already established in the book as well as in the
canon. See also, Leslie C. Allen, *The Books of Joel, Obadiah, Jonah, and Micah*, NICOT
(Eerdmans, 1976), 399. Note also the allusion to "days of old" in Mic 7:14 which seems
to connect with Amos 9:11 referring to the Davidic dynasty. Such terminology layers
Exodus, new Exodus, and new David.

Synthesis

Thus, David's wilderness sojourn is part of a larger "wilderness plotline" in Scripture. The prophets have woven this together via the term "wilderness" and other key scenes/images.

It begins with Moses and Israel and continues into David, whose experience intentionally embodies his people and predecessor (Moses) to form him into the proper leader of God's people. While David is raised up in the wilderness to deliver his people from it, he fails along with his entire dynasty. Because of this and the nation's own disobedience, Israel is also plunged into the wilderness of exile. The wilderness is not merely a past reality for Israel but their future.

Nevertheless, just like before, God will deliver His people again from this new wilderness sojourn. Like before, this will revolve around a new Moses/David. Like before, this demands that this new Moses/David be raised in the wilderness. However, this time though, the second David will definitively end God's people's sojourn.

All of this demonstrates that David is indeed a key "dot" or missing link in this biblical theological storyline. In this theme, he is the glue that ties together Moses, Israel, Elijah, wilderness, new wilderness, Exodus, new Exodus, David, and new David.

With that, the wilderness plotline moves to the NT with the expectation that not only Israel is in the wilderness, but their deliverer must ascend from the wilderness as well. He must succeed in what His predecessors could not so that He can raise up the ruins of Davidic dynasty and fulfill its role in redemptive history.

MATTHEW'S INTERTEXTUALITY: THE KING
HAS TRIUMPHED OVER THE WILDERNESS

Matthew picks up right where the OT wilderness storyline left off. After all, Matthew begins his narrative announcing Israel's exile (Matt 1:17) and a voice crying from that wilderness (Matt 3:3; Isa 40:3).[52] Even more, Matthew poses Jesus as the One who will bring His people from this wilderness. Jesus is the new David born in Bethlehem (Matt 2:1).

---

52 Hagner, *Matthew 1–13*, 6. Concerning Matt 1:17, The lack of repetition of the last name of group two in group three accentuates the exile.

Jesus also is the new Moses, who just like Moses, was delivered at birth from a murderous king (Matt 2:13–17; cf. Exod 1:15–2:10). Thus, Matthew begins not only speaking of Israel's wilderness sojourn but also the birth of the One who will deliver them from it.

Thus, we should not be surprised that Matthew takes us to Jesus' wilderness wanderings. Per the biblical theology of the wilderness, the new David must "arise from the wilderness to end it" and that is precisely where Matthew goes. Consistently, Matthew immerses the reader into the wilderness theme in discussing Jesus' trials. In the very first verse of the narrative, the gospel writer begins by speaking of the "wilderness" (ἔρημος, 4:1), a word Matthew so far has only used to refer to the wilderness motif of the OT (cf. Matt 3:1, 3). Moreover, in the next verse, Matthew states that Jesus fasted for forty days and nights. The number forty harkens back to Israel's own period in the wilderness for forty years.[53] It also is even more reminiscent of Moses' and Elijah's time in the wilderness.[54]

In a brief amount of text, Matthew has connected Jesus' trial to the full gamut of the biblical theology of the wilderness. With that, he deliberately addresses the issues that have developed in the flow of this theme. Is Jesus the One who will end the wilderness sojourn? Is Jesus the second David who is the culmination and fulfillment of all Israel's past leaders? Is He Israel's true king who will embody His people and will not fail like those before Him?

Matthew's presentation of the wilderness temptations definitively answers these questions. Jesus' trials recapitulate Israel, Elijah, Moses, and David. Point for point, He bears all that they endured. Point for point, He suceeds where they have failed. Point for point, He is not merely better than Israel, Elijah, Moses, or even David but the culmination of them all as Israel's ultimate king. His unbreakable character proves He is the One who will raise the Davidic house from its fallen state in the wilderness. And so He emerges triumphant from

---

53 Allison, *The New Moses*, 167–69. Allison will object to this, but it could very well be both in light of the cohesiveness of the wilderness tradition.

54 Allison, *The New Moses*, 166–69. The connection with Moses and Elijah is further confirmed by Jesus' final test. The language of Satan showing Jesus the kingdoms of the world (Matt 4:8–9) matches the language of how God showed Moses the Promised Land in the Greek translation of Deut 34:1–4.

the wilderness as the new David, the true final leader of Israel, and the One who will thereby end Israel's wilderness wanderings of exile. Matthew has continued right where the OT left off and shown how its anticipations are gloriously worked out in Jesus.

Conclusion

Where did David go? We asked this question when we noticed that David has been missing from the discussion of Matthew's depiction of Jesus' wilderness sojourn. We asked this question again in thinking through David's wanderings and discovered a biblical theology of the wilderness. David's wanderings tie together Israel and Moses for he has solidarity with them and encompasses their role. His wanderings also set up for a new David who must arise from the Davidic dynasty's regression back to the wilderness in order to deliver God's people from their own wilderness sojourn of exile. With that, David's wilderness wandering bridges together Israel, Moses, Elijah, and even a new David. In turn, Matthew follows this wilderness trajectory and shows that Jesus fulfills the demand of one who rises from the wilderness to end it.

As stated from the beginning, biblical theology is often akin to connecting the dots and by connecting the missing "dot" of David, we have gained a clearer picture of a major theme in Scripture.[55] This "dot" helps us piece together a complete biblical theology of the

---

55 A clearer picture does not mean a complete picture. To be sure, this individual thread of David and the wilderness participates in, contributes to, and even presumes larger biblical theological realities. For instance, the joint sonship shared between Israel (cf. Exod 4:22) and the Messiah (Ps 2:7) undergirds how the wilderness experience of Israel relates to David even as the David's wilderness experience reinforces the sonship connection. Likewise, the wilderness motif itself can be tied to how God sends Israel out in judgment in the wilderness but will in the end, make all things new in a new creation which overcomes the wilderness (cf. Isa 45:18; Jer 4:23). Such a connection between wilderness, creation, and this particular thread is not merely conceptual but anchored by the usage of wilderness in those prophetic contexts as well as by mention of forty days at Sinai, with Elijah, and with Christ. The forty days goes back to Noah whose salvation through judgment inherently embodies old creation to new creation as the language of the Flood imitates Gen 1 (see most clearly, Gen 9:1 and Gen 1:26–28). This essay may elucidate a particular "dot" which helps clarify a thread of biblical theology, however far more work can still be done.

wilderness flowing from OT to NT. This "dot" also helps us see more clearly Matthew's own agenda in his gospel. His use of the OT in Matt 4 is not random. Rather, his allusions pull on the entire thread of the wilderness and show that Jesus fulfills this specific expectation of a new David. He thereby is the final and true heir of the Davidic dynasty (cf. Matt 1:1).

With that, while biblical theology connects the dots, the aim is not merely to have the bigger picture but to appreciate it. In biblical theology, we do not merely discover a bunch of "dots" but a theology of a text. And in this case, such a theology shows that Matthew 4 is not merely about moral example or even that Jesus is better than some past OT characters. Rather, the big picture of Matthew 4 points to a poignant conclusion: Jesus is the confirmed final and ultimate King of Israel. He will raise up the tattered ruins of the Davidic dynasty. He is the culmination of the leadership of Israel. He thereby is the new Moses who will lead His people home from the wilderness of their exile. All of this because He has gone into the wilderness, withstood the tests none before Him could withstand, and emerged triumphant. At the beginning of His ministry, Jesus has established His person and role. He will now go about fulfilling it. Though biblical theology may involve connecting the dots, it is more than that. It brings together a big picture that ultimately honors the multifaceted glory of Christ. May that be our end in the discipline.

8

Paul's Usage of Psalm 69:9 in Romans 15:3 and Its Practical Implications

Geoffrey R. Kirkland

> *"[Christ] had power not to have been reproached, power not to have suffered what He did suffer, had He been minded to look to His own things" – John Chrysostom*

> *"For even Christ did not please Himself; but as it is written, 'THE REPROACHES OF THOSE WHO REPROACHED YOU FELL ON ME.'" – The Apostle Paul (Rom 15:3)*

I COUNT IT A TREMENDOUS PRIVILEGE to contribute to the Festschrift for my professor, mentor, and dear friend, Dr. Will Varner. Some of the most formative years in my study of Greek came under his instruction and discipling-care.

An interest that has captivated Dr. Varner for years is the study of how the biblical authors use biblical texts. I first became acutely aware of the study of the New Testament use of the Old in taking a course with Dr. Varner on the exegesis of Romans.

One of the hottest issues currently discussed in biblical scholarship focuses precisely on this topic of how the NT uses the OT. Because the biblical authors had saturated their minds with Scripture, they included many direct citations, allusions, and echoes in their writings. The goal in studying how the NT authors utilize the OT is to understand why they used the Scripture they used, whether they had respect for the original (OT) context, and the various hermeneutical and theological implications derived from such a usage. In the context of Romans, specifically, Paul deliberately and carefully uses the OT to enhance his argument.

This essay will examine how the Apostle Paul uses Psalm 69:9 in Romans 15:3. The methodology incorporated in this study follows the model of Beale and Carson in the *Commentary on the New Testament Use of the Old Testament*[1] to understand how Paul viewed and used Psalm 69 in his argument in the midst of the discourse in Romans 12–15. This study will look at the contexts of both Romans 15 and Psalm 69 so as to allow for a proper understanding of the hermeneutical and theological use of the NT use of the OT. To conclude, some practical implications will be drawn.

Background and Context of Romans 15

"This Epistle . . . is worthy not only that every Christian should know it word for word, by heart, but occupy himself with it every day, as the daily bread of the soul. It can never be read or pondered too much, and the more it is dealt with the more precious it becomes, and the better it tastes."[2] So wrote Martin Luther concerning Romans. In the epistle of Paul to the Romans, a magnificently divine and yet a supremely personal demonstration and realization of the gospel is displayed. Paul defines what could be seen as a thesis statement for the entire epistle in 1:16–17: "For I am not ashamed of the gospel, for it is the power of God for salvation to everyone who believes, to the Jew first and also to the Greek. For in it the righteousness of God is revealed from faith to faith; as it is written, 'But the righteous man shall live by faith.'"[3] The message originated from God, powerful enough to impart salvation to a sinner who believes, conjoins both believing Jews and believing Gentiles into a status of righteousness because of the imputed righteousness of Jesus Christ. Moo writes: "the bulk of

---

1 G. K. Beale and D. A. Carson, eds., *Commentary on the New Testament Use of the Old Testament* (Baker Academic, 2007).

2 Martin Luther, *Commentary on Romans*, trans. J. Theodore Mueller (Kregel, 1976), xiii.

3 Unless otherwise noted, all Scripture citations are from the *New American Standard Bible* (1995 updated edition).

Romans focuses on how God has acted in Christ to bring the individual sinner into a new relationship with himself (chaps. 1–4), to provide for that individual's eternal life in glory (chaps. 5–8), and to transform that individual's life on earth now (12:1–15:13)."[4]

The way this Pauline message of good news is defined in this particular epistle is inseparable with the person and work of the Lord Jesus Christ. This Son was born of a descendant of David according to the flesh (Rom 1:3). He was declared the Son of God with power by the resurrection from the dead according to the Spirit of holiness (v. 4). And He brings about the obedience of faith among all the Gentiles for His name's sake (v. 5). This Christological foundation lays a foundation for the entire epistle since Paul picks up the very same language near the end of the epistle, thus demonstrating cohesion in this discourse centering on the person and work of Jesus Christ (cf. 16:25–27).

Many of the predominant theological words and themes that Paul incorporates in this letter have their roots in the Old Testament and thus call the recipients to recall the Scriptures and surrounding contexts from which they come.[5]

In 1:18–3:20, Paul goes to great lengths to state his case that mankind is "all under sin" (3:9). This fundamental tenet of Christian theology comes at the outset of this epistle. Unless one sees his own severe sinfulness, his perilous plight before a holy God, and his utter helplessness in doing anything to redeem himself, he will not see the gospel message as glorious. But for the one who sees that he is "accountable to God" (3:19), Paul introduces the great news of God's righteousness that is manifested through faith in Jesus Christ for all who believe (3:21–22). The justification whereby God Himself justifies the ungodly by crediting righteousness apart from works (4:5–6) brings about hope (5:5) and a life of progressive sanctification (chaps. 6–8). Paul substantiates his argumentation with chapters 9–11 where he shows the faithfulness of God to the nation of Israel. This serves as an encouraging impetus for the believers in Rome on which to base their confidence in the faithfulness of God in His dealings with them.

The major transition point in Paul's epistle comes at 12:1. The

---

4 Douglas J. Moo, *The Epistle to the Romans*, NICNT (Eerdmans, 1996), 28.

5 See Mark A. Seifrid, "Romans," in *Commentary on the New Testament Use of the Old Testament*, ed. G. K. Beale and D. A. Carson (Baker Academic, 2007), 607.

doxology in 11:33–36 clearly marks the end of the first major section of the discourse and 12:1 begins the parenesis section of Paul's discourse.[6] In 12:1 continuing all the way to 15:13 Paul provides the believing community in Rome specific instructions on how to honor God by "presenting their bodies a living and holy sacrifice" (12:1).

The introduction to the entire parenesis part of the discourse is 12:1–2 where all of life is to be offered to God as an acceptable service of worship. This section provides exhortations as to the right use of spiritual gifts (12:3–8), Christian love toward one another and toward all men (12:9–21), the imperative of submitting to government (13:1–7), the crowning virtue of love in the last days (13:8–14), and relating to the weaker brother with a Christ-like, others-focused, gospel-centered mindset in areas of the conscience (14:1–15:13).

One cannot read chapters 14–15 divorced from the immediate context where Paul has just pleaded with the church to love without hypocrisy (12:9) and where he has elevated love as the "fulfillment of the law" (13:10). This discourse, joined together by the phraseology of accepting one another (14:1; 15:7), reminds the Christians in Rome to not pass judgment on the opinions of those weak in the faith (14:1)—that is, one who only eats vegetables (14:2). Stott remarks: "They are evidently weak in faith or conviction, rather than in will or character. They must have been mainly Jewish Christians, who believed they should still observe both the food laws and the feasts and fasts of the Jewish calendar."[7] The peak of this section in the epistle comes at 14:7–9 where Paul connects Christian living toward one another with the essential outworking of one's relationship to the Lord. The predominant principle in this section comes in 14:5 where each person must be fully convinced in his own mind concerning conscience issues. Paul affirms that, for the believer, no one lives for himself and no one dies for himself (14:7). The foremost aim of the Christian life is to live for the Lord and die for the Lord which impacts everything in life

---

6 Concerning parenesis, Stanley Porter, writes: "the parenesis section of the Pauline letter is concerned with proper Christian behavior. The parenesis often specifies what is proper Christian behavior, and expresses this using various traditional forms of moral instruction" (Stanley E. Porter, "Exegesis of the Pauline Letters, Including the Deutero-Pauline Letters," in *Handbook to Exegesis of the New Testament*, ed. Stanley E. Porter [Brill, 2002], 548).

7 John R. W. Stott, *The Message of Romans*, BST (InterVarsity, 1994), 42.

(14:8). In a typical Pauline fashion, he directly relates Christian living to the death and resurrection of Christ (14:9). Thus, the one who believes in the risen Christ has the power of the risen Christ in him to pursue the things which make for peace and the building up of one another (14:19; cf. Phil. 2:12–13; Col. 1:28–29).

The believer acting in love towards others does not do anything by which another brother would stumble (14:21). Those in the believing community who are strong must bear with the weaknesses of the weak and not be consumed with pleasing themselves (15:1). The Pauline focus of being others-centered arises yet again (cf. 12:9–13; 13:8–10). And including himself in his own exhortation to the Roman church, he states that each person must please his neighbor for his good (15:2). True love and Christlike edification begins with an others-focused perspective. Indeed, the goal of Christians living to please one another is edification (πρὸς οἰκοδομήν; 15:2b). The language Paul uses is stronger than some English translations render it, as Paul speaks with an imperative (ἀρεσκέτω). This notion of pleasing one's neighbor (πλησίον) recalls the previous two times Paul has used this word in the letter where he strongly pleaded with the believers to love one another and do no wrong to a neighbor (13:9, 10). Paul adds a theological statement to this exhortation, namely, the person and work of Jesus Christ which Paul will mention repeatedly in the following verses.[8] The best model (καὶ γὰρ) that Paul could provide points to the self-denial of Christ (15:3). This self-denial culminates at the crucifixion[9] when Christ did not please Himself but bore many reproaches (15:3b). Paul quotes (γέγραπται) Psalm 69:9 and puts the words of the psalm on Jesus' lips to serve as a model for the Roman Christians to imitate. Paul shows the believers that his usage of the Old Testament appropriately fits his purpose since everything written in earlier times was written for the believers' instruction (15:4). Indeed, through perseverance and the encouragement of the Scriptures, God gives hope (15:4). And the goal of what Paul says in this immediate context culminates when Paul wishes that the Roman believers be "of the same mind with one another according to Christ Jesus" (15:5). This is all for the greater purpose

---

8 See Stott, *Romans*, 369.

9 Cf. Moo, *Romans*, 868.

of glorifying God with the Christian community living in harmony (15:6).[10]

The gospel message radically changes one's life. Indeed, in this section of Romans (chaps. 12ff), Paul lays out the works that a Christian does for the statement rings true that "faith takes no holidays."[11]

BACKGROUND AND CONTEXT OF PSALM 69

That the Apostle Paul quotes from Psalm 69 should not come as a surprise since this psalm, along with Psalm 22, it is one of the most often-quoted psalms in the New Testament. Psalm 69, a psalm of David, is an individual lament where the psalmist presents his distresses to God. This psalm has elements of individual laments in which a speaker sets forth to God complaints about adverse situations and sufferings, along with strong petitions for divine action to relieve the distress.[12] The situation of the psalmist finds expression in clear detail and with honest anxiety. David reveals that many hate him vehemently (v. 4), even his closest relatives have spurned him (v. 8).

The intensity of David's suffering is evidenced by the anxiety of a sick person feeling the nearness of death (vv. 2–3, 14–17). Reproach has broken his heart (v. 20a), he has no comforters (v. 20b), he is in distress (v. 17b), and he describes his suffering with the metaphor of the muddy mire (v. 1b, 14, 15; cf. Jonah 2:3–7). As for an outline, one could see the psalm divided as follows:

1. Hear my cry, O God (1–12)
2. Answer me quickly, O God (13–19)
3. Curse my enemies, O God (20–28)
4. Receive my worship, O God (29–36)

Distressed of soul, David begins this lament cry to Yahweh. The address of God immediately fuses with the urgent petition for deliverance (v. 2a) and without hesitation flows into a lengthy complaint (v.

---

10   Thomas R. Schreiner, *Paul, Apostle of God's Glory in Christ: A Pauline Theology* (IVP Academic, 2001), 340.

11   Luther, *Romans*, xxiv.

12   Marvin E. Tate, *Psalms 51–100*, WBC (Thomas Nelson, 2000), 192.

2b–5).[13] David begins and ends the psalm with the similar expression of "save" (root: יׁשע) that provides unity and cohesion to the poem (cf. vv. 13, 29).[14] In v. 1, David begins by crying "save me, O God" (הֹוׁשִׁיעֵֽנִי אֱלֹהִים) and he concludes the psalm in v. 35 by affirming that "God will save" Zion (אֱלֹהִים יֹוׁשִׁיעַ). After crying for God to save him (v. 1a), David speaks of his terrible predicament (vv. 2–4) and he affirms that he has suffered much of this calamity for God's sake (v. 7–12). With a clear transition in v. 13a (וַאֲנִי),[15] David begs God to answer him (vv. 13, 16, 17) and to draw near to his soul and to redeem it (v. 18). Beginning with v. 22, David calls upon God to act and to judge his enemies. David's imprecations include a command for God to pour out indignation on them (v. 24) and to make their camps desolate (v. 25) so that they are blotted out of the book of life as to not be recorded with the righteous (v. 28).

With another clear break in the psalm (וַאֲנִי), David reminds God that he agonizes in affliction and in pain (v. 29). Nevertheless, he longs for Yahweh's full deliverance (יְׁשֽוּעָתְךָ, v. 29) and he praises the Lord, magnifies Him (v. 30) and remembers that the Lord does hear the needy (v. 33). To be sure, Psalm 69 is a psalm of protest and plea, yet it also closes with a declaration of trust based on the conviction that God does hear such prayer.[16] The conclusion of the psalm consists of a call to worship for the heavens, the earth, and everything in them to praise the Lord (v. 34) for God's deliverance that will soon come to His people (vv. 35–36).

Turning to vv. 7–12 specifically, the predominant focus is on David and his own suffering (note all the "I" statements). Goldingay remarks that these verses "suggest someone with a distinctive religious commitment, suggesting that the attackers are people with other forms of religious commitment, whom God should remove from the community."[17] David suffers not because of a whim nor because of some hei-

---

13 Erhard S. Gerstenberger, *Psalms, Part 2, and Lamentations*, FOTL 15 (Eerdmans, 2001), 47.

14 See Mitchell Dahood, *Psalms II: 51–100*, AB (Doubleday, 1968), 156; Leslie C. Allen, "The Value of Rhetorical Criticism in Psalm 69," JBL 105, no. 4 (Dec 1986): 581.

15 Tate sees this as the major transition point of the psalm (*Psalms 51–100*, 192).

16 John Goldingay, *Psalms Volume 2: Psalms 42–89*, BCOTWP (Baker Academic, 2007), 338.

17 Goldingay, *Psalms*, 338.

nous crime he has committed; rather, it is for God's sake that he bears reproach (כִּי־עָלֶיךָ נָשָׂאתִי חֶרְפָּה). These words closely resemble the experience of Jeremiah when he prayed to the Lord to take notice of him and take vengeance on his persecutors since it was for His sake that he endured reproach (שְׂאֵתִי עָלֶיךָ חֶרְפָּה, Jer 15:15; cf. 20:8). A window into the excruciating pain that David felt comes to light in v. 8 when he notes that he has been estranged (LXX: ἀπηλλοτριωμένος [Ps 68:9]) from even his brothers. Those once closest to David now show themselves to adamantly be distant from him. Far from being unrelated to Yahweh, David has a zeal for Yahweh's house that consumes him (v. 9a). So passionate is his worship of Yahweh that the reproaches of those who reproach Yahweh fall upon David (v. 9b). He suffers together with the Lord (cf. Rom 8:17). The pounding intensity of these reproaches brought David to sorrow (v. 10–11). This description shows the grief at what goes on in the temple. Ironically, this is what turns David into a byword among the peoples (cf. 44:14). People infer from the signs of David's penitence that he has sinned against God and needs forgiveness for his wrongdoing (v. 12).[18]

One must realize, however, that suffering can be transforming. An amazing feature in this psalm is that the Davidic king, who should be sharing in the Lord's triumphs, suddenly appeals for divine aid in a critical moment (v. 1).[19] David suffers not unjustly nor because he has lived in persistent sin. Rather, he faces severe suffering because of "his enthusiasm for God's cause."[20] The reproaches (חֶרְפוֹת) of those who reproach Yahweh (חוֹרְפֶיךָ) have fallen on David. He receives and feels what God's enemies direct to Him. The key word functioning as the unifying thread in this section is "reproach" (חֶרְפָּה). This word occurs 6 times in the psalm (vv. 7, 9 [2x], 10, 19, 20). In a sense, David understands what it is to suffer for God's sake and to be a sharer in the sufferings of Christ (1 Pet 4:13). Calvin ably sums up the application:

By this example we are taught, that whereas we are naturally so tender and delicate as to be unable to bear ignominy and

---

18 Goldingay, *Psalms*, 345.

19 Gordon J. Wenham, *Psalms as Torah: Reading Biblical Song Ethically* (Baker Academic, 2012), 171.

20 Wenham, *Psalms as Torah*, 171.

reproach, we must endeavour to get quit of this unhappy state of mind, and ought rather to be grieved and agonised with the reproaches which are poured forth against God. On account of these, it becomes us to feel deep indignation, and even to give expression to this in strong language; but we ought to bear the wrongs and reproaches which we personally suffer without complaining. Until we have learned to set very little value upon our own reputation, we will never be inflamed with true zeal in contending for the preservation and advancement of the interests of the Divine glory.[21]

Jesus knew this psalm and even spoke of himself being the fulfillment of it at certain points (Ps 69:4 and John 15:25; Ps 69:9a and John 2:17; cf. Ps 69:21 and Mark 15:36; Matt 27:34; Luke 23:36; John 19:29–30). As Evans has noted: "the Lament Psalms clarified aspects of Jesus' Passion and the suffering and persecution many of his followers experienced.[22]

EXAMINING THE USE OF PSALM 69 IN ROMANS 15

Paul quotes the OT frequently in Romans. Not only is it important to note that he quoted or alluded to a particular OT text but also one must see how Paul used the OT in addition to asking why he chose that particular text to enhance his point.

Text Types

Paul quotes the LXX verbatim without any changes whatsoever. Paul has done this already in the letter and even in the immediate context of chapter 15 he quotes from the LXX (vv. 9–12).

---

21 John Calvin, *Commentary on the Book of Psalms* (Eerdmans, 1949), 3:56.

22 Craig A. Evans, "Praise and Prophecy in the Psalter and in the New Testament," in *The Book of Psalms: Composition and Reception*, ed. Peter W. Flint and Patrick D. Miller, VTSup 99, FIOTL 4 (Brill, 2005), 551. Evans later notes that the Psalter had a crucial importance in aiding the early Church in its efforts to "understand and clarify the ministry, death, resurrection, and ascension of Jesus. That the Psalter functioned in this way is in itself intriguing, for it testifies to a convergence of worship and prophecy that characterized the charismatic nature of the early Christian community" (*Praise and Prophecy*, 578).

Hermeneutical Use

In trying to understand the reason why and the way in which Paul used Psalm 69 in Romans 15, one must begin with a proper understanding of both the larger context and the immediate discourse of Romans 15. The context of Romans 15 speaks of refusing to look out for one's own interests only. Paul served as a model of this kind of mindset even at the outset of the epistle when he wrote that he unceasingly prayed for the saints (1:9) and how he longed to come to them to impart a spiritual gift to them (1:10–11) so they may be mutually encouraged by one another's faith (1:12). His driving passion comes to light in 1:14–15. Paul eagerly longs to preach the gospel to those in Rome as well as to all Greeks and barbarians. Thus, the beginning verses of this epistle in Paul's attitude and ambitions demonstrates in a microcosm the greater macrocosm of the utter selflessness and devotion to the Lord that Jesus perfectly exemplified for the sake of others.

After presenting a cohesive, air-tight, compelling discourse on the gospel in 1:18–11:36, Paul transitions to how believers should live having experienced the salvation and benefits therein. In a sense, the entire parenesis section of the letter is framed by a call to utter self-abandonment and humility. In 12:3, Paul says to every believer "not to think more highly of himself than he ought to think; but to think so as to have sound judgment" and in 15:2, Paul again writes that "each of us is to please his neighbor for his good, to his edification." There is to be a remarkable sense and an obvious attitude about the person of God who lives not for himself but for others—which finds at its root a yearning to emulate Christ and live to God's glory.

Understanding this causes one to see a clear connection between Paul's exhortation to the believers in Romans 15 and Psalm 69 by picturing the reproaches that Christ bore for God's sake and the suffering of the psalmist who actually felt as though he partook in the sufferings directed toward God Himself. Just as David felt weary in his suffering (Ps 69:1–3) and was hated without a cause (Ps 69:4; cf. John 15:25), the Lord Jesus in the last few hours of his life found himself severely weak and sorrowful (see, e.g., Mark 15:32–42; Heb 2:18; 4:15).

Yet differences arise in the parallels between Jesus and David. David confessed that God knew his folly and his wrongs (Ps 69:5) whereas Jesus had no sin (Heb 4:15; 1 John 2:3). All the while, both David and Jesus had a God-centered focus that compelled them to live in such a way so as to bring about the greatest glory of God (Ps 69:6; John 8:28). David felt as though the reproaches that his enemies directed toward God fell upon him since he had a zeal for God's pure worship (Ps 69:9). Similarly, Paul puts David's words in the mouth of Christ as saying that the reproaches of those who reproached the Father also fell upon Him because of His passion to glorify God the Father (Rom 15:3, 6).[23] Yet this extends beyond the individual sufferings of David and Jesus. The very fact that Paul brings this Scripture out in this particular context of bearing with the weaknesses of those who are without strength (Rom 15:1) shows that Paul may have anticipated that believing Gentiles in the Roman church may receive reproaches from others. Yet, in this very act of bearing reproaches, they partake in the very act of suffering with Christ and with God.

The enemies of David's in Psalm 69 may serve as a pattern that the Roman Christians may experience as these Gentile believers gladly welcome, accept, and fellowship with their Jewish brothers in the faith. Thus, as they identify with believing Jews, they may very well receive hostility from their pagan neighbors. As this occurs, they follow in their Messiah's footsteps who also received reproach in similar manner.[24]

The closer the disciple relates to God, the more he feels what God feels. In Romans 15, Paul does not speak of Christ's love for humans (as an example of bearing with the weaknesses of the weak) but rather he speaks of the Messiah's devotion to God.[25] In so far as David and Jesus suffered by bearing the reproaches aimed at God, so the disciples of Jesus will face similar reproaches as they bear the blows that were intended for God.

Similarities also arise between the psalmist who experienced estrangement and alienation from even his own family (Ps 69:8), the Lord Jesus who was abandoned by his closest friends on the night of his arrest (Mark 14:50), and the Roman believers who enter into the

---

23 Paul does the same thing by putting the words of Scripture in Jesus' mouth in Rom 15:9–11; cf. C. E. B. Cranfield, *Romans 9–16*, ICC (T&T Clark, 1979), 733.

24 Seifrid, "Romans," 686.

25 Seifrid, "Romans," 686.

same rejection from intimate companions just as David the Messiah had previously.[26]

What comes to light then from this usage of Psalm 69 in the NT is an illustration of the sense of corporate solidarity between the righteous founder of the community (i.e. Jesus) and his following.[27] Ellis agrees as he notes: "the concept of solidarity has a bearing on Paul's OT interpretation."[28] That is to say, whatever befalls the founder also happens to his followers. The analogy between texts is evident but more specifically the particular usage of corporate solidarity comes to light as both texts are examined and compared carefully.[29] This God-centered perspective and self-giving for the benefit of others provides believers in the church at Rome—and all believers—a model to imitate.[30]

Theological Use

The Lord Jesus as the perfect Son of God models for all his sons whom He leads to glory the reality of suffering—and even suffering from the closest of friends.[31] The Pauline theology of Christian suffering finds its apex as the Christian life causes one to follow in the footsteps of his Savior. Jesus lived not to serve himself, but he lived so resolutely for God's glory that he felt the reproaches that the enemies directed to the Father. Paul understood this and put the Davidic words from the psalm on the lips of Jesus in Romans 15:3. Thus, the section on Christians living selflessly, accepting the weaker brother, and conducting themselves with a singular passion to edify the Christian community finds its fullest expression in a God-centered life that endures

---

26 Seifrid, "Romans," 686.

27 Evans, "Praise and Prophecy," 569.

28 E. Earle Ellis, *Paul's Use of the Old Testament* (Wipf & Stock, 1981), 139.

29 More generally, Paul uses Ps 69 to indicate an analogical or illustrative use of the OT (see G. K. Beale, *Handbook on the New Testament Use of the Old Testament: Exegesis and Interpretation* [Baker Academic, 2012], 67–71), but Paul may particularly be utilizing corporate solidarity to drive home his point.

30 Moo, *Romans*, 869; cf. Jeremy Moiser, "Rethinking Romans 12–15," NTS 36, no. 4 (Oct 1990): 579.

31 See Willem VanGemeren, "Psalms," rev. ed., EBC, ed. Tremper Longman III and David E. Garland (Zondervan, 2008), 5:529.

sufferings because it has joined itself to Jesus Christ—the suffering, crucified, and risen Messiah.[32] A truly Christian life is a God-centered life; and one who lives the God-centered life will feel the reproaches that are directed toward God.

Another theological implication arises when one looks at the larger discourse of Romans 15. Not only does Paul quote from a Messianic Psalm in verse 3 but he later also quotes a string of OT Scriptures to show that the Gentiles can glorify the sovereign Christ (vv. 9–12).[33] This observation helps one to understand that, in the larger discourse at hand, Paul sees Christ as worthy to receive worship from among all peoples (v. 11) since He alone is the glorious and sovereign Hope (v. 12). It is the God of hope who fills His people with all joy and peace in believing, so that they will abound in hope by the power of the Holy Spirit. This culminates in the person, work, sufferings, and glorious resurrection of Jesus Christ. God provided Him with joy and peace in entrusting Himself to His Father in all things which caused him to trust in His Father perfectly and entirely in the power of the Holy Spirit. Even in the dark hours of loneliness, despair, and abandonment—and even when he felt the reproaches that others directed toward His Father—he persevered with hope in the power of the Holy Spirit. And so in a similar way, all Christ's followers must give praise to the sovereign Christ—even in the harshest of times—because of the confident hope that Christ promises to His followers (cf. 15:4–6). After all, the very next verse after Paul's quote in Rom 15:3 speaks of the hope that the Scriptures provide for God's people (v. 4). Paul's understanding and usage of the Old Testament evidences that he has the light and power of the Old Testament with him.[34] This internalization of the Word grants hope and perspective so that Christians endure and thrive in the school of suffering—just as Jesus Himself did.

---

32 This point is further supported by Tom Schreiner who remarks that "[Paul's] sufferings are a corollary of the sufferings of Jesus" (Schreiner, *Paul*, 87). And later Schreiner notes that "suffering was central to the Pauline mission" (*Paul*, 87).

33 One should note that in the OT texts from which Paul quotes, he uses texts from all three major sections of the Hebrew Bible [the Law, the Prophets, and the Writings]: Rom 15:9 quotes from 2 Sam 22:50 [or Ps 18:49], Rom 15:10 quotes Deut 32:43, Rom 15:11 quotes from Ps 117:1, and Rom 15:12 quotes Isa 11:10.

34 Luther, *Romans*, xxvi.

PRACTICAL APPLICATIONS

Proper hermeneutics should always lead to Christian holiness. In so far as the Christian rightly divides the Word, sees the gospel in its beauty displayed, and receives instruction from the Scriptures, he will grow in the grace and knowledge of the Lord Jesus Christ (2 Pet 3:18). The following list provides just a few ways that believers can apply these texts examined in this study.

First, Christian Humility

Christ's emptying should serve as a model for humility. God emptied Himself by taking up human flesh and was perfected through his sufferings (Heb 2:10) and felt the blow of hardships, especially from those closest to him. In like manner, God's people should clothe themselves with humility and have the same mind as He had (1 Pet 5:5). Ware continues this thought when he says:

> [Believers must] see the heights from which he came and the depths to which he descended in coming as the suffering Servant who would bear our sin. We will belittle the magnitude of what Jesus has done if we fail to see the kind of obedience he rendered and the extent to which he was willing to go is ensuring that he fulfilled the will of his Father.[35]

Second, Hope in Suffering

Paul's usage of the OT can provide Christians a model for how to live with a Christ-centered, God-glorifying perspective in suffering. Christ, like David, bore such harsh treatment and soul-wrenching pain from his own kin and yet he lived not to please Himself but others. The hope of Christ was indelibly fixed to the glory of God and performing exactly what the Father had commissioned Him to do. This was the engine that gave Him hope even in suffering.

---

35 Bruce A. Ware, *The Man Christ Jesus: Theological Reflections on the Humanity of Christ* (Crossway, 2013), 27.

Third, Word-Centered Biblical Counseling

Biblical counseling provides hope for God's people who rest in and cling to the Word.[36] The Scriptures instruct the child of God and impart hope to the believer who comes to the Word for strength, sustenance, and encouragement. Just as Paul utilized the Scriptures to authoritatively exhort believers how to live and relate to one another, so believers today must incorporate the Scriptures in counseling and discipling relationships so as to "admonish the unruly, encourage the fainthearted, help the weak, be patient with everyone" (1 Thess 5:14). The Scriptures that Paul quoted from testify about this Christ and are "sufficient to cure souls."[37]

Fourth, Unity in the Body of Christ

Finally, Unity in the Body of Christ. The immediate discourse of chapters 14–15 underscores the unity that the church in Rome must exhibit. They must accept one another (14:1; 15:7) as they serve to please others for their edification (15:2). Thus, ecclesiological unity will come about as believers live out righteousness in Christian community. This all flows from God who gives perseverance and encouragement so that God's people may be of the same mind with one another according to Christ Jesus (15:5). This is not works-righteousness; this, rather is "worked-out righteousness."[38]

CONCLUSION

To sum up, Cranfield provides a timely word:

> The purpose of the reference is to indicate the lengths to which Christ went in His not pleasing Himself rather than specially to

---

36 Heath Lambert speaks to this: "All biblical counselors continue to believe in the authority, wisdom, relevance, and sufficiency of the Bible to help people with any problem that requires counseling" (*The Biblical Counseling Movement After Adams* [Crossway, 2012], 45).

37 David Powlison, "The Sufficiency of Scripture to Diagnose and Cure Souls," JBC 23, no. 2 (2005): 13.

38 Powlison, "Sufficiency of Scripture,"28.

encourage the strong Christians in Rome to imitate this particular element of Christ's endurance. If, for our sakes, He was willing to go as far as this in His not pleasing Himself, how ungrateful should we be, if we could not bring ourselves to renounce our self-gratification in so unimportant a matter as the exercising of our freedom with regard to what we eat or whether we observe special days—for the sake of our brothers for whom He suffered so much![39]

---

39 Cranfield, *Romans 9–16*, 733.

9

Opposition at the Gate:
Psalm 118 and Its Usage in Passion Week

Daniel Forbes

INTRODUCTION

P SALM 118[1] HAS BLESSED MULTITUDES with its transcendent message. However, this psalm raises some interpretative questions. What are the "gates of righteousness" (שַׁעֲרֵי־צֶדֶק)? Why does the speaker shift to addressing Yahweh directly in verse 21 ("I praise *you* that *you* have heard me..."), when previously he had only spoken of Yahweh in the 3rd person? Who or what is the stone in verse 22, and how does this statement fit in context? Who are the builders who reject this stone? Why does the psalmist use a plural suffix in verse 26 when the worshipper entering is conceivably alone ("Blessed is *he* who comes...")? Also, what bearing does the "gate entry" motif in the Old Testament (e.g. Isa 26:2; Ps 24:7–10) have on this psalm?

Further difficulties arise when we consider the psalm's usage in the Gospels. While scholars recognize the importance of Psalm 118 in Jesus' self-understanding during Passion Week (Matt 21:9, 42; 23:39; Mark 11:9; 12:10–11; Luke 13:35; 19:38; 20:17; John 12:13),[2] they also have

---

1 Unless otherwise stated, all versification and references to Greek and Hebrew texts are taken from Karl Elliger and Wilhelm Rudolph, eds., *Biblia Hebraica Stuttgartensia*, 5th ed. (Deutsche Bibelgesellschaft, 1997); Barbara Aland et al., eds., *Novum Testamentum Graece*, 28th ed. (Deutsche Bibelgesellschaft, 2012); Alfred Rahlfs and Robert Hanhart, eds., *Septuaginta*, rev. ed. (Deutsche Bibelgesellschaft, 2007).

2 Andrew C. Brunson, *Psalm 118 in the Gospel of John*, WUNT 158 (Mohr Siebeck, 2003); Hyukiung Kwon, "The Reception of Psalm 118 in the New Testament: Application of a 'New Exodus Motif'?" (PhD diss., University of Pretoria, 2007); Todd Michael Kinde, "The Use of Psalm 118 in Matthew 21–23" (ThM thesis, Calvin Theological

some questions. Why does Jesus suggest that further Hosanna cries are necessary (Matt 23:39; Luke 13:35) when the crowds earlier welcomed him into the temple precincts (Matt 21:9; Mark 11:9; Luke 19:38; John 12:13)? Why also does Mark's Gospel record that Jesus came into the temple, looked around, and then quickly departed (11:11)? Why did the scribes and chief priests react so violently to Jesus' quotation of Psalm 118:22–23 in their presence (Matt 21:45; Mark 12:12; Luke 20:19)?[3]

In my judgment, commentators have not adequately answered these two sets of questions (and the relationship therein). In brief, I believe that *Psalm 118 has not been fully understood*. In its original context, the psalmist is not welcomed in to worship *carte blanche*, but rather is *implicitly opposed* at the gate. When read this way, I argue that the questions posed above on Psalm 118 can be answered, and the way the Gospel writers used Psalm 118 makes better sense of the psalm's original meaning and context.

To see this, we will first examine Psalm 118 itself, then two other "gate-entry" texts (Isa 26:2; Ps 24:7–10), and lastly, we will reconsider the use of Psalm 118 in the Synoptic versions of the Passion Week Narrative.[4]

Seminary, 2004); Seyoon Kim, "Jesus—The Son of God, the Stone, the Son of Man, and the Servant: The Role of Zechariah in the Self-Identification of Jesus," in *Tradition and Interpretation in the New Testament: Essays in Honor of E. Earle Ellis*, ed. Gerald F. Hawthorne and Otto Betz (Eerdmans Publishing, 1987), 134–48; Rikk E. Watts, "The Lord's House and David's Lord: The Psalms and Mark's Perspective on Jesus and the Temple," *BibInt* 15 (2007): 307–22; Deborah Krause, "The One Who Comes Unbinding the Blessings of Judah: Mark 11.1–10 as a Midrash on Genesis 49.11, Zechariah 9.9, and Psalm 118.25–26," in *Early Christian Interpretation of the Scriptures of Israel: Investigations and Proposals*, ed. Craig A. Evans and James A. Sanders; JSNTSup 148 (Sheffield Academic Press, 1997), 141–53; J. Ross Wagner, "Psalm 118 in Luke-Acts: Tracing a Narrative Thread," in *Early Christian Interpretation*, 154–78; James A. Sanders, "A Hermeneutic Fabric: Psalm 118 in Luke's Entrance Narrative," in *Luke and Scripture: The Function of Sacred Tradition in Luke-Acts*, ed. Craig A. Evans and James A. Sanders (Fortress Press, 1993), 140–53.

3   To be sure, the Gospel writers make clear that they responded negatively because they were the wicked tenants of Jesus's parable, but this does not explain how Psalm 118 according to Jesus's *hermeneutic* would have angered them (more on this below).

4   One of the courses I took with Dr. Varner was a "Life of Christ" seminar. I recall fondly the energy and passion he brought to the subject and its different components—the Synoptic Problem, the chronology of Jesus' life and death, Messianic

AUTHORSHIP AND SETTING

Views on the authorship and original setting of Psalm 118 vary,[5] but the view that situates it within the monarchial period is preferable, for it provides the easiest solution for the imagery of war in verses 10–13 and the high status of the Temple entrant.[6] Kaiser has extended the monarchial setting to a case for Davidic authorship. Following Dahood, he sees verses 10–12 as an allusion back to 1 Samuel 18:25–27 and the foreskin tribute David gave to Saul in exchange for marriage to Michal. This view is provocative, but impossible to prove with any certainty.[7] It does seem most likely, however, that the psalmist is a royal figure like David (if not David himself) for several reasons. First, throughout the psalm the main voice "seems to act in some representative capacity," a capacity best suited to someone of royalty.[8] For

prophecies, and the relationship of the New and Old Testaments. These last two components he showed particular interest in and encouraged many of his students to continue studying them. This paper was written to that end, and it is with joy that I have rewritten it to honor Dr. Varner for his faithfulness to the Lord and his Word.

5 Briggs assigns it to the Maccabean period (Charles Augustus Briggs, *A Critical and Exegetical Commentary on the Book of Psalms*, ICC [T&T Clark, 1909], 2:404), while Dahood contends that it is pre-exilic given the royal and wartime motifs present (Mitchell Dahood, *Psalms III: 101–150*, AB 17A [Yale University Press, 1970], 155–56). Between these two extremes, many argue for a post-exilic date in the days of Ezra and Nehemiah. Delitzsch sees in Psalm 118:22 a reference to the finalization of the second temple in Ezra 6:15–18 (Franz Delitzsch, "Psalms," in K&D 5:720–21), whereas Perowne opts for the assembly of Nehemiah 8 (J. J. Stewart Perowne, *Commentary on the Psalms* [Kregel, 1989], 338–39). Oesterley argues for a "late post-exilic" date, but does not specify beyond this (W. O. E. Oesterley, *The Psalms: Translated with Text-Critical and Exegetical Notes* [S.P.C.K., 1959], 480–81).

6 Cf. Gen 24:31 (thus John H. Eaton, *Kingship and the Psalms*, 2nd ed., The Biblical Seminar [JSOT Press, 1986], 62). See other supports for this view in Jamie A. Grant, *The King as Exemplar: The Function of Deuteronomy's Kingship Law in the Shaping of the Book of Psalms*, SBLAcBib 17 (Society of Biblical Literature, 2004), 127–28.

7 Walter C. Kaiser Jr., *The Messiah in the Old Testament*, SOTBT (Zondervan, 1995), 100; cf. Dahood, *Psalms III*, 157. There are also a number of similarities between Psalm 118 and other allegedly Davidic psalms (e.g. Ps 18:18–20; 22:13, 17; 27:3); see Leslie C. Allen, *Psalms 101–50*, rev. ed., WBC 21 (Thomas Nelson, 2002), 165. One may argue that the psalm has no Davidic superscription, but Gerald Wilson has pointed out that the fourth and fifth books of the Psalter are frequently unspecified ("Shaping the Psalter: A Consideration of Editorial Linkage in the Book of Psalms," in *The Shape and Shaping of the Psalter*, ed. J. Clinton McCann, JSOTSup 159 [JSOT Press, 1993], 72–82).

8 Allen, *Psalms 101–150*, 164.

example, the salvation Yahweh brings to the psalmist in verse 14 transfers over to the people in verse 15: "Glad songs of *salvation* are in the tents of the righteous." Second, in several places the psalmist's speech fits best in the mouth of a royal figure. Verse 7 alludes to military triumph, with a king or royal person being the most fitting to "look in triumph" on the conquered army. Verses 8–9 seems to allude to military alliance, which would have been brokered by royalty (as, for example, in Isa 7:1–13).[9] And as noted above, the language of war in verses 10–13 best fits as spoken by the leader/commander of the army, who could have been royal. Last, as we will see below, Psalm 118 is closely related to the other "gate-entry" psalms 15 and 24, both of which were authored by David.[10]

A Passover *Sitz im Leben* is very likely for Psalm 118 given its use in Jewish tradition,[11] its allusions to Exodus 14–15 (see vv. 14, 21),[12] and its placement at the end of the Egyptian Hallel (Pss 113–118).[13] Other

---

9 Allen, *Psalms 101–150*, 166; Grant, *King as Exemplar*, 135–37. Willem A. VanGemeren, ("Psalms," in *The Expositor's Bible Commentary*, rev. ed., David E. Garland and Tremper Longman III [Zondervan, 2008], 5:854) argues that the parallelism of "man" and "princes" in vv. 8–9 is a merism for all people, those of high and those of low estates. However, the only other text that uses this exact wording of "trusting" (בטח) in "princes" (נדיב), Psalm 146:3, implies that the princes can supply salvation. This would not be the case of just anyone, but rather far more likely would apply to the military help another person of royalty could provide.

10 Grant notes several other theological affinities between Psalm 118 and Psalms 2 and 18–21, which suggests at least on a surface level that there are royal concerns in Psalm 118 as well (Grant, *King as Exemplar*, 121–48). This is also a rabbinic view of the passage; see *b. Tamid.* 32b.

11 *M. Pes.* 5:7; *m. Suk.* 3:9; *m. Suk.* 4:4; *b. Shabb.* 21b; *b. Suk.* 44a-b; *y. Meg.* 2:6; Louis Finkelstein, "The Origin of the Hallel," *HUCA* 23 (1950–51): 319–37; Solomon Zeitlin, "The Hallel: A Historical Study of the Canonization of the Hebrew Liturgy," *JQR* 53, no. 1 (1962): 22–29.

12 Ps 118:14 repeats Exod 15:2: עָזִּי וְזִמְרָת יָהּ וַיְהִי־לִי לִישׁוּעָה ("my strength and my song is Yah, and he has become my salvation"). "... Psalm 118 is to be read and understood in light of the situation of Israel and of Israel's song in Exodus 14–15. Song and situation are not identical with the psalm, but when the ambiguous language of the psalm is read in the light of the Exodus situation and song, much is decided" (James Luther Mays, *The Lord Reigns: A Theological Handbook to the Psalms* [John Knox Press, 1994], 141).

13 Elizabeth Hayes, "The Unity of the Egyptian Hallel: Psalms 113–18," *BBR* 9 (1999): 145–56; Erich Zenger, "The Composition and Theology of the Fifth Book of Psalms, Psalms 107–145," *JSOT* 80 (1998): 77–102; Michael K. Snearly, *The Return of the*

interpreters see the psalm's genesis in the Feast of Tabernacles,[14] but this view is unlikely given the lack of internal evidence to support it.[15] It is important to state, however, that irrespective of *which* day the psalm was originally meant to celebrate, it is clear that the psalm was meant to celebrate *a* day (v. 24), and this day was most likely one of the yearly pilgrimage festivals.[16] Finally, we note that the psalm is antiphonal, with the opening verses enjoining the community to join in with the song, a fluid interchange between singular and plural verbs, and changes of geographic location in the psalm's progression that also suggest changes in speaker.[17]

INTERPRETATIVE QUESTIONS

As noted, Psalm 118 has a number of interpretative questions that must be answered. What are the "gates of righteousness"? Why does the speaker shift from speaking of Yahweh in the 3rd person to addressing Yahweh directly in verse 21? What is the identity of the stone and function of the stone statement (118:22) in context? Who are the builders? Why the switch from singular to plural in verse 26 ("Blessed is *he* ...We bless *you* ..." [plural –כֶם])? And how do other gate-entry texts bear upon the interpretation of Psalm 118? We will proceed to answer them respectively here.

The Gates of Righteousness (118:19–20)

In verse 19 the psalmist enjoins someone, presumably the gatekeeper or gatekeepers, to open the gates to him so that he may enter. The phrase itself, "gates of righteousness" (שַׁעֲרֵי־צֶדֶק) presents some difficulty. Briggs believes צֶדֶק is "an ancient proper name of the

---

King: Messianic Expectation in Book V of the Psalter, LHBOTS 624 (T&T Clark, 2015), 112–13.

14 John P. Peters, "Notes on Some Ritual Uses of the Psalms," *JBL* 29, no. 2 (1910): 114–15; Perowne, *Psalms*, 338–39; Oesterley, *Psalms*, 480–81.

15 Allen, *Psalms 101–150*, 164–65.

16 Artur Weiser, *The Psalms: A Commentary*, trans. Herbert Hartwell, OTL (Westminster Press, 1962), 724. Derek Kidner argues for this based on the usage of חַג in v. 27 (*Psalms 73 – 150*, TOTC [IVP Academic, 2008], 450–51). Cf. Adele Berlin, "Psalm 118:24," *JBL* 96, no. 4 (1977): 567–68.

17 *Tg. Ps.* 118; *b. Pesah.* 119a.

Holy City."[18] Dahood translates "gates of victory" given his militaristic readings earlier in the psalm (v. 15).[19] Verse 20 seems to suggest that the name of the gates derives from the character of the entrants: the gates are "righteous" (צֶדֶק) because the "righteous ones" (צַדִּיקִים) go in there.[20] Perowne argues that it refers to the character of the place and the worshippers coming there. The controlling image, as these last two commentators suggest, appears to be the character of the entrant: the gates are "righteous" (צֶדֶק) because the "righteous ones" (צַדִּיקִים) go in there. Based on Yahweh's possession of the gate (singular) from verse 20, in all likelihood the temple is the edifice in view.

Within the issue of the gates of righteousness, an additional question is why the psalm shifts from plural "gates" (v. 19) to a singular "gate" (v. 20). *Targum Psalm* 118 and the Babylonian Talmud account for this by suggesting that the shift is indicative of a repartee between those outside and inside the gates. Having called for the gates (note plural) to be opened, someone on the other side responds, "*This* is the gate that belongs to Yahweh; the righteous may enter in it." Allen suggests that the gatekeepers "willingly accede" to this request,[21] but no accession is explicitly granted, only the qualifications for entrance. Then too, those allowed to enter are most likely the צַדִּיקִים of verse 15, that is, the warriors who just recently witnessed the victory of their commander (see vv. 10–12). The psalmist is doubtless among their ranks, but his *singular* request ("open to *me*") and his *singular* intent ("*I* will enter in them") seems to expect a *singular* response, which is lacking. Why did the respondent not answer that way? It is possible that the change is intended to highlight a relationship of solidarity between the psalmist and the warriors.[22] But if this were the case, we

18 Briggs, *Psalms* 2:406.

19 Dahood, *Psalms III*, 158–59.

20 Perowne, *Psalms*, 342–43; cf. Oesterley, *Psalms*, 484; VanGemeren, "Psalms," 5:855. In the words of Weiser: "Certain conditions are ... attached to this invitation, as Psalms 15 and 24 make quite clear" (*Psalms*, 728). The collocation "opening gates" and "entering in" appears only here and in Psalm 24:7–10, further strengthening this contention.

21 *Psalms 101–150*, 167.

22 Mays argues that the "theological identity" of this psalm "is corporate" ("Psalm 118 in the Light of Canonical Analysis," in *Canon, Theology and Old Testament*

might expect a tighter connection to be drawn between them earlier in the psalm; instead, after the first four verses, we find the psalm emphasizes the singular actions and Yahweh's action for him individually (vv. 5–7, 10–13, 17–18). I suggest, then, that the verse could communicate opposition from within, a welcome to the people rescued by the psalmist's victory *but implicit opposition to the psalmist himself.* It is not an explicit sign of unwelcome, but the context allows for the interchange to be implicitly unwelcoming.[23]

Interlocutory Shift (118:21)

In verse 21 the psalmist's attention shifts from those at the gate(s) to Yahweh himself: "I praise *you* that *you* have heard me, and *you* have become my salvation" (אוֹדְךָ כִּי עֲנִיתָנִי וַתְּהִי־לִי לִישׁוּעָה). Apart from verse 13, arguably a statement issued to the psalmist's enemy,[24] this is the first time anyone is directly addressed in the psalm. Further, it is the first direct address to Yahweh. This is an instance of "interlocutory shift," a common feature of Biblical Hebrew poetry. Structurally, it may serve as (1) a dividing marker, (2) a marker of beginning and end of discourse, or (3) a foregrounding device.[25] Psalm 23:4 illustrates this poetic device well. There David states, "Even though I walk in the valley of deep darkness, I will not fear disaster *for you are with me* (כִּי־אַתָּה עִמָּדִי)." In context, the switch to the 2nd person highlights the

---

Interpretation: Essays in Honor of Brevard S. Childs, ed. G. M. Tucker, D. L. Petersen, and R. R. Wilson [Fortress Press, 1988], 299–311). Grant further argues that the king sets the example in righteousness for the rest of the community to follow (*King as Exemplar*, 142–43).

23 S. B. Frost also notes the response of the entrant is different than expected ("Asseveration by Thanksgiving," *VT* 8, no. 4 [1958]: 380–81). Kidner calls these verses a "challenge and a counter-challenge" (*Psalms 73–150*, 449–50).

24 Goldingay writes, "...with vividness the leader now addresses the foe ... as if present..." (*Psalms 90–150*, 359). *Pace* Kraus, *Psalms 60–150*, 394.

25 L. Zogbo, "Enallage: Shifting Persons in Old Testament Texts" (presented at the United Bible Societies Triennial Translation Workshop, Chiang Mai, Thailand, 1994), 1–27. See also Steven W. Boyd, "Statistical Determination of Genre in Biblical Hebrew: Evidence for an Historical Reading of Genesis 1:1–2:3," in *Radioisotopes and the Age of the Earth: Results of a Young-Earth Creationist Research Initiative*, ed. Larry Vardiman, Andrew A. Snelling, and Eugene F. Chaffin, vol. 2 (Institute for Creation Research and the Creation Research Society, 2005), 647–48, 718–19.

vividness of the psalmist's dire situation *and* the hope he found in Yahweh. Similarly, I would argue that Psalm 118:21 is the psalm's emotional zenith, and marks the psalmist's singular hope for salvation.[26] The shift from 3rd to 2nd person reference to Yahweh here, immediately after the gatekeepers speak in verse 20, communicates the vividness of not only the psalmist's thankfulness and praise for rescue in battle, *but also the vividness of his rescue at the gate*. It seems that the salvation needed was not just provided in battle, but even (ironically) from those at the gate. Rather than answering the gatekeepers' challenge, he turns to Yahweh directly, knowing that only *He* has truly listened.[27] In this fashion, victory is implied, even if at the moment it is in question.

The Identity of the Stone (118:22)

Past scholarship on this psalm has mostly revolved around the sort of stone that is in view here.[28] For our purposes, it is sufficient to say that רֹאשׁ פִּנָּה is ambiguous. רֹאשׁ certainly denotes both the honorific role of the stone, but whether it is the "capstone" or the "cornerstone" of a building is uncertain.[29] More important for our discussion is the identity and purpose of the stone in context. There is virtual unanimity that the psalm depicts a processional from battle into the temple for worship; everything in the psalm points to this. If the temple is the destination of the processional, then it stands to reason that this אֶבֶן, "stone," was a part of the temple building.[30] The psalmist is therefore declaring that a certain temple stone, regarded as unimportant and unnecessary to its construction, is found to be the key to the temple itself. The phrase "Yahweh has done this" (v. 23) points back to the earlier description of Yahweh's actions in the psalm, how He helped

---

26 Zogbo notes that, "... the 'trade-off' ... between declarations about God and intimate interaction with Him is very characteristic of the Psalms in general ..." ("Enallage," 4).

27 Even the statement "you have answered me" seems to point in this direction, for had not the gatekeeper(s) just answered him?

28 For an introduction to the issues, see Joachim Jeremias, "λίθος," in *TDNT* 4:268–80.

29 Cf. Perowne, *Psalms*, 343–44.

30 Delitzsch, "Psalms," in K&D 7:723–24.

the psalmist (vv. 6–7, 10–14) and disciplined the psalmist (v. 18). The one who has seen a reversal of fortunes up to this point is the psalmist, so it follows that it is the psalmist who is cast as the rejected stone, opposed but triumphant.[31] This also fits well with other messianic "stone" texts in the Old Testament, which we will take up later (Isa 8:14–15; 28:16; Dan 2:34–35).

The Identity of the Builders (118:22)

The "builders," like the stone, seem to appear out of nowhere. Who are they, and what is their function in the psalm? Most commentators would hold that pagan nations are the builders, given the earlier context of battle between the psalmist and the nations (vv. 10–13). However, this view has several difficulties. First, why would the psalmist use this metaphor to describe the nations? A strong explanation for this is lacking. Second, given the immediate temple context, it is easier to regard the metaphor as referring to those involved in some sense with the temple. Third, the nations have already been defeated, "cut off," earlier in the psalm; why would they be introduced again? At the risk of circular reasoning, then, if my understanding thus far is correct, the builders are most likely to be identified as the opposing voice(s) on the other side of the temple gate (v. 20), or the priests.[32] This accords with the ancient Jewish view that the priests were known as "builders."[33]

---

31 See VanGemeren, "Psalms," in *EBC* 5:857; Allen, *Psalms 101–150*, 167;

32 With Delitzsch, "Psalms," in K&D 7:723–24; *pace*, e.g., Briggs, *Psalms* 2:407; Perowne, *Psalms*, 343; Dahood, *Psalms III*, 159.

33 Herman L. Strack and Paul Billerbeck (*Kommentar zum Neuen Testament aus Talmud und Midrasch*, 4 vols. [C H. Beck, 1922–1928], 1.876) note that the "building" with which the priests and rabbis were associated was that of the knowledge and learning of Torah (cited by Kim, "Zechariah," 146). Kinde is agnostic about the identity of the builders in the psalm's original context ("Use of Psalm 118," 26), but the identification of the priests with the builders is, to me, the most logical conclusion. Further, based on Jesus' use of the Old Testament throughout his ministry, it is unlikely he lighted on this text whimsically (see G. K. Beale, "Did Jesus and His Followers Preach the Right Doctrine from the Wrong Texts? An Examination of the Presuppositions of Jesus' and the Apostles' Exegetical Method," *Them* 14 [1989]: 89–96). Sanders comments helpfully, "A select group of priests from within the temple would ponderously intone v. 20 to remind all that they were guardians of the gate of the Lord's house and had sole authority for granting admission" ("Hermeneutic Fabric," 145).

Blessed Is the One Who Comes (118:26)

This verse is a snarl in my argument regarding the reception of the psalmist in vv. 19–21. Indeed, it appears from the first colon that those on the other side of the gates are excited to see him! In response, first, the word "blessed" (בָּרוּךְ) is not unequivocally a warm welcome; it is a greeting whose sense, whether positive or negative or neutral, must be derived from the context.[34] Second, it is interesting that the singular הַבָּא, "he who comes," becomes a plural second person suffix on בֵּרַכְנוּכֶם, "we bless *you all*."[35] Few Psalms commentators attempt to deal with this conundrum.[36] The previous example of shifting referent in the psalm is the shift of addressing Yahweh as "you" instead of in the 3rd person (v. 21). There, I argued that the reason for this shift was to show the heightened emotion of the psalmist and the tacit opposition he felt from the gatekeepers. Here, tacit opposition may be at play as well; those who say, "We bless *you all*" do not welcome the psalmist directly even though he requested the gates be opened to *him specifically*.[37] So the first half of the verse may be read as a general statement ("the one who comes is blessed"), while the second half gives a greeting to those coming through the gate. To be sure, this does not disallow the psalmist's inclusion in this throng coming through the gate; *but neither does this make his coming certain*. The phrase "from the house of Yahweh" (מִבֵּית יְהוָה) establishes the location of the ones giving the blessing, probably the builders.[38] In other words, the gatekeepers bless whoever enters through the gates, but it is not

---

34 See 1 Kgs 21:10, 13; Ps 10:3; Job 1:5, 11; 2:5, 9 (BDB 139; *NIDOTTE* 1:752). It is noteworthy that Yahweh is the referent for each of these euphemistic uses of בָּרוּךְ, so on balance it is at least unlikely that a euphemistic sense would be present here. Granting this, I am not saying here that the sense of the greeting *is* negative here, but merely that we must not *assume* it is positive; it could be a neutral greeting.

35 The LXX follows this with εὐλογήκαμεν ὑμᾶς.

36 It is not discussed in Delitzsch, Weiser, Kraus, Perowne, VanGemeren, or Allen. Goldingay points it out but does not say anything about it (*Psalms 90–150*, 354).

37 Alternatively, Dahood (*Psalms III*, 160) reads the suffix as a plural of majesty. I would contend that this reading is only necessary because of the inherent difficulty of the referent switch, which I believe is more easily explained via my reading of tacit opposition.

38 Kraus, *Psalms 60–150*, 400. *Tg. Ps.* 118:26 puts these words in the mouth of David

certain that the psalmist is one of those entrants. The phrase which is ordinarily translated to suggest the psalmist is blessed in his coming through the gate, *need not be read this way.* In context, I think it is better read as a general statement, leaving open for question whether the psalmist entered or not. Considering this, I suggest that the psalmist's welcome at the gate remains in question. And given the victory he had secured for the people, a questionable welcome could well be construed as opposition, or even rejection.

Synthesis

I have sought to demonstrate that common readings of Psalm 118 may have missed a major point of conflict in the processional drama. I believe that the kingly entrant, upon his request for admission, *is opposed at the gate.* The priests on the other side, by not giving him a clear welcome, *have opposed him.* I have shown that this reading fits the psalm's context and flow. Now, as noted at the beginning, Psalm 118 is not the only "gate-entry" text in the Old Testament. It is not necessarily a common theme, but gate-entry is a concern with several important passages in Psalms and Isaiah. If it can be shown that these other gate-entry texts imply a sense of opposition or challenge for the entrants to overcome, it will strengthen my argument so far that Psalm 118 should be read this way. So below, we will look at these other instances of the gate-entry motif.

GATE-ENTRY ELSEWHERE IN THE OLD TESTAMENT (ISAIAH 26; PSALM 24)

Psalm 118 is not the only text in the Old Testament dealing a call for gates to be opened. In the ancient world, a city's wall and gates played an important role in its defense and government. Business and interpersonal matters were conducted at city gates in the presence of the prevailing authorities, as in the famous case of Ruth 4:1–12 (cf. Prov 24:7). As evidenced in Jeremiah, kings or other invading leaders would set up their thrones at the gates of the cities they conquered as a sign of their takeover.[39] Other texts depict open gates as a weakness in city

---

39 *NIDOTTE* 4:210.

fortification (cf. Nah 2:6; Neh 7:3; Isa 24:12). In the same vein, Ezekiel 33:1–9 describes the prophet as a watchman, presumably on watch on the city walls or at the city gate, whose role is to sound the alarm to the inhabitants of impending doom. In Psalm 118, then, the call for city gates to be opened is a call for protection and safety for the entrant on the outside. It may also signal a time of peace, for the entrant has just overcome in battle with Yahweh's help (vv. 10–16), and gates opened voluntarily would suggest no impending harm on the outside (cf. Isa 60:11). While these OT passages provide some historical background for the gate situation in Ps 118, two passages in particular, Psalm 24 and Isaiah 26, deal with the specific motif found in the text. These parallels help us to further understand what is happening in this text. In what follows we will look at each of these texts in turn.

Psalm 24:7–10: "Lift Up Your Heads, Oh Gates!"

At first glance, this well-known text may not seem to fit the picture described in Psalm 118 or Isaiah 26. The psalm begins with praise to God for His work in creation (vv. 1–2) and follows with a recitation of the requirements to "ascend the hill," that is, to approach the dwelling place of Yahweh (cf. Ps 15:1–5). However, Ps 24:8 praises Yahweh as "strong and mighty, Yahweh mighty in battle" (וְגִבּוֹר יְהוָה גִּבּוֹר מִלְחָמָה). This implies that war, or a previously-overcome opposition, stands in the background of the psalm. The name Yahweh of hosts, יְהוָה צְבָאוֹת, also seems to signify conquest, or at the very least a general sense of power. Craigie offers, "The language describing God in these verses is thoroughly military in tone," and suggests as well that the psalm would have been used liturgically after Israel returned from battles. He further argues that 24:7–10 is antiphonal, with the personification of gates and doors in vv. 7 and 9 referring to the "gatekeepers of the temple" (priests) who would ask the people entering, "Who is this King of glory?"[40] Both arguments for Psalm 24 accord with what we have seen in Psalm 118. Additionally, the exodus-like language in Ps 118:14–15, 19–21 appears in 24:5: "He will get a blessing from Yahweh, *righteousness*

---

40 Peter C. Craigie, *Psalms 1–50*, WBC 19; (Word, 1983), 213–14. Craigie's views on the Ark of the Covenant being used frequently in Israel's battle are suspect, as the only example of this occurring in the Old Testament is highly denigrated (1 Samuel 4–7), but his overall conclusion on Psalm 24's liturgical use is instructive.

from *the God of his salvation.*" Last, Psalm 24 is explicitly Davidic (24:1), aligning it at least on the surface with the implicitly Davidic Psalm 118.

Another, more involved argument may connect the two psalms as well. There is some warrant for reading Psalm 24 as the climax of a progression found in the prior Psalms 22–23, and perhaps as the final bookend of a chiasm of Psalms 15–24.[41] Caution should be exercised when drawing connections between adjacent psalms, for Psalms is full of stock language for praise, worship, lament, and victory.[42] The upshot of such a view for our purposes, however, is that the entrance through the gates would at least implicitly be an entrance after opposition is overcome—the opposition of battle (24:8) and perhaps even the opposition of messianic suffering (Ps 22) and the valley of deep darkness (Ps 23:4).

Isaiah 26:2: "Open the Gates."

This passage is situated in the middle of what has sometimes been referred to as the "Isaiah Apocalypse" (Isaiah 24–27). It is a shocking picture of what Yahweh will do in the end times, bringing judgment on the whole earth as 24:1 bears out: "Behold, Yahweh is about to empty the earth and desolate it...." At the end, Yahweh will make all things right by defeating His people's enemies and even defeating Satan himself, as stated explicitly in 27:1: "On that day Yahweh will bring a hard and strong sword against Leviathan, the fleeing serpent, Leviathan the twisting serpent. He will slay that dragon in the sea."[43] This massive victory will also be accompanied by a reverse of the effects of the Fall, as Yahweh announces He keeps a pleasant vineyard and has no thorns or thistles to battle (cf. Gen 3:18).[44]

---

41 Philip Sumpter, "The Coherence of Psalms 15–24," *Bib* 94.2 (2013): 186–209; Nancy L. Declaissé-Walford, "An Intertextual Reading of Psalms 22, 23, and 24," in *The Book of Psalms: Composition and Reception*, ed. Peter W. Flint and Patrick D. Miller, VTSup 99 (Brill, 2004), 139–52.

42 See Declaissé-Walford, "Psalms 22, 23, and 24," 143. Her suggestions on connections between Psalms 22 and 23 are stronger in my judgment than are those with Psalm 24, but the broader chiastic structure of Psalms 15–24 maintains the set bound together at least superficially.

43 This interpretation of Leviathan as Satan is debated, but see Revelation 12:9 which takes this position.

44 Paul L. Redditt, "Isaiah 26," *RevExp* 88, no. 2 (1991): 195; John N. Oswalt, *The*

Turning to the earlier chapters of the Isaiah Apocalypse, we see numerous oracles of judgment. There the judgment Yahweh brings is spoken of in military terms, as in Isa 24:10, "The empty city is broken down; every house is closed so no one may come in." Returning to the motif in question, it is striking that this military victory is depicted by the enemies' battered gates, as in Isa 24:12: "Desolation remains in the city; the gates are battered to ruins." This image contrasts sharply with the exultant tone and manner of Yahweh's people, who will say, "'Behold, This is our God. We waited for Him, and He saved us. This is Yahweh. We waited for Him, now let us shout for joy and rejoice in His salvation'" (25:9). The context clarifies that the people were in great need, oppressed by their enemies, and Yahweh delivered them (25:4–5). This deliverance sparks praise, as within this context of exultation,[45] the inhabitants of Judah will sing, "Open the gates (פִּתְחוּ שְׁעָרִים), so that the righteous nation who keeps faithfulness may come in." Thus, we see in Isaiah a juxtaposition of gate images—the broken down, ruined gates of Israel's enemies, and the open gates of jubilant Israel who was rescued. Open gates for Israel and ruined gates for Israel's enemies signify Yahweh's salvation for Israel. The righteous nation may enter through the open gates of Jerusalem for its enemies have been defeated, and Yahweh has wrought salvation on their behalf.

In summary, the notion of gate entry in the Old Testament carries with it the ideas of battles won, peace secured, and lofty place of Yahweh as the one bringing salvation and indeed entering through the gates Himself. Psalm 118 especially fits this description, as the entrant has overcome in battle, overcome opposition at the gate, entering "against the odds." Psalm 24 and Isaiah 26 pick up different facets of the same motif, emphasizing that the righteous enter through the gates in victory. We might say that Psalm 118 emphasizes the "front" of the gate motif, showcasing in full the opposition that must be overcome, specifically by the royal entrant. On the other hand, Psalm 24 and Isaiah 26 emphasize the "back" of the gate motif, where the opposition has been overcome and both Yahweh and His people, by extension, enter through the gates victorious. In the next section, we

---

Book of Isaiah Chapters 1–39, NICOT (Eerdmans, 1986), 440.

45 Note the repetition of "on that day" (בַּיּוֹם הַהוּא) in 25:9 and 26:2 (see also 24:21; 27:1–2, 12–13).

will consider how the Gospel writers pick up on this motif and these nuances in their Passion Week quotations of Psalm 118.[46]

Use in the Passion Week
"Blessed Is He Who Comes in the Name of the Lord"?
Matt 21:1–11; Mark 11:1–11; Luke 19:28–40

As the first major event of Passion Week, Jesus entered Jerusalem from the east, coming down out of the Mount of Olives, entering the temple area on the back of a donkey's colt and met with shouts of Hosanna (ὡσαννά, Hebrew נָּא הוֹשִׁיעָה, "save now"). From the outset, the Gospel writers consider this entrance not that of an ordinary pilgrim. Jesus' entrance from the Mount of Olives on a donkey's colt was meant to evoke the prophet Zechariah, as Matt 21:5 makes explicit.[47] What is striking, however, is that the crowd who welcomes Jesus into the city does not refer to Zechariah; this is part of Matthew's portrayal but not necessarily the crowd's reception. Instead, they recite the antiphonal Psalm 118: "Blessed is he who comes in the name of the Lord." The reason for this has to do with the crowd's expectations. Jesus had already been labeled the "Son of David" on his way from Jericho to Jerusalem (Matt 20:30–31). The crowd wished to further ascribe Davidic pedigree to Jesus based on their Davidic conception of Psalm 118. The label of "prophet" that the crowds give him also fits with early Jewish notions that David was a prophet (Matt 21:11).[48] However, in the case of Matthew, the point of Jesus' meekness and humility (cf. Zech 9:9) was lost in the din of the procession.[49] My earlier reading of בָּרוּךְ הַבָּא בְּשֵׁם יְהוָה, "the one who comes in the name of Yahweh is

---

46 For brevity, I limit my survey to the explicit quotations of Ps 118:22, 25–26, and to these quotations only as they appear in the Synoptics.

47 N. T. Wright calls this "symbolic action" (*Jesus and the Victory of God*, Christian Origins and the Question of God 2 [Fortress Press, 1996], 490–91). Cf. Zech 9:9–10; 14:4; Kim, "Zechariah," 134–48.

48 Joseph A. Fitzmyer, "David, 'Being Therefore a Prophet' (Acts 2:30)," *CBQ* 34, no. 3 (1972): 332–39.

49 I am not sure I would agree with Turner when he says that Jesus' humility "perplexed" Jerusalem, but I do agree that they did not assimilate the humility aspect into his symbolic action (David L. Turner, *Matthew*, BECNT [Baker Academic, 2008] 493–97).

blessed," is thus agreeable to Matthew's presentation: the coming one may be greeted, but something is amiss in the greeting. The crowds welcome the entrant Jesus, but his entrance is one of weakness.

Mark adds to the crowd's recitation of Ps 118:26 the phrase "Blessed is the coming kingdom of our father David!" (ESV). Watts argues that Mark incorporates the psalm into a broader framework of new exodus motifs, most of which were either original to Psalm 118 and the Egyptian Hallel or were birthed by their earliest interpreters. The psalm's entrant, then, is the conquering hero who will restore the kingdom of David.[50] However, Mark adds a twist to the story by underscoring the tying and untying of the colt (vv. 2, 4–5). In light of the Old Testament background of Zechariah and also Gen 49:8–12, it is more than likely that Mark is playing on the words δέω and λύω, that the coming one is in some sense rescinding the prophecy of blessing on Judah with the image of the donkey tethered to a vine.[51] The story ends on an anticlimactic note, with Jesus surveying the temple precincts, and leaving as quickly as he had come in (v. 11). Both Evans and Watts are struck by how this goes against (their reading of) the psalm, and thus they opine that this lack of reception would have been an insult.[52] However, the lack of surprise apparent in Mark's presentation *a priori* militates against this. It seems best to believe that Mark too anticipated opposition at the gate even if the crowds missed it.

As for Luke, Bock posits that the addition of ὁ βασιλεὺς, "the king," in the chorus evinces the influence of Zech 9:9.[53] The further reference to "Peace in heaven and glory in the highest!" takes the place of ὡσαννά, "hosanna," and is probably an echo of Psalm 148 and connects back with the angel's proclamation in the birth narrative (Luke 2:14).[54]

---

50 Watts, "Lord's House," 307–22 (especially 313–15).

51 As argued forcefully by Deborah Krause, "Unbinding the Blessings," 141–53.

52 Evans remarks: "If Ps 118 gives us any guidance, especially as it is paraphrased in the Aramaic targum, then Jesus may very well have anticipated a priestly greeting. But none is recorded. This is admittedly speculative, but it could explain the awkward, anticlimactic ending of the entrance narrative" (Craig A. Evans, *Mark 8:27–16:20*, WBC 34B [Thomas Nelson, 2001], 146). And Watts: "Unlike Psalm 118 ... Jesus receives no such greeting from the temple authorities ... and Israel's unwelcome king remains outside the city" ("Lord's House and David's Lord," 315).

53 Darrell L. Bock, *Luke 9:51–24:53*, BECNT (Baker Academic, 1996), 1558.

54 David W. Pao and Eckhard J. Schnabel, "Luke," in *Commentary on the New Testament Use of the Old Testament*, ed. G. K. Beale and D. A. Carson (Baker Academic,

Luke's Gospel also records that the religious leaders chastened Jesus on His way in for allowing the crowds to attribute such grandeur to Him (19:39), picking up on the opposition nuance of the gate-entry motif. Jesus' statement that "the stones would cry out" if the entrance praises ceased probably functions in the narrative as another play on Psalm 118 as well.[55] The main difference in Luke's narrative resides in the paragraph that follows, verses 41–44. Here Jesus weeps over the city of Jerusalem after having entered it, for "you did not know the time of your visitation" (ESV). With clear allusions to the future destruction of Herod's temple, the Gospel record chides Jerusalem for rejecting the kingdom on "this day" (cf. Ps 118:24), for it was to be a day of God's action on the behalf of his people.[56] Considering the parallel to this passage in Matt 23:37–39, we see that the proposed allusion to Ps 118:24 in Jesus' weeping obtains, for he ends his diatribe with, "... you will certainly not see me again until you say, 'Blessed is the one who comes in the name of the Lord.'" Had the crowds not already issued this call when he came into the city? Of course, at least verbally even if not with full understanding. *But had the religious leaders issued the call along with them?* No. Rather, they chided Jesus for not rebuking his disciples when they issued this call (Luke 19:39).[57] The Gospels' usage of Psalm 118:25–26 fits well, then, with the opposition nuance of the gate motif. Jesus is given what appears to be a royal welcome, but his entrance is not without struggle, notably against the "builders."

"THE STONE THE BUILDERS REJECTED"
MATT 21:33–46; MARK 12:1–12; LUKE 20:9–18[58]

The parable of the wicked tenants has received much attention in the

---

2007), 355–56.

55 These would probably be temple stones, just as I have argued for the אֶבֶן in Ps 118:22.

56 Cf. Wright, *Jesus*, 333–35; Brent Kinman, "Parousia, Jesus' 'A-Triumphal' Entry, and the Fate of Jerusalem (Luke 19:28–44)," *JBL* 118, no. 2 (1999): 279–94.

57 On the surface, they did not think Jesus was the Messiah he claimed to be (Sanders, "Hermeneutic Fabric," 143–44, 151), yet even in their rejection of him they prove him to be the Messiah (cf. Isa 52:13–53:12).

58 In this section I will not deal with the differences between the Synoptics on the psalm quotation as I did in the previous section. *In nuce*, Luke drops Ps 118:23

past, and I cannot hope to add much to the discussion in general.[59] To begin, as mentioned previously, several Old Testament texts describe the Messiah as a stone (Isa 8:14–15; 28:16; Dan 2:34–35), and these also play a role in Jesus' parable and message.[60] In the Isaiah texts, Yahweh declares that the foundational stone He laid in Zion will not crumble for the one that hopes in it. Conversely, it is implied in 28:16 and stated explicitly in 28:17–22, that those who do not trust in Yahweh will stumble over the stone (cf. 8:14–15). In Daniel the stone cut from the mountain shatters the feet of the statue representing the four empires and establishes "a kingdom that can never be destroyed" (2:44–45, ESV).[61]

And what of Psalm 118? The verse in question is v. 22 and the famous phrase, "The stone the builders rejected has become the cornerstone." Here, as most commentators note, Jesus makes a wordplay on the Hebrew words for son (בֵּן, *ben*) and stone (אֶבֶן, *eben*).[62] The vineyard tenants reject the *Son* (υἱός), but they fail to realize that in so doing they have rejected the very foundation on which they stand, the *Stone*. Jesus pulls the rug out from under them, as it were: their place (the temple) and nation will be relinquished to Rome, in part due to their rejection of the true King and Lord of the temple. And this will come while the rejected Son continues to build His kingdom, a kingdom which, in Daniel's language, will never be destroyed. The Gospel writers are therefore sensitive to both the opposition *and* the victory sides of the gate-entry motif. Wright's comments are excellent:

The prophetic story of the rejected servants climaxes in the rejected son; he, however, is the messianic stone which, rejected by the builders, takes the chief place in the building. Those who oppose him

---

whereas Matthew and Mark retain it (cf. Bock, *Luke 9:51–24:53*, 1603–604).

59 John Dominic Crossan, "The Parable of the Wicked Husbandmen," *JBL* 90, no. 4 (1971): 451–65; K. R. Snodgrass, "The Parable of the Wicked Husbandmen," *NTS* 20 (1974): 142–44; J. A. T. Robinson, "The Parable of the Wicked Tenants," *NTS* 21 (1975): 443–61.

60 These same Isaiah texts are drawn together elsewhere in the New Testament (Rom 9:30–33; 1 Pet 2:4–10), on which see helpfully Norman Hillyer, "'Rock-Stone' Imagery in 1 Peter," *TynBul* 22 (1971): 58–81; George J. Brooke, "4Q500 1 and the Use of Scripture in the Parable of the Vineyard," *DSD* 2, no. 3 (1995): 268–94.

61 J. Alec Motyer, *The Prophecy of Isaiah: An Introduction & Commentary* (InterVarsity Press, 1993), 233–34; Edward F. Siegman, "Stone Hewn from the Mountain (Daniel 2)," *CBQ* 18, no. 4 (1956): 364–79.

62 Similarly, see *Tg. Ps.* 118:22.

will find their regime (and their Temple) destroyed, while his king-dom will be established. The psalm text indicates, cryptically, what will later become clear: when the owner of the vineyard acts against the wicked tenants, the son will be vindicated.[63]

Matthew's final word on the parable is worth noting in closing: "And when the chief priests and Pharisees heard his parables, they knew that it was concerning them that he spoke" (Matt 21:45). To be sure, Jesus' usage of the passage itself could not be missed on them. Then too, the prophetic missive against Judahite leaders in Isaiah 8 and 28, which are echoed here, could have added to their recognition. Even more, Jesus' own adaptations of the Isaiah 5 parable, especially the existence of the tenants themselves, point in the direction of this understanding. But Jesus' question, "Have you never read in the Scrip-tures…?" is immediately followed by the quotation from Psalm 118, not one of the Isaiah texts. This is to say, Jesus assumes that his audience would have understood the meaning of his parable, and his underly-ing critique of the religious leaders, *from Psalm 118*. And the fact that they did not challenge his interpretation seems to argue for its au-thenticity and applicability.[64] Drawing these threads together, Jesus saw Himself as Psalm 118's temple entrant who overcomes an implicit opposition to get there, and as the rejected-turned-victorious stone. The Gospel writers and religious leaders understood it the same way and, as I have argued, this is how Psalm 118 was intended to be read all along.

Conclusion

In this chapter I looked at Psalm 118 with the goals of (1) understand-ing it fully in context, (2) considering related Old Testament "gate-en-try" texts, and (3) seeing how the psalm is used in the Gospels. I have argued that the psalm in context allows for the interpretation the New Testament gives to it, namely that the stone rejected by the builders is

---

63 Wright, *Jesus*, 501 (see all of 497–501).

64 Turner, *Matthew*, 515. Incidentally, this means that if Jesus had misinterpreted the psalm, it is highly unlikely that he would or could have convinced the religious leaders of his reading. The scandal of their acceptance of his interpretation argues for its authenticity and its veracity.

the psalmist himself who is opposed, if not rejected, at the gate when he comes in to worship. I have argued that this is the experience Jesus endured when he came into Jerusalem during Passion Week. The Gospel writers picked up on the complex nuances of Psalm 118 and its theology well, demonstrating their command of the Scriptures and their theological profundity. And Psalm 118 is merely one case study of this reality. Throughout the New Testament we see that the New Testament writers wrote with great precision concerning prior revelation, skillfully and convincingly drawing out the nuances of the theology of the Old Testament. Some of them may have been "unschooled and ordinary" in the eyes of the religious elite (Acts 4:13), but they knew their Bibles extremely well, putting that knowledge on display for the church of their day and generations to come. They learned the Old Testament from the greatest Old Testament exegete of all, its author and our Lord, Jesus.[65] And I know I speak for many when I say that the ministry of Dr. William Varner has exemplified for decades what this kind of careful exegesis and sound theologizing can look like, both in the church and in the classroom. He too learned how rightly to handle the Word of truth from his Master, and the results of this learning are evident in every corner of his ministry.

---

65 On which see Abner Chou, *The Hermeneutics of the Biblical Writers: Learning to Interpret Scripture from the Prophets and Apostles* (Kregel Publications, 2018), to whom I am indebted for the opportunity to contribute to this volume.

10

Earliest Christian Jesus-devotion and Metaphysics

Wyatt Graham

L ARRY HURTADO HAS STUDIED JESUS-DEVOTION in light of Jewish monotheism to show the bi-nitarian shape of the earliest Jesus-devotion.[1] Responding to such proposals, Daniel Kirk argues that the synoptic Gospels portray Jesus as a man and not as one included in the being of God.[2] For Kirk, Hurtado may rightly understand Paul and John's early High Christology, but he misunderstands the story that the Synoptic Gospels present.

How can two astute scholars look at the same evidence and come to such different conclusions? Part of the answer has to do with how Hurtado and Kirk conceive of the Jewish intellectual context of the first century. Martin Hengel explains, "our modern understanding of nature and its reality seems to be different from the world of early Christian texts."[3] And one such difference involves a Jewish-Hellenistic awareness of metaphysics.[4]

By retrieving this metaphysical awareness, a stronger case can be made for the plausibility of an early high Christology. This chapter modestly aims to outline a number of passages from the Old

---

1 Larry W. Hurtado, *Lord Jesus Christ: Devotion to Jesus in Earliest Christianity* (Eerdmans, 2003).

2 J. R. Daniel Kirk, *A Man Attested by God: The Human Jesus of the Synoptic Gospels* (Eerdmans, 2016).

3 Martin Hengel, "Problems of a History of Earliest Christianity," in *Studien Zum Urchristentum: Kleine Schriften VI*, WUNT 234 (Mohr Siebeck, 2008), 302.

4 To this awareness of metaphysics, I would also add cosmology—the way in which Israel viewed the universe and its structures.

Testament that suggest an awareness of metaphysics on the part of the biblical authors. With this background in mind, the synoptic presentation of Jesus may entail metaphysical reasoning. What might confirm this is the Gospel according to John. It contains eye-witness testimony of Jesus that the evangelist reflected upon for about 60 years.[5] And this eyewitness account reflects on the metaphysical implications of Jesus' coming. Hence, it is plausible that the Gospel according to John shows readers how to reflect metaphysically upon the Jesus of testimony as found in the synoptic Gospels.

The World of the Old Testament

The Old Testament fundamentally speaks of the world in supernatural ways. Heavenly beings exist. The temple of God sits in the heavens. Miracles change the created world. Yet these two realities—heaven above and earth below—do not exist separately. They correspond to each other like two ends of a spectrum. What happens in heaven really does change what happens on earth. The following discussion illustrates how heaven and earth unite through the operation of angels and through the temple wherein heaven and earth meet.

Angels

Possibly the most under-valued characters in the Bible are angels.[6] They are everywhere but almost always forgotten. But they play a key role in the Bible and in the world to which the Bible testifies.

For example, Moses writes in Deuteronomy 32:

Remember the days of old; consider the years of many generations; ask your father, and he will show you, your elders, and they

---

5 Richard Bauckham, *Jesus and the Eyewitnesses: The Gospels as Eyewitness Testimony*, 2nd ed. (Eerdmans, 2017).

6 Early Christian and Jewish authors spent time reflecting on angels and their relationship to creation. Pseudo-Dionysius (fl. 5th or 6th ce.) laid out a vast paradigm for understanding celestial hierarchies in his writings. Similarly, the Book of Enoch (e.g., 1 Enoch 64–69) discussed the angelic realm. The modern period saw the eclipse of discussion on angels. One exception to this rule is Michael Heiser who has recently written *Angels: What the Bible really Says about God's Heavenly Host* (Lexham Press, 2018).

will tell you. When the Most High gave to the nations their inheritance, when he divided mankind, he fixed the borders of the peoples according to the number of the sons of God. (Deut 32:7–8)[7]

When God divided humanity, he did so according to the number of the sons of God, or angels.[8] The implication being that each nation has an angel overseeing it.

The book of Daniel illustrates what this looks like when an angel comes to Daniel and says:

The prince of the kingdom of Persia withstood me twenty-one days, but Michael, one of the chief princes, came to help me, for I was left there with the kings of Persia, and came to make you understand what is to happen to your people in the latter days. For the vision is for days yet to come. (Dan 10:13–14)

The prince of Persia, a spiritual being, stopped a foreign angel from crossing into his borders. The standoff lasted for three weeks until Michael, a chief prince, helped the angel infiltrate Persia to mediate God's message to Daniel.

Holy ones or watchers also execute God's judgment against the earthly power of Nebuchadnezzar (Dan 4:13–14). As Walther Eichrodt notes, "the real government of the world seems to have been transferred to them."[9] Angels oversee ("the watchers") and judge the nations. The angelic oversight of nations also carries over into churches. So Revelation 2–3 narrates Jesus' words not to the seven churches *per se*, but to the seven angels who have oversight of the churches.[10]

---

7 All translations are from the ESV unless otherwise noted.

8 As Walther Eichrodt notes, Job 1:6, 2:1, and 38:7 define angels as "Sons of God." Walther Eichrodt, *Theology of the Old Testament*, trans. J. A. Baker, vol. 2 (The Westminster Press, 1967), 195.

9 Eichrodt, *Theology*, 2:199. Eichrodt pointed me to Dan 4 and the role of the watchers and holy ones there.

10 It is equally possible that angels here refer to pastors. On this see, Peter J. Leithart, *Revelation 1–11*, International Theological Commentary (T&T Clark, 2018), 123–128. In this case, John may have used the term "angels" to indicate that Christian pastors have replaced the angels in the economy of God as those who have oversight over his people.

Angels rule over nations, battle at borders, and watch over churches. Small wonder then that Paul wants women to cover their hair "because of the angels" (1 Cor 11:10).

Why would angels need to oversee the church and why would our ethical behavior matter to them?

Paul explains in Ephesians that the mystery of the Gospel came "so that through the church the manifold wisdom of God might now be made known to the rulers and authorities in the heavenly places" (Eph 3:10). Note that the Gospel shows God's wisdom to rulers and authorities who exist in the heavenly or angelic realm. The church's preaching of Christ is meant to show God's wisdom to heavenly beings.

Our ethical behavior matters, therefore, for the sake of God's wisdom being manifest in the cosmos.

Paul provides further instruction about the spiritual realm that perhaps explains why John the Revelator speaks of angels overseeing churches. It is because our battle is not "against flesh and blood, but against the rulers, against the authorities, against the cosmic powers over this present darkness, against the spiritual forces of evil in the heavenly places" (Eph 6:12).

We know something of this invisible battle because Daniel records the conflict between Michael and the prince of Persia. Daniel provides few details concerning what this battle looks like. Likely, describing the angelic conflict would feel just as confusing as Ezekiel's vision of the divine chariot (See Ezek 1).

What we do know is that we battle spiritual powers through Gospel preaching and through our ethical behavior. And as Paul says in Ephesians 2:10, Christ recreated us "for good works."

In summary, nations have angels, angels battle over us, churches have angels, the Gospel shows God's wisdom to angelic beings, and our daily decisions matter at the cosmic level. So Paul can warn the Corinthians not to act untowardly "because of the angels" (1 Cor 11:10).

What seems clear is that what happens on earth corresponds to what happens in heaven; or what happens in heaven intersects with what happens on earth. The invisible truly affects the visible and vice versa.

The Tabernacle

The tabernacle represents the intersection between heaven and earth because God's glory abides in it (Exod 40:34; cf. 2 Sam 7:6–7; 1 Chr 17:5–6); Ps 78:60). Further, the design and articles within the tabernacle portray various elements that point to heavenly objects. Together the glory, the design, and the articles show earthly things pointing to or intersecting with heavenly realities. The following discussion will demonstrate these assertions.

The biblical text does not, however, provide sufficient details for a comprehensive explanation of the tabernacle's design. Instead, it highlights and repeats what has theological value since Exodus is a theological text. Duane Garrett explains:

> One may assume that many details are left out since the missing information could be filled in with common knowledge or common sense. Therefore, we should understand that the tent instructions only focus on details that are distinctive and religiously significant. This, in fact, helps to explain a curious feature about this text: there are many details left out, but instructions that are given are often repeated in what seems to be needless redundancy. But the point is to stress what has special meaning, not to state what is obvious or universal in tent making.[11]

What has special meaning in particular, then, are not, for example, the two outer layers of the tabernacle for which no information is given.[12] Rather, the following seven elements are important because they receive detailed instructions and repetition: the inner-two layers of the tent, the altar, the menorah, the table of showbread, the censor, the veil between the holy place and the most holy place, and the ark.

What is relevant to the current argument is that each of the seven elements and the tabernacle itself existed in heaven before Moses saw them and replicated them on earth. In proof of this, Exodus 24 narrates Moses entering into heaven to receive the pattern for the tabernacle and all its instruments.

11　Duane A. Garrett, *A Commentary on Exodus* (Kregel Academic, 2014), 571–72.

12　Garrett, *A Commentary on Exodus*, 571.

The story begins with the ascent of Moses into Mount Sinai where he entered into God's presence. Some way up the mountain Moses and few others "saw the God of Israel," and "There was under his feet as it were a pavement of sapphire stone, like the very heaven for clearness" (Exod 24:10).[13] They entered into the heavenly places.

But Moses ascends further than anyone else:

> Then Moses went up on the mountain, and the cloud covered the mountain. The glory of the LORD dwelt on Mount Sinai, and the cloud covered it six days. And on the seventh day he called to Moses out of the midst of the cloud. Now the appearance of the glory of the LORD was like a devouring fire on the top of the mountain in the sight of the people of Israel. Moses entered the cloud and went up on the mountain. And Moses was on the mountain forty days and forty nights. (Exod 24:15–18)

Moses not only entered into the heavenly places, he also entered into the very glory of God. The fiery glory of God enlightened Moses for 40 days in "thick darkness" (Exod 20:21). It took him seven days before he even spoke after God finally addressed him. He came the closest to the beatific vison than anyone up until his time had ever come, save perhaps Adam and Eve in paradise.

What he saw in God's glory, within the inner sanctum of God's glorious light, was the inner sanctum of the heavenly tabernacle. He received instructions on how to make the tabernacle (Exod 25:9). As Exodus 25:40 says, Moses made the tabernacle "after the pattern" which he saw on the mountain.

By saying "after the pattern," the text indicates that the earthly tabernacle models itself after a heavenly tabernacle. It follows the plans that Moses received from God (Exod 25:9). "The plans," writes John Goldingay, "correspond to the nature of God's already existent dwelling

---

13 Jeffrey Niehaus rightly sees Solomon's temple as replicating the heavenly pavement that Moses and others with him walked on and that John saw in Rev 4:6: "Solomon actually copied the supernal floor with gold pavement in both inner and outer rooms of his temple (1 Kings 6:30)." Jeffrey J. Niehaus, *Ancient Near Eastern Themes in Biblical Theology* (Kregel, 2008), 94.

in heaven."[14] The Wisdom of Solomon calls the temple "a copy of the holy tent that you prepared from the beginning" (9:8). The author to the Hebrews explains that the priests "serve a copy and shadow of the heavenly things. For when Moses was about to erect the tent, he was instructed by God, saying, 'See that you make everything according to the pattern that was shown you on the mountain'" (Heb 8:5).

But it is not just the tabernacle itself that existed in heaven. The seven key elements in the tabernacle also have a heavenly archetype. Numbers 8:4 confirms that Moses made the lampstand "according to the pattern that the LORD had shown Moses" (Num 8:4). We can plausibly infer therefore that the other elements beyond the lampstand also have heavenly forms. And this is exactly what Exodus 25:9 indicates: "Exactly as I show you concerning the pattern of the tabernacle, and of all its furniture, so you shall make."

Moses made what he saw in heaven on earth. Of the temple, Psalm 78:69 says, "He built his sanctuary like the high heavens, like the earth, which he has founded forever." The text here seems to mean that God's sanctuary somehow can be likened to both the "high heavens" and "the earth." G. K. Beale explains, "The psalmist is saying that, in some way, God designed Israel's earthly temple to be comparable to the heavens and earth."[15] Although the sanctuary (temple) came later, it seems clear that the temple followed the pattern of the tabernacle by portraying its visible form in accordance with the heavenly sanctuary.

In the New Testament, the author to the Hebrews asserts that Christ himself serves in the heavenly tabernacle. As Hebrews 9:11–12 states, the heavenly tabernacle in which Christ serves functions as the archetype for the earthly tent:

> But when Christ appeared as a high priest of the good things that have come, then through the greater and more perfect tent (not made with hands, that is, not of this creation) he entered once for all into the holy places, not by means of the blood of goats and

---

14 John Goldingay, *Old Testament Theology: Israel's Faith*, vol. 1 (IVP Academic, 2003), 395.

15 G. K. Beale, *The Temple and the Church's Mission: A Biblical Theology of the Dwelling Place of God* (IVP Academic, 2004), 32.

calves but by means of his own blood, thus securing an eternal redemption. (Heb 9:11–12)

The author continues:

> Thus it was necessary for the copies of the heavenly things to be purified with these rites, but the heavenly things themselves with better sacrifices than these. For Christ has entered, not into holy places made with hands, which are copies of the true things, but into heaven itself, now to appear in the presence of God on our behalf. (Heb 9:23–24)

The earthly tabernacle required purification through the mosaic system. Yet such rites could not purify the heavenly tabernacle since no earthly thing could do so. Only the man who came from heaven, Christ, could purify "the heavenly things themselves with better scarifies" than provided under the law of Moses. The correspondence between Christ's heavenly ascension and the heavenly reality of the temple illustrate how first century Christians perceived key theological (or metaphysical) realities about heaven and earth, which are present in the Exodus account.[16]

The tabernacle and its elements, therefore, replicate realities that already existed in heaven. Additionally, God's glory on earth plainly corresponds to God's glory in heaven (Exod 20:15–18, 22 with 40:34). It forms an intersection between heaven and earth.

A Sketch of the Tabernacle

Exodus 24 affirms that the sanctuary on earth replicates the one in heaven.[17] By closely describing the tabernacle and its elements, we may go beyond affirming *that* it replicates heaven but also specify the *ways* in which it corresponds to heavenly realities.

---

16   In more technical terms, this illustrates one trajectory of the reception history of the Exodus. Indeed, a number of earlier interpreters understand the tabernacle as intersecting with heaven (Wisdom 9:8; Josephus, *Ant.*, 3.181; Philo, *Life of Moses*, 2:98.

17   For a concise and clear description of the dimensions, shape, and look of the tabernacle, see Roland de Vaux, *Ancient Israel: Its Life and Institutions*, trans. John McHugh (Longman, and Todd, 1961), 295–96.

To visualize the following discussion, here is a brief sketch of the tabernacle's shape.[18] The tabernacle had three sections. The courtyard which one passes through to enter the tent is the first section (Exod 27:9–19). Next, one would walk into a space of about thirty feet inside the tent, which is called the holy place (Exod 26:1–2; 26:33). Afterwards, one would pass through the curtain into the most holy place that has a depth of fifteen feet (Exod 26:33).[19] The most holy place sits at the west side of the tent (Exod 26:22, 27), while the holy place and the entrance stand at the east side (Exod 38:13).

The Menorah

The entire tent, both the holy place and the most holy place, had no natural light except a seven candle menorah that Moses describes as having branches, blooms, and calyxes, which are basically the top of a flower.[20] So the menorah looks like a tree with a trunk or a stem and seven branches on top of it which are flower blooms, and it derives from a heavenly prototype according to Numbers 8:4.[21] Each of the seven calyxes would hold a candle, illuminating the room. This menorah would be on the left side of the tent from the point of view of the tabernacle's entrance.

On the walls of the room and on the veil between the holy and most holy place would be cherubim or angels sewn into blue or purple fabric (Exod 26:1, 31; 36:8, 35). It would look like the night sky with angels overhead and all around. This furthers the impression that the tree exists within the intersection of heaven and earth.

---

18 During the Summer of 2018, I enjoyed listening to Paul Martin's series on the Book of Exodus at *Muskoka Bible Centre*. These messages have enriched my understanding of the tabernacle and inform my discussion here.

19 The total length of the tabernacle was 30 cubits or about 45 feet. See Nahum M. Sarna, *Exodus*, The JPS Torah Commentary (The Jewish Publication Society, 1991), 167. The dimensions seem most easily discerned through the discussion of frames in Exodus 26:15–25.

20 The ESV translates גְּבִיעַ as "cups," but Garrett rightly argues that these "cups" probably refer to a blossom "since the word is described as something that has both calyx and petals." Garrett, *A Commentary on Exodus*, 556n18.

21 Sarna, *Exodus*, 164.

Additionally, the illumined tree would be both light and life. It symbolizes light because it illumines the room.[22] It points to life because it represents the presence of God, harkening back to the tree of life in the garden in Eden.[23] Like the tree of life provided life, so the tree in the tabernacle did the same.

The plausibility of this argument relies largely on seeing the garden as a primordial temple much like the tabernacle which was a mobile temple. Gordon Wenham has identified numerous connections between the garden and temple.[24] The same term that describes God's movement in Genesis 3:8 also describes God's presence in tent sanctuaries (Lev 26:12; Deut 23:15; 2 Sam 7:6–7). Cherubim block the eastern entrance to the garden as they do in the temple (1 Kgs 6:23–28, 29; Exod 25:18–22; 26:31). Adam's vocation "to work" and "to keep" the garden represents a word pair that only appears in the Pentateuch for Levitical duties (Num 3:7–8; 8:26; 18:5–6). Greg Beale adds, "When these two words occur together later in the OT, without exception they have this meaning and refer either to Israelites serving and guarding/obeying God's word (about 10x) or, more often, to priests who serve God in the temple and guard the temple from unclean things entering it (Num. 3:7–8; 8:25–26; 18:5–6; 1 Chron. 23:32; Ezek. 44:14)."[25]

Further, as the tabernacle divides into three sections, so also does the garden. Beale explains that "the outermost region surrounding the garden is related to God and is 'very good' (Gen. 1:31) in that it is God's creation (= the outer court); the garden is a sacred space separate from the outer world (= the holy place), where God's priestly servant worships God by obeying him, by cultivating and guarding; Eden is

---

22 Although he does not mention the menorah, Goldingay argues that the tabernacle "resumes the creation" story due various correspondences with the creation story. Goldingay, *Old Testament Theology*, 1:395–96. The menorah itself might remind readers of God's creation of light in Genesis 1.

23 L. Michael Morales, *Who Shall Ascend the Mountain of the Lord?: A Biblical Theology of the Book of Leviticus*, NSBT (InterVarsity Press, 2015), 102.

24 The evidence listed in the above paragraph derives from Gordon J. Wenham, "Sanctuary Symbolism in the Garden of Eden Story," in *I Studied Inscriptions From Before the Flood: Ancient Near Eastern, Literary, and Linguistic Approaches to Genesis 1–11*, ed. Richard S. Hess and David Toshio Tsumura, vol. 4 (Eisenbrauns, 1994), 399–404.

25 G. K. Beale, *A New Testament Biblical Theology: The Unfolding of the Old Testament in the New* (Baker Academic, 2011), 617–18.

where God dwells (= the holy of holies) as the source of both physical and spiritual life (symbolized by the waters)."[26]

Numerous other correlations appear,[27] but these suffice to communicate the point that the garden existed as a primordial temple. Ezekiel 28 confirms this interpretation because it calls Eden "the holy mountain of God" (Ezek 28:14; see also v. 13).

It is important to note that the Cherubim did not just guard the way to the garden. They blocked the way to the tree of life in Eden (Gen 3:24). Their purpose is to form a barrier between God and man.[28] Heavenly creatures guard the way to life. These same heavenly creatures surround God in heaven (Ezek 10:14) and representatively surround him on earth (Exod 25:18–22). Since they "guard the way to the tree of life" (Gen 3:24), the cherubim then block humanity from entering into life, God's presence. The illumined tree then represents the tree of life, entrance into God's very presence.[29] This further specifies how the tabernacle functions as the intersection of heaven and earth and replicates heavenly realities.

The Table

The table of God's presence stood on the right side of the tent from the point of view of the entrance. On it, twelve loaves of bread lay, symbolically pointing to the twelve tribes of Israel (Lev 24:8)[30] and harkening back to the manna from heaven that teaches Israel not to live on bread alone but on God's word (Deut 8:3).

---

26 Beale, *A New Testament Biblical Theology*, 621.

27 The temple connection has now become an established interpretive scheme. I refer readers to Beale's *A New Testament Biblical Theology* (617–48) for a full discussion. Beale's earlier work *The Temple and the Church's Mission* also outlines a theology of God's dwelling place throughout.

28 The cherubim probably kept out "the sinful and unclean." Beale, *The Temple and the Church's Mission*, 70.

29 Elsewhere in Scripture life and light together present God's presence, which further suggests that the illumined tree of life represents the life (and light) of God (e.g., Pss 27:1; 36:9). This background may partly explain why John writes, "God is light" (1 John 1:5; cf. John 8:12).

30 Jacob Milgrom, *A Continental Commentary: Leviticus: A Book of Ritual and Ethics* (Fortress Press, 2004), 291.

Two reasons suggest this conclusion. First, Exodus 16:4 calls manna bread from heaven. Since the tabernacle replicates heavenly realities, then it seems plain that the bread here replicates heavenly manna. Second, in the wilderness, Israelites did store manna in a jar within the tabernacle (Exod 16:31–34).[31] In this sense, heavenly bread was stowed away in the tabernacle. This storage may have seemed fitting because the bread on the table could have been seen to represent the heavenly bread which heaven provided.

The Incense

At the back of the tent but before the most holy place lay the altar of incense. The altar does not have any sacrifices laid upon it except once a year when the high priest put blood on the four corners of the altar, picked up some incense and coals, and walked into the holy of holies for the day of atonement. The incense symbolizes prayers ascending to God (cf. Rev 8:4).[32]

The Holy of Holies

At this point, the high priest would walk through the tree-illumined holy place with the cherubim watching and enter into the most holy place. He would peel back the curtain that signaled a movement into the most holy of all places, into the very presence of God (Exod 25:22).

Inside the most holy place, the high priest would put the incense into the coals to fill the room with the incense, an act which represents the prayers of the people going up to God in his presence. Then God's glory would appear between two cherubim that face each other over top of the ark of the covenant, which is a box with a slab on top of it; the slab is called the place of atonement, or the mercy seat, because the high priest atones for the people there, having already sacrificed an animal before entering the most holy place.

The cherubim in particular symbolize heavenly realties since actual cherubim guard God's presence (Ezek 10:14). Whatever Ezekiel

---

31 On this connection, see Brant Pitre, *Jesus and the Last Supper* (Eerdmans, 2015), 154. He makes this connection for a different argument than I do here, however.

32 Goldingay, *Old Testament Theology*, 1:398.

the prophet saw exactly in his visions, he did see cherubim guarding the throne of God (Ezek 1:16; cf. 10:20). And these cherubim ascend from the temple in Ezekiel 10. Thus, Ezekiel sees the genuine Cherubim leaving the temple in which the statues of cherubim stood (Ezek 10:18). The statues acted as signs, but Ezekiel saw the reality.

It is fitting therefore that Psalm 78:69 says, "He built his sanctuary like the high heavens, like the earth, which he has founded forever." The point being that the sanctuary somehow represents the heaven and the earth. What confirms this is the purple cloth in the tabernacle that is stitched with Cherubim. The heavenly creatures with a purple backdrop represent the cosmos. When the high priest went into the holy place, he pictorially transcended earth and heaven into the presence of God in which both heaven and earth meet. So God says in Exodus 25:22, "There I will meet with you."

In short, the tabernacle portrays itself as being heavenly and as being the place of God's presence much like the mountain was temporarily so when Moses ascended it.

The Cosmology of the Tent

The three sections of the tent also show how the tabernacle replicates heavenly realities. The partitions are the courtyard, the holy place, and the holy of holies. Given what has been said so far, these sections likely have theological import. Garrett explains:

> There was probably a cosmic dimension to this. That is, the outer chamber represented the lower heavens (what we would call the physical heavens) and the inner chamber, the holy of holies, would represent the upper heaven, God's abode. The Tent of Meeting was a microcosm of the created universe and of the heavenly throne room that was above the created universe. That is, God's glory fills all of creation, but there is yet a heavenly throne room that is above and beyond the physical universe. The Tent of Meeting is a smaller version of this cosmic reality. It is also the place where God who dwells in the highest heavens can be present or immanent in the world.[33]

---

33 Garrett, *A Commentary on Exodus*, 579–80.

The outer courtyard laid before one's eyes the place God became present. When one entered into the tent, they entered into the lower heavens and then into upper heaven where God dwells.[34] This also corresponds to Moses' threefold ascent into the mountain of God where Moses sees the heavenly tabernacle (Exod 24).

OTHER PATTERNS

Other patterns that illustrate heavenly realities intersecting with earth appear throughout Scripture. For example, humanity is created in the image of God (Gen 1:27). Now, sometimes this language seems so familiar to us that it loses meaning. But consider the word "image." An image reflects something. And that something is God. So, humanity was created in God's image. There is an archetype and a type—an essence and its image. Additionally, Proverbs 8:22–31 speaks about wisdom which becomes personified. Wisdom becomes something like a person that represents divine wisdom. These two patterns represent a small sampling of the biblical data.

SUMMARY

These patterns of angels and institutions show that the Old Testament views reality as comprising two overlapping realms: heaven and earth. And these two domains are not so distinct like they might be in the imagination of 21st century North Americans. Heaven often intersects with earth as when Moses ascended the mountain or when God's presence appears on the Day of Atonement in the Holy of Holies. And heavenly entities oversee earthly entities, such as when angels look after nations and churches.

Such a view of reality means that biblical authors and the divine

---

34 Garrett and my reading of the text have some precedent in the Christian tradition. Gregory of Nazianzus wrote in one of his justly famous theological orations: "Or, since Scripture recognizes the tabernacle of Moses as a symbol for the whole world (the world, I mean, of things 'visible and invisible') shall we pass through the first veil, transcending sense, to bend our gaze on holy things, on ideal and heaven transcending reality" (*Or* 28.31). Cited in *On God and Christ: The Five Theological Orations and Two Letters to Cledonius*, trans. Frederick Williams and Lionel Wickham (St. Vladimir's Seminary Press, 2002).

author himself deal signs and their archetypes.[35] As noted, the tabernacle is not merely a mobile tent. It is also a sign that points to a reality: the heavenly tent. The earthy tent points to something else, to its
exemplar. Whatever the precise connection between the tabernacle
in heaven and tabernacle on earth, Scripture affirms the two-fold reality of the tabernacle: the exemplar in heaven and the copy on earth.

This Old Testament impulse to understand the nature of things
represents part of the conceptual world of New Testament authors.
For example, John the Evangelist points to the tabernacle in order
to explain how the divine Logos could dwell among his people.[36] In
John 1:14, the word "dwelled" (ἐσκήνωσεν) could easily be translated
as "pitch a tent,"[37] evoking the tabernacle. Jesus becomes the temple, a reality that he himself attests to in John 2:19, "Destroy this temple, and in three days I will raise it up." And John explains that Jesus
meant his body (John 2:21). Christ becomes the place where heaven
and earth meet.

And as high priest, he serves in the heavenly places while Christians are united to his body on earth. Yet as Paul says in Ephesians
1:3, believers have every spiritual blessing in the heavenly places in
Christ. More could be said here, but this satisfies the point that later
Jewish-Christians readers of the Torah understood the tabernacle to
be an icon of the heavens.

Following this same instinct, Christians during the early centuries
developed a distinctly Christian view of the world, which meant that

---

35 In traditional Christian hermeneutics, Scripture is composed of signs and
things. For example, Augustine (354–430) writes, "All teaching is teaching of either
things or signs, but things are learnt through signs" (*On Christian Teaching*, trans.
R.P.H. Green [Oxford University Press, 1997], §1.4). A sign is also thing. In this case,
the tabernacle is both a sign and thing. It thus signifies the heavenly tabernacle without losing its status of being an earthly thing. What adds a layer of complexity is that
the earthly tabernacle signifies something more real and archetypal—something beyond the sensible world. We thus need to use the language metaphysics to understand what the Bible teaches. See the following section for more on metaphysics and
its relevance.

36 This impression did not just make its way to Christian authors. Josephus too
understood the tabernacle to be split into three sections: the land, the sea, and heav-
en (*Ant.* 3.181).

37 On this, see D. A. Carson, *The Gospel According to John*, PNTC (Eerdmans,
1991), 127.

they defined the essence of things in a Christian way.[38] The Trinity, for example, is shorthand for saying God is one substance in three persons. The essence of each person is divinity. When it comes to Christ, he has two substances: human and divine.

While older critical theories postulated that such views simply parroted Greek thought,[39] it seems clear that many of the intellectual concepts for such metaphysical reasoning already existed in the Old Testament.[40]

METAPHYSICS

The New Testament continues the metaphysical and cosmological trajectory that the Old Testament set. It uses contemporary Greek language to speak of biblical truth. Hence, Hebrews speaks about certain Old Testament institutions as shadows of the reality to come.[41] Paul

---

38 In the words of Bonaventure (1221–1274), "Metaphysics deals with the essence of things." "The Journey of the Mind to God" in *The Works of Bonaventure*, trans. José de Vinck (St. Anthony Guild Press, 1960), 1:34. Metaphysics more broadly seeks to explain what physics by itself cannot explain in the universe (mind, purpose, form, etc.).

39 Adolf Harnack writes, "The attempts at deducing the genesis of the Church's doctrinal system from the theology of Paul, or from compromises between Apostolic doctrinal ideas, will always miscarry; for they fail to note that to the most important premises of the Catholic doctrine of faith belongs an element which we cannot recognise as dominant in the New Testament, viz., the Hellenic spirit." Adolf Harnack, *History of Dogma*, trans. Neil Buchanan (Little, Brown, and Company, 1901), 1:72. For Harnack, the difference between the Hellenism and Judaism is not a mere gradual difference. He writes, "Judaism and Hellenism in the age of Christ were opposed to each other" (Harnack, 1:71).

40 Further, Paul Gavrilyuk has shown the inadequacy of simply imputing Greek philosophy to early Christians as the cause for their metaphysical reasoning about God in his *The Suffering of the Impassible God: The Dialectics of Patristic Thought* (Oxford University Press, 2004). Here, Gavrilyuk discusses impassibility, but his thesis may be applied more broadly to the criticism that early Christians simply adopted Greek Philosophy into their faith. Granted, Hellenism played a pervasive role in the linguistic and conceptual choices available to Christian theologians but the ideas themselves were deeply scriptural.

41 The letter to the Hebrews describes heavenly and earthly realities along platonic lines. Hence, Luke Timothy Johnson admits a directly platonic influence in the letter. He notes, "I have stated that the world imagined by Hebrews is one constructed imaginatively by Scripture and read through Platonic eyes" (*Hebrews: A Commentary*, NTL [Westminster John Knox Press, 2012], 45). The influence should be overplayed.

speaks of Old Testament festivals and says, "These are a shadow of the things to come, but the substance belongs to Christ" (Col 2:17). But Paul and the author of the Hebrews are not falling prey to Greek thinking; they are using the language of their day to define biblical realities.

In particular, the Gospel of John exemplifies the metaphysical sensibility of the Old Testament. John uses the imagery of the tabernacle to make sense of the divine logos' incarnation (John 1:14). This connection represents a particularly Jewish metaphysic expressed through first century Greek language. It seems fitting that John would draw on the deep explanatory power that the Old Testament provides for earthly and heavenly realities. The Gospel of John derives from John's eyewitness testimony that he mulled over for about sixty years; it represents a long reflection on the essence of the historical Jesus.

For Adolf Harnack, however, the Gospel of John is not a trustworthy report of the historical Jesus.[42] But such a position undervalues key data that shows that the Gospel of John derives from eyewitness testimony. Further, John's explanation of his eyewitness testimony draws on readily available metaphysical categories drawn largely from the Old Testament. In this way, John's eyewitness testimony allows future readers to see Jesus through his eyes—both as the man Jesus Christ and as the incarnate Word.

Eyewitness Testimony

The Gospel of John claims to flow out of eye-witness testimony. It therefore claims to be a historical record. This historical accent, however, does not prevent the Gospel writer from identifying heavenly realities in the historical and earthly ministry of the Christ. Just the opposite. The eyewitness testimony in conversation with the conceptual world of the Old Testament seems to have led John to consider how heavenly realities work out in the life of Jesus.

The New Testament exists in a Greco-Roman world in which public philosophy was relatively wide-spread. It would be almost impossible then to write a letter like Hebrews and not use common language that both truthfully described Scripture and used terminology common in Greco-Roman society.

42 Adolf Harnack, *What Is Christianity?*, trans. Thomas Bailey Saunders (Harper & Row, 1957), 19–20.

To confirm this interpretation, we need to consider the evidence that the Gospel of John derives from eyewitness testimony. In the first place, the evangelist claims to write eyewitness testimony about Jesus:

> This is the disciple who is bearing witness about these things, and who has written these things, and we know that his testimony is true. Now there are also many other things that Jesus did. Were every one of them to be written, I suppose that the world itself could not contain the books that would be written. (John 21:24–25)

As an eyewitness, John wrote the Gospel of John so that hearers would believe and have life in the name of Christ. He writes, "Now Jesus did many other signs in the presence of the disciples, which are not written in this book; but these are written so that you may believe that Jesus is the Christ, the Son of God, and that by believing you may have life in his name" (John 20:30–31).

Both John 20:30–31 and 21:24–25 function to conclude the Gospel. Richard Bauckham explains, "One reason the conclusion comes in two stages is that they serve to fence off the narrative in ch. 21 from the main narrative of the Gospel, thus indicating its status as an epilogue."[43]

The structural symmetry between the introduction and conclusion of John further evinces the importance of eyewitness testimony in the Gospel. The epilogue narrates Jesus speaking of the future, "If it is my will that he remain until I come" (John 21:23); his words here correspond to the opening of the Gospel that speaks of the past: "In the beginning" (John 1:1).[44] Additionally, the first stage of the conclusion speaks generally of disciples and signs (John 20:30–31), while the second stage speaks specifically about "the disciple" and Jesus' words in general (John 21:24–25).[45]

Bauckham also argues that the epilogue parallels the prologue by forming an *inclusio* of eyewitnesses.[46] According to John 1:7, John the Baptist "came as a witness, to bear witness about the light, that all

---

43 Bauckham, *Jesus and the Eyewitnesses*, 364.

44 Bauckham, *Jesus and the Eyewitnesses*, 364.

45 Bauckham, *Jesus and the Eyewitnesses*, 365–66.

46 Bauckham, *Jesus and the Eyewitnesses*, 366–67.

might believe through him," while the first stage of the conclusion states that the Gospel was "written so that you may believe that Jesus is the Christ." The second stage of the conclusion also finds a parallel in the prologue. John the Baptist "bore witness about him," according to John 1:15, while John 21:24 speaks of "the disciple who is bearing witness."

Bauckham explains:

> The conclusion enables readers finally to see how it is that John the Baptist's witness could be 'so that *all* may believe through him.' Incorporated in the Beloved Disciple's testimony and written, it continues to witness to all who read the Gospel, just as the Beloved Disciple himself does. So the Beloved disciple's present-tense testifying (*is* testifying) in 21:24 is matched by John the Baptist's present-tense testifying (he *testifies*) in 1:15.[47]

This two-stage conclusion finds earlier reverberations in John 19:35, "He who saw it has borne witness—his testimony is true, and he knows that he is telling the truth—that you also may believe." John 21:24 echoes "the language of 19:35."[48]

For these reasons, we can conclude that the Gospel according to John claims to be written by eye-witness testimony. While this evidence may not convince scholars like Harnack, the Gospel's focus on eyewitness testimony strongly argues for the historical plausibility of the Gospel.

John does not call *the Logos* God merely in imitation of cultural sensibilities. He draws on Old Testament metaphysical concepts to make sense of his eyewitness testimony while using common language of his day (e.g., John 1:14). The Gospel is therefore a plausible first-century Jewish account of the historical Jesus that meditates on a deeper layer of reality.

SIGNIFICANCE OF THE TESTIMONY

The significance of John's eyewitness testimony cannot be overstated.

---

47 Bauckham, *Jesus and the Eyewitnesses*, 367.

48 Bauckham, *Jesus and the Eyewitnesses*, 368.

The evangelist's testimony comes from a place of long reflection. Most affirm that the Gospel according to John was written sometime in the 90s. Hence, the evangelist wrote it some sixty years after Jesus died. We should thus read John as the mature testimony of a disciple of the Lord who has seen, touched, and proclaimed Christ.

The synoptic Gospels certainly reflect on Jesus. Yet their character is somewhat different than John's. For example, Luke self-consciously aims to write an historical narrative about Jesus on the basis of interviewing eyewitnesses (Luke 1:1–4). Tradition defines Mark as the recorder of Peter's recollections about the messiah.[49] We can infer a similar process of writing in the Gospel according to Matthew. Each appear within about forty years after Jesus' death and commit to writing what had been at that time in their mind or memory.

John likely writes about twenty to thirty-five years after these writings. He did not need to write down the events of Jesus' life in an orderly manner like Luke did (Luke 1:1–4). That had already been done. What he did do is what he said he has done: he bore eyewitness testimony to Jesus. We may safely presume that John spent his life attempting to discern what he saw, heard, touched, and proclaimed.

Testifying to the Nature of Jesus

John reflected on Jesus as an eyewitness, contemplating him in light of the metaphysical tradition of the Old Testament. In doing so, he concluded that in Jesus the invisible God became visible. Yet he does so by carefully affirming monotheism, the oneness of God (Deut 6:4). John witnessed Jesus speak, disciple, die, rise, and ascend. He knew Jesus was not *just a man*. Yet he was certainly that.

In his mature reflection, he identifies Jesus as the *Logos,* that principle of reason or unity in the mind of God (John 1:1). As our thoughts

---

49 Papias records, "Mark, having become Peter's interpreter, wrote down accurately everything that he remembered, though not in order of the things either said or done by Christ. For he neither heard the Lord nor followed him, but afterward, as I said, followed Peter, who adapted his teachings as needed but had no intention of giving an ordered account of the Lord's sayings. Consequently Mark did nothing wrong in writing down some things as he remembered them, for he made it his one concern not to omit anything that he heard or to make any false statement in them" (*Fragments of Papias*, 3.15).

are within us but not exactly the same as us, so similarly is God's *Logos*, his Word or reason, both God and with God.[50] Yet John does not leave readers with a vague analogy. He concretely roots his assertion in the Old Testament. By calling Christ *the Logos* or the Word in relation to creation (John 1:3), he identifies God's *word of creation* with the *Logos*. When God said, "Let there be light" (Gen 1:3) and "there was light," John identifies this act of God's Word with the Word (John 1:1, 3). Psalm 33:6 may also be echoed here: "The heavens were made by the word of the LORD (τῷ λόγῳ τοῦ κυρίου), and all the stars, by the breath His mouth (τῷ πνεύματι τοῦ στόματος αὐτοῦ)."

Proverbs 8 also provides a possible background to John 1. The analogy of *Logos* and God implies that the *Logos* is the reason, mind, or word of God. Each of these resonances are immaterial. Likewise, wisdom exists as an immaterial property. Hence, when Proverbs 8 identifies wisdom as the beginning of God's work (8:22) and "before the beginning of the earth" (8:23), it corresponds conceptually to the language of John 1:1–3. Further, the implication of Wisdom being with God in Proverbs 8 during creation implies that God created according to his Wisdom (e.g., in 8:27).

With this dual background in mind, John reasons, "In the beginning was the Word, and the Word was with God, and the Word was God. He was in the beginning with God. All things were made through him, and without him was not any thing made that was made." (John 1:1–3). Since he is the creative Word, he is life and "the light of men" (John 1:4). Unlike the lights that oversee creation (Gen 1:14–15), the *Logos* is the true light (τὸ φῶς τὸ ἀληθινόν)—no mere copy (John 1:9). And he enlightens all people (John 1:9).

As God's *Logos*, he was at the beginning (John 1:2). And anything at the beginning with God and anything through which God creates is excluded from the "All things" that "were made" through the *Logos*.

---

50 Peter Kreeft incisively clarifies John's symbolic language: "*Logos* means Reason or Mind or Inner Word or Thought; and your thoughts are both *with* you *and* they *are* you; the thinker and his thought are both one and two." (the original text appeared in parenthesis with a full stop) Peter Kreeft, *The Platonic Tradition* (St. Augustine's Press, 2018), 52. Kreeft may draw on the thought of Thomas Aquinas who wrote: "Just as the word of a human being is said to be the concept of the intellect, so the Word of God is the Son of God." *The Sermon-Conferences of St. Thomas Aquinas on the Apostles' Creed*, ed. Nicholas Ayo (University of Notre Dame Press, 1988), 115 [15.1].

Hence, the *Logos* is uncreated for "without him was not anything made that was made" (John 1:3). Therefore, the *Logos* must be divine and pre-existent. Yet John thereby does not affirm two deities. This is why he uses the brilliant analogy of *Logos* and God. The reason of God proceeds immaterially from God and so may be distinguished while still remaining identical to the essence of God.

Yet the *Logos* of God does not only eternally proceed from God as thought proceeds from the mind but also in the incarnation as a book follows from the idea to write it. The *Logos* became flesh: "And the Word became flesh and dwelt among us" (John 1:14). The eternal *Logos* of God became human. To further explain this reality, John draws on the Old Testament imagery of the tabernacle. The *Logos* "dwelt among us" or "pitched a tent" (ἐσκήνωσεν).[51] John draws his readers to see the *Logos* as the meeting place on earth where the invisible God becomes manifest.

His point becomes clearer in John 1:18: "No one has ever seen God; the only God, who is at the Father's side, he has made him known." The enfleshed *Logos* at the side of the Father makes God known.

For John, Jesus is the *Logos* of God through whom all things were made and in whom God is manifest. The evangelist invites readers to know Jesus not only as an earthly man but as divinity. While John certainly uses contemporary language and concepts to explain what he means, he also draws deeply on the Jewish scriptures.

Jesus is the tabernacle (John 1:14) and temple (John 2:18–22) because he makes God and humanity meet in his person. He unites divinity to humanity through the incarnation. Perhaps hinting at the union of heaven and earth in his body, Jesus says "Truly, truly, I say to you, you will see heaven opened, and the angels of God ascending and descending on the Son of Man" (John 1:51). In any case, John naturally adopts the biblical mindset that earthly signs point to heavenly realities. Rather than presenting something discontinuous with Old Testament revelation, John *draws precisely on the metaphysical concepts of the Old Testament* to make sense of his eyewitness testimony.

In the Old Testament, the tabernacle portrayed heavenly realities as copy. Yet Jesus does not merely portray heavenly realities in his earthly body *but is identified with them*. As Jesus claims elsewhere,

---

51 On this, see D. A. Carson, *The Gospel According to John*, 127.

"I tell you, something greater than the temple is here" (Matt 12:6). His body transcends the signs and shadows of the Old Testament because in him *are realties and not just copies of heavenly things*. He is God incarnate, the *Logos* of God. While John may draw on Old Testament imagery in surprising ways, his claim that Jesus is the incarnate Word builds on established metaphysical concepts in the Old Testament. It is an entirely plausible and coherent account of Jesus' relationship to God on the basis of Old Testament concepts.

CONTRIBUTION TO JESUS-DEVOTION STUDIES

Studies of early Jesus-devotion seem to avoid speaking about the metaphysical awareness of Jewish believers in the Old Testament as well as Christians writers of the New Testament. Yet as noted above, both groups care about the nature of things and the structure of the cosmos.

In particular, this means that the Synoptic Gospels may not highlight the divinity of Christ like John does, yet they do portray the earthly experience of Jesus of Nazareth. Early Christian readers later considered the person of Jesus, especially in light of his statements that "he has come." Where has he come from? The Gospel according to John provides a particularly powerful example of such meditation.

If this interest in the nature of things is granted, then studies like Simon Gathercole's *The Preexistent Son* will have an even stronger case for an early high Christology. On the basis of "I have come" + purpose statements in the synoptics, Gathercole argues that Jesus preexisted.[52] One kind of evidence that Gathercole uses is a comparison to angels who state, "I have come." In these cases, he reasons, they do not need to say I have come from heaven because it is obvious. As argued earlier, Jewish believers viewed reality as comprising both a heavenly and earthly realm. And so it is no surprise that angels would come from the former. In fact, it was assumed. The synoptic Gospels may in fact see the same kind of obvious entailment when Jesus says, "I have come."

---

52 Simon J. Gathercole, *The Pre-Existent Son: Recovering the Christologies of Matthew, Mark, and Luke* (Eerdmans, 2006), 83–87.

John thought about these questions for decades and wrote the Gospel according to John, which advances a careful reflection on Jesus Christ. Metaphysical questions about Jesus do not appear as some future development. Rather, these sorts of questions and concerns fill out the Old Testament and the Gospel according to John.

I wrote this chapter with the modest aim of describing certain biblical passages that evinced an awareness of metaphysical concepts. These concepts, integrated into a certain cosmology, supply some of the concepts that help make sense of what and who Christ is. In particular, the Gospel according to John illustrates what it looks like to meditate on the historical Jesus to deepen one's understanding of his heavenly origin and place in the cosmos. John then plausibly uses earlier scriptural concepts to conceive of the divine origin of Jesus. In short, the metaphysics of the Old Testament contribute, albeit in a partial way, to the historical plausibility of an early high Christology among the earliest Christians.

11

"You Are a Priest Forever":
An Exegetical and Biblical Theology
of High Priestly Christology

Clifford B. Kvidahl[1]

ONE OF THE MOST IMPORTANT CONTRIBUTIONS the letter to the Hebrews offers with respect to Christology is its unique emphasis on the high priesthood of Jesus. Not only is the author of Hebrews the only New Testament writer to utilize the appellation ἀρχιερεύς in reference to Jesus, Hebrews is further unique in its detailed description of Jesus's installation as high priest, his process of perfection, and his entrance into the heavenly sanctuary and subsequent offering for sin. Overall, the letter to the Hebrews provides the most vivid picture of Jesus's high priestly ministry in action, one that resembles the movement of the Levitical of high priest on Yom Kippur rather closely. This essay will explore the high priestly Christology of Hebrews, specifically as it relates to the death, resurrection, and ascension of Jesus into the heavenly sanctuary. Each of these events play an important role in the shaping of Hebrews' theology of priesthood.

The central focal point of this essay will address the following question: is there a discernible point in time when Jesus was appointed and installed as high priest? In light of the oath made by God to appoint Jesus high priest after the order of Melchizedek (Heb 5:6; 6:20; 7:17, 21), does Hebrews give any indication as to when this oath

---

1 It is with immense gratitude that I offer this contribution on the high priesthood of Jesus in honor of Dr. William Varner, which is an updated and expanded version of my article in *Conspectus* 29 (March 2020). It was during Dr. Varner's Advanced Greek Exegesis class at the Master's University that I was first introduced to the marvelous writing known as the Letter to the Hebrews, and ever since then the *auctor ad Hebraeos* and his letter have captivated my mind and heart.

was made, and consequently when Jesus took his place as high priest? While it may appear that a question such as this is making a distinction without a difference, it will be argued that this is in fact not the case; the timing of Jesus's installation as high priest is directly connected to the question of *when* and *where* the atonement occurred. Therefore, formulating a hypothesis as to the timing of Jesus's installation serves a crucial part in the overall cultic theology of Hebrews.

As will be exhibited in the following section, there has been several proposals put forward that attempt to answer the question of when Jesus became high priest. To address this issue, this essay will be structured around two main parts. Part one surveys proposals offered regarding the timing of Jesus's installation as high priest. Because Hebrews offers the most extensive description and sustained argument on this topic, the survey focuses exclusively on what commentators on Hebrews have concluded on this topic. Part two branches out from Hebrews to examine what other New Testament writers present regarding Jesus as high priest. The focus of part two is a brief examination of passages that are imbued with priestly connotation often applied to the person of Jesus. Simply stated, does the New Testament portray Jesus as functioning in a priestly manner during his earthly ministry? While it is important to map various themes across the landscape of Scripture, it will be evident from this brief survey that sometimes these themes are informed more by a certain theological tradition rather than by means of theological analysis of specific texts themselves.

A Survey of Hebrews' High Priestly Christology

The importance of the priesthood for the author of Hebrews cannot be overstated. In fact, an argument can be made that the priesthood of Jesus is *the* central theme of the entire letter.[2] Even in the central section of the homily (Heb 8–10), where the focus is on the once-for-all sacrifice of Jesus, the office and function of the priesthood lingers just beneath the surface; just as there is no offering without an officiant,

---

2 Alexander Nairne, *The Epistle of Priesthood: Studies in the Epistle to the Hebrews* (T&T Clark, 1913), 136; cf. Jerome Smith, *A Priest For Ever* (Sheed and Ward, 1969), 66–136.

in Hebrews, there is no sacrifice of atonement without a great high priest serving at the heavenly altar. The author's detailed depiction of Jesus and his earthly suffering comes to a crescendo in the carefully argued exposition of Ps 110:4, most notably in Heb 5–7, and Jesus's appointment as high priest and subsequent entry into the heavenly sanctuary, as portrayed in Heb 9–10. As Vanhoye rightly remarks, "the author describes the priesthood as *the purpose* of the incarnation and of the passion of Christ."[3]

Moving beyond Hebrews the references to Jesus operating in a manner consistent with that of high priest become fainter, with no more than possible echoes of priestly activities applied to the person of Jesus. And while there is debate as to whether Jesus is functioning in a priestly capacity outside of Hebrews, the testimony of Hebrews is unambiguous in its affirmation of Jesus's inability to serve at the altar while still present on earth (cf. Heb 7:13–14; 8:4).

In the ensuing section the following question will be addressed: is there a discernible point in time when Jesus was appointed and installed as high priest? Furthermore, in light of the oath made by God to appoint Jesus as high priest after the order of Melchizedek (Heb 5:6; 6:20; 7:17, 21), does Hebrews itself give any indication as to *when* this oath was made and the *moment* at which Jesus began his priestly duties as high priest? While such speculation may seem unimportant to the overall message of Hebrews, it will be argued that this is in fact not the case. Instead, the timing of Jesus's installation as high priest is directly connected to the question of *when* and *where* the atonement for sin occurred. Therefore, formulating a hypothesis with respect to the timing of Jesus's installation serves to situate Jesus's sacrificial self-offering within the framework of Yom Kippur and serves a crucial part in the overall cultic theology of Hebrews.

Eternal High Priest

One answer to this question is timeless in nature: Jesus always existed as high priest and there was never a moment in which he was anything other than high priest. In the opening chapter of Hebrews the

---

3 Albert Vanhoye, *The Letter to the Hebrews: A New Commentary*, trans. Leo Arnold (Paulist Press, 2010), 80, emphasis added.

author unequivocally applies eternal language to the Son. The author affirms the eternal nature of the Son in Heb 1:3, noting that Jesus is ἀπαύγασμα τῆς δόξης καὶ χαρακτὴρ τῆς ὑποστάσεως αὐτοῦ.[4] Unlike humanity, who was created in the image of God (בְּצַלְמֵנוּ כִּדְמוּתֵנוּ; κατ' εἰκόνα ἡμετέραν καὶ καθ' ὁμοίωσιν; Gen 1:26), the Son is the "exact imprint of God's nature and the very radiance of his glory." Furthermore, because the Son shares in the glory and nature of God, he is both the agent and sustainer of creation (Heb 1:2c, 3b).

The eternal nature of the Son is further affirmed through a string of OT passages that form a *synkrisis* (comparison) between the Son and the angels in 1:5–13.[5] For example, in Heb 1:6 the angels are commanded to pay homage to the Son upon his ascension and exaltation in heaven.[6] The author further applies eternality in 1:8–9, referring to

---

4 Cf. Phil 2:5–11; Col 1:15–18; 1 Tim 3:16 for similar language applied to the eternal nature of Jesus. It has been suggested by some that Heb 1:3, like Phil 2:5ff., Col 1:15ff., and 1 Tim 3:16, is a formulaic hymn that has been appropriated within New Testament Scripture. Some of the literary traits that are characteristic of early Christological hymns are 1) a change in reference from God to Son, marked by the presence of the nominative relative pronoun ὅς; 2) uncommon or rare words, which in the case of Hebrews are the NT hapax legomena ἀπαύγασμα and χαρακτήρ; 3) the humiliation and death of Jesus; and 4), language of exaltation (Paul Ellingworth, *The Epistle to the Hebrews: A Commentary on the Greek Text*, NIGTC [Eerdmans, 1993], 96; William L. Lane, *Hebrews 1–8*, WBC 47A [Word, 1991], 13; Craig R. Koester, *Hebrews: A New Translation with Introduction and Commentary*, AB 36 [Doubleday, 2001], 179; cf. Harold W. Attridge, *The Epistle to the Hebrews: A Commentary on the Epistle to the Hebrews*, Hermeneia [Fortress Press, 1989], 41).

Relevant to Heb 1–2 and Jesus's superiority over the angels, 1 Pet 3:22 succinctly outlines Jesus's post resurrection activity: "Who (ὅς) has gone into heaven and is at the right hand of God (ἐν δεξιᾷ τοῦ θεοῦ) with angels ... subject to [Jesus] (ὑποταγέντων αὐτῷ ἀγγέλων)." The language of subjection in 1 Pet 3:22c of angelic powers to the risen Christ mirrors that of the author of Hebrews' exposition of the superiority of Jesus over the angels. The language of subjection in Heb 1–2 plays a significant role in the author of Hebrews' exposition, most notably in the encompassing eschatological subjection of all things under the feet of the risen Jesus in Heb 2:8.

5 Luke Timothy Johnson, *Hebrews: A Commentary*, NTL (Westminster John Knox, 2006), 74.

6 There is disagreement regarding the meaning of Heb 1:6, particularly as it relates to the placement of πάλιν and the exact referent for οἰκουμένη. The location of πάλιν in the sentence has led to different translations of the temporal clause. It is possible to take πάλιν with εἶπέν in 1:4, thus introducing a third a question: "And *again* ... " (cf. πάλιν in 1:5; 2:13; 4:5; 10:30). It is also possible that πάλιν modifies the verb εἰσαγάγῃ, in which case the author is referring to a second bringing: "And when he

again brings ...." This reading segues into the second interpretive issue of 1:6: What is the οἰκουμένη that the Son enters?

Some commentators have suggested that this is a reference to the incarnation (Ceslas Spicq, *L'Épître aux Hébreux*, Études Biblique [Gabalda, 1952–53], 2:17; Hugh Montefiore, *A Commentary on the Epistle to the Hebrews*, BNTC [A. and C. Black, 1964], 45–46). They point to the account in Luke's birth narrative (Luke 2:13) where angels appear to shepherds and give glory to God as a possible allusion to God's command to worship the Son (Montefiore, *Hebrews*, 46). However, in Luke's Gospel the angels are engaged in singing praises to God's glory and not explicitly giving homage to the Son himself. Further evidence against this view is in Heb 10:5, where the author refers to Jesus's incarnation as a "coming into the world." Here, the more familiar κόσμος is used to speak of Jesus's first coming and not the οἰκουμένη of Heb 1–2 (cf. Vanhoye, *Hebrews*, 63).

A further possible referent for οἰκουμένη is the *Parousia*. Such an understanding rests on πάλιν modifying εἰσαγάγῃ, in which case the "second bringing" of the Son occurs at his second coming (B. F. Westcott, *The Epistle to the Hebrews*, 3rd ed. [Macmillan, 1909], 21–23; Jean Héring, *The Epistle to the Hebrews*, trans. A. W. Heathcote and P. J. Allock [Wipf and Stock, 2010], 9; Ernst Käsemann, *The Wandering People of God: An Investigation of the Letter to the Hebrews*, trans. Roy A. Harrisville and Irving L. Sandberg [Wipf and Stock, 2002], 101). While οἰκουμένη can and often does refer to the inhabited world (cf. Matt 24:14; Luke 2:1; Rom 10:18), the context of Heb 1–2 points in a different direction. In Heb 1:6 the οἰκουμένη in question is populated by angels; there is no mention of humanity being present. Further, the command to worship the Son in 1:6 is directed specifically to angels and does not include humanity, which is curiously lacking if this is indeed a reference to the *Parousia* (cf. Rev 1:7). What's more, in Heb 2:5, the only other occurrence of οἰκουμένη in Hebrews, the subjection of the world that is to come is not to angels (Οὐ γὰρ ἀγγέλοις ὑπέταξεν τὴν οἰκουμένην τὴν μέλλουσαν). And while the Son is for a time "lower than the angels" (because of his incarnation), he will again be crowned with glory and honor, and will have all things subjected under his feet (Heb 2:6–8; quoting Ps 8:4–6).

The most probable referent of οἰκουμένη is one that is informed by the author's use of exaltation language, particularly considering the author's use of Ps 110 in the overall structure and meaning of his homily (Otto Michel, *Der Brief an Die Hebräer*, KEK 13 [Vandenhoeck & Ruprecht, 1957], 116; David Peterson, *Hebrews and Perfection: An Examination of the Concept of Perfection in the 'Epistle to the Hebrews,'* SNTSMS [Cambridge University Press, 1982], 219 n. 19; Attridge, *Hebrews*, 55–56; Erich Gräßer, *An Die Hebräer*, EKKNT 1:1 [Neukirchener, 1990], 78; David A. deSilva, *Perseverance in Gratitude: A Socio-Rhetorical Commentary on the Epistle "to the Hebrews"* [Eerdmans, 2000] 96–97; Ardel B. Caneday, "The Eschatological World Already Subjected to the Son: The Οἰκουμένη of Hebrews 1:6 and the Son's Enthronement," *A Cloud of Witnesses: The Theology of Hebrews in its Ancient Contexts*, ed. by Richard Bauckham, et al., LNTS 387 [Bloomsbury T&T Clark, 2008], 28–39). Thus, when the author of Hebrews refers to the οἰκουμένη, he is speaking not of the inhabited earth (either with reference to the incarnation or the *Parousia*) but is referring particularly to a place that

the eternal throne of the Son. Finally, the author again applies the activity of creation to the Son, while also emphasizing the timeless nature of the Son (1:10–12). The catena of 1:5–13 is unambiguous in its claims of the Son's eternal nature. But does this eternality apply also to his role as high priest?

Unlike the Levitical high priest, who was chosen based on lineage, Jesus's appointment to high priest came by way of an oath (cf. Heb 7:20–21, 28). Quoting Ps 110:4 (109:4 LXX), the author of Hebrews affirms that the oath made to Jesus was that he would be "a priest *forever* (εἰς τὸν αἰῶνα) according to the order of Melchizedek" (5:6). Similarly, in 7:24 the author notes that in his office as high priest, affirming that "[Jesus] continues forever (εἰς τὸν αἰῶνα), [holding] his priesthood permanently (ἀπαράβατον)."

Further supporting the idea of an eternal priesthood is the author of Hebrews' midrash on Gen 14:17–20 and Ps 110:4 in 7:1–10 and 7:11–28.[7] In the opening verses of Hebrews 7, the author recounts the meaning of Melchizedek's royal names and lack of lineage (7:1–3). Important for the topic at hand is the author's assertion that Melchizedek has "neither beginning of days nor end of life." Alongside the lack of genealogical record, such vague and ambiguous assertions by the

---

is inhabited by angels, which most likely is heaven, or more specifically, the heavenly sanctuary of Heb 9:11–12, 24 (cf. 4:14; 6:19–20; 10:19–20). Therefore, instead of interpreting οἰκουμένη as a reference to the incarnation of Jesus or to his second coming, it is best to understand Heb 1:6 as a reference to Jesus's entrance into heavenly realm.

7 Cf. G. B Caird, "The Exegetical Method of the Epistle to the Hebrews," *CJT* 5 (1959): 47–48; Joseph A. Fitzmyer, " 'Now this Melchizedek …' (Heb 7,1)," *CBQ* 25 (1963): 305; Gareth Lee Cockerill, "The Melchizedek Christology in Heb 7.1–28" (PhD diss., Union Theological Seminary, 1976), 18; 288–307; Fred L. Horton, *The Melchizedek Tradition: A Critical Examination of the Sources to the Fifth Century A.D. and in the Epistle to the Hebrews*, SNTSMS 30 (Cambridge University Press, 1976), 12–53; James W. Thompson, "The Conceptual Background and Purpose of the Midrash in Hebrews VII," *NovT* 19 (1977): 209–223; Paul Ellingworth, " 'Like the Son of God': Form and Content of Hebrews 7.1–10," *Bib* 64 (1983): 258; Parsons, Mikeal C. "Son and High Priest: A Study in the Christology of Hebrews," *EvQ* 60 (1988): 212–213; Attridge, *Hebrews*, 186; William L. Lane, *Hebrews 9–13*, WBC 47B (Dallas: Word, 1991), 158–159; Deborah W. Rooke, "Jesus as Royal High Priest: Reflections on the Interpretation of the Melchizedek Tradition in Heb 7," *Bib* 81 (2000): 81–94; Eric F. Mason, *"You are a Priest Forever": Second Temple Jewish Messianism and the Priestly Christology of the Epistle to the Hebrews*, STDJ 74 (Brill, 2008), 25–26; Gard Granerød, "Melchizedek in Hebrews 7," *Bib* 90 (2009): 194–195.

author of Hebrews provide just enough scriptural precedent to allow for the possibility of Jesus's preincarnate priesthood. For the author of Hebrews, the lack of parentage and genealogy provides for him the exegetical soil necessary for the comparison between Melchizedek and the Son of God, while also allowing just enough room for speculation regarding the eternality of Melchizedek and the nature of his priesthood.

While language used to describe Jesus's priesthood has an eternal ring to it, this ringing is forward moving and does not echo back into the halls of eternity past. In the oath from Ps 110:4 in Heb 5:6 the promise that Jesus is a priest forever is not made before the incarnation. In the preceding verse the author of Hebrews again quotes from Ps 2:7, thus establishing a relationship between Jesus' sonship *and* his role as high priest.[8] The declaration of sonship took place upon Jesus's entry into heaven at his exaltation, and by connecting it with God's oath to make Jesus a priest after the order of Melchizedek, the author of Hebrews places the installation of Jesus as high priest subsequent to his entry into the heavenly sanctuary.

Likewise, the eternal language in Hebrews 7 is forward pointing and does not point the reader back towards eternity past. This is so in Heb 7:23–24, where the author provides a contrast between the multiplicity of Levitical priests and the singular priesthood of Jesus, indicated by the presence of a μέν ... δέ construction. In 7:23 the author emphasizes the need for continual priests at the altar because death prevented them from continuing their cultic ministry. However, things changed with the priesthood of Jesus. Unlike the mortal priests of Israel, Jesus's priesthood is forever *because* he holds it permanently. The key to understanding the meaning of "forever" and "permanently" is in the contrast between death and life. Whereas death brings about the termination of cultic ministry for the Levitical high priest, it is precisely this event that inaugurates the high priestly ministry of the great Melchizedekian high priest. Therefore, it is because of his perpetuity that Jesus is able to save those drawing near to God, "since he *always lives* to make intercession for his own (7:25, emphasis added).

One final point to emphasize regarding the timing of Jesus's

8 James Moffatt, *The Epistle to the Hebrews*, ICC (T&T Clark, 1924), 64.

installation as high priest is the language of "becoming" which the author utilizes with respect to Jesus's high priesthood. After expounding on the necessity of Jesus's participation in the human experience (2:10–16), the author concludes that such an experience was necessary in order that Jesus might "become (γένηται) a merciful and faithful high priest with respect to the things of God, thus making atonement for the sins of the people" (2:17).[9] Similar language is also used later in chapter five, where the author informs his hearers that "Christ did not glorify himself so as *to become* (γενηθῆναι) a high priest ...." (5:5a). Rather than operating as high priest before his incarnation, Jesus became high priest at a specific point in time, a point in time *after* his incarnation.

Earthly High Priest

Another way to answer the question regarding the timing of Jesus's installation as high priest is to perceive of his installation as high priest as an incarnational event. For example, Chrysostom states in no uncertain terms that Jesus became high priest at the moment of his incarnation: "And observe the mystery. First it was royal, and then it is become sacerdotal: so therefore also in regard to Christ: for King indeed He always was, but *has become Priest from the time that He assumed the Flesh*, that He offered the sacrifice" (*Hom. Heb.* 13:2, emphasis added).[10] Kistemaker and Scholer, on the other hand, are a

---

9 Space does not permit a prolonged discussion regarding the timing of the atonement in Hebrews. In the section below titled "Exalted as High Priest," it is presupposed that the author viewed atonement as something taking place *upon* Jesus's entrance into heaven. For support of such a view cf. the works of Kenneth M. Monroe, "Time Element in the Atonement," *EvQ* 5 (1933): 397–408; Walter Edward Brooks, "The Perpetuity of Christ's Sacrifice in the Epistle to the Hebrews," *JBL* 89 (1970): 205–214; David M. Moffit, *Atonement and the Logic of Resurrection in the Epistle to the Hebrews*, NovTSup 141 (Brill, 2011); Joshua M. Vis, "The Purification Offering of Leviticus and the Sacrificial Offering of Jesus" (PhD diss., Duke University, 2012), 256–308; R. B. Jamieson, "When and Where Did Jesus Offer Himself? A Taxonomy of Recent Scholarship on Hebrews," *CurBS* 15 (2017): 338–68; Jamieson, *Jesus' Death and Heavenly Offering in Hebrews*, SNTSMS 172 (Cambridge University Press, 2019); Clifford B. Kvidahl, "Atonement, the Heavenly Sanctuary, and Purgation of Sin: An Exegetical Study of Hebrews 9" (MTh thesis, South African Theological Seminary, 2019).

10 Cf. Spicq, *Hébreux*, 2:211; Aelred Cody, *Heavenly Sanctuary and Liturgy in the Epistle to the Hebrews: The Achievement of Salvation in the Epistle's Perspectives* (Grail

bit more ambiguous, concluding at most that the Son functions as a priest during his earthly ministry.[11]

It has also been noted that the "prayers and supplications" (δεήσεις τε καὶ ἱκετηρίας) that Jesus offers "in the days of his flesh" may be construed as a priestly act. Koester points out that the anguish of Jesus in 5:7 parallels the offering of "gifts and sacrifices" (δῶρά τε καὶ θυσίας) in 5:1 (cf. 8:3).[12]

A further solution to the question of timing suggests that Jesus is installed as high priest at the cross. In this manner, the cross functions not only as the place where atonement is accomplished, but also as the "starting point for the high priest's atoning work".[13] This view of Jesus's installation coheres nicely with the more traditional understanding of the cross serving as the place of atonement. In order to be consistent with the role of a priest and the presentation of his offering before God, it is necessary to hold to a view of installation that coincides with the cross. For the death of the Son of God to be considered as an offering for sin, Jesus must also be high priest for such

Publications, 1960), 97; William R. G. Loader, *Sohn und Hoherpriester: Eine traditionsgeschichtliche Untersuchung zur Christologie des Hebräerbriefes*, WMANT 53 (Neukirchener, 1981), 245–247; Gerald O'Collins and Michael Keenan Jones, *Jesus our Priest: A Christian Approach to the Priesthood of Christ* (Oxford University Press, 2010), 49–50; Christopher A Richardson, *Pioneer and Perfecter of Faith: Jesus' Faith as the Climax of Israel's History in the Epistle to the Hebrews*, WUNT 2/338 (Mohr Siebeck, 2012), 42; 47–48.

11 Simon J. Kistemaker, *Hebrews*, NTC (Baker, 1984), 252–253; John M. Scholer, *Proleptic Priests: Priesthood in the Epistle to the Hebrews*, JSNTSup 49 (Sheffield Academic Press, 1991), 87–89; cf. Thomas R. Schreiner, *Commentary on Hebrews*, BTCP (B&H, 2015), 160.

12 Koester, *Hebrews*, 109. Cf. deSilva, *Hebrews*, 189. Kleinig, however, correctly notes that the prayers and supplications offered by Jesus were not priestly in nature but rather the outworking of suffering through obedience that the Son had to endure in order that he could serve as high priest (John W. Kleinig, *Hebrews*, ConcC [Concordia Publishing House, 2017), 250–253.

13 Käsemann, *The Wandering People of God*, 223; cf. Peterson, *Hebrews and Perfection*, 195; Ellingworth, *Hebrews*, 397; Ian G. Wallis, *The Faith of Jesus Christ in Early Christian Traditions*, SNTSMS 84 (Cambridge University Press, 1995), 146; Sabastian Fuhrmann, *Vergeben und Vergessen: Christologie und Neuer Bund im Hebräerbrief*, WMANT 113 (Neukirchener, 2007), 102–117; Furhmann, "Christ Grown into Perfection: Hebrews 9, 11 from a Christological Point of View," *Bib* 89 (2008): 94–96; Herman V. A. Kuma, *The Centrality of Αἷμα (Blood) in the Theology of the Epistle to the Hebrews: An Exegetical and Philological Study* (Edwin Mellen, 2012).

an offering to be acceptable to God. Arthur Peake understands this to be the case, noting, "If, then, [Jesus] offered his body on the cross, he must have been a priest of this [Melchizedekian] order *before his death*. And this suggests an answer to the question, When did he become high-priest? *At the close of his Agony*, when he had learnt his sorest lesson of obedience and had achieved perfection."[14]

Exalted as High Priest

A final answer offered, and the one affirmed in this article, is the installation of Jesus as high priest upon his entrance into the heavenly sanctuary and subsequent exaltation to God's right hand.[15] One of the earliest proponents of such a view was the Italian theologian Faustus Socinus.[16] Socinus rightly grasps the logical connection between the activity of the Levitical high priest (immolation → entry into the tabernacle → manipulation of blood) with that of Jesus in Hebrews (cross → entry into heavenly sanctuary → offering of sacrifice). This led Socinus to conclude that the cross is the not the location of Jesus's self-offering; instead, Jesus's self-offering occurs in heaven. It is not until his exaltation and attainment of an indestructible life that Jesus was installed as high priest and was thus able to offer his atoning sacrifice for sin.[17]

---

14 Arthur S. Peake, *Hebrews*, NCB (T. C. & E. C. Jack, 1906), 137, emphasis added.

15 Brooks, "The Perpetuity of Christ's Sacrifice in the Epistle to the Hebrews," 207; Timo Eskola, *Messiah and the Throne: Jewish Merkabah Mysticism and Early Christian Exaltation Discourse*, WUNT 2/142 (Mohr Siebeck, 2001), 259, 264; Moffit, *Atonement*, 194–208; Ole Jakob Filtvedt, *The Identity of God's People and the Paradox of Hebrews*, WUNT 2/400 (Mohr Siebeck, 2015), 85–87; Michael Kibbe, *Godly Fear or Ungodly Failure? Hebrews 12 and the Sinai Theophanies*, BZNW 216 (de Gruyter, 2016), 162–163; Jamieson, *Jesus' Death*, 25.

16 While Socinus offers a view of Jesus's installation that is affirmed in some ways by the author of this essay, this affirmation is in no way a wholesale agreement with his theology *in toto* (cf. similar sentiments can be found in David M. Moffit, "Jesus' Heavenly Sacrifice in Early Christian Reception of Hebrews: A Survey," *JTS* 68 [2017]: 49–51). I am indebted to the example of Dr. Varner and his encouragement to always read those with whom you disagree, not with a suspicious eye, but rather with a humble spirit and critical mind. It was from his personal example that I learned the most important lesson in biblical interpretation: never throw the baby out with the bath water.

17 Bruce Demarest, *A History of Interpretation of Hebrews 7,1–10 from the*

The reason why this distinction is important is because the author of Hebrews is unambiguous in his affirmation that while Jesus was on earth, he was barred from serving as high priest (Heb 8:4). This prohibition is due in part to two important factors. First, Jesus's genealogy prohibited him from serving in the earthly sanctuary. Jesus was a descendant from the tribe of Judah, and as such, Judah had no priestly representation (7:13–14). This distinction is important for the development of the author's cultic theology, particularly in its relationship with the inauguration of a new covenant, and with it, a new priesthood (cf. Heb 7:11–22; 8:7–13; 9:15–21).

The second factor prohibiting Jesus from serving as high priest while on earth was the presence of the Levitical priesthood itself. While the Mosaic covenant and Levitical priesthood remained operative in Jerusalem the Melchizedekian high priest was unable to offer gifts or sacrifices within the holy sanctuary (Heb 8:4). Moffitt rightly notes that the problem Jesus faced with regard to his role as high priest while on earth was an ontological problem created by the incarnation. Although he is the Son of God and appointed by God to be high priest, his elevation to that office was prohibited by his tribal genealogy.[18] For these reasons the priesthood that Jesus assumes must be one that had no geographical or genealogical connection to the Mosaic covenant or Levitical cult.

Be that as it may, if it is the case that Jesus was prohibited from presenting his offering for sin while on earth—a case that Hebrews clearly makes—where then was his offering for sin made? As noted in Heb 5:1, the duty of a priest is "to offer gifts and sacrifices for sins" (ἵνα προσφέρῃ δῶρά τε καὶ θυσίας ὑπὲρ ἁμαρτιῶν). However, because Jesus was genealogically barred from presenting such an offering while present on earth, the logical conclusion is that Jesus presented his offering for sin upon his ascension into the heavenly sanctuary (8:1–4;

Reformation to the Present, BGBE 19 (J.C.B. Mohr, 1976), 22 n.2; Michael Kibbe, "Is it Finished? When did it Start? Hebrews, Priesthood, and Atonement in Biblical, Systematic, and Historical Perspective," *JTS* 65 (2014): 25–61; Kibbe, "You are a Priest Forever!' Jesus' Indestructible Life in Hebrews 7:16," *HBT* 39 (2017): 134–155.

18 David M. Moffitt, "It is not Finished: Jesus's Perpetual Atoning Work as the Heavenly High Priest in Hebrews," *So Great a Salvation: A Dialogue on the Atonement in Hebrews*, ed. Jon C. Laansma et al., LNTS 516 (Bloomsbury T&T Clark, 2019), 160.

cf. 9:11–12, 24–26).[19] As a result, Jesus obtained his role as high priest at a point in time *after* his resurrection.

Furthermore, this line of thought is supported by the author of Hebrews' declaration that the priesthood which Jesus received is not a matter of genealogy, but instead is based on the "power of an indestructible life" (ἀλλὰ κατὰ δύναμιν ζωῆς ἀκαταλύτου, 7:16). The word ἀκατάλυτος is a New Testament hapax legomena, occurring only in Hebrews and carries the sense of "endless" or "perpetual."[20] The only occurrence of ἀκατάλυτος in Second Temple literature is found in 4 Macc 10:11, where it refers to "eternal torments" (ἀκαταλύτους βασάνους). At the resurrection of Jesus God affirms the Son as high priest in perpetuity, which enabled him to present his offering upon his ascension into the heavenly sanctuary.

Important to the issue of timing is the concept of perfection. In Hebrews, particularly in chapters five and seven, the author organizes his homily in such a way as to illustrate the Son of God's qualification to serve as high priest. The various qualifications for appointment to the office of high priest can be grouped together under one rubric in Hebrews: the author's use of τελειόω and its related cognates. Perfection is the requisite characteristic that is required for the Son to function as the Melchizedekian high priest.

This is nowhere seen more clearly than in Hebrews 5:7–10, where the author outlines the steps the historical Jesus took on his way to perfection and ultimately his installation as high priest. In 5:7, the

---

19 David M. Moffitt, "Wilderness Identity and Pentateuchal Narrative: Distinguishing between Jesus' Inauguration and Maintenance of the New Covenant in Hebrews," *Muted Voices of the New Testament: Readings in the Catholic Epistles and Hebrews*, ed. Katherine M. Hockey et al., LNTS 587 (Bloomsbury T&T Clark, 2017), 162.

The *timing* and *location* of the atonement in Hebrews has been widely discussed of late. Beginning with David Moffitt's 2011 landmark study on the role resurrection plays in Hebrews and its relationship with the atonement, the question of *when* and *where* the atonement occurred has been debated in articles, essays, and academic conferences, all with a focus on the nature of Jesus's death in Hebrews. And while there has been pushback regarding Moffitt's thesis, his thesis has been heartily adopted and assumed in this chapter. Moffitt's thesis regarding Jesus' death, resurrection, exaltation, and purification of sin follows closely that which Richard Nelson refers to as a "ritual script," one that mirrored the "Day of Atonement ritual" ("'He Offered Himself:' Sacrifice in Hebrews," *Int* 57 [2003]: 252).

20 Cf. BDAG, 35; GE: s.v. ἀκατάλυτος LSJ, 48.

author provides a snapshot of the earthly life of Jesus, together with his Passion, and because of his reverence/fear (ἀπὸ τῆς εὐλαβείας) he is heard by God (εἰσακουσθείς). There is some debate as to the precise meaning of ἀπὸ τῆς εὐλαβείας in the context of 5:7. Most translations take ἀπὸ τῆς εὐλαβείας as a reference to Jesus's piety, hence the translation "because of his reverence/piety/reverent submission."

Another possible meaning is to understand the noun εὐλαβείας as a reference to fear, which provides the following translation, "because of his fear." This fear points back to the prepositional phrase πρὸς τὸν δυνάμενον σῴζειν αὐτὸν ἐκ θανάτου in 5:7. This fear of death is similar to Hebrews 2:14–15 and the universal fear of death (φόβῳ θανάτου) that continues to plague mankind ever since the Garden. By sharing in our humanity, Jesus likewise agrees to take on the shared experiences of humanity, none of which is more universal than the fear of death. It is this fear of death that the Son experiences during his Passion, deliverance from which he prayed for and was heard.[21] The content of Jesus's prayer is important in the context of perfection and installation as high priest; it is the plea of the Son for deliverance from death (ἐκ θανάτου). But what precisely does the prepositional phrase ἐκ θανάτου refer to in 5:7, and how does it relate to perfection and priestly installation?

Again, in the context of 5:7 Jesus is praying for deliverance from his impending crucifixion.[22] But this understanding introduces an inherent contradiction within Hebrews 5:7, namely that Jesus's prayer went unanswered. Montefiore attempts to solve this by proposing that his prayer was in fact answered, just not in the way one would expect. Montefiore suggests that instead of deliverance from the cross, the deliverance that was granted to Jesus was from the fear of death itself.[23] Given the context of Hebrews 2:14–15 and its reference to the "fear of death," this is a plausible interpretive option. Although not addressing the same issue as Montefiore, Bruce likewise suggests a possible double entendre for ἐκ θανάτου in 5:7, offering Hos 13:14 as a possible example of such an occurrence.[24] Attridge attempts to solve

---

21 Ellingworth, *Hebrews*, 290.

22 "Bitte um Bewahrung vor dem Tod." Herbert Braun, *An Die Hebräer*, HNT 14 (J.C.B. Mohr, 1984), 142.

23 Montefiore, *Hebrews*, 98–99.

24 F. F. Bruce, *The Epistle to the Hebrews*, rev. ed., NICNT (Eerdmans, 1990),

this conundrum by delaying God's answer to prayer until the time of Jesus's exaltation.[25] Unfortunately, none of these options adequately solve the contextual problem of Hebrews' affirmation that Jesus was in fact heard and his prayer answered.

Contextually, what Jesus prayed for was salvation *out of death* and not from the actual moment of death itself;[26] that is to say, the answer to Jesus's prayer was granted in the act of resurrection out of the realm of death (cf. Sir 48:5: ὁ ἐγείρας νεκρὸν ἐκ θανάτου). The earthly life of Jesus was one of learning obedience through suffering (5:8). This all culminated in 5:9, where "having been perfected, [Jesus] became the source of eternal salvation." This perfection, indicated by the aorist passive participle τελειωθείς, refers to the earthly completion of Jesus's sufferings in 5:8, after which he became the source of eternal salvation (ἐγένετο...αἴτιος σωτηρίας αἰωνίου) for all those who obey him.

The events in 5:7–10 are laid out in a sequential manner: Passion, suffering and death, perfection/resurrection, source of eternal salvation and installation as Melchizedekian high priest. Likewise, a similar sequence is found in Heb 9:11–12, where Jesus appears in heaven as high priest, enters through the perfect tabernacle and into the heavenly sanctuary where he obtains eternal redemption for his people. At his resurrection, Jesus achieved perfection and was made fit to enter the heavenly sanctuary and offer his sacrifice for the purification of sin and the cleansing of conscience from dead works.[27]

A Biblical Theology of the Priesthood of Jesus

While the letter to the Hebrews is unique among its New Testament counterparts in its presentation of Jesus as the great high priest, some

---

128 n.51. The LXX of Hos 13:14a reads: ἐκ χειρὸς ᾅδου ῥύσομαι αὐτοὺς καὶ ἐκ θανάτου λυτρώσομαι αὐτούς.

25 Attridge, *Hebrews*, 150; cf. Joachim Jeremias, "Hbr 5:7–10," *ZNW* 44 (1953): 109–110.

26 Matthew C. Easter, *Faith the Faithfulness of Jesus*, SNTSMS 160 (Cambridge University Press, 2014), 122–124; cf. James Kurianal, *Jesus our High Priest: Ps 110, 4 as the Substructure of Heb 5, 1–7, 28*, European University Studies 23/693 (Peter Lang, 2000), 70; David M. Moffitt, "'If Another Priest Arises': Jesus' Resurrection and the High Priestly Christology of Hebrews," *A Cloud of Witnesses*, 69–71; Christopher A. Richardson, "The Passion: Reconsidering Hebrews 5:7–8," *A Cloud of Witnesses*, 60.

27 Jamieson, *Jesus' Death*, 25–35; cf. Moffitt, *Atonement*, 194–214.

commentators have suggested that there are echoes in the Gospels and the letters of Paul of Jesus functioning in a priestly manner.[28] And while these echoes never rise to the level of Hebrews' overtly high priestly Christology, they nevertheless introduce incidents in the life of Jesus that may contain echoes to activities associated with the office of high priest.

Synoptic Gospels

Perhaps the definitive role associated with the Levitical priesthood is the officiating of the sacrifice and the duty of the high priest in assuming the burden of Israel's sin. The duty of bearing the burden of Israel's sin is first set out to Aaron in a chapter focused on a description of the high priestly garments. Moses is commanded by Yahweh to make a pure plate of gold and engrave on it the words "Holy to the Lord," after which he is to fasten it upon the turban with a blue cord (Exod 28:36–37). By wearing the engraving upon his forehead, Aaron assumed the guilt of the people (וְנָשָׂא אַהֲרֹן אֶת־עֲוֹן הַקֳּדָשִׁים; ἐξαρεῖ Ααρων τὰ ἁμαρτήματα τῶν ἁγίων), which transfers from the officiant to the high priest by means of the sacrifice. This transfer of guilt is also seen in Lev 10:17, where Moses chastises Eleazar and Ithamar for not eating the flesh of the goat of the sin offering and thus "bearing the iniquity of the congregation (נָתַן לָכֶם לָשֵׂאת אֶת־עֲוֹן הָעֵדָה; ἵνα ἀφέλητε τὴν ἁμαρτίαν τῆς συναγωγῆς)." What is of significance here is the transference of sin from one person/people group to that of the high priest, who alone is able to bear the transferred sin.

A prominent New Testament account that illustrates this transfer of sin is in Mark 2 (cf. Matt 9:1–8) and the healing of the paralytic

---

28 Oscar Cullmann, *The Christology of the New Testament*, rev. ed., trans. Shirley C. Guthrie and Charles A. M. Hall (The Westminster Press, 1963), 83–89; André Feuillet, *The Priesthood of Christ and His Ministers*, trans. Matthew J. O'Connell (Doubleday, 1975); Crispin Fletcher-Louis, "Jesus as the High Priestly Messiah: Part 1," *JSHJ* 4 (2006): 155–175; Fletcher-Louis, "Jesus as The High Priestly Messiah: Part 2," *JSHJ* 5 (2007): 57–79; Brant Pitre, "Jesus, the New Temple, and the New Priesthood," *Letter & Spirit* 4 (2008): 47–83; David H. Wenkel, "Jesus at Age 30: Further Evidence for Luke's Portrait of a Priestly Jesus?" *BTB* 44 (2014): 195–201; Nicholas G. and David S. Schrock, "You Can Make Me Clean": The Matthean Jesus as Priest and the Biblical-Theological Results," *CTR* 14 (2016): 3–13; Nicholas Perrin, "Jesus as Priest in the Gospels," *SBJT* 22 (2018): 81–91; Perrin, *Jesus the Priest* (SPCK, 2018).

man. After witnessing the faith of the associates of the paralytic, Jesus pronounces a pardon of forgiveness for the paralytic man (2:3–6). This verdict causes immediate consternation among the religious leaders, who rightly acknowledge that it is only within the purview of God to declare a pardon for sin (2:6–7). Knowing that the religious leaders were debating his pardon, Jesus also provides the healing that was first sought as a testimony to his ability to not only declare such a pardon, but also the power to actualize the forgiveness pronounced (2:9–11). The man who came to Jesus paralyzed and believing that he could be healed left not only walking away from the mat that carried him there, but also from the burden of his guilt (2:12). By declaring the paralytic forgiven Jesus appears to assume the duty of the high priest and his responsibility of bearing the burden of sin.

However, the context of Mark 2 does not support a priestly involvement in the forgiveness of sin. Instead, it is the ontology of Jesus that is emphasized in his declaration of forgiveness and its juxtaposition with the singular truth that only Yahweh has such authority to pronounce a pardon for sin. When the religious leaders reasoned that forgiveness was God's prerogative alone, they were correct in their estimation. The Old Testament is emphatic in its insistence that only God is able to forgive sin.[29] Jesus uses this event not only to provide temporal healing for a man long paralyzed, but also as a teaching moment to demonstrate to the crowd that he was the long-promised Messiah, the very God incarnate. Therefore, while Jesus does in fact remove the burden of this man's sin, there is no indication in the pericope that what the author of Mark's Gospel had in mind was an allusion to the high priest's role in bearing the burden of the sin.[30] Instead, Jesus' declaration of forgiveness and its connection to the healing of the paralytic was affirmation of Jesus's ontological claim to deity.

A further duty of Israel's priests involved those who were deemed to be ritually impure. As recorded in Lev 12–15, several factors could render one ritually unclean, thus preventing them from approaching God. One such state of being that prohibited any such approach of sacred space was the presence of leprosy.[31] Leviticus 13 gives a detailed

---

29 Exod 34:7; Num 14:18; 2 Sam 24:10; Neh 9:17; Job 7:21; Ps 51:2; 130:4; Isa 43:25; 44:22; Jer 31:34; 36:3; Dan 9:9; Micah 7:18; cf. Acts 5:31; Col 2:13.

30 R. T. France, *The Gospel of Mark*, NIGTC (Eerdmans, 2002), 125–126.

31 Although it is common for translations to refer to this specific malady as

account of the various manifestations of leprosy, noting that it is the responsibility of the priests to diagnose whether or not a person has been stricken with leprosy, thus rendering that person unclean. If the diagnosis is that of a leprous outbreak, the stricken person is removed and isolated from the congregation. Once healed, the person is brought to the priest for inspection, and if the priest determines that the leprosy is gone, the former leper must offer a sacrifice of cleanings, after which the leper is declared clean (Lev 15). The duty and responsibility of the high priest as it relates to leprosy is both diagnostic and cultic; the high priest diagnoses the condition of the afflicted and also declares one ritually clean from defilement.

With respect to Jesus one sees a very different, though altogether consistent, attitude towards leprosy and ritual purity. In Mark's account of the healing of the leper (Mark 1:44; cf. Matthew 8:4; Luke 5:14; Luke 17:14), Jesus commands the former leper to go and show himself to the priest and offer the appropriate sacrifice Moses commanded in light of his cleansing (προσένεγκε περὶ τοῦ καθαρισμοῦ σου ἃ προσέταξεν Μωϋσῆς; cf. Lev 13:2–14:32). By pointing the healed man to the priest for cleansing, Jesus acknowledges the legitimacy of the Old Testament cult for ritual purification.[32] For if Jesus had been high priest at that moment in his ministry, he would have been able to rectify this defilement himself, thus rendering the Levitical cult null and void (cf. Heb 8:13). However, as a faithful Jew, Jesus was demonstrating to his detractors that he in fact kept the commandments of Moses.

In contrast with the Gospels, the letter to the Hebrews is clear that not only are people cleansed of the outward ritual defilement of sin, but more importantly they are also cleansed of the inward defilement caused by sin, a defilement of the conscience now purified through the blood of Jesus's sacrifice (9:13–14). By healing the man

---

leprosy, this is unfortunately not helpful in ascertaining the precise nature of this disease. And while leprosy (or Hansen's disease) is caused by the bacteria *Mycobacterium leprae* and is known to cause severe nerve damage, along with debilitating skins deformities, most commentators today agree that what Leviticus and elsewhere refer to as leprosy is anything but (cf. Jacob Milgrom, *Leviticus*, AB 3 [Doubleday, 1991], 773; David P. Wright and Richard N. Jones, "Leprosy," *ABD* 4:277–282; Matthew Thiessen, *Jesus and the Forces of Death: The Gospels' Portrayal of Ritual Impurity within First-Century Judaism* [Baker Academic, 2020], 43–68).

32 Robert A. Guelich, *Mark 1–8:26*, WBC 34A (Word, 1989), 76.

of his leprosy, Jesus was demonstrating to the people his power over death and disease, and his role as God's Messiah;[33] but in the case of requisite ritual cleansing, he leaves this responsibility in the hands of those who are authorized to handle such matters of religious and social importance.

John 17

Perhaps the most well-known passage outside of Hebrews that is given the designation of "priestly" is the so-called high priestly prayer of Jesus in John 17. Although the textual basis for such a title in John 17 is debatable, ever since the Reformer David Chyträus[34] in the sixteenth century onward it has been assumed that the content of the prayer alone is more than enough to warrant such an appellation. This conclusion is no doubt in some ways heavily influenced by an overt dependence upon the high priestly Christology outlined in the letter to the Hebrews.[35]

One of the earliest to ascribe priesthood to Jesus in their interpretation of John 17 is Cyril of Alexandria. In his exposition on John 17:9–11, Cyril refers to Jesus as "our truly and all-holy High Priest." Jesus is "the Sacrifice, and is Himself our Priest, Himself our Mediator, Himself a blameless victim, the true Lamb which takes away the sin of the world." As our high priest and mediator, Jesus "prays for us as a Man," and "being a holy High Priest, blameless and undefiled, offered Himself not for His own weakness, as was the custom of those to whom was allotted the duty of sacrificing according to the Law, but rather for the salvation of our souls, and that once for all ...." (*In Joh.* 11:8; PG 74:505).

---

33 Adela Yarbro Collins, *Mark: A Commentary on the Gospel of Mark*, Hermeneia (Fortress Press, 2007), 179.

34 Edwyn Hoskyns, *The Fourth Gospel*, ed. Francis Noel Davey (Faber and Faber Limited, 1947), 494; Cullmann, *Christology*, 105; Rudolf Schnackenburg, *The Gospel according to St. John*, vol. 3, trans. David Smith and G. A. Kon (Crossroad, 1983), 433; Craig S. Keener, *The Gospel of John: A Commentary* (Hendrickson, 2003), 2:1051.

35 Cf. Ceslas Spicq, "L'origine johannique de la conception du Christ-prêtre dans l'Epître aux Hébreux," *Aux Sources de la tradition chrétienne: Mélanges offerts à M. Maurice Goguel* (Delachaux & Niestlé, 1950), 258–269; Cullmann, *Christology*, 105; J. Ramsey Michaels, *The Gospel of John*, NICNT (Eerdmans, 2010), 873–874; Daniel B. Stevick, *Jesus and His Own: A Commentary on John 13–17* (Eerdmans, 2011), 310.

Although Cyril's exposition is on John 17:9–11, one cannot help but note the influence of Hebrews upon his reading of John 17. The most obvious example of this influence is the use of the title "High Priest" with reference to Jesus. Outside of Hebrews, this title is nowhere else applied to Jesus, and any reading of this title into the prayer of Jesus in John 17 is no doubt directly tied to one's familiarity with the high priestly Christology of Hebrews. Further evidence of the influence of Hebrews upon Cyril's exposition is found in the expression "not for His own weakness." According to Heb 7, Jesus's sacrifice was once-for-all, and unlike the high priests of the Levitical cult, he was excluded from making any such sacrifice for himself. Also, because of the weakness of man and their inevitable death, the sacrifices of the Levitical priests were only operative so long as a high priest was serving in the sanctuary (Heb 7:27–28). Therefore, when Cyril refers to the lack of human weakness with respect to Jesus, he does so informed by Hebrews' high priestly Christology and its theology of atonement.

Regarding the structure and content of John 17, several issues should be noted that have been used to support a priestly reading. First, the structure of Jesus's prayer in John 17 is organized around three sets of prayers: Jesus prays for himself (17:1–8); Jesus prays for his disciples (17:9–19); and Jesus prays for the world (17:20–26). Some commentators suggest a connection between the tri-partite structure in John 17 and the liturgy of the high priest on the Day of Atonement.[36] On Yom Kippur, the high priest offers first a sacrifice for himself and his kin (Lev 16:6). This is followed by an offering for the people (16:15). Finally, there is the universal prohibition against entering the tent of meeting (16:17). While these similarities are curious, as Attridge notes, they are not "enough in itself to confirm that the evangelist is playing with priestly imagery."[37]

Second, much has been made of the intercessory nature of Jesus's prayer in John 17. As noted above, Jesus engages in intercessory prayer for himself, his disciples, and future believers. However, such intercessory prayer could easily be understood against the backdrop of

---

36 Harold W. Attridge, "How Priestly is the 'High Priestly Prayer' of John 17?" *CBQ* 75 (2013): 9–10; C. H. Dodd, *The Interpretation of the Fourth Gospel* (Cambridge University Press, 1953), 417–423.

37 Attridge, "High Priestly Prayer," 10.

ancient farewell discourses often found in Jewish literature.[38] For example, both Gen 49 and Deut 32–33 offer similar cases to that of John 17 (cf. *Jub.* 22:7–23). Similar to Jacob in Genesis 49 and Moses in Deut 32–33, Jesus is likewise involved in making preparations for his departure from this world and returning to his father in heaven (17:5, 11, 13, 24; cf. 7:33; 13:1, 3; 14:12, 28; 16:5, 28).

Such intercessory prayer is also common among the Old Testament prophets. Moses on many occasions stood between God's wrath and the people, interceding on their behalf that God would spare them from destruction (Exod 32:11–14; Deut 9:18, 26–29; cf. Ps 106:23). Such is similar with the prophet Samuel as well. For example, in 1 Sam 7, the people urge Samuel to cry out to the Lord on their behalf for deliverance from the hand of the Philistines (1 Sam 7:8–9; cf. 12:23). A further example intercessory prayer is also found in God's rebuke of his people in Jer 7, where God commands that Jeremiah "not pray for this people (אַל־תִּתְפַּלֵּל בְּעַד־הָעָם הַזֶּה) or lift up a cry or prayer for them (וְאַל־תִּשָּׂא בַעֲדָם רִנָּה וּתְפִלָּה), and do not intercede with me (וְאַל־תִּפְגַּע־בִּי), for I will not listen" (7:16; cf. 11:14; 14:11; cf. 2 Macc 15:14). Such intercession was not only a common occurrence among the prophets, it was also a duty of one's calling as a prophet.

When looking at the content of Jesus's prayer in John 17, much has been made of Jesus's use of ἁγιάζω in 17:17 and 17:19. Ramsey posits that it is at this point in Jesus's prayer that one gets their first taste of priestly language.[39] In John 17:17, Jesus asks that his Father would "sanctify/consecrate [his disciples] in [his] truth (ἁγίασον αὐτοὺς ἐν τῇ ἀληθείᾳ)." In 17:19, Jesus sanctifies/consecrates himself (ἐγὼ ἁγιάζω ἐμαυτόν) so that his disciples would be sanctified/consecrated in truth (ἵνα ὦσιν καὶ αὐτοὶ ἡγιασμένοι ἐν ἀληθείᾳ). While the language of sanctification and consecration is closely associated with Old Testament priests (cf. Exod 19:22: ἁγιασθήτωσαν; 28:41: ἁγιάσεις αὐτούς, ἵνα ἱερατεύωσίν μοι), it is also used for consecrating prophets for their prophetic mission.[40]

---

38   D. A. Carson, *The Gospel According to John*, PNTC (Eerdmans, 1991), 550–551; Herman Ridderbos, *The Gospel of John: A Theological Commentary*, trans. John Vriend (Eerdmans, 1997), 546; Keener, *John*, 2:1051; Andrew T. Lincoln, *The Gospel According to Saint John*, BNTC (Continuum, 2005), 432.

39   Ramsey, *John*, 872.

40   C. K. Barrett, *Gospel According to St John: An Introduction with Commentary and Notes on the Greek Text*, 2nd ed. (SPCK, 1978), 510; John W. Baigent, "Jesus as Priest:

A clear example of this is Jer 1:5: "Before I formed you in the womb, I knew you, and before you came out of the womb I have consecrated you (ἡγίακά); I have appointed (τέθεικά) you a prophet for the nations." Here, the prophet's consecration and appointment are parallel to one another and occur while Jeremiah was still unborn (cf. Gal 1:15a).

Finally, in John 10, similar language to that of 17:17 and 17:19 is used by Jesus in his confrontation with the Jewish leadership. Responding to the charge of blasphemy, Jesus comments that it is the Father who consecrated him and sent him into the world (ὁ πατὴρ ἡγίασεν καὶ ἀπέστειλεν εἰς τὸν κόσμον; 10:36). The language of consecration in 10:36 is connected to that of sending, so that what Jesus is sanctified/consecrated for is his mission to the world. Further, the prayer of Jesus for his disciples in 17:17, and again in 17:19b is that they would be sanctified "in truth" (ἐν τῇ ἀληθείᾳ / ἐν ἀληθείᾳ). In Jesus's self-consecration in 17:19a, this same purpose of consecration in truth is implied, so that what is explicit in his prayer for the disciples is understood in his prayer for himself.[41] Therefore, it is this sense of consecration for mission that Jesus certainly had in mind in both 17:17 and 17:19.[42]

An Examination of the Claim that the Concept of Jesus as Priest may Found in the New Testament Outside the Epistle to the Hebrews," *VE* 12 (1981): 38.

41 Raymon E. Brown, *Gospel According to John (XIII-XXI): Introduction, Translation, and Notes* AB 29A (Doubleday, 1970), 766.

42 Barrett, *John*, 510; Some have suggested a different nuance for Jesus's self-consecration (ἐγὼ ἁγιάζω ἐμαυτόν) in 17:19. Rather than reading all three instances of ἁγιάζω in 17:17, 19 as parallel, the meaning of Jesus's self-consecration has been turned into a reference to his impending death on the cross. Bultmann appears to suggest both the act of sending and sacrifice are in view in 17:19 (*The Gospel of John: A Commentary*, trans. George R. Beasley-Murray [The Westminster Press, 1971], 510–511, n.5). Furthermore, it is through this self-sacrifice that Jesus's disciples are consecrated to the ministry for which Jesus has called them to (cf. Ernst Haenchen, *John 2*, Hermeneia, trans. Robert W. Funk [Philadelphia: Fortress Press, 1984], 155).

However, such a break from the parallel uses in 17:17 and 17:19 does not fit the context of what Jesus is praying for. As noted in the commentary on these verses above, what Jesus is praying for is the consecration of both his and his disciples' mission to the world (cf. 10:36; 17:18). Lincoln correctly surmises, "When now Jesus speaks of sanctifying himself, this is in line with the way this Gospel portrays him as sharing what would normally be considered divine prerogatives and also as being in control of his own life and mission" (*John*, 438). Barrett likewise concludes along similar lines, noting that whatever one makes of the meaning of ἁγιάζω in 17:17 (and, it may

The Pauline letters

Moving outside of the Gospels, potential references to the priesthood of Jesus become harder to identify with any precision.[43] This is certainly the case with the writings of Paul, who speaks more about the sacrifice of Jesus than he does about his priesthood. In fact, Montefiore emphatically insists that Paul does not even regard Jesus as a priest anywhere in his writings.[44] Although lacking explicit and implicit references, there are a few verses that have been interpreted as references to Jesus's high priesthood.

Romans 8:34 is found within the crescendo of a prolonged discussion regarding justification by faith.[45] This final pericope (8:31–39) is a celebration of that work of justification, and subsequent future glorification, in the lives of those who have placed their faith in the work of Christ.[46] In 8:34, Paul concisely describes the redemptive work of Jesus in the following manner: Christ died (ὁ ἀποθανών), was raised (ἐγερθείς), and now intercedes for his own (ἐντυγχάνει ὑπὲρ ἡμῶν). This rather formulaic statement[47] rightly describes the procession of Jesus, from death to intercession. Furthermore, the intercession of Jesus echoes that of the Holy Spirit in 8:27 (ἐντυγχάνει ὑπὲρ ἁγίων / ἐντυγχάνει ὑπὲρ ἡμῶν). Rather than elements of priestly activity in the formulaic statement of Rom 8:34, the focus is on the legal advocacy (παράκλητος) involved in Jesus's intercessory ministry on behalf of his followers (cf. Heb 7:25; 9:24; 1 John 2:1).[48]

---

be added, 10:36), the meaning of Jesus's self-consecration in 17:19 cannot mean something altogether different (*John*, 510).

43 The possible exception being the book of Revelation, particularly John's description of Jesus among the seven golden lampstands, clothed in a long robe and golden sash (Rev 1:9–20; 15:6; cf. G. K. Beale, *The Book of Revelation*, NIGTC [Eerdmans, 1999], 208–209).

44 Montefiore *Hebrews*, 5.

45 James D. G. Dunn, *Romans 1–8*, WBC 38A (Word, 1988), 497.

46 N. T. Wright, "The Letter to the Romans: Introduction, Commentary, and Reflections," in *The New Interpreter's Bible*, vol. 10 (Abingdon Press, 2002), 609.

47 Dunn, *Romans*, 503; C. K. Barrett, *The Epistle to the Romans*, rev. ed., BNTC (A & C Black, 1991), 162.

48 Cf. Robert Jewett, *Romans: A Commentary on the Book of Romans*, Hermeneia (Fortress Press, 2007), 542; *pace* C. E. B., *The Epistle to the Romans*, vol. 1., ICC (T&T Clark, 1975), 439. Commenting on Rom 8:34, Calvin proclaims that "[Jesus] appears

Therefore, Paul's confessional formula of Jesus's death, resurrection, and intercessory activity in 8:34 supports the argument of this chapter, namely that Jesus became high priest upon his entry into the heavenly sanctuary, rather than describing any type of earthly intercessory work done by Jesus. For Jesus to engage in such a ministry of intercession he first must die and then rise from dead. Although the sequence of these events does not prove definitively the argument that Jesus became high priest after his entry into the heavenly sanctuary, it does argue against the idea that Jesus engaged in a priestly function of intercession before his death and subsequent resurrection.

One final passage that may have priestly overtones is found in the creedal statement of 1 Tim 2:5–6.[49] Similar in some respects to the formulaic statement in Rom 8:34, 1 Tim 2:5 portrays Jesus as both a sacrifice and one who stands between God and man. Whereas Jesus's activity of intercession is highlighted in Rom 8:34, in 1 Tim 2:5 Jesus is specifically referred to as the "one mediator between God and humanity (εἷς καὶ μεσίτης θεοῦ καὶ ἀνθρώπων)." While on the surface Jesus's role as mediator may invoke images of priestly intercession, such an understanding is most likely reading into 1 Tim 2:5 an idea that is not present in the meaning of the passage. Elsewhere, Paul uses the same word, μεσίτης, in reference to Moses's mediatorial work with respect to the giving of the law (Gal 3:19–20). A similar usage of μεσίτης is found in Hebrews, where Jesus is referred to as the mediator of a new covenant, one that is established by him and mediated through him (8:6; 9:15; 12:24). Therefore, rather than a priestly intercessor, Jesus is the negotiator between God and humanity of the new covenant inaugurated through his sacrificial offering.[50]

---

continually, as one who died and rose again, and as his death and resurrection stand in the place of eternal intercession, and have the *efficacy of a powerful prayer for reconciling and rendering the Father propitious to us*, he is justly said to intercede for us" (John Calvin, *Commentary on the Epistle of Paul the Apostle to the Romans*, ed. and trans. John Owen [Logos Bible Software, 2010], 325, emphasis added).

49 Cf. J. N. D. Kelly, *The Pastoral Epistles*, BNTC (A & C Black, 1963), 63; William D. Mounce, *Pastoral Epistles*, WBC 46 (Word, 2000), 87; Linda Belleville, "1 Timothy," *Cornerstone Biblical Commentary: 1 Timothy, 2 Timothy, Titus, and Hebrews*, vol. 17 (Tyndale House Publishers, 2009), 42.

50 Luke Timothy Johnson, *The First and Second Letters to Timothy: A New Translation with Introduction and Commentary*, AB 35A (Doubleday, 2001), 191–192.

Conclusion

The focus of this chapter has been twofold. Starting with the letter to the Hebrews, the question of timing with respect to the installation of Jesus as high priest was assessed. This examination attempted to answer the following questions: Was Jesus high priest from all eternity? Did Jesus become high priest at his incarnation or at some point during his journey along the *Via Dolorosa*? Was Jesus installed as high priest at the cross? And lastly, did Jesus' inauguration as high priest coincide with his entrance into the heavenly sanctuary? It was proposed that the evidence in Hebrews best supports a view of Jesus becoming high priest upon his entry into heaven.

Furthermore, Jesus's lineage also prevented him from serving as high priest while present on earth. Because he was a descendant of Judah, Jesus was excluded from serving in the earthly temple, and was thus unable to make any type of priestly offering for sin. This prohibition against making an offering presented a problem for Jesus, since it is the duty of high priest to offer sacrifices for sin. However, for the author of Hebrews this does not pose any serious problem. The once-for-all-time offering that Jesus presents for sin does not take place in the Jewish temple, which is a representation of the old covenant and its cult, but in the heavenly sanctuary, where Jesus inaugurated not only a new covenant but also a new cult. Therefore, the priesthood that Jesus assumes was established not according to a legal requirement, but on the basis of an oath and the power of an indestructible life.

The second part of this essay undertook a short biblical theology of priesthood in relationship to Jesus, built upon the premise that Jesus was unable to serve as high priest while still present on earth. This biblical theology was selective, constructed upon passages from the Synoptic Gospels, John 17, Rom 8:34, and 1 Tim 2:5–6. Each of these passages have in some way been understood as applying priestly activity to the person of Jesus. However, as was argued above, these activities are not exclusively priestly and can also be associated with functions related to ontology, office, or consecration for ministry. In this manner, the activities of Jesus portrayed in the Gospels and the writings of Paul are not exclusively connected to the role of high priest.

The main responsibility that sets the high priest apart from the rest of his kin was the sacrificial offering that he presented for the atonement of sin, and no other sacrificial offering was more important than the one presented annually on the Day of Atonement. Because Jesus was prohibited from making his offering of atonement while present on earth, this by extension negates the argument that it was at the cross that Jesus became both the offering and officiant of the atoning sacrifice for sin. Instead, just as the high priest slaughtered the victim outside the tent and then entered into the Holy of Holies and obtained atonement for sin by the manipulation of blood upon the mercy seat, so also Jesus, after he was sacrificed outside the gates, entered into the heavenly sanctuary whereby he offered himself to God as the once-for-all-time sacrifice of atonement.

12

"What Have I Done in Comparison with You?": The Itinerary of Gideon's Pursuit of the Midianites in Judges 7–8

Chris McKinny

INTRODUCTION[1]

BEFORE WE BEGIN OUR DISCUSSION of the geography of Judges 7–8, let us briefly examine the interaction between Gideon and the men of Ephraim at the fords of the Jordan (Judg 8:1–3). Their meeting occurred in the middle of Gideon's long pursuit of Midian from the Jezreel Valley to "Karkor" and then back to the fords of the Jordan. One should understand Ephraim and Gideon's discussion as a comparison between the accomplishments of Gideon, as the unlikely representative of Yahweh (e.g., Judg 7:2, 18–20), and the men of Ephraim. By one reckoning, both Ephraim and Gideon captured and executed two leaders of the Midianites, Ephraim caught and killed Oreb and Zeeb (Judg 7:25), whereas Gideon caught and killed Zebah and Zalmunna (Judg 8:18–21). Clearly, the author of the Book of Judges wanted readers to look further than this surface-level equality. With the princely heads of Zeeb and Oreb in their hands, the men of Ephraim leveled their complaint against Gideon.

---

1 I would like to express my deep and heartfelt gratitude to Will Varner. Will has had an enormous impact upon my personal and professional life. So much of my academic development and interests have been influenced by his scholarship and teaching in the classroom, the "field" (i.e., Israel), and the pulpit. As many of his students could attest, Varner's passionate teaching and scholarship clearly conveys that his "heart burns" (Luke 24:32) for his Messiah. For so many of us, Will's passion has been (and still is) quite contagious.

> Then the men of Ephraim said to him, "What is this that you have done to us, not to call us when you went to fight against Midian?" And they accused him fiercely. And he said to them, "What have I done now in comparison with you? Is not the gleaning of the grapes of Ephraim better than the grape harvest of Abiezer? God has given into your hands the princes of Midian, Oreb and Zeeb. What have I been able to do in comparison with you?" Then their anger against him subsided when he said this (Judg 8:1–3)." [2]

While Gideon's diplomatic response pacified the belligerent Ephraimites, one wonders if Gideon's question was meant to be genuine, sardonic, or a combination of these? Did Gideon really mean that Ephraim had done more than he had in defeating the Midianites?

To answer this question, we must compare Gideon and Ephraim's contrasting motivations and the distances travelled in the conflict. Despite several bouts of personal cowardice, Gideon portrayed humble obedience and, eventually, bravery in carrying out Yahweh's commands to save all of Israel from the menace of Midian and her allies. In contrast, Ephraim showed cowardice and pride, as well as a total disregard for his fellow tribes. These details are relatively clear from the text, and we will briefly discuss other literary aspects of Ephraim's hypocrisy and cowardice below. To modern readers, the geography of Judges 6–8 is less apparent. The goal of this paper is to demonstrate the incomparable nature of Gideon vis-à-vis Ephraim's contributions to the defeat of Midian. Put succinctly, Gideon and his 300 men travelled hundreds of miles/km to accomplish total victory over the Midianites while the Ephraimites essentially stayed in their own territory, captured some of the Midianites, and then bragged about a partial victory. We will discuss the details of Gideon's itinerary, but let us begin with a brief synopsis of Judges 7–8.

After a long prelude to the conflict (Judg 6:1–7:14), Gideon's small force of 300 men defeated the Midianites in the Jezreel Valley (Judg 7:15–22). While pursuing Midian, Gideon sent messengers to various tribes including Naphtali, Asher, and Manasseh (Judg 7:23), and then Ephraim (Judg 7:24). Before Gideon's forces were reduced by the Lord (Judg 7:1–8), the northern tribes had initially mustered to

---

2 All translations are ESV unless otherwise noted.

Gideon (Judg 6:35) to fight against the hosts of Midian, Amalek, and the people of the east (Judg 6:3). Significantly, Ephraim had not mustered with the other tribes to face the common foe. The Ephraimites blamed Gideon for not initially calling them to the battle (Judg 8:1–2). Their complaint should not to be taken seriously by careful readers of the Book of Judges. To understand this assertation, let us briefly examine the literary backdrop to the tension-filled meeting between Gideon and the Ephraimites at the fords of the Jordan (Judg 8:1–3).

Ephraim was the tribe of Joshua (Judg 2:9)—the great leader of Israel who had faithfully led Israel into Canaan. Subsequent to this, Ephraim readily responded to the call of Ehud—the Benjaminite judge—when he led Israel against the Moabites (Judg 3:27). In the preceding account to Gideon, Ephraim (Deborah's tribe; Judg 4:5) led the rebellion against Sisera in the same region where Gideon faced off against the Midianites (Judg 4:8–10, 14; cf. Ps 83:9–11). In fact, Ephraim was the first tribe mentioned in Deborah's song (Judg 5:14), which ironically ridiculed other tribes for not appearing at the battle (Judg 5:15b-17). In the story of Jephthah (Judg 10–12), the Ephraimites again complained that they were not called to the battle (Judg 12:1–3) despite the fact that they themselves had been invaded by the Ammonites (Judg 10:9). Jephthah's subsequent battle against the Ephraimites (Judg 12:5–7) underscores the negative portrayal of Ephraim from Judges 6–12. Finally, we will show that Gideon's hometown of Ophrah of the Abiezrites (Judg 6:11, 24; 8:27, 32) was actually located to the southeast of Shechem in immediate proximity to Ephraim (Figure 12.6). In light of all of this, Ephraim's absence from Gideon's initial mustering was completely inexcusable and their complaints for not being called to the battle should be understood as the hypocritical justification of a cowardly, glory-seeking, previously-great tribe.

THE HISTORICAL GEOGRAPHY OF THE GIDEON NARRATIVE (JUDG 6–8)

The Gideon Narrative (Judg 6–8) includes a high quantity of geographical details covering a large area of the southern Levant including sites in the central hill country (Ophrah of the Abiezrites; Judg 6:11, 24; 8:27–32), the Jezreel/Harod Valley (Hill of Moreh and En-harod; Judg

7:1), the Jordan Valley (e.g., Succoth and Penuel; Judg 8:8–9, 14–17), Gilead (Judg 7:3),[3] and perhaps even northwest Arabia (Karkor; Judg 8:14; but see discussion below). Before discussing the specific identifications of the towns in the itinerary, we will provide a brief summary of the route of Gideon's pursuit of the Midianites as recorded in Judges 7–8. In the conclusion, I will repeat this itinerary in more depth by adding in my suggested site identifications. We will then be able to better answer Gideon's question—"what have I done in comparison with you?" to the prideful Ephraimites at the fords of the Jordan (Judg 8:3). We will see that this narrative presents the itinerary of Gideon's efforts against Midian in a way that starkly contrasts with those of the Ephraimites. While Gideon's 300 men travelled a long distance and were the principle force in defeating the Midianites, the Ephraimites did not valiantly respond to Gideon's initial call to action, and when they later did they never even left their own territory.

Summary of Gideon's pursuit

Following the defeat of the Midianites[4] at the Hill of Moreh (Nebi Dahi), Gideon and his 300 men chased the Midianites down the Harod Valley (En-harod ='Ain Jalûd) to the Jordan Valley using the western Jordan Valley route[5] (Judg 7:22–23; Figure 12.1). The Midianites had apparently outpaced Gideon and his men. However, the Ephraimites captured the fords of the Jordan River (presumably at Adam) and assassinated Oreb and Zeeb, princes[6] of Midian (Judg 7:24–8:3). Upon reaching the fords, Gideon had to diplomatically pacify the jealous Ephraimites (see above) before crossing the Jordan. Upon crossing,

---

3 Some suggest that "Mount Gilead" in this passage should be read as Mount Gilboa in light of the geographical context of Gideon, e.g., J. F. Walvoord and R. B. Zuck, *The Bible Knowledge Commentary: Old Testament* (David C. Cook, 1983), 393.

4 The Midianites were joined by Amalekites and Kedemites. The Kedemites, i.e., the "people of the east" (Judg 6:3, 33; 7:12; 8:10), were probably associated with the Ishmaelites as can be seen in "Kedemah" the twelfth prince in Ishmael's genealogy (Gen 25:15; 1 Chr 1:29; cf. Isa 11:14; Jer 49:28; Ezek 25:4, 10).

5 Yohanan Aharoni, *The Land of the Bible: A Historical Geography*, trans. Anson F. Rainey, revised and enlarged (Westminster Press, 1979), Map 3-"way of the Jordan."

6 The designation of Oreb and Zeeb as "princes of Midian" (שָׂרֵי מִדְיָן) versus Zebah and Zalmunnah as "kings of Midian" (מַלְכֵי מִדְיָן) might imply a hierarchy of leaders in Midian.

Gideon and his men were refused provision by the cities of Succoth and Penuel, who were apparently afraid of retribution from Midian (Judg 8:4–9). Continuing his pursuit, Gideon ascended the Transjordanian hill country (via the "way of the tent dwellers") and caught up with the Midianites at "Karkor." At Karkor, Gideon thoroughly defeated Midian (Judg 8:10–12). Upon returning to Succoth and Penuel (via the "ascent of Heres"), Gideon punished Succoth and Penuel and executed Zebah and Zalmunna, captured kings of Midian.[7] We will now turn our attention to the specific toponyms mentioned in the text.

Beth-shittah

Beth-shittah is only mentioned in Judges 7:22 (cf. *Onom.* 54.11). The Midianite army clearly fled along the route from the western Harod Valley towards the east, as Abel-meholah can plausibly be identified with Tell Abu Sûs (see below). Therefore, Beth-shittah must be distinct from Abel-shittim/Shittim (Num 25:1; 33:49; Josh 2:1; 3:1; Mic 6:5), which should be located near the northeastern shores of the Dead Sea. Beth-shittah ("house of the acacia") has been identified with Shŭtta[8], which is located 2.5 km to the east of En-harod. While there does not appear to be an Iron Age site at Shŭtta, surveys at the nearby ruin of Murḥan[9] revealed remains from the Iron I and Iron II.[10] Another

---

7 Judg 8:13–21. For a discussion of textual issues in this narrative see e.g., D.I. Block, "Judges," in *Joshua, Judges, Ruth, 1 & 2 Samuel*, ed. J.H. Walton and D.I. Block, vol. 2 (Zondervan, 2009), 150–167; J.M. Sasson, *Judges 1–12: A New Translation with Introduction and Commentary*, Anchor Bible Commentary 6A (Yale University Press, 2014), 346–372.

8 E.g., J. J. Simons, *The Geographical and Topographical Texts of the Old Testament: A Concise Commentary in XXXII Chapters* (Brill, 1959), 293. See also the suggestion to associate Beth-shittah with Tell Sleihat in the eastern Jordan Valley in H.O. Thompson, "Beth-Shittah," in *Anchor Bible Dictionary*, ed. D.N. Freedman (Doubleday, 1992), 1:698. However, this site appears to be a natural hill with no archaeological remains, Simons, *Geographical and Topographical Texts*, 293.

9 This site is located just east of the modern settlement of Ein Harod near Qûmieh on the SWP (Survey of Western Palestine).

10 In this paper, I use the following archaeological periodization (only biblical periods included and all dates are approximate): Middle Bronze II (c. 2000–1550 BC), Late Bronze (c. 1550–1200 BC), Late Bronze I (c.1550–1400 BC), Late Bronze IIA (c. 1400–1300 BC), Late Bronze IIB (c. 1300–1200 BC), Iron I (c. 1200–1000 BC), Early Iron IIA (c. 1000–900 BC), Late Iron IIA (c. 900–800 BC), Iron IIB (c. 800–701 BC), Iron

possibility is the nearby ruin of Tell el-Farr (Tel Salwim), located less than a km to the south of Shŭtta, where surveys and excavations revealed remains from the Middle Bronze II, Late Bronze, Iron I, Iron II, and Persian-Early Islamic periods.[11] Either of these ruins is suitable for Beth-shittah as they match the geographical and archaeological requirements.

Zererah

Zererah (צְרֵרָה), which also only appears in Judges 7:22, is seemingly problematic from a textual perspective. The MT's צְרֵרָה—צררתה with the directional ה—is often understood to be a scribal error for צרדתה.[12] The latter form occurs as another scribal error in 2 Chronicles 4:17 in light of the parallel account of 1 Kings 7:46, which has the term Zarethan.[13] Attempts to associate Zererah with Zarethan[14] would require a double textual emendation and thereby are unwarranted. In my opinion, Zererah should be located between Beth-shittah and Abel-meholah because it is part of the itinerary of the Midianites' flight towards the southeast. Assuming that Beth-shittah can be related to Shŭtta, as we have argued above, then it is possible that Zererah should be located on the route from Beth-shittah to the "border" (שׂפת)[15] of Abel-meholah. One may possibly identify Zererah with

IIC (c. 701–586/539 BC), Persian (c. 539–332 BC), Hellenistic (332–63 BC), and Early Roman (63 BC-AD 70). N. Tzori and N. Shemesh, *Map of Ein Harod*, Online, Archaeological Survey of Israel 62 (Israel Antiquities Authority, 2015), site 21, http://survey.antiquities.org.il/index_Eng.html#/MapSurvey/2141.

11 N. Tzori and N. Shemesh, *Map of Ein Harod*, site 25.

12 Some manuscripts have this reading.

13 The readings of Γαραγαθα in LXXB and συνηγμενη in LXXA do not clarify the issue, e.g., Simons, *Geographical and Topographical Texts*, 292.

14 This is commonly identified with Tell es-Sa'idiyeh. N. Glueck, "Three Israelite Towns in the Jordan Valley: Zarethan, Succoth, Zaphon," *Bulletin of the American Schools of Oriental Research*, no. 90 (April 1, 1943): 2–23; H.O. Thompson, "Zarethan," in *Anchor Bible Dictionary*, ed. Freedman, 6:1042–1043; B. MacDonald, *East of the Jordan: Territories and Sites of the Hebrew Scriptures* (American Schools of Oriental Research, 2000), 149; but see Aharoni, *The Land of the Bible*, 34; A.F. Rainey and S. Notley, *The Sacred Bridge: Carta's Atlas of the Biblical World* (Carta, 2006), 176.

15 For the unique usage of שׂפת with a toponym see Simons *Geographical and Topographical Texts*, 293.

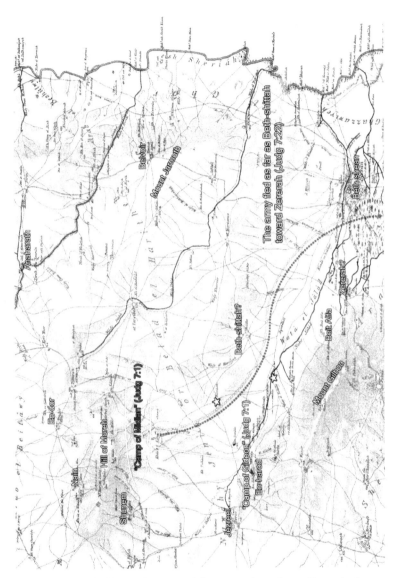

Figure 12.1—Survey of Western Palestine, with markings (by author)
showing sites mentioned in Judges 7, map is north-oriented,
© Todd Bolen/BiblePlaces.com used with permission.

Tellûl ez-Zahrah, which is located c. 4 km west of Beth-shean and just
north of the modern kibbutz Nir David. Tellûl ez-Zahrah has remains
from the Chalcolithic-Byzantine periods including remains from the

Iron I and Iron II.[16] From a toponymic perspective, Tellûl ez-Zahrah can plausibly be linked to Zererah. The geographical positioning of the site along the western road from the Harod Valley towards the fords of the Jordan River also matches the flight of the Midianites who fled towards the direction of Abel-meholah.

Abel-meholah

Judges 7:22 mentions Abel-meholah (אָבֵל מְחוֹלָה) in the retreat of the Midianites from Gideon to the Jordan River. It is associated with the otherwise unknown sites of Beth-shittah, Zererah, and Tabbath. It lies in Baana's district of Solomon's kingdom (1 Kgs 4:12), which contains the region between Beth-shean and Jokmeam. It also is the hometown of Adriel (1 Sam 18:19; 21:8) and Elisha (1 Kgs 19:16). Judges 7:22 and 1 Kings 4:12 clearly point to a location near the Jordan River in close proximity to Beth-shean. The name itself means the "plain of Mahlah."[17] Mahlah was a Manassehite clan (Num 26:33; 27:1; 36:11; Josh 17:3; 1 Chr 7:18).[18] These details indicate that Abel-meholah should be located within the territory of Manasseh and on a flat plain. During the Byzantine period, Eusebius provided a very precise identification of Abel-meholah with the site of Bethmaela. Eusebius stated that Bethmaela was "a village in Aulon (i.e., the biblical Arabah or the Jordan Rift Valley from Mount Hermon to the Dead Sea, cf. *Onom.* 14.9), ten milestones from Scythopolis" (*Onom.* 34.13). Jerome added that the direction from Scythopolis to "Bethmaula" was southward (*Onom.* 35.13). Consistently, Tell Abu Sûs (Figure 12.2) is located almost exactly ten Roman Miles (15 km) away from Scythopolis to the south and has remains from throughout the Iron Age, as well as Early Bronze, Middle Bronze, Late Bronze, and Persian-Byzantine.[19] Accordingly, Tell Abu Sûs appears to be the best candidate for Abel-meholah.[20]

---

16 Tzori and Shemesh, *Map of Ein Harod*, site 24, see also site 44.

17 Or perhaps "the plain of the dancing." See MacDonald, *East of the Jordan*, 206 with bibliography.

18 D.V. Edelman, "Abel-Meholah," in *Anchor Bible Dictionary*, ed. Freedman, 1:11.

19 N. Zori, *The Land of Issachar: Archaeological Survey* (Israel Exploration Society, 1977), site 56; A. Zertal, *The Manasseh Hill Country Survey, Vol. IV—From Nahal Bezeq to the Sartaba* (Tel Aviv, 2005), site 33.1977

20 Cf. Edelman, "Abel-Meholah," 11–12 for a thorough discussion of the other opinions; see also MacDonald, *East of the Jordan*, 205–206; A. Zertal, *The Manasseh*

Figure 12.2—Aerial of Abel-Meholah (Tell Abu Sûs) from northwest,
© William Schlegel/BiblePlaces.com used with permission.

Tabbath

If Abel-meholah can be identified with Tell Abu Sûs, then presumably Tabbath (טַבָּת), which only appears in Judges 7:22, should be located in close proximity. While acknowledging the difficulty with the passage, Aharoni suggested that Zererah/Zeredah (connecting it with Zarethan, see above) and Tabbath should be associated with Transjordanian destinations that the Midianite forces were attempting to reach in their flight from Gideon. In his view, Abel-meholah and Beth-shittah represented Cisjordan towns near fords.[21] In my opinion, this interpretation cannot be sustained. One might translate the passage as follows, "the camp fled as far as Beth-shittah toward Zererah (with directional ה) as far as the border of Abel-meholah [which is] across from Tabbath (Judg 7:22)." Thus, Beth-shittah and the border of Abel-meholah is the itinerary of the Midianites before they reached the fords of the Jordan, which is associated with Beth-barah (Judg 7:24). Tabbath is simply an additional geographical indicator for the location of Abel-meholah. Since Tabbath's relationship to Abel-meholah is described using the preposition עַל, then Tabbath could potentially have been located in either Cisjordan or Transjordan. Therefore, associating Tabbath with Ras Abu Ṭabat in the Ajlûn on the basis of a toponymic connection is possible.[22] However, Glueck noted that the site lacks adequate archaeological remains,[23] and the extended distance from Abel-meholah to Ras Abu Ṭabat remains problematic. Perhaps Ṭâbqath el-Hilweh preserves Tabbath. Ṭâbqath el-Hilweh is situated c. 8 km southeast of Tell Abu Sûs. The nearby small ruin (3.2 dunams) of Tell el-Ḥilu (SWP Tell 'Ain Sifry) possesses remains from the Middle Bronze-Byzantine period including from the Iron I and II.[24]

Hill Country Survey: The Eastern Valleys and the Fringes of the Desert, vol. 2 (Brill, 2008), 110.

21 Aharoni, *The Land of the Bible*, 284, note 222.

22 F.M. Abel, *Géographie de la Palestine: Géographie Physique et Historique*, 3rd ed. (Gabalda, 1967), 2.474; Simons, *Geographical and Topographical Texts*, 293; Aharoni, *The Land of the Bible*, 284; MacDonald, *East of the Jordan*, 206.

23 Glueck, "Three Israelite Towns in the Jordan Valley," 12.

24 Zertal, *The Manasseh Hill Country Survey*, 2: site 96.

Beth-barah

Beth-barah (בֵּית בָּרָה) should not be confused with Beth-arabah (בית הערבה) of Joshua 15:6, 61; 18:22.[25] Beth-barah (cf. *Onom.* 54.10) is associated with the fords of the Jordan where the Ephraimites joined the fight and captured Oreb and Zeeb, the princes of Midian (Judg 7:24–25). While the fords of Adam are not mentioned in the narrative of Judges 8, the Midianites likely crossed near Adam (Tell ed-Dâmiyeh),[26] since the town is probably referenced in Psalm 83:10 [11 MT].[27] Accordingly, Beth-barah should be located somewhere in this vicinity, presumably on the western side of the Jordan River. One possible candidate for Beth-barah is Tell el-'Abayad, which is situated directly across from Adam on the southern edge of Wadi Far'ah as it enters the Jordan Valley. Surveys at Tell el-'Abayad revealed two Iron Age fortresses[28] in close proximity to one another that undoubtedly policed the major intersection of the Jordan Valley, Wadi Far'ah, and Adam fords. Ṣartaba/Alexandrium, which is located in the hills to the west of Tell el-'Abayad, is probably a later iteration of these fortresses (Hellenistic-Roman) that guarded the junction of these important routes. While this suggested identification certainly fits the geographical context, it should not be considered certain, as the location of Beth-barah with regards to the Jordan River (whether west or east) is unclear. Yet, the text of Judges 7:24–8:4 indicates that the Ephraimites first captured the Jordan River (where Beth-barah is mentioned), then crossed the Jordan and captured Oreb and Zeeb on the other side. This was prior to returning with their severed heads to Gideon, who had yet to cross over the fords (Judg 8:4)[29] If Beth-barah can be

---

25 For a discussion of Beth-arabah see Chris McKinny, "A Historical Geography of the Administrative Division of Judah: The Town Lists of Judah and Benjamin in Joshua 15:21–62 and 18:21–28" (Ph.D. Dissertation, Bar Ilan University, 2017), 57–58.

26 See the recent excavations which have revealed a late Iron Age sanctuary, L. Petit and Z. Kafafi, "Beyond the River Jordan: A Late Iron Age Sanctuary at Tell Damiyah," *Near Eastern Archaeology* 79, no. 1 (2016): 18–26.

27 רמן לאדמה, "dung for the ground," Rainey and Notley, *The Sacred Bridge*, 139.

28 Including pottery from the Iron I and Iron II, Zertal, *The Manasseh Hill Country Survey*, site 98, site 99.

29 See Barry J. Beitzel, *The New Moody Atlas of the Bible* (Moody Publishers, 2009), Map 51 for a suggestion that puts Beth-barah in this vicinity.

identified with Tell el-'Abayad, then it might represent the location where Gideon and the Ephraimites met (Judg 8:1–3) before Gideon crossed over the Jordan.

Mahanaim

Mahanaim does not appear in Judges 7–8. However, both Mahanaim and Penuel appear as the name of the location where Jacob wrestled the angel of Yahweh near the Jabbok River (Gen 32:2, 31).

Mahanaim[30] and Penuel are often identified with the dual ruin of Tulul edh-Dhahab in the Jabbok River—known as Tell edh-Dhahab esh-Sharqiyya (the eastern hill of Tulul edh-Dhahab) and Tell edh-Dhahab al-Garbiyya (the western hill of Tulul edh-Dhahab).[31] Gordon and Villiers' survey at Tell edh-Dhahab esh-Sharqiyya revealed ceramic remains from the Iron Age.[32] A team led by Pola excavated Tell edh-Dhahab al-Garbiyya from 2005–2011. On the western slope of Tell edh-Dhahab al-Garbiyya, Pola revealed a fortification wall that was dated, on the basis of ^{14}C dating, to between 1305–978 BC.[33] Tell edh-Dhahab esh-Sharqiyya is a smaller site (60 x 30 m on the summit) that was primarily inhabited during the Iron Age and Hellenistic period.[34] Remains from the Middle Paleolithic, Neolithic, Early Bronze, (apparently) Middle Bronze were also noted in the survey and excavations of the sites.[35]

---

30 Gen 32:3; Josh 13:26, 30; 21:38; 2 Sam 2:8, 12, 29; 17:24, 27; 19:32; 1 Kgs 2:8; 4:14; 1 Chr 6:60; Shishak Karnak List No. 22.

31 E.g., MacDonald, *East of the Jordan*, 139–142; H.M. Hutton, "Mahanaim, Penuel, and Transhumance Routes: Observations on Genesis 32–33 and Judges 8," *Journal of Near Eastern Studies* 65, no. 3 (July 1, 2006): 161–178.

32 R.E. Gordon and L.E. Villiers, "Telul Edh Dhahab and Its Environs Surveys of 1980 and 1982: A Preliminary Report," *Annual of the Department of Antiquities of Jordan* 27 (1983): 275–283.

33 T. Pola et al., "A Preliminary Report of the Tulul Adh-Dhahab (Wadi Az-Zarqa) Survey and Excavation Seasons 2005–2011," *Annual of the Department of Antiquities of Jordan* 57 (2013): 88.

34 Gordon and Villiers, "Telul Edh Dhahab and Its Environs Surveys of 1980 and 1982: A Preliminary Report," 287; Pola et al., "A Preliminary Report of the Tulul Adh-Dhahab (Wadi Az-Zarqa) Survey and Excavation Seasons 2005–2011," 83–84.

35 Pola et al., "A Preliminary Report of the Tulul Adh-Dhahab (Wadi Az-Zarqa) Survey and Excavation Seasons 2005–2011."

The recently exposed archaeological evidence seems to further confirm the hypothesis that Mahanaim should be related to Tulul edh-Dhahab. On the other hand, it remains unclear if both ruins should be related to Mahanaim, as suggested by the dual ending of Mahanaim. Some scholars maintain that Mahanaim should be associated with both ruins and that Penuel should be located in the Jordan Valley at Deir 'Allā.[36] In my view, Mahanaim should be related to Tell edh-Dhahab esh-Sharqiyya and Penuel to Tell edh-Dhahab al-Garbiyya.[37]

Penuel

Penuel is mentioned in three narratives in the Bible. According to Genesis 32:32, Jacob gave the name "Peniel" to the ford of the Jabbok River and the site of his wrestling match with the "prince of God" and then limped to "Penuel" as the sun was rising. This passage also indicates that Penuel was near Mahanaim (cf. Gen 32:2) and east of Succoth and the Jordan River (cf. Gen 33:17). Penuel is next mentioned in Gideon's pursuit of the Midianite kings Zebah and Zalmunna when both Succoth and Penuel refused to answer Gideon's request for help (Judg 8:8–9). This resulted in Gideon's destroying the "tower of Penuel" and then killing the men of the city (Judg 8:17). Finally, Penuel was re-built by Jeroboam following becoming king of Israel (1 Kgs 12:25).

Outside of the biblical text, Penuel possibly appears in the Shishak/Sheshonq I conquest list from the Karnak temple (no. 53).[38] In this list, it appears near Succoth and Adam (Nos. 55–56).[39] The possible reference to Penuel in the Shishak city-list presents a problem

36 Cf. MacDonald, *East of the Jordan*, 139–142; E. Lipiński, *On the Skirts of Canaan in the Iron Age: Historical and Topographical Perspectives* (Peeters, 2006), 282–283.

37 Aharoni, *The Land of the Bible*, 34; R.A. Coughenour, "A Search for Maḥanaim," *Bulletin of the American Schools of Oriental Research*, no. 273 (February 1, 1989): 57–66; Hutton, "Mahanaim, Penuel, and Transhumance Routes"; Rainey and Notley, *The Sacred Bridge*, 115.

38 But note Rainey's hesitation to consider the reading certain, *The Sacred Bridge*, 186.

39 Despite LaSor's statement that Penuel should be related to "the city of Panili" of later "Assyrian documents," W.S. LaSor, "Penuel," in *International Standard Bible Encyclopedia*, ed. G.W. Bromiley (Eerdmans, 1986); see also J.C. Slayton, "Penuel," ed. D.N. Freedman, *Anchor Bible Dictionary*, 5.223; Block, "Judges," 163., I could find no such

for the association of Penuel and Mahanaim with Tulul edh-Dhahab. As we noted above, the list also includes Mahanaim (no. 22) between geographical contexts that are connected by the Jezreel and Beth-she-an Valleys (nos. 14–18—Taanach, Shunem, Beth-shean, Rehob, and Haphraim) and the regions of Judah and Benjamin (nos. 23–25—Gibeon, Beth-horon, Kiriath-jearim?, and Aijalon).[40] Despite this is-sue, it is possible to connect Ma-ḥa-n-ma with the geographical con-text of the preceding itinerary, which actually continues in the third line of the relief (nos. 27–39—e.g., Megiddo).[41]

Succoth

The biblical references to Penuel (Gen 33:17; Josh 13:27; Judg 8:5–16; 1 Kgs 7:46; 2 Chr 4:17; Ps 60:6; 108:7) as well as the possible occurrence of the name in the Shishak list (no. 55), provide a lot of geographical details concerning Penuel's location. Succoth should be located in the central Jordan Valley, near the fords of the Jordan River at Adam, and east of Penuel. If Penuel and Mahanaim can be localized at Tu-lul edh-Dhahab, then Succoth can be confidently identified with Deir

---

toponym in the Neo-Assyrian corpus, see S. Parpola and M. Porter, *The Helsinki Atlas of the Near East in the Neo-Assyrian Period* (Casco Bay Assyriological Institute, 2001).

40 Rainey and Notley, *The Sacred Bridge*, 186ff. which is the determining ratio-nale for associating Ma-ḥa-n-ma [no. 22] with Mahane-dan [Judg 13:25; 18:12].

41 On a related point, it would seem possible to identify the preceding town of Ša-au-di/Šawdî (no. 21) in Shishak's list with the ruin of Khirbet es-Sûweideh (32°17′29.85″N, 35°31′31.90″E). The site is dominated by a large Late Roman military camp, whose plan was studied by Zertal over an area of 40 dunams, see Zertal, *The Manasseh Hill Country Survey*, 2:site 239. Remains from the Iron I (5%) and Iron II (5%), as well as Middle Bronze II and Persian-Byzantine periods, were also noted at the site. Since the site is situated just above the main Jordan Valley route from the Beth-shean Valley to the fords of the Jordan, seemingly has remains from the time pe-riod in question (i.e., the 10th century BC), and theoretically could retain the ancient name, I propose that Khirbet es-Sûweideh should be identified with Ša-au-di (no. 21) of Shishak's conquest list at Karnak. For a discussion of the other towns mentioned by Shishak in the Jordan Valley, see Petit "What Would the Egyptian Pharaoh Shoshenq I Have Seen If He Had Visited the Central Jordan Valley?" *Palestine Exploration Quar-terly* 144, no. 3 (October 2012): 191–207.

*Figure 12.3—Warren's Reconnaissance of the Jordan Valley 1867
with identified locations and routes marked in the text.*

'Allā.[42] In addition, the Talmud (*Šebiʿit* 9. 2)[43] connected Deir ʿAllā with
Succoth, which was a major site in the Late Bronze and Iron Ages.[44]

42 Rainey and Notley, *The Sacred Bridge*, 115; see also Lipiński, *On the Skirts of Canaan in the Iron Age*, 286–288 for a discussion that opts for identifying Deir ʿAllā with
Penuel and Succoth with the nearby ruin of Tell el-Aḥsâs.

43 See discussion in H.J. Franken, "Tell Deir ʿAllah," in *Anchor Bible Dictionary*,
ed. Freedman; Lipiński, *On the Skirts of Canaan in the Iron Age*, 286–288.

44 H.J. Franken, *Excavations at Tell Deir ʾAlla. The Late Bronze Age Sanctuary*
(Peeters, 1992); G. van der Kooij, "Deir ʿAlla, Tell," in *New Encyclopedia of the Archae-
ology of the Holy Land*, ed. E. Stern (Carta, 1993); P.M. Fischer, *The Chronology of the
Jordan Valley During the Middle and Late Bronze Ages: Pella, Tell Abu Al-Kharaz, and
Tell Deir ʿAlla* (Austrian Academy of Sciences, 2006).

Figure 12.4—Map showing different locations for Karkor with sites mentioned in text, markings by author on Google Earth satellite image.

Figure 12.5—View of Baqaʻa Valley (Karkor?) from Tell Ṣafuṭ,
© *Todd Bolen/BiblePlaces.com used with permission*

Karkor and the Way of the Tent Dwellers

Karkor[45] (קַרְקֹר) was the destination of the Midianite army's flight from Gideon (Judg 8:10).[46] Midian may have have attempteded to regroup at Karkor following their defeat. Since Penuel and Succoth are mentioned before Karkor, the site or region must be located southeast from the central Jordan Valley, but the exact location remains unclear. Most scholars suggest that Karkor should be identified with al-Qarqar in the northern region of Wadi Sirḥân (Figure 12.4).[47] Given the context of Gideon's demand for provisions for his weary men at Penuel and Succoth (c. 85 km from the En-harod to Succoth), it would seem unreasonable that Karkor should be located at such an extended distance beyond Nobah and Joghebah (most likely located between Deir ʿAllā and Amman, see below). On the other hand, the author of Judges could possibly be demonstrating the extraordinary extent of Yahweh's provision of Gideon's 300 men by contrasting the relatively short distance from the Jezreel Valley to Succoth/Penuel (c. 85 km) vis-à-vis to al-Qarqar in Wadi Sirḥân (c. 200 km to the east of Jogbehah, located east of the modern Saudi Arabian town of al-Qurrayat). While this remains a possible identification, Ephʿal compared the flight of Midian to the Assyrian pursuit of Arab camps by Ashurbanipal, which he suggests were only "20–25 kilometers from the settled area."[48] If so, this analysis makes an extended Israelite pursuit deep into Arabia less likely. Another possibility would be to equate Karkor to an "epithet meaning watering holes" on the basis of *qr* from Ugaritic, which means "water-holes, springs, or wells" (HALOT 1148). While it seems likely that the proper place name is derived from this

---

45 The toponym only occurs here.

46 Eusebius relates Karkor to the "fort of Karkaria, a day's journey from the city of Petra" (*Onom.* 116.7), but the direction is not given in the passage and, in any case, a location in Edom would be too far south to fit the context.

47 Following A. Musil, *The Northern Hegaz: A Topographical Itinerary* (New York, 1926), 284; e.g., Aharoni, *The Land of the Bible*, 264; Rainey and Notley, *The Sacred Bridge*, 139.

48 I. Ephʿal, *The Ancient Arabs: Nomads of the Borders of the Fertile Crescent, 9th-5th Centuries B.C.* (Brill, 1982), 153; cf. E.J. Payne, "The Midianite Arc in Joshua and Judges," in *Midian, Moab and Edom: The History and Archaeology of Late Bronze and Iron Age Jordan and North-West Arabia*, ed. J.F.A. Sawyer and D.J.A. Clines (A&C Black, 1983), 172.

generic meaning, it seems clear that a proper toponym is intended in Judges 8:10 (cf. LXX's εν Καρκαρ). One possible location for Karkor is the Baqaʻa Valley (Figure 12.5), which is located just north of the modern limits of Amman (modern ʻAin Al-Basha). This well-watered valley is a logical endpoint of a route leading from Succoth and Penuel to Jogbehah (see below) and into the desert west of Amman that was apparently known as the "way of the tent dwellers (Figure 12.3)."[49]

Nobah and Jogbehah

The region north of Amman up until the Jabbok River was not well-surveyed in the various expeditions of the late 19th and early 20th century. The SWP's sheet of "Eastern Palestine" does not include any territory north of Wadi Nimrîn. Schumacher's excellent and highly detailed surveys of northern Jordan, "Karte des Ostjordanlandes," do not continue south of the Jabbok River. In comparison with other parts of the southern Levant, modern maps of this region of Jordan are also lacking, which makes it difficult to even locate ruins much less suggest an identification with an ancient site.

Nobah and Jogbehah were situated near the "way of the tent dwellers" (דֶּרֶךְ הַשְּׁכוּנֵי בָאֳהָלִים). The context of Judges 8:10 indicates that this route was controlled by the Midianites, as Zebah and Zalmunna's "army felt secure" (Judg 8:11). The end of this route is presumably at Karkor, but may have also led beyond into north Arabia.[50] Nobah also occurs in Numbers 32:40–42 as the name of a Manassehite clan, who conquered Kenath (Qanawât) and renamed it Nobah (cf. 1 Chr 2:23). Given the different geographical contexts of the two passages, the two sites are clearly distinct.[51] Nobah should be located between Penuel/

---

49 An additional consideration for placing the location of the Midianites' retreat in central Transjordan comes from Numbers 31:1–12, which places the five Midianite "kings" (Evi, Rekem, Zur, Hur, and Reba –Num 31:8; cf. Josh 13:21) in the vicinity of the "plains of Moab" and Baal-peor of the Medeba Plateau (cf. Num 25:18; 31:16). Regardless of a possible geographic relationship, the four leaders of Midian during the time of Gideon (Oreb, Zeeb, Zeba, and Zalmunna—Judg 7:25- 8:21) should probably be related intertextually to the five kings mentioned in Numbers.

50 Aharoni, *The Land of the Bible*, Map 3.

51 Cf. MacDonald (*East of the Jordan*, 124), who also summarizes different suggestions for identifying Nobah.

Succoth and Jogbehah (Jubeihâh?). Lemaire's suggestion to identify Nobah with Tell el-Ḥajjâj[52] would seem to fit the geographical and archaeological criteria for Nobah. A survey by Gordon and Villiers revealed remains from the Iron I and Iron II.[53] Tell el-Ḥajjâj is situated on a tributary wadi of the Jabbok River (Wadi Ḥajjâj), which could have carried traffic from the fords near Adam towards Amman (Ammonite Rabbah).[54]

Besides the reference in Judges 8:11, Jogbehah is mentioned as a Gadite settlement in Numbers 32:35, where it occurs between Jazer and Beth-nimrah. The ancient name of Jogbehah may be preserved at Jubeihâh.[55] Glueck surveyed an "Ammonite Tower" (*rujm malfuf*) with walls 2 m thick at Jubeihâh, where he found remains from the Iron I and II.[56] MacDonald summarizes the evidence for other Iron Age sites in the vicinity of modern Jubeihâh, and concludes that it is "a good candidate for the location of biblical Jogbehah."[57] On the other hand, Tell Ṣafuṭ is the largest site in the vicinity and has remains from the Middle Bronze, Late Bronze, Iron I, Iron IIB, Iron IIC, and Persian, as well as later periods, and could theoretically also be identified with either Nobah or Jogbehah (Figure 12.3).[58]

---

52 A. Lemaire, "Galaad et Makîr: Remarques Sur La Tribu de Manassé à l'est Du Jourdain," *Vetus Testamentum* 31, no. 1 (1981): 55.

53 Gordon and Villiers, "Telul Edh Dhahab and Its Environs Surveys of 1980 and 1982: A Preliminary Report," site 25; and perhaps also Late Bronze/Iron I transitional see E.J. van der Steen, *Tribes and Territories in Transition: The Central East Jordan Valley in the Late Bronze Age and Early Iron Age: A Study of the Sources* (Peeters, 2004), 231; Hutton, "Mahanaim, Penuel, and Transhumance Routes," 164.

54 See Hutton, ("Mahanaim, Penuel, and Transhumance Routes," 175), who expresses similar logic but suggests that Nobah should be located at sites east of Jogbehah.

55 See MacDonald, *East of the Jordan*, 119–120 with extensive bibliography.

56 Nelson Glueck, "Explorations in Eastern Palestine, III," *The Annual of the American Schools of Oriental Research* 18/19 (1939): 172; cf. MacDonald, *East of the Jordan*, 119.

57 MacDonald, *East of the Jordan*, 120.

58 D.H. Wimmer and S. Farajat, "Tell Safut Excavations: 1982–1985 Preliminary Report," *Annual of the Department of Antiquities of Jordan* XXXI (1987): 159–174, PL.557–558; O. Chesnut, "The Hellenistic Period at Tall Safut," *Liber Annuus*, no. 63 (2014): 415–422; cf. D.H. Wimmer, "Tell Ṣafuṭ," in *The Oxford Encyclopedia of Archaeology in the Near East*, ed. E. Meyers American Schools of Oriental Research (Oxford University Press, 1997) who prefers to identify the site with Nobah.

Ascent of Heres

Following the battle with the Midianites, Gideon and his 300 men returned to the vicinity of Succoth and Penuel by a different route than they had taken in their pursuit of Midian (i.e., the "way of tent dwellers"). This route is referred to as the "ascent of Heres" (Judg 8:13; cf. *Onom.* 32.4),[59] which can be translated as the "ascent of the sun"[60] (מַעֲלֵה הֶחָרֶס—compare Judg 1:35; 2:9; HALOT 1.355). Notably, Gideon arrived at Succoth before Penuel (Judg 8:14–17), which would seem to indicate that travel along the ascent of Heres caused Gideon to approach Succoth from the south. One possible route is a road descending from the vicinity of es-Salt (west of Baqaʿa Valley) towards Beth-nimrah where it connects with the main eastern Jordan Valley route heading towards the fords of Adam and Succoth.[61] This route is marked on Warren's Map of the "Reconnaissance of the Jordan Valley" (Figure 12.3)[62] which runs along the ridge just south of Wadi Shaîb. If the ascent of Heres can be connected with this route, then it would explain why Gideon encountered Succoth before Penuel in his punitive return.[63]

CONCLUSION

This paper has discussed the historical geography of the Midianite retreat from Gideon as recorded in Judges 7–8. I have provided an

---

59 The ascent of Heres can hardly be related to Kir-haresheth (e.g., 2 Kgs 3:25) as suggested by the editors of the *Onomasticon, The Onomasticon by Eusebius of Caesarea*, ed. R.L. Chapman III and J.E. Taylor, trans. G.S.P. Freeman-Greenville (Carta, 2003), 113.

60 Regardless of the location of the route in Transjordan, the name probably indicates a western perspective from the central hill country of Cisjordan as it would seem to imply that the route could be associated with the rising of the sun over the hill country of Transjordan.

61 Cf. Aharoni, *The Land of the Bible*, Map 3; the "way of the plain" (2 Sam 18:23).

62 C. Warren, "Reconnaissance of the Jordan Valley" (Palestine Exploration Fund, 1867), http://www.iaa-archives.org.il/zoom/zoom.aspx?folder_id=89&type_id=6&id=8359.

63 See discussion in Hutton, "Mahanaim, Penuel, and Transhumance Routes," 177–178 who suggests that the ascent of Heres was a short route connecting Succoth with Tell el-Ḥajjâj.

updated archaeological and bibliographic information for the sites of Abel-meholah (Tell Abu Sûs), Mahanaim and Penuel (Tulul edh-Dhahab), Succoth (Deir ʿAllā), Nobah (Tell el-Ḥajjâj?), and Jogbehah (preserved at Jubeihâh and possibly located at Jubeihâh or nearby Tell Ṣafuṭ?). I have also suggested new identifications or refinements to past identifications for the sites of Beth-shittah (Tell el-Farr?), Zererah (Tellûl ez-Zahrah?), Tabbath (Tell el-Ḥilu?), Beth-barah (Tell el-ʿAbayad?), Karkor (within the Baqaʿa Valley?), and the ascent of Heres (route following the ridge above Wadi Shaîb).

Putting the itinerary together (Figure 12.6) produces the following sequence:

(1)[64] Gideon and his men attacked the Midianites in front of the Hill of Moreh.

(2) Then, Gideon's men chased the Midianites from the Hill of Moreh towards the east using the Harod Valley passing the nearby towns of Beth-shittah and Zererah (Judg 7:22). The Midianite army continued south using the western Jordan Valley road south of Beth-shean passing the area of Abel-meholah and Tabbath, which were presumably located on the western side of the Jordan River (Judg 7:22).

(3) As the Midianites were crossing over the Jordan River, men of Ephraim, who had been alerted by messengers from Gideon, descended to the fords of the Jordan (likely via Wadi Fârʿah) and took control of the fords of Adam (including Beth-barah). Presumably, the Ephraimites attacked the rear guard of the Midianites, and assassinated Oreb and Zeeb—princes of Midan—on the east side of the Jordan (Judg 7:24–25). The Ephraimites then brought the heads of the Midianite "princes" to Gideon as he approached the fords (Judg 7:24–8:3).

(4) After an argument over tribal superiority that ended in Gideon's acquiescence (Judg 8:1–3), Gideon sought provision for his weary men, who had by this point travelled c. 85 km. He first sought support at the nearby site of Succoth (12 km northeast from Adam), and then at Penuel (6 km east of Succoth), who both refused to provide aid in fear of retribution from Midian (Judg 8:4–9).

(5) During this time, Midian had presumably re-gathered its remaining forces at Karkor (Judg 8:10), which I have suggested should

---

64 These numbers are connected to the sequence of events on Figure 12.6.

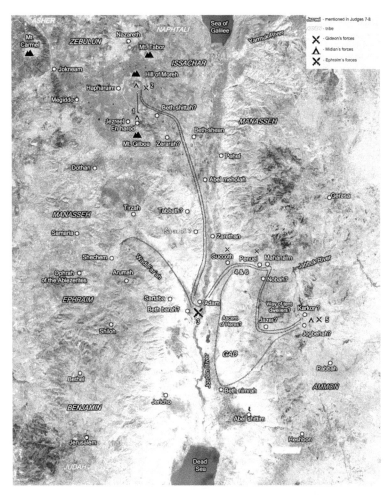

Figure 12.6—Map of Judges 7–8 with sites mentioned in text,
markings by author on Google Earth satellite image.

be related to the Baqaʻa Valley north of modern Amman (c. 28 km
from Penuel). After pledging his own brand of retribution on the inhabitants of Succoth and Penuel, Gideon and his men continued their
pursuit of Midian by using the "way of the tent dwellers," which ran
through the western hill country of Transjordan past Nobah and Jogbehah towards Karkor (Judg 8:10–11). After defeating Midian and cap-
turing Zebah and Zalmunna, the "kings" of Midian, Gideon descended via the "ascent of Heres" (Judg 8:13), which may have descended

unto the eastern Jordan Valley near Beth-nimrah along the natural ridge route above Wadi Shaîb (c. 30 km from the Baqaʿa Valley).

(6) Approaching Succoth from the south (the distance from Beth-nimrah to Succoth is c. 35 km), Gideon captured a young man from Succoth and compelled him to list the 75 "officials and elders of Succoth," whom he disciplined with "thorns and briers" before breaking the "tower of Penuel and killing the men of the city" (Judg 8:14–17).

Assuming that these identifications are correct or at least in close proximity to the intended towns, the writer of Judges portrayed Gideon and his 300 men as travelling c. 190 km from the initial battle. Even without a journey into northern Arabia,[65] Gideon's accomplishments over the course of his campaign against Midian certainly overshadowed the Ephraimites boastful complaint in Judges 8:1–3.

In light of the above, we can re-ask and answer the question—what did Gideon "do in comparison" with the Ephraimites? The answer—Gideon did a lot more than Ephraim. Ephraim avoided conflict with the oppressing Midianites until Gideon in the instruction and power of Yahweh had already caused the Midianites to flee in defeat. When Gideon sardonically asked the question at the fords of the Jordan (Judg 8:3), he had already done more than the Ephraimites until that point. But this was just the beginning of the total defeat of the Midianites at the hands of Gideon. With no help from Ephraim or Gad (i.e., Succoth and Penuel), Gideon and his 300 men continued on to face and defeat the vast host of Midian at Karkor (Judg 8:10–12). Gideon's triumphant return with captured Midianite "kings" instead of "princes," as well as calls for Gideon's kingship further contrast Gideon with the Ephraimites (Judg 8:18–26).

---

65 If Karkor is to be related a northern region of Wadi Sirḥân then c. 400 km would have to be added to Gideon's pursuit, which would result in a total journey of c. 600 km.

13

Economic Ethics in the Didache

Todd A. Scacewater

W IILLIAM VARNER HAS BEEN FOR ME a mentor, a colleague, a partner, and a friend. His teaching ministry, in which he cares so deeply about his students, and his pastoral heart are both admirable and imitable. He has partnered with me in my online efforts to promote continued education in the biblical languages, to great effect.[1] I was thrilled to have the opportunity to publish his magnum opus, a thoroughly exegetical commentary on the book of James, which is a treat for pastors and scholars alike.[2] Like many other students, pastors, and scholars, I have benefitted greatly from his Facebook group, Nerdy Biblical Language Majors, which he moderates and participates in daily, providing a lively yet helpful academic forum for discussion of biblical language and linguistic issues.[3] More than all these aspects of our relationship, Dr. Varner has been a gracious and humble friend to me, and I am honored to contribute to this Festschrift.

In honor of Dr. Varner's interest in and use of discourse analysis, as well as his commentary on the Didache, I will do my best to pique his interest with an essay utilizing discourse analysis to analyze the

---

1 Exegetical Tools provides video courses that walk the viewer through translating entire biblical books from the original languages. All series, including Dr. Varner's, may be found at http://www.exegeticaltools.com.

2 William Varner, *James: A Commentary on the Greek Text* (Fontes Press, 2017). I have also had the pleasure of editing and publishing his *Passionate about the Passion Week: A Fresh Look at Jesus' Last Days* (Fontes, 2020) and *Anticipating the Advent: Looking for Messiah in All the Right Places* (Fontes, 2020).

3 https://www.facebook.com/groups/NerdyLanguageMajors.

Didache.[4] My aim is not to provide an exhaustive discourse analysis. Rather, I will limit my investigation in two ways. First, I will examine the entire document, but only at the higher levels of the discourse, and not down to the minutiae of each sentence. Second, I will not use the full range of tools that discourse analysis provides, but only the ones that serve the purpose of this study. My desired result is to demonstrate how economic concerns are pervasive (perhaps preeminent) throughout this writing, especially at prominent points of the discourse. Many Christians, pastors, churches, and organizations shy away from discussing or teaching about economic issues and ethics, either from a fear of congregational repercussions or a lack of real interest in these issues. However, economic matters were for some reason a central concern for the community receiving this writing, and we might learn from the Didache how central economic ethics can and should be in our own ethical concerns.

Discourse Analysis Methodology

For the sake of space, I will only provide a few comments on my methodology in this essay.[5] There is a distinction between theoretical discourse analysis and applied discourse analysis. The former is concerned with how language above the level of the sentence operates. What are the properties of a text? How is a text coherent? How do receivers process texts? How do we discover the topic of a discourse? These are only a few of the questions that have been explored. In applied discourse analysis, an analyst takes the insights from theoretical discourse analysis and applies them to a specific text, often for specific purposes. Sometimes that purpose is simply to analyze an entire document in a more rigorous manner, using as many insights from

---

4 William Varner, *The Way of the Didache: The First Christian Handbook* (University Press of America, 2007). He has demonstrated his use of discourse analysis in William Varner, *The Book of James—A New Perspective: A Linguistic Commentary Applying Discourse Analysis* (Kress Biblical Resources, 2010); and in his larger James commentary, cited above.

5 For further elaboration on the areas of research in discourse studies, see my "Introduction" in Todd A. Scacewater, ed., *Discourse Analysis of the New Testament Writings* (Fontes, 2020). For further examples of my own methodology, see my chapters "Ephesians" and "Colossians" in the same volume. And of course, see Varner's contribution in the same volume on "James."

theoretical discourse analysis as possible. Sometimes the purpose is to utilize some of these insights to solve a problem or to deepen our understanding of a text.

In this essay, I am concerned with applied discourse analysis. The main aspects of a discourse that I will be concerned with are that of macrostructure, coherence relations, and cohesion analysis. These are the main tools often employed in applied discourse analysis, so just a few comments about them should suffice.

Macrostructures are representations of an entire discourse. One might also refer to them as "discourse topics." Often, macrostructures are understood to be simple (or sometimes more complex) outlines of a writing, as one would find in any commentary introduction. But what I mean by macrostructure is the output of a function applied to a discourse. That is, the analyst applies certain operations to a text in a methodical manner with the end result being the macrostructure of the discourse.

There are different methodologies to uncover the macrostructure of a text. Some assume that texts are hierarchical. Both Rhetorical Structure Theory (RST) and Semantic Structural Analysis (SSA) view macrostructure as a series of coherence relationships between propositions (or sentences), constructed in a hierarchical manner from the entire document. At the apex of the pyramid, so to speak, is the most important proposition of the text, so the macrostructure is that most prominent proposition insofar as it organizes the entire discourse.[6] T. van Dijk, on the other hand, created macrorules for reducing an entire discourse to a semantic representation in the same way he surmised that a human

---

6 For SSA, see John Beekman, John C. Callow, and Michael F. Kopesec, *The Semantic Structure of Written Communication*, 5th ed. (Summer Institute of Linguistics, 1981) as well as the series Semantic Structural Analysis published by SIL International. For RST, see William C. Mann and Sandra A. Thompson, "Relational Propositions in Discourse," *ISI/RR-83-115* (1983): 1–28; William C. Mann and Sandra A. Thompson, "Rhetorical Structure Theory: Description and Construction of Text Structures," *ISI/RS-86-174* (1986): 1–15; William C. Mann and Sandra A. Thompson, "Rhetorical Structure Theory: A Framework for the Analysis of Texts," *ISI/RS-87-185* (1987): 1–22; William C. Mann and Sandra A. Thompson, "Rhetorical Structure Theory: Toward a Functional Theory of Text Organization," *Text* 8, no. 3 (1988): 243–281; William C. Mann, Christian M. I. M. Matthiessen, and Sandra A. Thompson, "Rhetorical Structure Theory and Text Analysis," *ISI/RR-89-242* (1989), 1–60. The last mentioned 1988 essay lays out the mature theory of RST and provides a sample analysis of a brief fundraising letter from a political organization.

receiver does so cognitively.[7] The result is not so much a hierarchical representation of the discourse, but a semantic representation similar to a summary, which entails the semantic content of the entire discourse. These methodologies are not mutually exclusive, since van Dijk's macrorules make a discourse much easier to analyze after reducing and combining a vast majority of the sentences into much more concise semantic representations, which can then be related by coherence relations. Other methodologies do not view macrostructures as hierarchical. R. de Beaugrande theorized a related network of concepts, all connected to a "control center," which is the central topic of the macrostructure.[8] R. W. Todd uses the terminology "discourse topics" and is more interested in the way topics shift and change throughout a discourse, making his view of macrostructure more linear.[9]

My own view is that macrostructures are hierarchical insofar as one overarching discourse topic, which hierarchically organizes the entire span of text, can be determined.[10] In many texts, the entire document can be considered one discourse with one macrostructure, and such is the case with the Didache.

Coherence relations are significant because they help us understand how two sentences, or two units of a discourse, relate to one another.[11] It is easy to see how "I'm hungry. Pass the bread" is a coherent

---

7 Teun van Dijk, *Macrostructures: An Interdisciplinary Study of Global Structures in Discourse, Interaction, and Cognition* (Erlbaum, 1980).

8 Robert de Beaugrande and Wolfgang Dressler, *Introduction to Text Linguistics* (Longman, 1981), 95–110.

9 Richard Watson Todd, *Discourse Topics*, P&BNS 269 (John Benjamins, 2016).

10 There is a question of whether macrostructures are represented by noun phrases ("Bob"), propositions ("Bob went to the store"), concepts ("shopping"), or other less popular proposals. For a variety of reasons, I believe macrostructures should be represented by propositions, since noun phrases and concepts are too broad to function as an organizing principle for an entire coherent discourse. Think of a macrostructure as similar to a "big idea" of a sermon, to which (according to proper homiletical theory) everything in the sermon must be connected, and which organizes everything in the sermon hierarchically (ideally, the three or four main points are semantically entailed by the big idea, and the audience can see how to combine the main points into the big idea). See further, Dijk, *Macrostructures*, 94–98; Gillian Brown and George Yule, *Discourse Analysis*, Cambridge Textbooks in Linguistics (Cambridge University Press, 1983), 106–124; Rachel Giora, "Notes toward a Theory of Text Coherence," *Poetics Today* 6, no. 4 (1985): 699–715.

11 Other terms for coherence relations include rhetorical predicates, functional relations, propositional relations, and interclausal or intersentential relations.

series of utterances with a problem-solution relationship. The solution is more prominent because it could stand alone and achieve the speaker's purposes, while simply uttering the problem ("I'm hungry") would not be as effective.[12] Coherence relations help us understand the organization of a discourse, help us discover prominent elements of the discourse (and to do so recursively up to the highest levels), and force us to ask what the relationships are between every unit of a discourse. Rather than a series of bullet-points, a discourse becomes an intricate web of semantic and pragmatic relationships that are structured in a particular way to achieve some purpose(s). Coherence relations are necessary for forming macrostructures, for determining unit boundaries, for relating all microstructures together as part of a hierarchy, and more. A full list of these relations is available in many other publications, and there is no need to list them all here.[13]

Finally, cohesion is the use of explicit linguistic features to bind a text together, to help create texture and coherence in a text, and to give clues to the receiver on how to process the communicative intent of the producer.[14] Cohesive devices include discourse markers (including conjunctions), co-referential forms, lexical relationships, syntactical constructions, and grammatical features such as verbal aspect and tense-forms. Analyzing cohesive devices in a text reveals much about a discourse. They help in determining unit boundaries, discourse topics (especially at lower units of the discourse such as para-

---

12 See Mann and Thompson, "Framework," 5–10.

13 These relations were first given systematic attention (to my knowledge, and according to Joseph Grimes) in Daniel Fuller's *The Inductive Method of Bible Study*. See other treatments in Joseph Grimes, *The Thread of Discourse* (Mouton, 1975), 207–229; and most exhaustively in Rhetorical Structure Theory and Semantic Structural Analysis. Among biblical scholars, see Peter Cotterell and Max Turner, *Linguistics and Biblical Interpretation* (InterVarsity Press, 1989), 188–292; George Guthrie, "Discourse Analysis," in *Interpreting the New Testament: Essays on Methods and Issues,* ed. Black and Dockery (Broadman & Holman, 2001). Tracing coherence relations has been adopted by many biblical scholars as the totality of what discourse analysis is, but one should be aware that coherence relations are only one of dozens of topics within theoretical discourse analysis, and that most use coherence relations to deal only with the semantic aspect of the text, not the pragmatic.

14 The seminal study was M. A. K. Halliday and Ruqaiya Hasan, *Cohesion in English* (Longman Group Limited, 1976). From another perspective, see W. Gutwinski, *Cohesion in Literary Texts: A Study of Some Grammatical and Lexical Features of English Discourse* (de Gruyter, 1976).

graphs), pervasive themes, links between discourse units (e.g., the use of hook words to create head-tail or tail-head linkage), and more. Some forms of discourse analysis make cohesion the main concern, especially those concerned with analyzing ancient texts, since the explicit linguistic features of the text are accessible, but sociolinguistic factors are less so. Yet, cohesion is neither necessary nor sufficient for a text to be received as coherent, which means it is one of the less important factors in discourse studies.[15] Perhaps it is fair to say that cohesion analysis is more useful in applied discourse analysis with written texts than it is in theoretical discourse analysis.

With these methodological concerns behind us, I now turn to the Didache. I will first propose a macrostructure for the Didache, providing enough substantiation to warrant moving forward with the analysis (further warrant would require analyzing all the way down to each sentence, which space will not allow). Within the confines of the macrostructure I propose, I will then argue that economic concerns arise at pivotal moments in the discourse. I conclude with some reflections on the results.

---

15 Initially, cohesion was one of the main topics of discourse analysis. It was seen by Halliday and Hasan (*Cohesion in English*), as well as by Beaugrande (*Introduction to Text Linguistics*, 48–83), as necessary for a series of utterances to be considered a "text," and Halliday and Hasan believed cohesion was necessary for coherence. However, it became clear in the 1980s that texts could lack any cohesion and still be coherent because of so many cognitive and pragmatic elements of discourse. Many linguists also produced plenty of paragraphs that exhibited great cohesion but lacked coherence (e.g., a paragraph in which the topic continually changes from one sentence to the next through head-tail linkage, or the discourse of a schizophrenic). Thus, from the 1980s on, cohesion was downgraded as a central concern, and coherence took its place as the most studied aspect of discourse. See Brown and Yule, *Discourse Analysis*, 194–197; Robert A. Dooley and Stephen H. Levinsohn, *Analyzing Discourse: A Manual of Basic Concepts* (SIL International, 2001), 33; Yuan Wang and Minghe Guo, "A Short Analysis of Discourse Coherence," *Journal of Language Teaching and Research* 5, no. 2 (2014): 460–465; J. R. Martin, "Cohesion and Texture," in *The Handbook of Discourse Analysis*, 2nd ed., ed. Deborah Tannen, Heidi E. Hamilton, and Deborah Schiffrin (Wiley Blackwell, 2015), 71; Patricia L. Carrell, "Cohesion is Not Coherence," *TESOL Quarterly 16* (1982): 479–483; H. G. Widdowson, *Discourse Analysis*, Oxford Introductions to Language Study (Oxford University Press, 2007), 49. On coherence as the key concept in discourse analysis by 1999, see Wolfram Bublitz, "Introduction: Views of Coherence," in *Coherence in Spoken and Written Discourse: How to Create It and How to Describe It*, ed. Wolfram Bublitz, Uta Lenk, and Eija Ventola (John Benjamins, 1999), 1.

THE MACROSTRUCTURE OF THE DIDACHE

The first step in determining the macrostructure of a discourse is to discover the unit boundaries. If macrostructures are hierarchical, then each unit (starting from the top) can be divided into one or more subordinate units. Each unit has its own macrostructure, and units on the same level are combined to form the macrostructure of the superordinate unit. There are many indicators of unit boundaries. The most prominent marker is probably lexis; when one clustering of lexis is replaced by another clustering, there is likely a new unit. Discourse particles may explicitly signal a new unit in the discourse. Potential literary markers include the vocative, imperative, asyndeton, a formula, a newly expressed topic, definite noun phrases instead of anaphoric substitutes, and the complete lack of anaphora. Thankfully, there are plenty of explicit boundary markers in the Didache, which makes the task of discovering unit boundaries somewhat simple.

The First and Second Parts of the Didache (*1.1–6.2; 6.3–16.8*)

The Didache divides easily into two Parts (1.1–6.2; 6.3–16.8), which is obvious because the author provides explicit labels for the first section:

> "There are two ways, one of life and one of death..." (1.1).[16]
>> "Now, the way of life is this..." (1.2)
>> "Now, the way of death is this..." (5.1).[17]

This Two Ways material is a standard Jewish literary form that the Didachist has adapted for his purposes, making it easier to find the end of this unit.[18] The author adds a hortatory post-script in 6.1–2, which

---

16 Translations of the Didache are my own.

17 The Didache was only re-discovered in the modern era in 1873, and even the earliest commentators after its rediscovery recognized this simple two-part division of the document. E.g., J. Armitage Robinson, *Barnabas, Hermas and the Didache* (SPCK, 1920) 43–44.

18 Source and redaction criticism have been a huge part of Didache scholarship, generally fragmenting the document into various sources with sometimes clumsy editorial stitching ("a clumsy collage constructed by gathering, trimming, and pasting

should be included as part of the Two Ways unit because (1) it contains similar lexemes (ὁδός, διδαχή/διδάσκω) and (2) the phrase τέλειος ἔσῃ (6.2) echoes the same phrase in 1.4.[19]

The second part of the Didache concerns matters of church worship and Christian community ethics. The author provides instructions on various topics one after another. As demonstrated below, no other major parts are evident within the Didache, so I turn now to discussing the sections within each of the two parts. Once we have seen how the document flows, we will be poised for examining how economic concerns appear prominently in the discourse.

Microstructures of Part 1 (1.1–6.2)

The biggest problem in determining the units within Part 1 is some ambiguity in the author's discourse orienters.[20]

> "There are two ways, one of life and one of death…" (1.1)
>   "Now this is the way of life" (1.2)

---

together preexisting sources," Aaron Milavec, *The Didache: Faith, Hope, and Life of the Earliest Christian Communities, 50–70 C.E.* [Newman Press, 2003], xv). Discourse analysts (especially those in biblical studies) tend to react to these results of source and redaction criticism by relying on the assumption of coherence that discourse analysis requires (a receiver will assume that a discourse is coherent and do everything he or she can via cognition, social knowledge, etc. to figure out the speaker's meaning and communicative intent). The result is that the documents analyzed become perfectly coherent documents with hundreds of years of problems waved away by the magic wand of discourse analysis. Instead, I think that results of source and redaction criticism, when reasonable, can be useful for discourse analysts in a number of ways, including the discovery of unit boundaries. More research on this topic would be incredibly welcomed.

19 Some commentators include 6.3 in the post-script, but they seem to be operating by chapter numbers for unit boundaries rather than giving a linguistic justification. E.g., Kurt Niederwimmer, *The Didache: A Commentary*, Hermeneia (Fortress Press, 1998), 120–125; Paul Sabatier, *La Didachè: L'Enseignement des Douze Apôtres* (Librairie Fischbacher, 1885), 68. However, the use of περὶ δὲ beginning at 6.3 is part of a series of topics introduced by the same transition (see below), so 6.3 is not part of the post-script.

20 A discourse orienter is a statement that explicitly states what is about to happen in the discourse. Orienters are therefore a great help in discerning the author's communicative intent.

> "First, you shall love God" (1.2)
> "Second, you shall love your neighbor" (1.2)
> **"The teaching of these words is this..." (1.3)**
> [Positive commands, 1.3–6]
> **"The second commandment of the teaching is..." (2.1)**
> [Prohibitions, 2.1–7]
> [More commands, 3.1–4.13]
> "This is the way of life" (4.14)
> "But the way of death is this" (5.1)

The orienters at 1.1, 1.2, 4.14, and 5.1 are clear enough. The bolded lines are the problems. After introducing the way of life, he lists the two great commandments, love of God and love of neighbor. He then says, "The teaching of these words is this" and proceeds with positive commands. By "these words" in 1.3, he may refer to both of the great commandments or only the second. Either way, he never expounds on love of God in the rest of Part 1, making us wonder why he mentions it; everything that follows 1.2 is an elaboration on love of neighbor (even the way of death is simply a list of sins against neighbor).[21] This observation is useful, though, because it tells us that while love of God is the greatest commandment, the author's more prominent concern in Part 1 is love of neighbor.

Equally problematic is 2.1, "the second commandment of the teaching is..." At first it seemed that the author would divide the Way of Life into love of God and love of neighbor. Now it seems he wants to divide it into "the teaching" and "the second commandment," orienters that do not match each other.[22] Despite the ambiguity (or in-

---

21 Thomas O'Loughlin, *The Didache: A Window on the Earliest Christians* (Baker Academic, 2010), 35, takes 1.3–6 to explain love of God, but the teaching is all about how to treat others. Perhaps the Didachist considered love of God to be evidenced by love of neighbor, but here we are exercising that great principle of the assumption of coherence, by which we not only (sometimes over-zealously) explain away problems, but also (more productively) assume that the author had a communicative intent and look beyond any inefficiencies or linguistic problems that mask that intent. Even written documents are not perfect, but that does not mean that the author's meaning is incoherent or lost.

22 Better would be, "the first commandment of the teaching," and "the second commandment of the teaching.

efficiency) of the orienters, these two units are still clearly distinguished by the two orienters and by the fact that 1.3–6 gives positive commands while 2.1–7 gives prohibitions.

It seems to me that the best reading of the Way of Life is that he first summarizes it as love of God and love of neighbor. He then decides to expound only on love of neighbor, dividing it first into positive commands (1.3–6), second into prohibitions (2.1–7),[23] and finally into a mixture of commands and prohibitions framed by the frequent vocative "my child" (τέκνον μου, 3.1, 3, 4, 5, 6; 4.1). Thus, the Way of Life has three sections.

Now we can determine the hierarchical structure of Part 1. The main units of Part 1 are the introduction (1.1) the body (1.2–5.2), and the post-script (6.1–2). Within the body, we have an introduction to the Way of Life (1.2), three sections expounding the Way of Life as love of neighbor (1.2–4.13), a conclusion to the Way of Life (4.14), an introduction to the Way of Death (5.1), and one section expounding the Way of Death as hatred of neighbor (5.1–2). The three sections of the Way of Life divide by positive commandments to love one's neighbor (1.2–6), negative commandments against hatred of neighbor (2.1–7), and a mixture of commandments to love one's neighbor mostly introduced by τέκνον μου (3.1–4.13).[24] These units are charted in hierarchical fashion in Figure 13.1 below.

The few potential problems for this structure, such as the problems with the orienters and the fact that ch. 2 ends with three positive commands (albeit, as stating the inverse of a negative command), are probably the result of the author's use and redaction of sources (or less charitably, the author's slight lack of literary skill). The result is a coherent Part 1 that requires a slightly higher cognitive processing load than would otherwise be required if these structural problems did not exist.

We are now poised to suggest a macrostructure for Part 1. As stated earlier, I take macrostructures to be semantic representations of a

---

23 The three final positive commands at the end of 2.7 simply provide the inverse (ἀλλά) of "you shall not hate anyone."

24 The last instance of τέκνον μου is at 4.1, and there does not seem to be a unit division after 4.1 until the conclusion of the Way of Life in 4.14, so I consider 3.1–4.13 a unit mostly characterized by the use of τέκνον μου.

Figure 13.1: Constituent Organization of Part 1

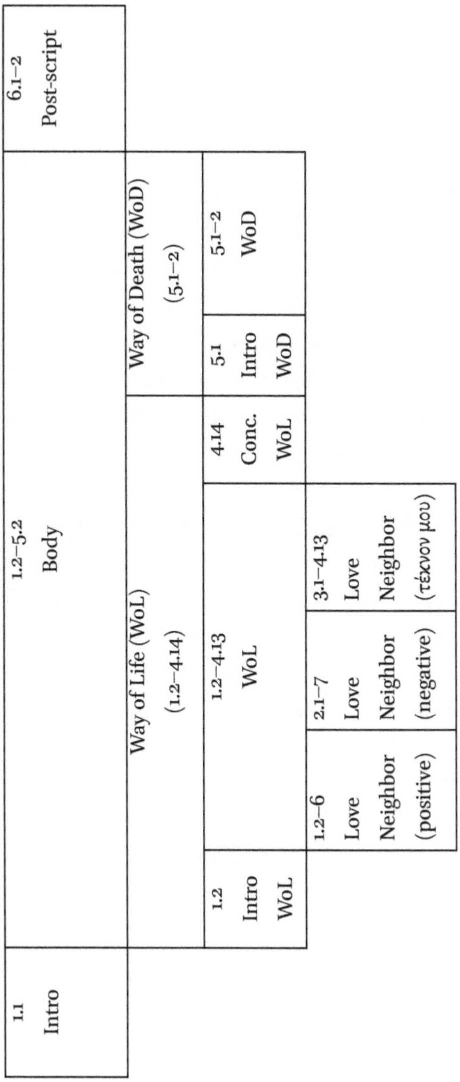

discourse that hierarchically organize the entire discourse that is subordinate to it, and they should be represented by propositions. Whatever the proposed macrostructure, all microstructures of a discourse should be entailed by it.

As Figure 13.1 above shows, the entire Two Ways document boils down to love of neighbor, which is a concept to which all else connects.

The macrostructure might then be "The way of life is to love your neighbor and the way of death is to hate your neighbor." The macrostructure of the post-script is "Ensure that no false teachers lead you astray from the way of life." How these macrostructures relate to each other is debatable. As a post-script, we could segment it off from the body, making the macrostructure of the Two Ways the most prominent part of Part 1. On the other hand, the macrostructure of the body is expository ("Now this is the way of life..."), while the post-script is hortatory, and in an expository discourse-type, the hortatory is more prominent because the expository is less central to the author's communicative purposes than the hortatory.[25] That is, the hortatory could fulfill the communicative intention of the author without the expository (simply with less efficacy), but the expository could not fulfill the communicative intention without the hortatory. Since this post-script is clearly integral to the letter (it relates to the false teachers that are such a concern in Part 2 of the Didache), is hortatory, and is not a formulaic conclusion as in epistles, it most likely functions as the most prominent concern of the Two Ways, demonstrating the author's most important communicative intention. By making the post-script prominent over the body and combining the macrostructures, I propose that Part 1's macrostructure is "Don't let false teachers lead you away from loving your neighbor because loving your neighbor is the way of life."

The function of Part 1 is to persuade the audience not to be led away from the teaching of the Two Ways by false teachers. By lauding and praising the Way of Life, while denouncing the Way of Death so harshly, the author attempts to provide ample motivation to obey his exhortation to avoid false teachers.

Microstructures of Part 2 (6.3–16.8)

The second division concerns proper church (or more broadly,

---

25 Some commentators suggest 6.1 was part of the original source, with the Didachist beginning his own expressions at 6.2 (e.g., Niederwimmer, *Didache*, 121). If this is true, then 6.1 was still a post-script in the original manuscript. Had all of 6.1–2 been added by the Didachist, perhaps we would give it extra prominence, since he saw a need to add it to his existing material. Again, more research on the relationship between source and redaction criticism and discourse analysis is needed.

Christian community) order. Four of the topics are introduced by περὶ δὲ, stretching from 6.3–13.7:

περὶ δὲ τῆς βρώσεως ("now, concerning food" [6.3])
περὶ δὲ τοῦ βαπτίσματος ("baptism" [7.1])
περὶ δὲ τῆς εὐχαριστίας ("thanksgiving [at the Eucharist]" [9.1])[26]
περὶ δὲ τῶν ἀποστόλων καὶ προφητῶν ("the apostles and prophets" [11.3])

It is unclear why the author continues to the final two topics without introducing them with περὶ δὲ. Instead, they are introduced by asyndeton and an imperative:

Κατὰ κυριακὴν δὲ κυρίου συναχθέντες κλάσατε ἄρτον καὶ εὐχαριστήσατε ("now, on the Lord's day, when you gather, break bread and give thanks" [14.1])[27]
Γρηγορεῖτε ὑπὲρ τῆς ζωῆς ὑμῶν ("keep watch over your lives" [16.1])

Perhaps, as with the structural imperfections in Part 1, the author's use and redaction of sources has affected his literary plan.[28] In any case,

---

26 This topic further divides into three more topics, two of which are introduced by περί, one of which includes a δέ (9.3), which at first makes it seem (incorrectly) like a main unit of Part 2:

πρῶτον περὶ τοῦ ποτηρίου ("first, concerning the cup," 9.2)
περὶ δὲ τοῦ κλάσματος ("now concerning the broken [bread]," 9.3)
μετὰ δὲ τὸ ἐμπλησθῆναι οὕτως εὐχαριστήσατε ("and after you are full, give thanks thus," 10.1).

Dr. Varner also recognizes the repetition of περὶ δὲ as a literary organizer in Part 2 (*Didache*, 58–59).

27 This unit includes three subordinate units. 14.1–3 provides a command to ensure that worship on the Lord's day is pure from sin and strife. A two-part inference (οὖν, 15.1) is then drawn; apparently both sets of inferred instructions are to assist in obeying the command for the Lord's day. First, they should appoint elders and deacons (15.1–2). Second (δέ, 15.3), they should reconcile with each other in peace (15.3–4). Thus, the entire unit of 14.1–15.4 is concerned with the purity of worship on the Lord's day.

28 Although this is a conjecture, perhaps the units beginning with περὶ δὲ are taken from a source, while the units that do not begin with περὶ δὲ come either from his own hand or from other sources. On the other hand, Paul uses περὶ δὲ in 1 Corinthians to introduce his answers to questions the Corinthians had asked him. See R. Bruce Terry, "1 Corinthians," in *Discourse Analysis of the New Testament Writings*

there are six topics total in Part 2, whose macrostructures combine to form the macrostructure of Part 2.[29] Figure 13.2 shows the six main units and topics of Part 2.

6.3	7.1–8.3	9.1–11.2	11.3–13.7	14.1–15.4	16.1–8
Food	Baptism	Eucharist	Apostles & Prophets	Lord's Day	Watch Yourselves

Figure 13.2: The Six Topics of Part 2

The following six macrostructures of these units are approximate. More precision would require a full exegesis of every sentence, which I admit is beyond my current scope and intention:

6.3: Obey food laws to the best of your ability.

7.1–8.3: Baptize according to the prescribed instructions.[30]

9.1–11.2: Take the Eucharist according to the prescribed instructions.

11.3–13.7: Handle apostles and prophets according to the rule of the gospel.

14.1–15.4: Ensure that your Sabbath worship is undefiled by sin or strife.

16.1–8: Watch over your lives and gather frequently to ensure your perfection in the last days.

(Fontes Press, 2020). Is it possible the Didachist is also responding to questions he had been asked by his audience? I subsequently found that Dr. Varner makes the same observation and asks the same question (*Didache*, 58–59).

29 Two units that seem at first like main units of Part 2 are 11.1–2 and 16.3–8. However, both are subordinate to their preceding contexts and belong with them. 11.1–2 is a chiastic admonition to therefore (οὖν) receive true teachers and reject false teachers. Much like the post-script of the Two Ways (6.1–2), this little post-script to the sacramental instructions warns against being led astray from the teaching by false teachers. The second passage, 16.3–8, should be subordinated to its immediately preceding admonition to "watch over your lives" in 16.1–2 because of the tail-head linkage and the subordinating γάρ (ἐν τῷ ἐσχάτῳ καιρῷ τελειωθῆτε [16.2]. ἐν γὰρ ταῖς ἐσχάταις ἡμέραις [16.3]). There are no orienters to consider, as in Part 1.

30 This unit has three topics, linked in tail-head fashion. The baptism instructions say the one to be baptized must fast for one or two days beforehand (7.4). A progressing thought (δὲ) is that these fasts should occur on different days than those of the hypocrites (8.1). The mention of hypocrites prompts the remembrance of Jesus' teaching not to pray like hypocrites (8.2–3; cf. Matt 6:5). The three topics of baptism, fasting, and prayer are therefore all part of the baptism preparation regimen. Perhaps our churches today could learn something from the Didachist!

The difficult task now is to figure out how to combine these six macrostructures into one overarching macrostructure. One of the tests would be to see if all six units share any lexemes, from which we could extrapolate a topic. However, this method is not helpful in this case. Lexemes in the first unit (6.3) are shared at most by only 2 other units. Other prominent lexemes (προφήτης, ψευδοπροφήτης, διδαχή/ διδάσκω, δύναμαι, δίδωμι, ἅγιος) also span only 1–3 units maximum, with the exception of κύριος, which occurs in every unit except 6.3 (a lexeme to be expected in units discussing Christian community and worship). Thus, clusterings of lexemes do help us determine unit boundaries, but in this case they are of little help in determining an overarching macrostructure.

There are, however, some general linguistic clues that can help us. First, the imperative mood is used to address the recipients forty-one times in Part 2, suggesting that the most prominent part of the macrostructure should be hortatory in nature.[31] Second, there is a general theme of order in church worship and Christian community, which is also evident from the pervasive reference to the Lord. Third, the first five units all begin with δέ, a discourse marker that functions to advance the discourse.[32] The sixth and final unit, however, transitions uniquely via asyndeton. It therefore stands out in the way the author introduces it, and it also stands out by being the most general of exhortations: "Watch over your lives" (16.1). This exhortation is not specifically related to church worship or interpersonal community matters, but rather zooms out to the most general of concerns: be watchful, be ready. This general exhortation entails all the matters of church order and community relations that the first five units expound. Being watchful and ready means observing worship properly, avoiding false teachers, housing the true prophets, etc. Thus, the final unit is the most prominent part of Part 2 because it is a generalization that entails the first five units.

---

31 6.3 (x2); 7.1 (x2), 2, 3, 4; 8.1 (x2), 2 (x2); 3; 9.1; 5 (x2); 10.1, 7; 11.1, 2, 3, 4, 6, 12; 12.1, 2, 3 (x2), 4, 5; 13.4, 5, 6, 7; 14.1 (x2); 15.1, 3 (x3), 4; 16.4.

32 Stephen Levinsohn says δέ represents "a new step or development in the author's story or argument" (*Discourse Features of New Testament Greek: A Coursebook on the Information Structure of New Testament Greek* [SIL International, 2000], 72). Similarly, Steven Runge, *Discourse Grammar of the Greek New Testament: A Practical Introduction for Teaching and Exegesis* (Hendrickson, 2010), 28–36.

Further evidence that 16.1–8 is the most prominent unit of Part 2 is the formal resemblance of 16.1–2 to the post-script of 6.1–2. Similarities include the transitional use of asyndeton, an initial imperative (ὅρα, γρηγορεῖτε), a following supportive passage connected by γάρ (6.2; 16.3), and the location of the unit as the final unit of the Part (hence, post-script). Given the uniqueness of the sixth unit, and its formal resemblance to the post-script of 16.1–2, I suggest that the sixth unit is the most prominent part of Part 2's macrostructure. Since the other five units comprise proper church worship and Christian community relations, we might combine the macrostructures thus: "Watch over your lives in the last days, especially by ensuring that you engage properly in worship and with fellow believers."

All that is left is to combine the macrostructures of Part 1 and Part 2:

> Part 1: "Don't let false teachers lead you away from loving your neighbor, because loving your neighbor is the way of life."
>
> Part 2: "Watch over your lives in the last days, especially by ensuring that you engage properly in worship and with fellow believers."

The greatest problem with combining these macrostructures is that the transition between the two parts is made by περὶ δέ. Because περὶ δέ is a formula to introduce topics in Part 2, it does not help us understand how the author intends the two Parts to relate. We must surmise a coherence relation. I do not find any discussion of this coherence relation in the commentaries, and so I am left to my own conjecture. I propose that the macrostructure of Part 2 is more general than that of Part 1, and therefore the more prominent. Avoiding false teachers in order to remain committed to loving one's neighbor is a part of the more general task of watching over one's life. Thus, there is a specific—GENERAL relation to the two parts. The general concern of the Didache is that, in these last days, believers watch over their lives, and that they do so in a way that is relevant for their community. Put formally, and by taking the most prominent aspects of the macrostructures of Parts 1 and 2, the macrostructure of the Didache is, "Watch over your lives in these last days, especially by not letting false teachers lead you away from loving your neighbor."

Now that we have determined a macrostructure for the Didache and sketched its major microstructures, we may examine how economic concerns tend to appear in prominent ways throughout the discourse.

PROMINENT ECONOMIC ETHICS IN THE DISCOURSE

Economic concerns arise quickly in the discourse, but continue throughout. I will discuss them as they arise in the writing.

Give to All Who Ask (1.3–6)

The Way of Life is said to be love of God and of neighbor (1.2), with the rest of the Two Ways expounding what love of neighbor is. In the first Way of Life unit (1.3–6), which contains eleven imperatives, the final four are economic in nature.

> "if someone takes your cloak, *give* your tunic also" (1.4)
> "if someone takes what is yours, *do not demand back*" (1.4)
> "*give* to all who ask of you and *do not ask for it back*" (1.4)

Since the final four imperatives are all in the same ethical sphere, the eleven imperatives possibly build to a climax. If so, these last four economic imperatives are of greatest concern for the author.

Even if the list does not progress to a climax, the author expands on the final economic imperative, suggesting that at least this specific economic imperative is significant. Following the imperative to give to all who ask (and not ask for it back) is a lengthy grounds section beginning with "for the Father desires to give to all from his own gifts..." (1.5) and extending to the end of 1.6. Inferring some coherence relations, the logic of the higher level ideas of 1.5–6 is:

> Give to all who ask
>> For, the Father desires to give to all from his own gifts
>>> Therefore, the giver is blessed

> On the contrary, woe to the one who takes without needing
> On the other hand, let your alms sweat in your hands until you
> know to whom you should give

We are to give because the Father desires to give to all from his own gifts; i.e., Christians are to be the agents through whom the Father gives gifts. From this fact the author draws the inference that "the one who gives according to the commandment is blessed" (1.5). On the contrary, woe to the one who takes if he does not need it. In this case, he will face a great judgment. The author in 1.5 employs Jesus' saying about the man who is imprisoned until he can pay the last penny (Matt 5:26; Luke 12:59).

The command to give is neither absolute nor naïve. Verse 6 provides a mitigation: "but (ἀλλά), also concerning this, it is said, 'Let your alms sweat in your hands until you know to whom you should give.'" The demonstrative τούτου ("this") likely refers back to the initial command to "give to all who ask" and its subsequent grounding. Thus, while one should give, one must give with prudence. The proverb that the author cites is not extant in any other writing and is therefore otherwise unknown, but its meaning is clear enough.[33] Money should be given wisely to those who truly need it. But in that case, it should be done without reservation and with no expectation of repayment. The person who gives in this way will be blessed and will be innocent before God. In the case that someone takes advantage of a Christian's obligation to give to all who ask, the giver may find consolation in the harsh judgment awaiting such a greedy swindler.

One further related note is the eight-fold use of the δίδωμι word group in 1.4–6. If someone slaps you on the cheek, give them your other cheek. If someone takes your cloak, give them your tunic also. Give to anyone who asks, because the Father wants to give from his own gifts. We must give according to the command (of love of neighbor). The one who takes when he does not need it will give (i.e., yield, as a crop) judgment to himself. This person will be imprisoned and will not be released until he has given back (ἀποδίδωμι) every last penny. As the proverb in 1.6 says, we should let our gift sweat in our hands

---

33 BDAG s.v. ἱδρόω. A similar saying, with the same word "sweat" (ἱδρόω), does appear in Sib. Or. 2.79: "Of your grain give to the needy with sweating hand."

until we know to whom to give it. The predominant concern for the Christian here is that we are givers—both of our bodies and of our resources for the cause of love. In giving, we are imitating our Father and are the agents through whom he distributes his own gifts. Those who fail to abide by the law of love with regard to giving will yield (δίδωμι) their own judgment (1.5).

Be Generous, Not Stingy (4.5–8)

The "giver" theme from 1.3–6 appears again in the third Way of Life unit (3.1–4.13). The paragraph is not in a prominent location of the overall structure of the discourse, but its length of development in contrast to the surrounding commands and prohibitions gives it more prominence than the other ethical concerns. Of the five slippery ethical slopes in 3.1–6, the list of commands and prohibitions in 3.7–4.4, and the further string of imperatives in 4.9–13, none are developed with more than a simple supporting clause. On the other hand, the economic command in 4.5 is developed at length in 4.6–8.

The opening command is "do not strive toward receiving by stretching out your hands but withdrawing from giving." This general concern echoes the final command in 1.4 to give to all who ask and not ask for it back. The repetition of the topic brings it further prominence in the discourse because of the rhetorical effect of repetition.[34] Following the opening command are a result clause and five elaborations of the general command. The structure is thus:

COMMAND: Receive but do not withdraw from giving (4.5)
> RESULT: You will give a ransom for your sins, if you have [earned the money] through your hands.[35]
> MANNER: You shall not hesitate to give

---

34 Niederwimmer, *Didache*, 107n42 says the repetition occurs because 1.5–6 is the Didachist's composition, while 4.5–8 was included in his Two Ways source. Even if so, the Didachist gives 4.5–8 more prominence by adding the same topic in 1.5–6.

35 Under the condition that the money is earned "through your hands." The idea that almsgiving earns merit toward salvation appears in Tob 2:14; 4:10–11; 12; 8–10; Sir 3:30; 31:5. See especially among these Tob 4:10–11 (NRSV): "For almsgiving delivers from death and keeps you from going into the Darkness. Indeed, almsgiving, for all who practice it, is an excellent offering in the presence of the Most High." This subject

MANNER: You shall not grumble while giving
EXTENT: You shall not turn away from the needy one
EXTENT: You shall share everything with your brother
GROUNDS: You shall not claim anything to be your own[36]

This command to give freely, particularly with one's brother in the community, clearly stands out from its context with both its repetition of the similar idea in 1.4 and its elaboration in 4.6–8, which is unique among all the commands and prohibitions in the third Way of Life unit.

Mistreatment of the Poor and Oppressed (5.1–2)

The way of death is described generally as "above all evil and completely cursed" (5.1). The author continues to list specific acts of evil with a list of 22 vices (all nouns without modifiers). Only three of these vices are economic, none of which have any particular prominence (thefts, robberies, and greed). In 5.2, the author shifts from vices to evildoers (nouns with modifiers).[37] 5.2 is the final part of the Way of Death, and thus also the conclusion of the Two Ways (excepting the post-script), so it is significant that many economic concerns arise here. The eighteen evil-doers are listed below. Those in bold are definitely economic in nature, while those in italics are possibly so.

persecutors of good
haters of truth
lovers of falsehood
those who do not know the reward for righteousness,
those who do not cling to good or righteous judgment,
those who care not for the good, but for evil

---

is treated fully in Gary A. Anderson, *Charity: The Place of the Poor in the Biblical Tradition* (Yale University Press, 2014).

36 There are no conjunctions to help determine these coherence relations, except δέ and καί, which are not much help for semantic relations. One might label the relations differently, but what matters is that they all five elaborate on the main command in 4.5.

37 Niederwimmer, *Didache*, 116–119 is helpful for discerning the groupings of the vices and evildoers.

those who are far from humility and patience
lovers of worthless things
pursuers of rewards
those who do not have mercy on the poor
those who do not labor for the oppressed
those who do not know the one who made them
murderers of children
corrupters of what God has molded
those who turn away the needy
oppressors of the distressed
advocates of the rich
lawless judges of the poor

The author sums up these vices and evil-doers by saying they are "altogether sinful!"

It is difficult to determine whether each of the italicized lines describes economic misdeeds. "Worthless things" may refer to ephemeral possessions in the world, which moths destroy (*à la* Jesus), while the "rewards" that the wicked pursue may be possessions for their labor (perhaps done dishonestly, contrary to the condition in 4.6 to earn possessions through proper labor). On the other hand, they may be general vices: having misguided priorities and seeking the rewards (accolades) of virtue that they do not deserve.[38] "Murderers of children" may have economic connotations, since in the first-century Greco-Roman world infants were often exposed for economic reasons, such as high dowry prices (thus females were exposed more often) and the prohibitive cost of children for the poor.[39]

As in 1.3–6, the author again signals prominently his economic concern by completing this list with four serious economic

---

38 Cf. Niederwimmer *Didache*, 117.

39 See Donald Engels, "The Problem of Female Infanticide in the Greco-Roman World," *Classical Philology* 75 (1980): 112–120; W. V. Harris, "Child-Exposure in the Roman Empire," The *Journal of Roman Studies* 84 (1994): 1–22; Michael J. Gorman, *Abortion and the Early Church: Christian, Jewish and Pagan Attitudes in the Greco-Roman World* (IVP, 1982). David Instone-Brewer, "Infanticide and the Apostolic Decree of Acts 15," *JETS* 52, no. 2 (2009): 301. P. Oxy. 4.744 says "I beg and entreat you, take care of the little one, and as soon as we receive our pay I will send it up to you. If by chance you bear a child, if it is a boy, let it be, if it is a girl, expose it." Thanks to Sean du Toit for sharing these references with me.

condemnations, preceded by two others. It seems he has saved the elements for the end that best serve his communicative purposes. The evil-doers lack mercy for the poor (πτωχός) and do not labor (πονέω) for the oppressed (καταπονέω).[40] The verb πονέω can refer to emotional concern or physical toil, and perhaps both are intended here.[41] Simple almsgiving is insufficient to meet the ethical demands required of serving the poor; we must also labor on their behalf (they are powerless and cannot defend themselves). In case anyone wondered how the poor became oppressed, the author lets us know. The wicked are the oppressors (καταπονέω) of the distressed (θλίβω). More than that, the wicked not only "turn away" the needy but they "advocate for the rich." Even if the poor wanted justice, they would not find it, for the wicked are "lawless judges of the poor." This is the Way of Death.

Economic Exploitation by False Teachers and False Brothers (11.3–13.7)

The final and most dense section discussing economic ethics is in the fourth topic of Part 2, where the author provides instruction for itinerant apostles and prophets. Many of these instructions concern economic matters of practical importance. The prominence of this teaching comes not from its place in the overall literary structure, but from the relative amount of space spent discussing economic matters and the connection between these matters and false teachers. Recall that the false teachers are the concern in the two most prominent parts of the discourse's macrostructure, i.e., in both post-scripts. False teachers could lead the recipients astray from the Way of Life (6.1–2) and keep them from watching over their lives (16.1–3). By connecting the false teachers with economic concerns, the author again shows that these concerns are at the top of his ethical itinerary.

---

40 The variety of lexemes used here and in other ancient Jewish and Christian texts demonstrates the complex nature of the concept of poverty in antiquity. There are clear economic, socio-political, and religious connotations to the variety of lexemes (and there are dozens) that are used to describe the poor. See Todd A. Scacewater, "The Dynamic and Righteous Use of Wealth in James 5:1–6," *Journal of Markets and Morality* 20, no. 2 (2017): 227–242.

41 See Pss. Sol. 2:14; In Jos. Asen. 25.3; Josephus *Ant.* 12.240; 15.33; Philo, *Leg.* 1.80; *Det.* 11; *Migr.* 27.

The Didachist begins by providing several ways to snuff out false prophets. First, if one teaches what is not in accord with the teaching in the Didache, then he is a false prophet (11.2). This would include all the teachings on money and work. Second, if he takes advantage of the church community's hospitality, he is a false prophet. Apostles and prophets should be welcomed "as the Lord" (11.3), but they are only allowed to stay one day, or two if there is need (11.5). "But if he stays three days, he is a false prophet" (11.5). The teaching seems to presuppose that the itinerant apostles and prophets would be following Jesus' command to the seventy-two in Luke 10:1–16 to take nothing with them, to stay with those who would lodge them, and to eat their food. The Didache gives limits to the required generosity of the hosts so they will not be taken advantage of economically. Given the subsistence-level living of many in the early church, staying more than one or two days could become an extreme economic burden in a household. Just as they should give prudently (1.6), so they should host prudently. Third, if he demands a meal in the Spirit and then eats it, he is a false prophet (11.9). Such a ruse would swindle believers out of their meager food supply. Fourth, if a prophet demands money in the Spirit, he is a fraud. But if he commands believers to give the money to the poor, "let no one judge him" (11.12).[42]

12.1–5 shifts to the testing of incoming believers. "All who come in the name of the Lord" are allowed three days maximum of free lodging (12.2, one more than apostles and prophets). If they wish to join the community, however, they are not allowed to become a community leech. They must work for their living (12.3). If a new community member is not a craftsman, the community will find him some way to make a living so that he is not idle (12.4). If he tries to mooch indefinitely, he is χριστέμπορος. This adjective does not appear before the Didache, but means something like "dealing in Christ."[43]

---

42 This phrase, which occurs also in 11.11, could mean either that he is a true prophet, or that the prophet may or may not be true, but the action is consistent enough with a true prophet to leave him alone.

43 Ὁ ἔμπορος is one who travels as a merchant, selling wholesale in distant lands. The adjective χριστέμπορος would then mean that the person is making a profit on the name of Christ. The Didachist may have created the word as a contrast to Χριστιανός. See Niederwimmer, *Didache*, 187 for a brief word study.

In 13.1–7, the author shifts back to prophets and teachers. To compensate them for their work (if they settle in the community), they are to be given the first-fruits of food and livestock, "for [the prophets] are your high priests" (13.3). Even if there are no prophets, they must still give these first-fruits to the poor (13.4). There is more freedom with money and clothes and "any other possessions," for they may "take the first fruit that seems right" to them and give them "according to the commandment" (13.7), which surely refers to the commandment to love their neighbor.

Thus this entire unit about the apostles and prophets (both itinerant and resident) and visiting Christians provides detailed economic instructions for the community. Echoing teaching from earlier in the discourse, they must be generous, but not so generous that they enable swindlers and leeches, or that they endanger their own family's well-being. That is, they should be prudently generous. The community should also encourage each member to find a trade and be industrious and self-supporting—presumably both because it will keep from over-burdening others and because then they too can provide hospitality. If any do not abide by these economic prescriptions, then they are false prophets or false brothers.

Since the entire document is framed by two post-scripts that warn against false teachers, and these economic ethics provide standard tests by which false prophets and false brothers could be outed, it seems that the economic ethics of the Didache were vital to the faith of the recipient community. Figure 13.3 shows the locations of economic concerns in the Didache and, to the best of a figure's ability, the amount of space devoted to these concerns.

CONCLUSIONS

There is a definite literary structure and a discernable macrostructure to the entire Didache. The author had a rhetorical purpose, the most prominent concern of which was to warn them against succumbing to false teaching, which would lead them astray from the Way of Life and from watching over their lives with regard to proper worship and community relations. That the two post-scripts both warn against false teachers, and that the majority of the section on teachers (11.3–13.7) is concerned with distinguishing true and false teachers, demonstrates how central this concern was to the author.

The second part of this essay attempted to connect economic concerns to the warnings against false teachers. First, such teachers might persuade them away from the Way of Life, which includes three prominent sections teaching about economic ethics. Second, not only do false prophets teach poor economic ethics, they also practice poor

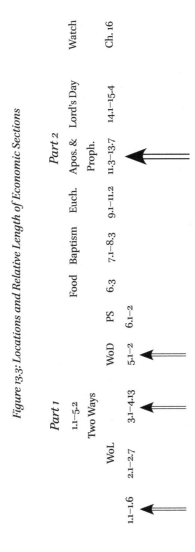

Figure 13.3: Locations and Relative Length of Economic Sections

economic ethics. The entire section on apostles and prophets contains various economic tests that root out true and false prophets. You will know them by their economic fruits.

Are there any lessons here for today? I am not aware of any contemporary faith community that takes the Didache as authoritative, so it certainly is not prescriptive, but I put forth the following observations for the reader's consideration. First, the economic ethics are private, not public. They are for the Christian community, pertaining to personal work ethic and interpersonal hospitality. To apply these ethics to the public sphere would require sophisticated interdisciplinary knowledge of political and modern economic theory.[44] Second, just as some NT passages teach (e.g., Matt 6:21; 1 Tim 3:3; 6:10; 2 Tim 3:2), economic teaching and behavior can be a litmus test for true and false teachers. Third, the instructions for each member to have an industrious work ethic, to take when truly in need, but always to be willing to give are consonant with many New Testament passages (e.g., Matt 5:42; Eph 4:28; 1 Thess 2:9; 2 Thess 3:8). This work ethic is not only for the sake of not troubling others, but also so that each member of the community might have the means to provide the hospitality that was shown to them when they arrived. Fourth, it is obvious how central economic ethics were to this early Christian community, and it should be no less so today. Within a global economy, where even local choices can affect our global neighbors, Christians should become aware of basic economic principles and their ethical implications so that they can best love their neighbor through their own economic choices. Finally, while the hospitality ethics of the Didache somewhat fall in line with ancient expectations, perhaps we modern Christians

---

44 Contra, e.g., Aaron Milavec ("The Economic Safety Net in the Didache Community," *Proceedings: Eastern Great Lakes & Midwest Biblical Societies* 16 [1996]: 73–84), who applies the personal ethics directly to the public sphere by suggesting Christians should advocate for governmental welfare. This application is possible, but the simple one-to-one correspondence between personal ethics for a first-century Christian community and public policy for a twenty-first century Western democratic and capitalistic society is lacking in sufficient warrant. The spirit of the Didache is to be concerned with what is best for both the poor and the giver. Certainly, Christians should be concerned to apply this ethic to the public sphere (especially since it aligns with the Bible's teachings), but Christians must take account of the workings of modern politics and economics to discern how public policies will affect all classes of citizens, and especially what will best help the poor.

should take more seriously this obligation as hosts in our communities.[45] We may have more obligations to our Christian brothers and sisters, as the Didache teaches, but may we also demonstrate such neighborly love among those who do not yet know our Lord. And may we do so with eschatological urgency, for we "do not know the hour when our Lord is coming" (16.1).[46]

45 See especially Rosaria Butterfield, *The Gospel Comes with a House Key: Practicing Radically Ordinary Hospitality in Our Post-Christian World* (Crossway, 2018).

46 My thanks go to David J. Clark, Kyle J. Keesling, Jr., and the editors, Abner Chou and Christian Locatell, all of whom provided penetrative comments and questions to help me think further about my analysis and conclusions.

Index